AI Game Develop

Synthetic Creatures with Learning and Reactive Behaviors

Contents at a Glance

AI Game Development

Synthetic Creatures with Learning and Reactive Behaviors

Alex J. Champandard

New Riders

800 East 96th Street, 3rd Floor, Indianapolis, Indiana 46240
An Imprint of Pearson Education
Boston • Indianapolis • London • Munich • New York • San Francisco

AI Game Development

International Standard Book Number: 1-5927-3004-3

Library of Congress Catalog Card Number: 2002112970

Printed in the United States of America

First printing: December 2003

08 07 06 05 04 03   7 6 5 4 3 2 1

Interpretation of the printing code: The rightmost double-digit number is the year of the book's printing; the rightmost single-digit number is the number of the book's printing. For example, the printing code 03-1 shows that the first printing of the book occurred in 2003.

Trademarks

Warning and Disclaimer

Publisher
Stephanie Wall

Production Manager
Gina Kanouse

Executive Development Editor
Lisa Thibault

Senior Project Editor
Sarah Kearns

Copy Editor
Keith Cline

Indexer
Brad Herriman

Proofreader
Sheri Cain

Composition
Ron Wise

Manufacturing Coordinator
Dan Uhrig

Interior Designer
Kim Scott

Cover Designer
Aren Howell

Media Developer
Jay Payne

Marketing
Scott Cowlin
Tammy Detrich
Hannah Onstad Latham

Publicity Manager
Susan Nixon

Table of Contents

About the Author

 **Alex J. Champandard** has a strong academic background in artificial intelligence, with science and engineering degrees from York and Edinburgh. He often speaks about his AI research, notably at the Game Developers Conference, where he also hosts a roundtable on learning AI. As the lead programmer of FEAR (an open source game AI project), he consults with professional programmers to integrate state-of-the-art prototypes into commercial games. Founder of AI-Depot, a popular community AI site, he brings regular tutorials to an audience of AI enthusiasts. Alex has also contributed multiple articles to the *AI Game Programming Wisdom* series. He is part of the AI Interface Standards Committee, which intends to define a common specification for game AI techniques.

About the Technical Reviewers

These reviewers contributed their considerable hands-on expertise to the entire development process for *AI Game Development*. As this book was being written, these dedicated professionals reviewed all the material for technical content, organization, and flow. Their feedback was critical to ensuring that *AI Game Development* fits our readers' need for the highest-quality technical information.

Eric Dybsand is currently finishing up a series of articles on AI middleware, scheduled to appear later this year. He has consulted on an extensive list of computer games, including designing and developing the AI for *Full Spectrum Command*, a tactical command simulator used by the U.S. Army. He also has designed strategic AI for MOO3, AI for racing, baseball, and wrestling games. He developed the AI opponents for the real-time strategy game *Enemy Nations*, and for the first-person shooter games *Rebel Moon Revolution* and the *War in Heaven*, and a number of turn-based war games. Eric has been involved with computer game AI since 1987, doing game design, programming, and testing, and is a contributing author on AI to the *Game Programming Gems* and *AI Wisdom* series.

Neil Kirby is a member of the technical staff at Bell Laboratories, the research and development arm of Lucent Technologies. He currently develops .NET solutions. His previous assignments included building speech-recognition software and teaching at the university level. Neil holds a masters degree in Computer Science from Ohio State University. In his spare time, he designs multiplayer, tactical combat computer games. Neil is one of the moderators of the AI Roundtables at the Game Developers Conference. He lives with his spouse and son in central Ohio.

François Laramee has been involved the interactive entertainment industry since 1991. He has designed, produced, written, or programmed more than 20 games for all sorts of platforms. He has also published two books for game developers—*Game Design Perspectives* and *Secrets of the Game Business*—as well as countless articles and a handful of short stories. He has earned graduate degrees in administration and computer science from two different universities, moonlights as a comedy writer, and despite going freelance in 1998, he hasn't starved to death yet. Visit his web site at http://pages.infinit.net/idjy.

Acknowledgments

Apparently, this section is the only one I can be sure anyone will read—at least that would be the case if this were an academic dissertation. That's one advantage of writing a book instead; everyone's already downloading the final demo and skimming through Part VII! I guess that's not a bad thing; this section no doubt has the weakest content anyway.

This book probably wouldn't have seen the light of day without the persistent help of Andy Coates and the encouragement from Linden Hutchinson. I'm also eternally grateful to my family for their support over the past few months; they've been quite intense (both the family and the months). Special thanks go to my sister Jess for not carrying out her threat to help write this book—although it did cost me an extra few lines of acknowledgment.

I'm in debt to AI gurus extraordinaire Neil Kirby, Eric Dybsand, and François Dominic Laramee for their technical reviews of my early drafts. Without their insightful comments and critical analyses, this book wouldn't be what it is today—and I mean that in the best possible way. Thanks to Steve Woodcock for writing the Foreword. Acknowledgments also go to Lisa Thibault and Stephanie Wall from New Riders for making this whole experience seem that much easier!

Finally, I want to acknowledge the people involved with the FEAR project for their company and great debates, particularly Max Dennis Lüsebrink and Thomas Webber. I'm also deeply indebted to the gang in the AI department at the University of Edinburgh, especially Tim Lukins, Jay Bradley, and Ignasi Cos Aguilera, for the many ideas and discussion topics that made it into this work.

Tell Us What You Think

As the reader of this book, you are the most important critic and commentator. We value your opinion and want to know what we're doing right, what we could do better, what areas you'd like to see us publish in, and any other words of wisdom you're willing to pass our way.

As the publisher for New Riders Publishing, I welcome your comments. You can fax, email, or write me directly to let me know what you did or didn't like about this book— as well as what we can do to make our books stronger. When you write, please be sure to include this book's title, ISBN, and author, as well as your name and phone or fax number. I will carefully review your comments and share them with the author and editors who worked on the book.

Please note that I cannot help you with technical problems related to the topic of this book, and that due to the high volume of email I receive, I might not be able to reply to every message.

Fax: 317-428-3280

Email: stephanie.wall@newriders.com

Mail: Stephanie Wall
          Publisher
          New Riders Publishing
          800 East 96th Street
          3rd Floor
          Indianapolis, IN 46240 USA

Foreword

The first thought that came to my mind as I was looking over this book's drafts was: "Well, it's about time."

About time that somebody wrote a book on game artificial intelligence (AI) that focused more on the techniques actually *used* by game developers instead of reiterating the same old academic studies.

About time that somebody focused less on the basics of AI—pathfinding, architecture, scripting—and more on building nonplayer characters (NPCs) that look and feel more *real* than players have seen before.

About time that somebody took a look at what the future of game AI might be and how the techniques presented in this book might help developers reach those goals.

About time, in short, that somebody wrote *AI Game Development*.

About Alex

It makes perfect sense that Alex was the one who did it. I've known Alex for several years now, and I guess he's a bit too modest to say these things himself, so I suppose it's up to me.

Alex has been a regular contributor to various discussions on game AI on the web and at the Game Developers Conference (GDC), and he has even made a couple of presentations there. His knowledge of game AI is vast and his wit is keen. In any GDC AI session with a Q&A portion at the end, he was nearly always first in line to question the speaker on some detail of his presentation. Over the years, he's written a number of excellent papers on various aspects of AI, and I've watched as he's slowly evolved his *nouvelle game AI* approach through several GDCs. One can look back a few years to his earlier presentations and clearly see elements of his ideas taking root there.

It was perhaps inevitable that he would eventually put all his thoughts and ideas and experiences into a book. *AI Game Development* is the result.

Something Different

AI Game Development is a bit of a different beast in the AI field, particularly when compared with other game AI references. Although many quite excellent books are on the market, *AI Game Development* is better than most at providing one core focus: helping the reader learn the techniques to build reactive, *learning* AIs.

Throughout this book, Alex expands on the concept of what he terms nouvelle game AI, a design concept that combines elements of reaction architectures and learning algorithms. This combination enables developers to develop AIs that are autonomous unto themselves.... They use the same basic algorithms and AI engine functions, but they are independent agents that can act and react to their environment in their own way. These autonomous agents have a natural capability for adapting to (or at least not looking stupid in) new environments, such as the ones found in the ever-unfolding and evolving world of an online role-playing games (RPGs).

These design concepts are sound and represent much of what I've been saying in the industry for many years. The recent popularity of "open-ended" games, such as *The Sims*, *Freelancer*, and *GTA3: Vice City*, show that the game-playing public loves games that "feel" real, which have NPCs and wingmen and passers-by that just "act right."

Meeting those desires are exactly what this book is all about. From the initial chapters on basic navigation behaviors to the more detailed chapters on designing AIs with perception and emotion, *AI Game Development* provides readers with the tools needed to answer the demands of players over the next few years.

Useful for Everybody

Alex manages to do all this while keeping the book light and fun, which is a bit different from what one might find in other tomes. Instead of offering a series of, at best, loosely connected techniques with no obvious design interconnections, Alex focuses instead on trying to teach design skills and working techniques. The idea is to give the user a set of undoubtedly useful AI techniques, of course, but also to help provide him with the skill set to *understand* the theory behind the techniques and use them to better design his AI engine in the first place. Alex manages to pull this off without descending into the academic staleness that one often finds in similar books, which is frankly refreshing to somebody who has seen a *lot* of books cross his desk.

AI Game Development should be useful to just about anybody. Whether the reader is a hobbyist looking to build a new bot for the latest first-person shooter, a game developer who has some time between projects to pick up a few new techniques, or just a casual seeker of information to better understand the games he plays, this book will have something for you. The demos are fun to play with even if readers don't enjoy browsing through code, and the principles presented are done simply enough that players can at last bug their favorite developers on the forums to focus more on better game AI. (Trust me; we game AI developers need all the player support we can get!)

So sit back, pull up a laptop, and prepare to have some fun learning about game AI. This book talks about the future of game AI; it's worth paying attention.

Steven Woodcock
Founder of GameAI.com

Introduction

AI Game Development explains how to create synthetic characters with realistic behaviors, focusing on individual *animats*. These are autonomous creatures with an artificial body situated in a virtual world. Our job as AI programmers is to give them unique skills and capabilities so that they can interact with their environment.

Throughout this book, we will learn how to build such autonomous AI characters and get them to react intelligently. A realistic 3D game is used as a test bed, rather than programs running from the command prompt or dealing with simple grid worlds.

To achieve satisfactory levels of intelligence and realism, this book introduces a variety of technologies, including modern AI techniques (such as neural networks, decision trees, genetic classifiers, and reinforcement learning) as well as standard control mechanisms that have been at the heart of the game industry for decades (such as rule-based systems and finite-state machines). Each technique is described theoretically using brief descriptions, intuitive examples, and formal insights based on mathematics. To complement these abstract notions, this book covers practical applications for building realistic nonplayer characters (NPCs). This theoretical and practical understanding will enable us to apply AI techniques to other problems as exercises.

From just programming skills, we will build up a set of methodologies for creating autonomous characters, and explore the AI development process from the ground up. Using the examples, we will gain insights into common problems game AI engineers face and establish how to approach them in a structured manner.

AI Game Development provides a unique combination of theory, practice, and concepts about AI development. Within the space of three chapters, for instance, we will discover neural networks, get bots to blast each other with rockets, and learn a lesson about understanding AI problems in general. Apart from being a valuable educational experience, this will also be a particularly entertaining one!

Why Learning and Reactive Behaviors?

The animat approach emphasizes the creation of intelligent behaviors in genuine creatures. This underlines the essence of AI development, instead of just programming and optimizing academic algorithms. A balance of responsibilities is necessary in professional game AI.

This approach—which we dub *nouvelle game AI*—shows how to deal with modern academic AI in practice by blending it with popular technology. As game AI development faces new challenges (such as increasing intelligence, efficiency, and realism), wisdom from other well-established disciplines becomes indispensable. The approach to game AI in this book can be seen as a combination of three fields of research:

➤ Nouvelle AI studies **embodied** systems that are actually situated in realistic worlds (such as game characters).

➤ **Reactive architectures** provide control with distributed components that react instantly to the environment.

➤ **Learning** techniques used for the simulation of adaptive behaviors produce creatures with intelligent capabilities.

This book sheds light on nouvelle game AI as the application of these contemporary ideas to computer games. We believe that they are applicable to games in four ways (as discussed in the following subsections), improving believability and simplifying the development.

> **NOTE**
> Naturally, there are some drawbacks to this approach compared with "standard" game AI. We will present both approaches when possible, deciding when nouvelle game AI is applicable, and when it's not as desirable. Notably, we will find ways to combine learning with fixed approaches and make embodiment efficient. This will enable us to use an ideal blend of technology to create the most suitable AI for NPCs, combining the advantages of both approaches.

Embodiment Makes Synthetic Creatures More Genuine, Which Improves Believability

Behavioral research shows that believability flows from accurately simulating the body of creatures, notably their interaction with the environment. When imposing such biologically plausible constraints on the perceptions and actions, realism is a byproduct of applying the AI as a brain. Each detail of the design no longer needs to be faked, and animats remain believable outside of their intended domain.

Situatedness Facilitates NPC Development and Improves the Benefits of Learning AI

Embodied systems are mostly affected by their immediate surroundings. Using senses, only local information is gathered, similar to the way humans or animals interact with their environment. This automatically filters out less-relevant information, and tremendously simplifies the problem of developing intelligent behaviors—both in theory and practice. The process of computing an action based on the perceived situation is almost straightforward. Learning techniques perform better for this same reason, reducing potential problems and increasing efficiency.

Reactive AI Architectures Are Ideally Suited to Controlling Game Characters

Like living creatures, animats must react to stimuli from the environment. Because there are various types of situations, it is often appropriate for different AI components to provide reactions. Together, these independent components can be organized into reactive architectures to increase their capabilities. There are many architecture types, but reactive ones are suited to intelligent control because of their reliability and simplicity, often providing a foundation for more elaborate techniques.

The Game AI Development Pipelines Can Benefit from Methodologies Used to Create Embodied Creatures

Embodiment separates the brain and the body. In the game engine, this explicitly distinguishes the AI from the game logic and even the world simulation itself—greatly simplifying design decisions. As for development, the animats are usually built incrementally, validating the system by experimentation. This is a great methodology to ensure realism and robustness. Finally, reactive architectures are intrinsically modular, allowing the divide-and-conquer paradigm during both implementation and testing.

Who Is This Book For?

AI Game Development targets readers who want to learn about AI and apply their knowledge practically to games. Particularly, this book is intended for the following people:

➤ **AI enthusiasts who want to learn the trade in the best practical way: using computer games**

Most people only understand AI when it is applied practically. Synthetic characters in computer games bring AI to life with palpable behaviors. In this book, we hide the complexity of the game engine to expose the essence of game AI—ideal for educational purposes.

➤ **Hobbyist game developers wanting to add intelligent creatures to their favorite games (or even to their own)**

In this book, we present generic interfaces between the AI and the game engines. Re-implementing these interfaces allows easy integration of the AI into custom games. All the demos and AI techniques are applicable to most video games.

➤ **Programmers interested in modern AI techniques and methodologies to create synthetic creatures**

Creating believable and realistic behaviors is about more than just programming. *AI Game Development* explains how to use AI techniques both in theory and practice, and identifies the benefits of this approach. The methodology during the AI production pipeline is also discussed.

➤ **Professional game developers eager to investigate new AI approaches to improve their NPCs**

Two new concepts are right around the corner in game AI development: *learning* and *embodiment*. Along with reactive systems, their applicability to commercial games is scrutinized throughout this book.

General skills in game AI engineering are discussed, not just descriptions of algorithms. Some experience with the C++ language is assumed for those who want to use the existing code; knowledge of game engine structure is a distinct advantage for integrating the ideas into custom games. However, the latter is not required, because a game framework is provided.

How Is the Book Organized?

AI Game Development is divided into parts, chapters, sections, sentences, and words; nothing revolutionary there! In the practical spirit of game AI, however, each part of this book covers an aspect of the creation of NPCs, such as movement or combat. Creature capabilities are built up step by step, culminating in an AI that can learn to play a deathmatch game in a first-person shooter. Along the way, we will explore the concepts behind the development, lessons that will prove invaluable for becoming independent game AI engineers.

The chapters in each part correspond to different steps of the AI production:

1. *Analyzing* the platform
2. *Understanding* the problem
3. *Designing* the specification
4. *Implementing* a simple prototype
5. *Researching* AI theory
6. *Developing* a modular component
7. *Applying* the technique to the problem
8. *Experimenting* with the results
9. *Testing* the solution
10. *Optimizing* the model

This is the basic blueprint for each part, although we'll use artistic variations in the chapters as we progress through this book.

Where Is the Web Site?

There is a web site dedicated to this book at `http://AiGameDev.com/`. The site is a valuable online resource that extends the content of this book in many ways, making this a truly multimedia experience. All the source code for the framework is available online, as are demos and extra material, including the following:

➤ Step-by-step guides for each demo

➤ Exercises with hints and solutions

➤ Game AI Specialists Forum

➤ Mailings lists for announcements

The framework supporting the demos is an open source project called Flexible Embodied Animat 'Rchitecture (FEAR). The project provides a great foundation to reduce the amount of preparation required to implement the AI and test the animats. The codebase is evolving rapidly, but the development can be followed on the SourceForge page at `http://fear.sf.net/`. We strongly encourage involvement in the project, and welcome contributions to the initiative. FEAR has already become the reference open source game AI framework; just imagine what it could become with your help!

Which Software Is Required?

The primary operating system supported for this book is Windows—any recent flavor. Most importantly, you need a C++ compiler to be able to extend the demos and try the exercises. Both Visual C++ 6.0 and .NET are suitable choices, but the code also compiles with Dev C++ (a free development environment).

The recommended game platform for the AI is id Software's *Quake 2*. It is possible to run the examples using the assets from the *Quake 2* demo only (available for free), but there are a few visual limitations. You need to own the full game if you want to see all the maps, textures, and objects.

Part I
Overview

Chapter 1

Artificial Intelligence in Computer Games

Right from the very beginning, since the days of *Pong* and *Pac-Man*, artificial intelligence (AI) has played an undeniable role in computer games. Although far from the primary concern of developers, AI was still a necessity to produce entertaining games. Now that other aspects of games (for example, graphics and sound) have reached impressive levels, more attention is being focused on AI. Over the past few years, game AI has suddenly burst out of the shadows—even taking center stage in recent games.

This chapter describes the role of AI in games, and how it fits in with the development. Specifically, this chapter covers the following topics:

➤ What is AI?

➤ Why do we need AI in games?

➤ How can AI help in game development?

➤ What are the major problems?

The next sections emphasize the link between AI and design and attempt to clarify the role of AI in this relationship.

Overview of Artificial Intelligence

To a great majority of the population, AI is the brain behind powerful cybermachines—the kind found in sci-fi films. To software developers, it's a buzzword for technology that repeatedly failed to deliver on its promises throughout the twentieth century. To academics, it's a seemingly endless source of challenges and excitement.

But how is AI relevant to game developers?

Artificial intelligence has *two* separate meanings; both types are beneficial to game development:

➤ First, AI is a form of intelligence that has been artificially re-created using machines.

➤ Second, AI is a set of academic techniques, research methods, and problems that fall into one sub-branch of science.

Machine Intelligence

Historically, it seems "intelligent" is a term mankind found to describe itself. Intelligence is just a human ability that distinguishes us from animals or plants. Nowadays, intelligence is commonly used as a distinguishing trait among humans; everyone implies that "intelligent" means an especially clever person.

Universal Ability

Conceptually speaking, a generic form of intelligence undoubtedly exists. Humans and animals have small subsets of this ability, particular instances of *universal intelligence*. Humans seem to have inherited a larger portion of this universal skill. However, our biological intelligence lacks some characteristics of universal intelligence (for instance, exhaustiveness and neutrality).

Most computer-science researchers assume that biological intelligence can be reproduced, and that intelligence is not exclusively human. This statement essentially gifts machines with a subset of universal intelligence. AI can therefore be seen as an artificial counterpart of the intelligence produced by our biological brains. Naturally, engineering produces different results than evolution, explaining why AI has different properties than human intelligence (for instance, thoroughness). AI is another instance of universal intelligence.

It's difficult for us to understand universal intelligence because we have few advanced examples. However, we can try to define human intelligence.

Definition of Intelligence

For lack of a better definition, intelligence is a set of skills that allows humans to solve problems with limited resources [Kurzweil02]. Skills such as learning, abstract thought, planning, imagination, and creativity cover the most important aspects of human intelligence.

Given this wide variety of abilities, there is no unique problem to put them all to the test. Animals are intelligent in some ways: they are capable of surviving and managing their time, for instance. Insect colonies can adapt quickly to their environment to protect their nest. Popular IQ tests are very specific and require training more than the gift of "intelligence." These tests measure what is known as *narrow* intelligence.

Each problem requires different abilities. We're particularly interested in a problem that can become surprisingly complex—behaving autonomously within a realistic virtual environment. Playing games isn't just about wrist power and rudimentary reflexes! Games present interesting challenges because most humans find entertainment in solving such problems.

Computer game AI is an artificial version of this human ability. AI controls computer characters purposefully, meaning that actors and background cast don't have to be hired (as they must be in films). We'll refer to this first interpretation of AI as nonplayer character (NPC) intelligence, which implies that it's *machine* intelligence.

Field of Science

The second interpretation of AI is as a set of technologies. The definition on the introductory page of the *AI Depot* has served well over the past couple years:

> "Artificial intelligence is a branch of science that helps machines find solutions to complex problems in a more human-like fashion. This generally involves borrowing characteristics from biological intelligence, and applying them as algorithms in a computer-friendly way."

AI algorithms can be applied to practically anything—they're not just limited to re-creating human intelligence. For instance, they could be applied to managing a production chain, or perhaps to pattern recognition in medical data. The common properties of AI techniques and biological intelligence (for instance, learning or abstraction) make these techniques part of the field of AI.

As a discipline, AI sits at the crossroads of many subjects (for instance, computer science, psychology, and mathematics). These subjects all share a significant body of common knowledge. Given such a wide variety of influences, it's difficult to say what belongs to AI and what doesn't. It seems to vary from year to year, depending on the popularity of each field. There is an increasingly large overlap with other disciplines anyway, which is a good thing; it reveals the maturity of the field and its consistency with other theories.

Historically, AI tended to be very focused, containing detailed problems and domain-specific techniques. This focus makes for easier study—or engineering—of particular solutions. These specific techniques are known as *weak* AI because they are difficult to apply outside of their intended domain.

This weakness of AI has become a roadblock—one that can't be driven around. Weak AI has been extremely successful in many domains, but human experts need to apply it manually. When trying to assemble techniques together to solve bigger problems, it becomes evident that techniques are too focused.

This is one reason why we need AI engineers. If AI were good enough, programmers wouldn't be needed. This is (at least) a few decades off, however; until then, we need humans to develop the systems. This is the case for AI technology in computer games, too; rest assured, programmers are still necessary!

Computer Games and AI

As mentioned previously, AI means two different things. Which kind of AI do we mean when we say "computer game AI"? What good is AI for computer games?

It's understandable that we want intelligent characters in our games because they add to the experience and improve gameplay. Intelligent NPCs make single-player games possible, and improve multiplayer experience, without having to rely on an existing community of (biological) people.

We want useful sidekicks, worthy deathmatch opponents, hordes of enemies that get shot in particularly entertaining fashion, and background characters that add depth to the game. Regardless of the game type—whether real-time strategy (RTS), first-person shooter (FPS), or massively multiplayer online game—intelligent NPCs are absolutely necessary to create the illusion of playing with other intelligent players.

Fundamentally, these examples revolve around synthetic characters. Because the essence of the problem is to develop a single NPC, that seems an obvious place to start (from an educational point of view). Focusing on one creature leaves vast quantities of processing power available, which provides a perfect test bed for experimentation.

> **NOTE**
> In AI, a smart entity is known as an *agent*. A system that handles more than one game unit in coordination is known as a *multi-agent system*. Developing multiple agents involves scaling down the AI enough so that it's feasible to scale up the number of NPCs. In essence, it's about using simpler AI using less memory and processing power—although this is a challenge in its own right!

From an external point of view, NPCs need only to display a certain level of intelligence. This is one key realization; computer game AI requires the result. It doesn't really matter how NPC intelligence is achieved, as long as the creatures in the game appear believable. So AI *technology* is not justifiable from this outsider's point of view, because standard software engineering techniques could be used equally well to craft the illusion of intelligence (for instance, scripting).

The State of Game AI

Remember the dawn of 3D graphics in games? Only a few companies were willing to take the plunge: the proverbial penguins. Some mastered the subject, but the games still had many bugs. Visual artifacts slowly disappeared, eventually becoming unacceptable. Nowadays, even when new technologies are introduced, they are integrated seamlessly; the development pipeline is well established. There is much experience in the field, assisted by a strong hardware industry.

In AI, we're still in the first stage. Common techniques that have been used over the years—such as scripted behaviors and A* pathfinding—could be compared to 2D graphics. Although improvements still need to be made, these two techniques have matured tremendously; scripted behaviors and A* pathfinding in most AI systems nowadays don't make obvious mistakes. This is an amazing feat. We've even reached a stage where such AI techniques shine in some games (for instance, *Unreal Tournament 2003* and *Return to Castle Wolfenstein*).

However, AI (both kinds) is set to revolutionize the way we make games. AI technology is modernizing the development, and intelligent creatures are transforming game design.

Technological Revolution

Some companies have ventured into more advanced technology borrowed from the field of AI (for example, decision trees or reinforcement learning). In these applications, the superior AI generally achieves similar design goals, only the means of production change. (For instance, *Colin McRae Rally 2* uses learning and neural networks, which means the AI doesn't have to be programmed manually [Hannan01].) Despite the standard gameplay design, the game engine needed to be adapted to accommodate the AI techniques and the development process (usually involving less scripting). This is the *technological AI revolution* in the trenches.

Nevertheless, a certain amount of skepticism still exists within the game-development community—and justifiably so. Why is better AI technology actually needed? Given a standard design, does it help the development in any way? The answer is that AI techniques are not a *requirement* per se. There's no *need* for awesome technology if it produces the same gameplay! In development, we *could* do fine without AI; in fact, most professional game programmers have the skill to do without any form of AI if they so desire.

However, AI technology has the potential to improve the development process by boosting efficiency, speeding up design and experimentation, and generally improving the quality of the final product—when chosen in the right context. We spend the rest of this book on this subject, learning from successful prototypes and making mistakes.

Design Revolution

Few other games use modern AI to actually push levels of NPC intelligence beyond designs possible with "standard" AI (that is, scripts and pathfinding). Together, the stronger AI techniques and adventurous designs have led to obvious improvements in gameplay. For example, *Black & White*'s gameplay revolves around the interaction with an intelligent creature with learning abilities.

On the whole, these more intelligent creatures have had a great reception from the press and the public (including AI enthusiasts). Capturing this amount of attention has only been possible with ambitious designs, which the game community now seems to crave. This is the *AI design revolution*, and it's just starting.

There's a calm certainty that a golden age in AI NPC is looming, despite some hesitations about how to make it happen. There is little doubt that the AI revolution will be mainly design driven. The savings generated by a better AI production pipeline compare meekly to the lucrative market for AI games. This market in itself is enough to drive any progress.

The technology to bring these AI designs to life has been available for years—if not decades. Granted, the necessary processing power and experience have been lacking anyway. Only recently has it matured enough; nowadays, practical wisdom has increased dramatically and computational power is less of a problem. In this book, we explore such techniques capable of bringing AI designs to life efficiently.

Designers Versus AI

How do stronger AI technology and the potential for intelligent NPCs affect game design? It's clear that improvements in the field of AI have opened up possibilities for the design. In the near future, advancements will undoubtedly lead to other expansions in "design space."

However, intelligent NPCs are changing the methods of game design, too. These issues discussed in this section are causing tension within the development teams, and the subject is very topical. Clashes are a recurring theme—even among the very best developers.

Obstacles

Beyond any technical details, a major problem is making room for intelligent behavior in the design, and dealing with those behaviors:

➤ Intelligent game characters can behave autonomously.

➤ Designers need to control the behavior of NPCs.

An undeniable clash exists in these roles; do we actually need AI? If AI is present, do we need designers? The overlap lies between the designers' wishes and what the AI can provide. A reasonably intelligent NPC can challenge the authority of the designer!

Two Types of Games

Different attitudes toward control have led to two distinct varieties of video games. In the first variety, designers implement their vision in a *top-down* fashion, controlling every detail of the game. This is the *explicit design* approach. It's particularly common in games based on a single story line (*Doom 3*, *Unreal 2*).

When the design script is extremely detailed, such as in single-player scenarios, there is little need for AI techniques. It's even arguable whether NPCs are "intelligent" characters at all. (They do the same thing every time regardless of changes in the situation.) Standard programming or scripting can bring the design to life. The less detail there is in the story, the more AI technology is necessary.

The second type of game results from *bottom-up* design, whereby the AI and the environment combine and emerge into an interesting game. The key observation is that there is no master script. Working together, all the characters in the game create an interesting world that makes a game (that is, an emergent story line, as in *Pizza Tycoon*).

This is *implicit design*, because the story is not controlled directly by the designer, although each individual NPC behaves as told (low-level explicit control). If the NPCs are intelligent rather than scripted, the designer's control lies in the environment only!

Many games are built in the implicit fashion, but very few of these actually have a story line (for instance, *SimCity*, *Transport Tycoon*). The story line is whatever path the player decides to take. In these games, designers can't easily control how the AI comes together to affect the gameplay.

The combination of top-down and bottom-up approaches to game design is a topical problem in AI research. One practical solution that's already been used (in *Grand Theft Auto III*, for instance) is to alternate sequences of explicit control (to set up the story line), and implicit control (to allow the player to play it). In this case, the behavior of the NPC is overridden during the "cut scenes" and left to autonomous AI control otherwise.

What Conflict?

These distinct types of games reduce the overlap between the AI and the design. In general, the designer's job is to craft the game, from the low-level behaviors to the overall story line. Animating characters is a crucial part of this. It's the AI's responsibility to control the behavior of in-game characters, bringing the vision to life.

Conflict can arise when the designer wants explicit control of an intelligent NPC. In this case, the AI has to perform a particular action in a specific situation as told. This is the easiest problem to resolve—even with standard AI techniques—because the AI can be directly overridden (as in cut scenes).

Further conflict can arise when designers want the story line to emerge in a different fashion (for instance, get the characters to force the player into this situation instead). This cannot be resolved as simply because the control is implicit; there's often no easy way to tell the NPC directly what to do for a particular situation to emerge.

Designers of games with story lines seem to have particular issues with implicit control, not realizing the challenges presented to the AI programmer. Identifying the situation can help. As a rule of thumb, control is implicit when it requires more than one operation to achieve.

For example, making sure that there is another player—any player—behind the door when it opens is explicit control; it's just a matter of spawning a new entity into the game world. However, guaranteeing that teammate Marvin is behind the door when it opens is implicit control. Just moving Marvin would make the game world inconsistent. (He might have been visible at the time.) So he actually needs to go through the door, which takes more than one operation; it's implicit control.

The solution is for designers to *agree* with the AI programmer upfront about all types of implicit control required, and then to *specify* explicit control as necessary. The idea is that the AI system needs to be engineered specially to provide "handles" for implicit control, whereas explicit control is just a matter of overriding the system.

Setting up guidelines allows the AI developers to exploit the freedom they are given to build the AI system. Designers will make the most of the AI system with the agreed forms of control—harnessing their power to improve the gameplay.

AI in Game Programming

In practice, the purpose of the AI system in the game engine is to control every aspect of the NPC. For example, within computer games—and not only first-person shooters—the AI must provide the following:

➤ **Primitive behaviors** such as picking up items, pressing switches, using objects, performing purposeful gestures, and so on

➤ **Movement** between areas of the game environment and dealing with obstacles, doors, or platforms

➤ **Decision making** on a higher-level to decide which actions are necessary for the NPC to accomplish its tasks, and in what order

To develop systems capable of providing such control, a minimal amount of technology is necessary. Although standard programming techniques allow the implementation of intelligent NPCs, techniques from the field of AI can provide the following:

➤ Elegant solutions for explicit control

➤ Technology to support implicit control efficiently

Compared to standard scripting techniques, AI technology can be computationally more efficient and can generate better quality behaviors. Such improvements are possible thanks to various aspects of AI, discussed throughout this book:

➤ AI techniques providing functionality such as motor control, pattern recognition, prediction, or approximation

➤ Design patterns inserted at a system level to assemble these components together

➤ Methodologies used to design and test behaviors within realistic environments

These AI methodologies allow the synthetic characters to come to life, but they also serve a particular purpose in games. Game development has common requirements that need to be taken into account when engineering the AI system. Two properties are important in games:

➤ **Entertainment**—The AI can call upon the skills of human players. This involves providing them with various challenges and testing different abilities with increasing levels of difficulty. The AI also can play on emotions to increase entertainment value. The AI can trigger amazement by arranging cool events, or fright by building scary atmospheres.

➤ **Believability**—The AI characters can improve immersiveness by doing their job in a way that does not distract attention from the mission of the game. As for realism, AI allows each individual NPC to behave in a plausible way that seems logically feasible to human players.

In summary, AI game development is about providing control to NPCs to produce entertainment (assisted by believability or realism). The next chapter takes the engineer's approach, using AI technology to assist in the creation of systems capable of such tasks.

Chapter 2

The Design of Intelligence

This chapter looks under the hood of game engines, revealing how designs are brought to life by the artificial intelligence (AI). As expected, developing a system capable of providing nonplayer characters (NPCs) with intelligence is an imposing engineering task.

The next few pages tackle the following topics:

➤ How to move from the design to the AI development

➤ The traditional approach to game AI

➤ A different approach to game AI, relying more on learning and embodiment

➤ The background knowledge required to pull this off

➤ An outline of the AI development process, examining the important stages

The principles presented here apply throughout the rest of this book.

An Engineer's Perspective

Relying on a solid design is important for game developers. However, creating an AI system requires a more pragmatic approach.

Entertainment and realism are undoubtedly goals for game developers. In fact, these objectives are often worshipped—as if placed on a pedestal. Such an attitude is often counterproductive, leading to comments such as these:

"We don't need feature *x*, we're looking for entertainment."

"Do it first, then I'll judge if it's realistic enough."

This attitude is acceptable from a player's point of view, but the goal is more cooperation within the development team! Thinking of entertainment and realism as the Holy Grail really dodges the issue. English is ambiguous, and leaving these values as fuzzy terms such as *entertainment* and *realism* certainly doesn't help understanding. By not even trying to define these terms, the development teams—and particularly the AI engineers—are sentencing themselves to hours of forced labor, fastidious tweaking in the search of what closely resembles an illusion.

The aim of game designers and AI programmers is to bring these objectives onto the dissecting table and divide them into small parts. These atomic concepts are easier to identify and analyze, revealing what *entertainment* and *realism* are all about. Engineering relies on the capability to quantify goals; removing all ambiguity from these goals makes it possible to refine the design into specific NPC behaviors. Under these conditions, the development team can perform at its best.

Traditional Approach

How do developers tackle this problem generally? Creating game AI is certainly not the most formal of processes in software development; it requires many ad-hoc modifications and hours of empirical evaluation. The games industry is somewhat immature as a whole, but game AI is probably the furthest behind.

Until recently, AI code took barely a few hundred lines of code, being hacked together with a couple of months to spare before the deadline. Since the turn of the millennium, AI has suddenly been propelled into the limelight and it is expected to scale up—often becoming a centerpiece of the design.

A few different aspects about the typical approach to creating game AI merit analysis, notably the integration with the engine, the design of the system, and the guidelines used throughout the development.

Integration and Design

Historically, in-game agents were simulated as part of the game logic. The 2D positions of the characters were updated at each iteration, like in *Pac-Man*. Since then, things have moved on slowly. Thankfully, the AI code now is generally separated from the logic. However, the agent is generally given direct access to the game data, free to extract whatever it needs. The separation is only a programming trick to simplify the codebase.

As for software design, AI subsystems are often created as separate libraries (to handle movement, for example). Naturally, these are created in different ways, depending on the development style. The most common approach in game development is the hands-on approach, where you incrementally build up the interface and required functionality from scratch. This might not sound formal—at least in terms of classical software design—but modern *agile* approaches acknowledge the benefits of such rapid iterations. This is certainly well suited to AI because a large amount of experimentation is required.

Beyond these modular components, the code can become somewhat unmanageable because the unexpected complexity of the task or the deadline pressures sometimes catch programmers. For example, the AI for *Return to Castle Wolfenstein* uses C function pointers to simulate a finite-state machine, an approach that quickly becomes almost impossible to understand by anyone but the original developer.

Guidelines

Because of the limited resources available, the only important guideline for AI developers is to cut corners wherever possible yet still achieve efficiency. The responsibility of the AI itself is to control characters in a realistic fashion. How this is achieved under the hood is irrelevant. Many applicable techniques could be borrowed from AI research, but few are used in practice. All the common techniques used in classical game AI (for instance, search and scripting) arguably have their roots in computer science instead.

Often, the combination of these two requirements (efficiency and realism) leads to simple AI solutions, such as scripts. This approach is entirely justifiable because it solves the problem in a way that designers can easily control.

Discussion

This typical approach to game AI has been finely tuned over the years and seems to have reached satisfactory levels. AI in games is competent enough to not stand out. The standard design and integration has immediate benefits (such as simplicity), but can prove inconvenient in many ways.

First, letting the AI access information in the game directly is both dangerous and unnecessary. Second, manually developing all the behaviors for the AI can be tedious using plain programming and causes an exponential growth in time required.

There is undoubtedly room for improvement over these standard approaches, as shown by recent progress in game AI. There is an underlying trend in these innovations.

A Modern Approach

Traditionally, AI is viewed as a code fragment that manipulates data. These small programs are generally known as *agents*. These agents are like software systems; they have *layers*. One central processor acquires information, processes it, deliberates a bit more, and executes some actions. Acting on behalf of the user, agents solve narrow problems with a human quality.

This view is problematic for building large and intelligent systems; the theory scales up poorly, and does not transfer from lab examples to other domains. *Nouvelle AI* rejects such focused AI, instead believing that true intelligence is about performance in the real world.

The 1980s witnessed a revolution based in robotics that eventually shook most of AI. The ideas, initially from Rodney Brooks (1986 and 1991), proposed using a different model for intelligence, allowing working systems to be built with more suitable methodologies [Brooks86, Brooks91].

This leads to studying embodied systems situated in realistic environments (such as robots or game characters). To solve the problems that occur in practice, new approaches to AI are needed (such as the behavior-based approach).

Brooks advocates that no central processor has to deliberate every move; instead, the system is distributed into behaviors that react instantly to their environment. Using this reactive approach, full systems are built up incrementally, by testing each set of components.

This revolution has continued since, notably influencing a group of researchers to focus on the simulation of adaptive behavior (SAB). The first conference was organized back in 1990 by the International Society for Adaptive Behavior [ISAB02].

> *"Every two years, the Animals to Animats Conference brings together researchers from ethology, psychology, ecology, artificial intelligence, artificial life, robotics, engineering, and related fields to further understanding of the behaviors and underlying mechanisms that allow natural and synthetic agents (animats) to adapt and survive in uncertain environments."*

Animats are essentially synthetic creatures that live within a virtual environment. Because they are *embodied*, they interact with the world using only their body—making them fully autonomous. Animats can also adapt to their environment by using a variety of learning algorithms. But are these approaches suitable to games?

Animats in Games

Many game players, and even developers, would consider animats the "proper" way of dealing with AI NPCs. Wouldn't it be impressive to have each bot in the game as an accurately simulated creature? As far as game AI techniques are concerned, this *nouvelle game AI* approach is the opposite of standard techniques.

Are Animats Applicable to Games?

The major goal of game developers is believability; the accuracy of the simulation itself is not a concern. Still, animats have much to offer to computer games. By simulating the creatures accurately, fewer aspects of the behaviors need to be "faked." Because the AI is genuine, it can handle situations unforeseen by designers.

Already, similar (diluted) ideas are starting to leave their mark on the industry. Recent trends in game AI lean toward embodiment, notably in the simulation of sensory systems (*Thief*), the addition of noise to some actions (*Quake 3*), and even perceptual honesty (*Black & White*).

By extrapolating this progression, the result is fully embodied animats. This will certainly happen within a few years, but whether this is three or ten years away is anyone's guess. In the mean time, preliminary research in synthetic creatures shows that properties of animats, such as embodiment, actually lead to more genuine behaviors, which in turn improves believability [Isla02, Blumberg01].

As far as software engineering is concerned, the animat approach has much to offer from a design point of view. Embodiment is an elegant way of modeling the role of the AI in the game engine. The formal definitions of interfaces between the body and the brain is good practice (notably separating the AI from the logic and simulation). As for developing AI behaviors, animat and behavior-based research has revealed many ways of dealing with experimentation, such as incrementally building the AI system.

How Do We Create Animats Effectively?

How can such radical ideas be applied within game engines? Is it even feasible given time and computational constraints? As a matter of fact, it's more than feasible; different aspects of animats have already been demonstrated in popular games. This is the crucial observation; it's possible to integrate properties of animats into the standard AI design, which enables us to compromise between typical game AI approaches and the animat approach.

To date, no *genuine* animats have been shipped in commercial implementations, but this isn't too far in the future. Some animat prototypes have closely matched the skill level of standard game bots. In some cases, animat prototypes prove to be more reliable and realistic than game bots.

Instead of games using standard agents, animats can in fact be more efficient in many respects. The interaction of an animat with its environment is formalized so it can be optimized in the most appropriate format (for example, passing messages, function calls, shared variables). Learning techniques can minimize the processing power used to perform a particular behavior.

A Healthy Compromise

The animat approach has many benefits, regardless of policies on learning or embodiment. These advantages include improvements in the design and in the development pipeline. Naturally, genuine undiluted animats have the potential to be extremely successful within games, and the rest of this book investigates this noble goal. However, far from being on an idealistic crusade, this discussion attempts to identify places where the animat approach isn't appropriate in games, while trying to extract its advantages.

The remainder of this chapter investigates further these issues by tackling the two major characteristics of animats separately (embodiment and learning), looking into their potential benefits and pitfalls.

Embodiment

Embodiment is a different way of dealing with in-game creatures. Typically, NPCs are just agents: "smart" programs that manipulate data, like chatbots or web spiders. Such entities are purely virtual, whereas embodied agents live in a simulated world and have a synthetic body. Regardless of whether they are 2D sprites or complex 3D models, these bodies cannot do some things. Indeed, the bodies are influenced by the physical rules of the world.

Definition

An *embodied agent* is a living creature subject to the constraints of its environment.

Because the bodies of animats are physically constrained, the actions of their brains are limited. In general, the possible actions that can be executed by the body—and hence the AI—are restricted to the subset of actions consistent with the laws of the simulation. These actions often turn out to be physically plausible. However, embodiment generally does not limit what the AI can achieve; it just restricts how it is done.

Some characters in games represent human players who get to control the bodies. Many other characters are synthetic, similarly controlled by the computer. The AI itself can be understood as the brain, and the body offers the means for interaction with the game's physics and logic.

Consider a classical example: a standard agent can change its position itself to reach any point in space. An animat—with embodiment—needs to move itself relatively to the current position, having to actually avoid obstacles. It will not even have the capability to update its position directly. Nowadays, many games do this, effectively enforcing the simplest form of embodiment.

Actually simulating the body enables developers to add biologically plausible errors to the interaction with the environment. Errors might be present when information is perceived from the environment and in the actions. For example, animats could have difficulty perceiving the type of characters in the distance. There could even be parametric noise in the turning action, so aiming is not perfect (as with humans). Including such biologically plausible details allows the NPC to behave more realistically.

Motivation

Increasingly, agents with full access to the game data are becoming inconvenient. Having no restrictions on the reading and writing of data often results in internal chaos within the design of the engine. Because there is no formalized interface, the queries for information are left to the client (AI). Developers are actually starting to impose restrictions on these queries, notably limiting the subset of information available to the AI, such as preventing bots from seeing through walls.

For large games (such as massively multiplayer online games), it's essential to develop such hooks for the AI in the game engine. Using formal interfaces is essential because doing so allows the server to be distributed so that agents can reside on different machines if necessary. The AI can thereby be fully separated from the game logic and from the simulation of the world (physics).

So it seems formal interfaces, such as those that the *AI Interface Standards Committee* is attempting to define [AIISC03] will become increasingly important. Whether these can be standardized is another issue, but embodiment provides useful guidelines for drafting custom interfaces as the exchange of information between the body and the brain. Sensory data flows from the body to the brain, and actions are passed from the brain to the body.

This book anticipates the trend and uses such formal interfaces. In terms of code complexity, major improvements result from separating the acquisition of the data from its interpretation. As for efficiency, using embodiment often allows better optimizations.

Technology

With a formalized interface, the engineer can easily decide on the most appropriate format to communicate data to the AI—and do so mostly transparently using mechanisms such as messages, callbacks, abstract function calls, shared variables, and so on. Because a standard interface exists, its implementation can be particularly optimized for speed using the most appropriate mechanism.

Implementing embodiment efficiently requires a few common techniques to be used. These tricks are the major reasons why formal interfaces can actually outperform an AI implementation with direct access to the data:

➤ **Lazy evaluation** means that no information is gathered from the world until it is actually requested by the AI. This prevents redundant computation.

➤ **Event-driven** mechanisms mean that the AI does not need to check regularly for data. When relevant information is available, the AI is notified in an appropriate fashion.

➤ **Function inlining** still allows the interfaces to be separated, but also optimized out by the compiler (if necessary). This is suitable for small functions, but larger ones benefit from being separate.

➤ **Custom optimizations** can be used often to speed up the queries. By using spatial partitions of the world, only necessary information can be checked by visibility to gather the information.

➤ **Batching** refers to collecting many queries or actions so that they can be processed later. Within the engine, the implementation can then decide the best way to deal with them to maintain memory coherence.

Used appropriately, these techniques can significantly reduce the cost of exchanging information between the AI and the engine, and make formal interfaces and embodiment a desirable property.

Learning

Learning is the second property of animats and characteristic of nouvelle game AI. Instead of the designer crafting fixed behaviors, the process is automated by adaptation and optimization techniques.

Definition

Regardless of their actions in the world, living creatures are constantly presented with a flow of sensory data. Biological animals are capable of assimilating this information and using it to adapt their behavior. There are no reasons why animats are not capable of learning; they too are presented with a stream of information from the environment, which they can interpret.

> "*Learning* is the acquisition of new knowledge and abilities."

This definition identifies two kinds of learning: information and behavior. As far as the result is concerned, there is little difference between the two. Indeed, it's often possible to learn knowledge as a behavior; conversely, behaviors can be expressed as knowledge. So intrinsically, both these subtypes of learning can be considered identical in outcome.

In practice, a distinction exists between the two. A part of the animat does not change (*phylogenetic*), and another part can be adapted (*ontogenetic*). If the AI system itself is changed at runtime, the adaptation is called *direct*, and *indirect* otherwise [Manslow02] (Again, there's a fine line between the two.)

Motivation

Two main scenarios encourage the use of learning in computer games. Different terms are used for each of these cases—optimization and adaptation, respectively—during the development and within the game:

➤ **Optimization** is about learning a solution to a known puzzle. This is essentially used to simplify the development process (offline) because learning might produce a better answer to the problem in less time than the manual approach.

➤ **Adaptation** is about learning in unknown situations, and how best to deal with them. This scheme requires the AI to continuously update itself—to deal with different player styles during the game, for example (online).

Fundamentally, these scenarios may be considered as the same problem, too! Indeed, the exact same techniques can be used to perform either. However, both learning schemes are suited to different domains, implying different AI techniques are more appropriate.

The design of the AI can exploit these different types of learning, too. Optimization is often much easier to integrate into the development pipeline as a useful tool for creating believable characters. Adaptation, on the other hand, has repercussions within the game, so it requires a few more precautions in the design.

Technology

Many AI techniques can be used to perform both varieties of learning: neural networks, decision trees, genetic algorithms, reinforcement learning, classifier systems, and so forth. These different solutions are discussed throughout this book. From a conceptual point of view, there are the following four categories of algorithms:

➤ **Supervised learning** algorithms need to be presented with examples. Apart from assimilating facts or behaviors, they can recognize patterns in the training samples. This allows the learning to *generalize*, and perform well on unseen examples.

➤ **Reinforcement learning** evaluates the benefit of each action using a scalar number, instead of providing specific examples. This reward feedback is used to adapt the policy over time.

➤ **Evolutionary approaches** provides scalar feedback for a sequence of actions, evaluating the fitness of episodes instead of giving a continuous reward.

➤ **Unsupervised learning** does not rely on direct training. Instead, the designer provides high-level guidance, such as a performance metric.

Naturally, there are often ways to integrate these approaches—or even use one approach to solve the other (for example, self-supervision). These design issues come into consideration after the problem is identified.

Given techniques that learn (either supervised or not), the animats can be taught in different ways:

➤ **Teaching** involves humans providing a set of examples that help the animat to behave until it's managed to understand what to do.

➤ **Imitation** allows the animat to copy another player, who is usually human. It can thereby learn its behavior from a third-party experience.

➤ **Shaping** sets up successive trials from which the animat can learn. After the animat learns to accomplish simple tasks, more complex ones are presented.

➤ **Trial and error** places the animat in its environment and expects it to learn by trying out all the different approaches on its own.

Each of these methodologies can be followed during the development stage or during the actual game. Although these different approaches are presented in a practical fashion throughout this book, Chapter 35, "Designing Learning AI," specifically covers general technical and design issues.

For Skeptics

The key to successfully integrating learning within games is to use it with consideration. Some things are just not suited to learning. There will always be a need for "static" AI, even if it just acts as the glue between adaptive components.

The benefits of learning are undeniable! Learning enables the developer to save time whenever possible, and to add to the game's appeal by bringing ambitious designs to life.

However, it's debatable whether learning is capable of performing reliably within games. One of the major advantages of learning techniques is that they can be combined with other solutions. This enables the designer to modify or override the results of the learning. This book covers ways to indirectly control the learning, but directly supervise the outcome.

Finally, the fact that techniques can be applied to learning facts or behaviors, online or offline, and with so many different methodologies undoubtedly means that one flavor is suitable for every purpose.

Required Background

Before discussing the process of creating such animats in games, it seems appropriate to list what skills are required to develop AI. This book assumes the reader has a few years of programming experience, but creating AI is an interdisciplinary process. The AI part of the software sits at the crossroads between the game engine and the AI data; the AI engineer also mediates with the other programmers and designers.

Programming

An important skill needed by an AI developer is programming knowledge. AI can get relatively complex in places, but a reasonable knowledge in programming can help significantly. In fact, most programmers would be able to produce rudimentary NPCs without much AI knowledge. That said, programming is rarely the bottleneck of an AI developer.

> **NOTE**
> In this book, the theory behind the algorithms is described in pseudo-code for the sake of simplicity. As such, it's possible to implement them in almost any language. Because the code available on the web site is C++, most of the programming idioms focus on that language.

Computer Science

Most programming skills are accompanied with elementary knowledge of computer science. Being comfortable with data structures (for example, lists, trees, and graphs) and basic algorithms is a tremendous help for creating AI, too. Don't worry, however; the necessary principles are covered by the book.

Mathematics

Math is essential improving as an AI programmer. Just like 3D programmers need knowledge of geometry to push the application programming interface (API) to its limits, mathematical understanding enables AI programmers to integrate cutting-edge theory from academia, and to optimize the theoretical aspects of each algorithm. It is possible to avoid the math by relying on pseudo-code and example implementations, but a more permanent solution requires that you not shy away from theory. This book gives ample opportunities for dedicated readers to understand the theory and make a step toward academic papers.

Software Engineering

Designing an intelligent system that can control a creature in a complex 3D world is no easy task. Applying common design patterns to the problem certainly helps simplify the system. This book explains the design patterns commonly used in AI and how they can be adapted to different problems.

Game Engine Architecture

Preliminary steps need to be climbed before the actual AI development itself can start. This generally involves preparing the engine architecture so that it can support AI. In most cases—especially when human players are already supported—this job is straightforward.

As a good framework is in place, it's actually possible to code AI without knowing too much about the underlying game. Chapter 4, "FEAR: A Platform for Experimentation," presents the framework used as the basis of this book, which is extremely useful from an educational or experimental point of view.

In a professional environment, groups of developers work together to build the game architecture. Experienced developers (those who know best?) can thereby assist the integration of the AI in design and implementation. AI developers can rely on other programmers to assist them when necessary.

AI Development Process

Developing AI is often an informal process. Even starting out with the best of intentions and ending up with the perfect system, the methodology will often be left to improvisation, especially in the experimental stages. In fact, most developers will have their own favorite approach. Also keep in mind that different methodologies will be suited to different problems.

In a somewhat brittle attempt to formalize what is essentially a dark art, I developed the flow chart shown in Figure 2.1. This flow chart describes the creation of one unique behavior. Jumping back and forth between different stages is unavoidable, so only the most important feedback connections are drawn.

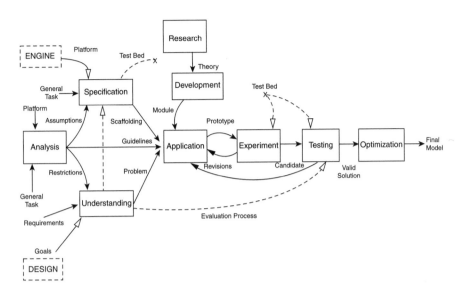

Figure 2.1   An interpretation of the dark art that is the AI development process.

Hopefully, Figure 2.1 makes the process seem less arbitrary! At the least, this method is the foundation for the rest of this book. We'll have ample opportunities to explore particular stages in later chapters, but a quick overview is necessary now.

Outline

The process begins with two *informal* stages that get the development started:

➤ The **analysis** phase describes how the existing design and software (platform) affects a general task, notably looking into possible restrictions and assumptions.

➤ The **understanding** phase provides a precise definition of the problem and high-level criteria used for testing.

Then, there are two more *formal* phases:

➤ The **specification** phase defines the interfaces between the AI and the engine. This is a general "scaffolding" that is used to implement the solution.

➤ The **research** phase investigates existing AI techniques and expresses the theory in a way that's ready to be implemented.

All this leads into a couple of *programming* stages:

➤ The **development** phase actually implements the theory as a convenient AI module.

➤ The **application** phase takes the definition of the problem and the scaffolding, using the module to solve the problem.

This is where the main *testing* loop begins:

➤ The **experimentation** phase informally assesses a working prototype by putting it through arbitrary tests that proved problematic in previous prototypes.

➤ The **testing** phase is a thorough series of evaluations used only on those prototype candidates that have a chance to become a valid solution.

Finally, there is a final *postproduction* phase:

➤ The **optimization** phase attempts to make the actual implementation lean and mean.

These phases should not be considered as fixed because developing NPC AI is a complex and unpredictable process. Think of this methodology as agile—it should be adapted as necessary.

Iterations

These stages share many interdependencies, which is unavoidable because of the complexity of the task itself (just as with software development). It is possible to take precautions to minimize the size of the iterations by designing flexible interface specifications that don't need changing during the application phase.

The final product of this process is a single behavior. In most cases, however, multiple behaviors are required! So you need to repeat this process for each behavior. There is an iteration at the outer level, too, aiming to combine these behaviors. This methodology is in spirit of nouvelle AI, which is directly applicable to game development.

Luckily, it's possible to reduce the number of outer iterations by using a clever AI architecture design, which is discussed in the next chapter.

Summary

AI development is fundamentally an engineering task:

➤ The requirements and design goals must be quantified.

➤ The traditional approach to game AI is highly controllable, closely integrated with the game engine.

Recent developments in modern games have improved upon this, notably by borrowing modern ideas from AI. This trend progresses toward embodied animats with learning capabilities:

➤ Genuine embodiment can improve behaviors and reduce the need to "fake" behaviors individually.

➤ Embodiment is good practice because it formalizes the interfaces between body and brain, providing guidelines to separate the AI from the logic and simulation.

➤ Learning comes in a variety of different flavors, appropriate in many situations.

➤ Learning can be done online or offline, in supervised or unsupervised forms.

Achieving this can be surprisingly difficult:

➤ Much background knowledge is required; programming skills are assumed in this book.

➤ There are guidelines for the AI development process, but this is a rough sketch that needs customizing.

➤ Iteration and testing is the backbone of success in AI, just as in game development.

The next chapter covers reactive techniques and AI architectures, showing how they can help improve game development.

Chapter 3

Reactive Approach

The AI techniques and behaviors used in this book share a common trait: They are all *reactive* components. The reactive approach is ideally suited to computer games because it's so simple and efficient. The predictability is also a tremendous advantage for design and testing. Contrary to popular belief, mostly reactive systems can be made to be extremely competent, rivaling approaches based on planning. This chapter shows how to achieved this in the design of the AI system, combining reactive components together.

This chapter covers the following topics:

➤ The definition of the term *reactive*, in mathematical and practical terms

➤ The difference between reactive techniques and planning, and two different approaches to solving similar problems

➤ The numerous benefits of reactive AI in games

➤ Reactive architectures that combine reactive behaviors and techniques

Reactive techniques are the most successful in the field of AI and have been demonstrated in a great majority of computer games. Before this discussion turns to the benefits and pitfalls of this approach, we need to understand the capabilities of reactive AI.

Definitions

The term *reactive* has two meanings. The first sticks to the formal description—not too common during practical applications. The second is a much slacker meaning, allowing for small deviations from the theory.

Reactive by Definition

Whether behaviors or techniques, all AI components take an input and produce an output. For reactive AI, there is a particular property about the output; given a specific input, it will always be the same.

This can be interpreted as a function in the mathematical sense (see Figure 3.1). Each configuration in the domain (input) corresponds to only one configuration in the codomain (output). Naturally, these functions can take multiple input *values* and return multiple outputs, but this can be understood as one single *configuration* on the input and output.

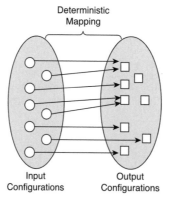

Figure 3.1 A reactive mapping from the input to the output. The mapping is deterministic, because no ambiguity exists. All the inputs are assigned to one output only, but outputs may correspond to multiple inputs (many-to-one function).

Often, these functions are known as *many-to-one*. None of the inputs correspond to multiple outputs, so there is no ambiguity. Each output is fully predictable for this reason. Such components are therefore known as a *deterministic*.

Practically speaking, a reactive behavior always does the same thing in the same situation. A reactive component makes the same decisions, and outputs the same predictions for identical input conditions, which is particularly appropriate for computer games. Designers and producers tend to prefer predictable results.

Reactive in Practice

In theory, a reactive component would have absolutely no sense of *state*; it has no memory, however small. If it did, the mapping between domain and codomain would not be deterministic; an output that depends on a state variable potentially varies output based on the same input.

Strictly speaking, internal feedback is not reactive either for the same reason. If the preceding output is used to determine the next value, the same input could also lead to a different output. Both these examples reflect *nondeterminism*.

Using a small trick, it's also possible to consider these techniques as reactive (see Figure 3.2). If we consider the internal state, or the feedback connection, as another input, the mapping is once again reactive! There is no longer any ambiguity when the internal variables that would make the component nondeterministic are instead exposed as inputs.

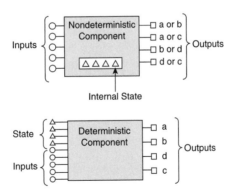

Figure 3.2   A nondeterministic component can be interpreted as reactive if the internal state values are considered as an input. The state also may be updated reactively.

So in practice, components with a small sense of state or feedback connections are considered as reactive. Even when a small random factor is used to perform the mapping, it can be considered as reactive, too; the random number could be interpreted as an additional input.

Behaviors: Planning Versus Reactive

One interesting theory about biological intelligence is that even humans do little planning [Heuer99]. Neither animals nor insects are notorious for deliberating what to do next. In most situations, instinct makes it possible to act intelligently just by reacting to external or internal conditions. This is how evolution has allowed us to survive.

Although it can be demonstrated that humans can actually plan, this ability is certainly used less often than expected. Recent research has shown that even playing *chess* or *go* is more a matter of intuition [Chen02, Atherton02]!

Goal-Oriented Planning

Theoretically speaking, what's the difference between planning and just reacting to certain situations? The obvious answer is that planning actually thinks ahead.

Planning is generally seen as a nondeterministic process, also known as *deliberative* algorithms. From a given situation, multiple actions can be taken depending on many factors, such as the current goal. A planning algorithm can scan through the possible options and find the sequence of actions that matches the goal.

In essence, planning is nondeterministic because of the goal. But what if the goal is part of the situation? This is like modeling all the "hidden" factors as additional inputs. Then, it's possible to use reactive techniques to achieve exactly the same results.

Using reactive techniques to compute plans in such a way is known as *reactive planning*. This differs from standard *deliberative planning*, which generally uses search algorithms to scan through all the possible options. Generally, when planning is mentioned, a search algorithm is often implied.

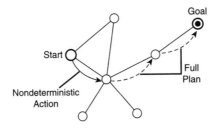

Figure 3.3   Planning through a set of situations to reach a predetermined goal.

Planning in Games

A wide variety of techniques exist to build plans for different situations. However, theoretically, there is no difference between planners and reactive techniques. It's just a question of expressing the problem differently. Therefore, justifying the use of planning by claiming that reactive techniques cannot handle goal-oriented behavior is provably false.

So, is planning actually needed in games? Of course. In practice, planning is well-suited to particular types of problems. This is notably the case with a large number of possible goals, because modeling them as additional inputs increases the number of input configurations dramatically. Here, approximating the entire problem in memory with reactive techniques is not always possible; instead, planning uses more computation rather than memory to search a solution.

This is the case with movement. Game developers have found that so-called *pathfinding* is best done with planning techniques. These algorithms essentially search the terrain for the best possible path.

In this example, the planning component actually uses knowledge of the terrain; this is called a *world model*. As discussed, it's possible to use reactive techniques to plan based on this world model. However, generally, reactive behaviors use little memory (no state), so a component that contains a world model would not theoretically be classified as reactive.

Reactive Substitutes

However, there are surprisingly few cases where planning is actually *necessary*. In many situations, reactive decisions appear very intelligent—especially high-level tactical decisions. Such instinctive decisions are surprisingly close to the way human experience works in most cases. To use reactive behaviors rather than deliberative algorithms, it's necessary to use properties of the situation as input, and use the output directly as a decision.

In fact, even movement can be handled with reactive behaviors. The problem can, for example, be treated as one of obstacle avoidance. Then, using a combination of information about the obstacles and the target, many scenarios can be handled. Usually, this approach is not as robust as the planning approach, because pathfinders use global knowledge of the terrain, and not only local obstacle information. A reactive planning approach, however, would be very competitive with a planner based on search.

Generally, however, reactive behaviors are extremely robust solutions. When combined with learning, they can significantly reduce the need for planning. When deliberative algorithms are needed, they are often enhanced by reactive techniques—both in performance and efficiency.

So, although the general use of planning algorithms is debatable, reactive techniques as discussed in this book have an undeniable place in games and AI.

Reactive Techniques in Game Development

Just like the behaviors, reactive—or *reflexive*—techniques have many advantages. In fact, reactive AI techniques have been at the core of most games since the start of game development. As explained, these techniques are often enhanced to provide non-determinism, but this can often be simplified into a deterministic mapping.

Advantages in Standard Game AI

The major advantage of reactive techniques is that they are fully deterministic. Because the exact output is known given any input pattern, the underlying code and data structures can be optimized to shreds. The debugging process is also trivial. If something goes wrong, the exact reason can be pinpointed.

The time complexity for determining the output is generally constant. There is no thinking or deliberation; the answer is a reflex, available almost immediately. This makes reactive techniques ideally suited to games.

Success stories of such approaches are very common, and not only in computer games. Historically, these are the most widely used techniques since the dawn of game AI:

➤ **Scripts** are small programs (mostly reactive) that compute a result given some parameters. Generally, only part of the programming language's flexibility is used to simplify the task.

➤ **Rule-based systems** are a collection of "if...then" statements that are used to manipulate variables. These are more restrictive than scripts, but have other advantages.

➤ **Finite-state machines** can be understood as rules defined for a limited number of situations, describing what to do next in each case.

These standard techniques have proven extremely successful. Scripts essentially involve using plain programming to solve a problem (see Chapter 25, "Scripting Tactical Decisions"), so they are often a good choice. Rule-based systems (covered in Part II) and finite-state machines (discussed in Part VI) can be achieved with scripting, but there are many advantages in handling them differently.

Advantages for Animats

The reactive approach also has benefits for animats, improving learning and dealing with embodiment extremely well.

Embodiment

With *embodiment*, most of the information perceived by the animat is from the surroundings, which needs to be interpreted to produce intelligence. Reactive behaviors are particularly well-suited to interpreting this local information about the world (as animals have evolved to do).

Also, it's possible to make the reactive behaviors more competent by providing the animat with more information about the environment. Thanks to their well-developed senses, humans perform very well with no advanced knowledge of their environment. Instead of using better AI, the environment can provide higher-level information—matching human levels of perception. Essentially, we make the environment smarter, not the animats.

Learning

Most learning techniques are based on learning reactive mappings. So if we actually want to harness the power of learning, problems need to be expressed as reactive.

Additionally, it's often very convenient to teach the AI using the supervised approach: "In this situation, execute this action." Reactive behaviors are the best suited to modeling this.

Architectures

Designing (game) AI is about assembling many weak components together. The components provide functionality for each other and communicate together to collectively solve the problem. This set of nested components is known as an *architecture*.

These architectures are *reactive* when they are driven by sensory input, and decide on output actions deterministically. Such architectures are very common for systems that need to react in a timely fashion, whether to external requests or stimuli from the environment (for instance, robots and washing machines).

Components

A component can be understood as a black box with a mystery AI technique inside. Alternatively, the component may be built as a subsystem of smaller components. Components interact with others via their interfaces, using inputs and outputs.

Internally, as mentioned previously, there is no theoretical difference between a deliberative component and a reactive component. This correspondence applies for the interfaces, too! Any deliberative planning component can be considered as reactive. All the necessary information is provided via the interfaces in the same fashion; only the underlying technology changes.

This is a tremendous advantage during the design phase, because the underlying implementation can be disregarded. Then, if a reactive technique is not suitable, a deliberative component can be inserted transparently.

Another consequence of the black box paradigm is that you can use other components during implementation. These components are nested inside others. This is the epitome of modularity in AI.

Organization

Naturally, there are many ways to combine components together. This is the purpose of architectures, because they define the relationship between components. Figure 3.4 shows three example architectures with different internal organizations:

➤ **Monolithic** architectures include only one component.

➤ **Flat** architectures have many components in parallel.

➤ **Hierarchical** models have components nested within others.

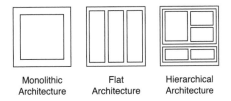

Monolithic   Flat   Hierarchical
Architecture Architecture Architecture

Figure 3.4   Three example architectures with different internal organizations. From left to right, monolithic, flat, and hierarchical architectures.

As an example of a hierarchical architecture for games, the brain may be built as a collection of behaviors (for instance, hunt, evade, patrol), which are components within the brain. Each behavior in turn may depend on components for moving and shooting. This is a three-level hierarchy.

In general, selecting the organization of an architecture is about problem complexity. Simple problems will manage with monolithic architecture, more sophisticated problems may need flat architectures, whereas hierarchical architectures can handle almost any problem by breaking it down. (Chapter 21, "Knowledge of the Problem," and Chapter 28, "Understanding the Solution," discuss these points further.)

Decomposition

Instead of thinking of an architecture as a combination of components (bottom-up), it can be understood in a top-down fashion: "How can this problem be split up?" This concept of *decomposition* is central to AI development in general.

There are many types of decompositions. The idea is to split the problem according to certain criteria—whichever proves the most appropriate for solving it! This applies equally well to software design as to the creation of game AI:

➤ **Structural decomposition** splits the solution according to the function of each component. For example, there may be a component responsible for movement, and another for handling the weapon. These are different functions.

➤ **Behavioral decomposition** is based on the distinctive activities of the system. These can be understood as different modes such as hunting, fleeing, collecting ammo, or celebrating. Different components would handle these behaviors.

➤ **Goal decomposition** uses the overall purpose of the system to determine how to split it into components. In game AI, goals depend on the behavior (for instance, finding a weapon). Although goals do not provide clear policies for decomposing the problem, they are always a criteria in the decisions [Koopman95].

Naturally, the decomposition can happen on multiple levels using many different criteria. For example, the initial problem may be decomposed as behaviors, then each behavior may be expanded as different functionality, using different criteria known as a *hybrid* decomposition, as opposed to using one criteria throughout the architecture (or *pure* decomposition).

Behavioral decompositions are very appropriate for computer games. The functional decomposition is also used in this book, as we develop common abilities that can be reused by the nonplayer character (NPC) AI.

Arbitration

Given a set of subcomponents, how are they connected together? Specifically, how are all the outputs interpreted to form the output of the component itself? There are four different ways of doing this:

➤ **Independent sum** essentially connects each component to different outputs so no clashes can occur.

➤ **Combination** allows the outputs of different components to be blended together to obtain the final result.

➤ **Suppression** means that certain components get priority over others, so weaker ones are ignored.

➤ **Sequential** arbitration sees the output of different components alternating over time.

There really is no right or wrong method of arbitration. Each of these methods is equally applicable to computer games.

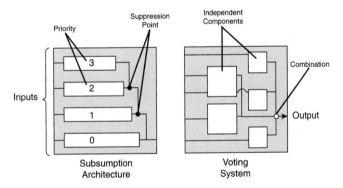

Figure 3.5   Two popular reactive architectures. On the left, the subsumption architecture with its horizontal layers. On the right, a voting system that combines the votes of four nested components.

Examples

There are many different combinations of architectures. Figure 3.5 shows two common examples to illustrate the issue.

Subsumption

The subsumption architecture is a behavior-based decomposition, using a flat organization with suppression on the outputs [Brooks86].

The system can be seen as a set of horizontal layers. The higher the layer, the greater the priority. Layers can thereby *subsume* the ones beneath by overriding their output. This architecture is explained further, and applied to deathmatch behaviors in Chapter 45, "Implementing Tactical Intelligence."

Voting System

Voting systems generally use a functional decomposition, with a flat organization using combination to merge the outputs together. Chapter 25 uses a voting system for weapon selection.

The system can be interpreted as a set of distributed components that are all connected to a smaller component responsible for counting votes. The output with the most votes becomes the output for the global output.

Summary

This chapter covered the theory and common properties behind reactive techniques:

➤ A reactive component is a deterministic mapping from inputs to outputs.

➤ Components with some internal memory are often considered reactive, despite not being so in theory.

➤ It's possible to express nondeterministic components (with internal states) as a reactive mapping by using additional inputs.

We've also learned the difference between reactive behaviors and planning:

➤ Planning algorithms are nondeterministic, because the output depends on the goal.

➤ Planning generally uses an internal model of the world, whereas reactive behaviors generally do not.

➤ Planning is better suited to some problems because it sacrifices computation in favor of memory.

This chapter also covered the many reasons for using reactive behaviors and techniques:

➤ Reactive behaviors are suited to games due to their efficiency, reliability, and predictability.

➤ Reactive behaviors are ideal for animats because they enhance embodiment as well as learning.

➤ Reactive techniques are often at the base of more sophisticated systems.

Finally, this chapter covered reactive architectures as amalgamation of hierarchical components:

➤ Components are treated as black boxes with the same interfaces regardless of the implementation. Components can be nested transparently.

➤ Reactive architectures must react quickly to external requests or stimuli from the environment.

➤ There are different ways to decompose the problem to build architectures, simplifying the development.

➤ Many approaches to combining the output of multiple components were discussed.

The next chapter looks at ways to put all these ideas together practically so that the actual development of NPCs is slightly easier!

Chapter 4

FEAR: A Platform for Experimentation

KEY TOPICS

- Technical Overview
- World Interface
- Modules
- Flexible Architecture
- Creating an Animat

Game AI generally takes a lot of work to implement—not directly for the AI techniques, but to integrate custom AI, or even middleware, within the game. This is an unavoidable consequence of current engine design, and can be difficult to deal with when starting out in AI development.

This book provides a real game for testing the AI, and not just a toy environment or command prompt. For this, the open source FEAR project is used, integrated with a commercial first-person shooter game engine. Some other game engines use similar frameworks to assist the AI development (but they're not as flexible). FEAR provides some helpful facilities, including the following:

➤ World interfaces for the AI to interact with the game engine (physics simulation and logic)

➤ Modules that implement AI functionality on their own or by depending on other modules

➤ Flexible architectures that enable engineers to assemble arbitrary components together

➤ Tools to create animats and their source files using minimal programming

As the combination of these elements and more, FEAR provides an ideal foundation for the examples in this book—and many other prototypes, thanks to its flexibility.

Technical Overview

This book is based on a framework called FEAR, a Flexible Embodied Animat 'Rchitecture! It's an open source project that provides portable support for the creation of game AI, as well as building blocks that can be combined.

All the code available with this book—both for AI modules and example animats—compiles with FEAR. This book's web site at `http://AiGameDev.com/` contains step-by-step instructions on how to install FEAR. This book itself is a resource for learning AI, and not a technical guide to FEAR. For further details about how FEAR works, or to follow recent progress, see the project web site at `http://fear.sf.net/`.

FEAR is based on many of the ideas explained in this book, combined with other design principles. FEAR can be understood as one way of putting the ideas in this book into practice.

Specification

FEAR uses a high-level specification to describe all aspects of the AI [FEAR03a]. FEAR uses a minimal *domain-specific language* based on XML for this purpose. AI is essentially about manipulating data at different levels, so this is formalized as three separate parts, as follows:

➤ **Interfaces** provide a set of functions (with inputs and outputs) that can be called, messages that can be passed back, type definitions, and constant declarations.

➤ **Modules** are the implementation behind the interfaces. Most interfaces are run-time (that is, implemented in C++), but the storage of persistent data can be considered as an interface with the disk (for instance, writing binary files during shutdown). To formalize dependencies between modules, each module imports and exports interfaces.

➤ **Architectures** are built from nested components (instances of modules) forming a hierarchy. The root of the hierarchy is usually the *brain* of the animat.

These high-level definitions are processed by the toolset to create source files, based on customized templates. This is known as *meta-programming* (a.k.a. code generation). The programmer can thereby create new definitions (for example, modules and interfaces) and have them running in FEAR with minimal coding. Already, most of the repetitive programming work can be automated.

Framework

The purpose of the framework is to implement the specification. FEAR does not impose a particular framework, but recommends a simple application programming interface (API) that common code should comply with [FEAR03b]. The developer can thereby build the system with one of many different types of implementations (for instance, static, dynamic, different styles of C++). This is achieved by expressing parts of the framework as templates, processed by code-generation tools to customize the system for each module and interface.

The framework can be tailored to almost any situation. At the moment, the FEAR team is focusing on a dynamic C++ framework, designed to be very flexible during initialization. This book uses this framework because it is ideal for educational and experimental prototypes. The demo animats are configured and loaded with little or no recompilation.

A static C++ framework will remove all the runtime customization for the sake of speed. The FEAR team is working on such a static framework that is fully compatible with the API and design patterns used in the dynamic framework. The architectures and modules can thereby be hard-coded and linked together, with most of the overheads optimized out.

Status of Development

FEAR has been going since early 2002, supporting other animat projects at first, but as a self-standing initiative since. There have been three major iterations already, but much work remains to be done—both in research and development. That said, the codebase is mature enough to support experimentation for educational and research purposes.

FEAR aims to become a general-purpose framework for state-of-the-art game AI development. Any kind of feedback on the project is extremely welcome. The developers also strongly encourage any kinds of contributions! Don't hesitate to get in touch via the web site at `http://fear.sf.net/` or directly by email.

World Interface

The exchange of information with the world is an extremely important part of AI. For animats, this takes the form of interfaces between the brain and the body. In terms of information flow, this leads to two different types of interfaces:

➤ **Sensors** provide a way to acquire information from the surrounding environment.

➤ **Effectors** allow the brain to control the body to act upon the world.

Although it is possible to separate these two types of interfaces in the implementation, FEAR no longer imposes this. Respecting this convention is unnecessary and leads to overly complex code. Instead, it's more convenient to group world interfaces by functionality:

➤ **Weapon** interface allows query of the state of the weapon, change and reload, and then actually use it.

➤ **Movement** interface allows forward/backward and side steps to be performed, as well as turning actions.

➤ **Physics** interface allows the animat to query its internal state: in water, midair, or colliding with a wall.

This approach generally reduces the amount of code required to implement the interfaces. Also, this separation enables you to import different functionality into the AI independently.

The implementation of the world interfaces is called the *backend* (as far as the AI is concerned). FEAR's framework can be plugged in to arbitrary platforms (for instance, game engines) that implement the backend for the interfaces.

Currently, the recommended platform supported by FEAR is *Quake 2*. The engine offers a great variety of game types, enabling programmers to develop animats for deathmatch, single player, or even capture the flag. The low-key graphics leave much computational power to the AI. There is tremendous community support for the game, including custom levels and various tools. The entire source code is available, too, making *Quake 2* one of the best choices for pure AI development.

Modules

Modules are essentially implementations of AI techniques. When the modules are instantiated within the architecture, they're called *components*. For example, there is only one rule-based system implementation (module), but different rule-based behaviors can be used for movement and tactical decisions (components).

Interfaces

The module interfaces are purposefully made high level. Only the core functionality is exposed by the interfaces (for instance, movement requests). This approach emphasizes the purpose of the module, which helps understanding and the design.

Such interfaces have many advantages in terms of modularity—just as in software development in general. Essentially, the implementation can be completely abstracted from the other components, which reduces dependencies.

Many AI techniques have similar capabilities, such as pattern recognition, prediction, function approximation, and so on. This functionality can often be expressed as one concise interface, but implemented in different ways.

Data Loading

Special interfaces are used to store data on disk. These interfaces are also specified formally, so the meta-programming tools generate functions that save and load data from disk. The low-level details of the storage are thereby handled automatically. The programmer is only responsible for postprocessing the data as appropriate after it has been loaded.

Dependencies

Each module may import specific interfaces. Conceptually, this means the module depends on other implementations to provide its own functionality.

At runtime, this translates into nested components. The internal components are called on when their output is needed to produce the final result. For example, nested components could be used to implement a subsumption architecture for navigation, or even a voting system handling combat—as explained in the preceding chapter.

Flexible Architecture

FEAR supports entire architectures, defined as hierarchies of components. A hierarchy is the most generic type of architecture, because both monolithic and flat can be considered a specific subtype.

Each component has access to its children. (This access is called the *scope* of the component.) FEAR's dynamic C++ framework initializes the components automatically during initialization, so none of the standard code to import interfaces needs to be written manually (as with DirectX).

At the time of writing, all forms of arbitration (independent, suppression, combination, sequence) are supported indirectly; the programmer can implement each as modules in a customized fashion.

Creating an Animat

The process of creating an animat in FEAR is threefold, as described in this section.

Description of the Architecture

Create a file with the description of the architecture. This specifies which components the brain of the animat needs and other recursive dependencies for those components.

Generating the Source Code

To create all the project files, we need to process this architecture definition with the toolset. The resulting animat should compile by default, effectively creating a brain-dead animat!

Adding behaviors to the animat involves adding code to a few files—usually those with "to-do" comments inside them. Other generated files are managed by the toolset (stored in the Generated folder of the project) and should not be edited manually; their content may disappear when the tools are used again.

Preparations for the Game

The compiled files need to be accessible by the game engine. This involves copying the brain dynamic link library (DLL) into the correct directory, along with a descriptive file to tell the framework about the architecture required. All the data files for the animats are stored in their own directory, too.

INSTALLATION NOTE

Each of the animats can be downloaded separately, or in a complete package. The full source is available as well as the compiled demos. It's best to start by running the demos to get a feel for the platform. The instructions for installing the tools and building each animat are detailed on the web site at `http://AiGameDev.com/`.

Summary

This chapter provided a preliminary overview of FEAR. Details about the tools and procedures used to develop animats and AI models are detailed as necessary throughout this book. The design decisions for particular world interfaces and AI implementations are also discussed in respective chapters.

Readers interested in advanced use of FEAR, or the design and implementation behind the project, should consult the *Technical Overview* [FEAR03c] and the *Library Reference* [FEAR03d]—each available from `http://fear.sf.net/`.

Part II

Moving Around

This part is dedicated to creating a fully mobile game character, capable of reactive activities such as obstacle avoidance and wall following. The concepts of movement are explained, and two different solutions are proposed—one for each behavior. Our knowledge of rule-based systems will also be cultivated, and the first few stages of the AI development process are presented. Most importantly, by the end of this part, we'll have a basic AI to build upon.

Motivation

Even the simplest living creatures can move; it's a fundamental skill for most of them. In games, the background cast pretty much only moves around, so after this chapter, we could have lots of "extras"—like in films!

Movement is an ability that can be re-created relatively simply. It takes much effort to improve on that, but it's a good place for us to start. The abundance of existing work on the subject will come in handy as guidance.

More elaborate behaviors (for instance, hunting and gathering) are almost always based on movement. So, before we get too ambitious, it seems wise to spend some time on this fundamental activity. By the time we develop more sophisticated AI, our experience will have grown enough to enable us to handle it without whimpering!

Outline

This part consists of eight chapters, providing an ideal blend of theory, practice, and concepts—at least partly related to movement or its development.

Chapter 5, "Movement in Game Worlds." First, the importance of the game environment is analyzed, because it can be a challenge even for human players. We also discuss the handling of movement by the engine.

Chapter 6, "Moving Abilities." The problem of navigation in computer games is understood by examining the human approach to movement, revealing how AI characters can copy their behavior. This chapter defines the ability in detail, and provides a set of criteria for evaluating the motion of the animats.

Chapter 7, "Analysis and Understanding." Next, we suspend our quest for movement to explain the importance of the *analysis* and *understanding* phases in AI development generally. These are crucial stages for creating artificial intelligence—and not only movement behaviors.

Chapter 8, "Formalizing Motion." Back to movement again, we build on the assumptions we identified by establishing a formal specification of the problem. This provides a set of interfaces with the environment and an empty code skeleton; this is a good base waiting for the right solution to be implemented.

Chapter 9, "Specifications and Knowledge Representation." This chapter discusses the importance of specifying the problem. Notably, this relies extensively on the subject of knowledge representation, which we explain in detail. Then, we show how to conduct the *specification* phase generally.

Chapter 10, "Steering Behaviors for Obstacle Avoidance." The development focuses on the problem of obstacle avoidance first. As a simple technique for this task, an approach from artificial life is explained; steering behaviors can be applied to create an animat that can prevent collisions. This simple implementation will reveal a few problems, so better alternatives are investigated.

Chapter 11, "Rule-Based Systems." Rule-based systems will come to the rescue, and the concepts are explained. Taking a game developer's approach to the technique, this chapter presents commonly used tricks.

Chapter 12, "Synthesizing Movement with Rule-Based Systems." Once described, an expert system is applied to another movement problem: wall following—with practical issues explained along the way. Then, a few exercises enable us to apply our recently acquired knowledge.

Assumptions

This is the first practical part, so there's little to rely on. We'll assume the following tools and software are available:

➤ A **game engine** that is ready for AI characters. This will need to support movement with a simple physical model and animation system. This is a lucky position for us to be in, because the AI is often developed alongside the engine. However, the same critical analysis can be applied when the engine is being developed.

➤ A variety of **different environments** that will be used to develop and test the animat's moving abilities. These can—and should—be game levels used by human players.

➤ A **development framework** to support the development of the AI, namely FEAR—as described in Part I.

These basic requirements will serve as a basis for all the other parts, too. The remaining support facilities are explained as we go through the development process.

Chapter 5

Movement in Game Worlds

Before getting carried away thinking about the implementation, it's a good idea to analyze the platform for the AI (that is, the engine and the environment's design). Luckily, this book reuses an existing game, so the specification is already established! In most cases, the specification is not frozen at this stage of development. Nonetheless, the game design has already focused on these issues as they also apply to human players. The aim here is to explain parts of the design to be reused and customized by the AI, to fulfill general requirements from the rest of the development team (for instance, efficiency and realism).

This chapter covers the following topics:

➤ A study of the environment as it implicitly defines movement down to every possible step, and restrictions on the behaviors of animats

➤ The types of movement supported by game worlds, which will reveal some assumptions reused during the specification phase

➤ How the game engine ties everything together, with a focus on the simulation of the world itself

➤ A description of the ideal environment, providing testing conditions and guidelines to assist when creating movement

The analysis from this chapter provides a foundation for the specification of a world interface for controlling movement and for the understanding of behaviors relating to movement.

The Environment and Space

Let's focus on the game world where movement takes place. The environment is planned by the designer, created with modeling tools by the graphics artist, and updated and displayed within the game by the programmer's engine. A wide variety of technologies can be used along this production pipeline, but it is mostly inconsequential from the AI's perspective.

What's important is the information contained implicitly within the world. Most environments are split into two components: structure and detail. After discussing them separately, this section looks at how they combine to define space.

Sum of Its Parts

The information about the environment provided to the players can be conceptually divided into two main components: structure and detail. This is more than just a theory, because most game engines strongly distinguish the two for efficiency reasons. The physics simulation handles the structure, and the detail is for graphics rendering. In the real world, of course, the boundaries between them are much more debatable, so we should consider ourselves lucky to be dealing with computer games!

➤ The **structure** is the part of the environment that can physically affect movement. Naturally this includes the floor, walls, doors; chairs, tables, and other furniture; trees, roads, and bridges; and so on. This list is not exhaustive, and should include all the elements in the world that are mostly static—those the players cannot trivially push aside.

➤ As for the **detail**, it consists of the "cosmetic" part of the environment: the things game characters cannot collide with (or if so, insignificantly)—books, kitchen utensils, or bits of food; grass, shrubs, and small ledges; among many others.

There is one important omission to notice from the preceding definitions. What happens to living creatures and other mobile entities? Although not necessarily created with the same tools as the rest of the game world, they too are arguably part of the environment. We could argue that game characters have properties of both the structure and the detail. However, some developers (and robotics researchers) believe that they should be treated separately, as an entirely different set. Generally in games, the set of living creatures ends up being forced into one category or the other (for instance, players are detail that's ignored during movement, or players are part of the environment structure that movement takes into account).

Essentially, the problem is about combining these three components of the environment together to create an understanding of space. We want to understand space as best possible to develop high-quality movement. Considering moving creatures as either detail or structure can have a negative effect on the movement, especially when the problem has not been identified beforehand.

Fortunately, we have the luxury of being able to decide how to handle living creatures as we design the AI. In a deathmatch, for example, it's fine to ignore the other animats for movement; they can be blown up with a rocket if they get in the way! In cooperative mode, however, a separate category is needed for nonplayer characters (NPCs) so that they can ask each other to move. Finally, other players can be considered as obstacles in large crowds.

Each of these three interpretations is a way of understanding the environment, but most importantly space—which relates to the NPC AI.

Defining Space

Fundamentally, the game world describes space. As the shape of the environment, the structure plays an important role; as far as the physics engine is concerned, all the movement is defined by the structure. However, both human players and AI characters cannot always match this physical knowledge of space; it will be extremely difficult, if not impossible, for them to understand the environment perfectly.

In some cases, when a simple world is stored in an explicit fashion (for instance, a 2D grid), understanding it can be a manageable task. As the design becomes more complex, many elements combine to define the environment in an intricate fashion (for example, a realistic 3D world). However, no matter how well the environment is defined or how accurate its physical rules are, it is not necessarily as clear to players and NPC.

➤ **Human players** have to assimilate the environment based on imperfect visual information. The detail of the environment plays an important part visually.

➤ **AI characters** usually get a simplified version of this world before the game starts (offline), in both an imprecise and incomplete fashion (for instance, waypoints as guides). Alternatively, the environment can be perceived and interpreted online (as humans would).

For all intents and purposes, space is an abstract concept that cannot be fully understood. Different techniques will have varying degrees of precision, but all will be flawed. Don't see this as a problem, just accept it and embrace it; perfection is overrated! This lesson was learned in robotics thanks to the wave of *nouvelle AI* robots.

After space has been figured out, it's possible to determine which parts are free space and which can be considered solid. This implicitly defines all movement: what is possible and what isn't. Only then can intelligent movement be considered.

Types of Game Worlds

It's surprising how many games rely on movement as their most fundamental concept. They range from chiefly strategic logic games such as *Chess* or *Diplomacy*, or the more entertaining alternatives such as *Horses* or *Downfall*. Let's not forget computer games of course; first-person shooters, real-time strategy, or even role-playing games would be extremely dull without motion!

Despite virtual worlds being widespread, they come in many varieties. Notably, there are worlds of different dimensions (for instance, 2D or 3D), with different sizes and precision. Some worlds are based on grids (discrete), and some are free of restrictions (continuous).

Conceptually, there is a big difference between these variations, which translates into the feel and style of the gameplay. Behind the scenes in the engine, distinct data structures and implementation tricks are used in each case, but this discussion focuses on the consequences for the AI.

On Dimensions

Some games can take place in 2D levels like top-down worlds (*Warcraft II*), or side views with moving platforms and smooth scrolling (*Super Mario Brothers*). Alternatively, the world itself can be fully 3D, with different floors in buildings (*Half Life*), or even tunnels (*Descent 3*).

It's important to note that the dimensions of the game world are independent from the rendering. For example, the original *Doom* is in fact a 2D world with the floors at different levels. Even recent 3D first-person shooters have a lot in common with *Doom*. This leads to the assumption that the underlying properties of the environment are very similar. Indeed, much of the technology is applicable in 2D and 3D.

Most academic research projects deal with top-down 2D AI movement algorithms, for example [Seymour01], which provides a nice amalgamation of past research. The same goes for the most of the figures here; they show the problem projected onto the floor. This is primarily because 2D movement is simpler than its 3D counterpart.

As a justification, one often read that "2D generalizes to 3D," so it's fine to focus on the simpler alternative. With an algorithm defined for two dimensions, the same concept is re-applied again to an additional dimension! This is mostly the case, although special care needs to be taken to devise a solution that scales up with respect to the number of dimensions.

For movement in 3D games, this simplification is also acceptable. In realistic environments, gravity plays an important role. All creatures are on the floor most of the time, which *almost* simplifies the problem to a 2D one. It is not quite 2D because the floor surfaces can superimposed at different heights (for instance, a spiraling staircase); this type of world is often known as *2.5D*, halfway between the complexity of two and three dimensions.

In the process of applying, or generalizing, our 2D solution to 3D, watch out for a couple of pitfalls:

➤ Complex environments often exhibit tricky contraptions (for example, jump pads or lifts), which are quite rare in flat worlds.

> ➤ Instead of naively applying an original algorithm, it can be tailored to make the most of the problem at hand.

These factors influence the design the solution.

Discrete Versus Continuous

Another property of game worlds is their precision, in both time and space. There are two different approaches, *discrete* and *continuous* events (in space or time), as shown in Figure 5.1. A discrete variable can accept only a finite number of values, whereas a continuous variable theoretically takes infinite values.

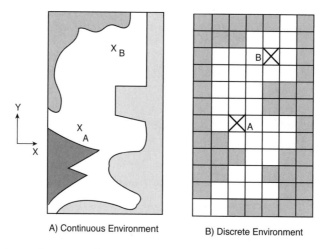

A) Continuous Environment   B) Discrete Environment

Figure 5.1   Two types of game environments observed top-down. On the left, space is continuous, whereas the world on the right is based on a grid (discrete).

Conceptually speaking, there is little difference between a continuous domain and a discrete one. Indeed, when the discretization is too fine to notice, the domain appears continuous. This doesn't apply mathematically, of course, but on modern computers, there are hardware limitations. To simulate continuous media, current software must select an appropriate discrete representation.

Using examples for space and time in game worlds shows how it's not only a game design issue, but also a fundamental element for the AI. (It's an independent AI design decision.)

Space

The game environment can be limited to cells of a grid; it's discrete if there are a finite number of grid coordinates. Continuous environments have unlimited locations because they are not restricted to grids.

To store the coordinates in the world, data types must be chosen. These are usually single precision floating-point numbers, which essentially allocate 32 bits to discretize those dimensions. Although there are benefits to using a double representation (64 bits), single representations are enough to make each object seem like it can take every possible position and orientation in space.

Time

Actions can be discrete in time, taking place at regular intervals—like in turn-based strategy games. Alternatively, actions can be continuous, happening smoothly through time as in fast-pace action games.

Similar floating-point data types can be chosen to represent this dimension. However, this choice is slightly more complicated because the programmer can't "manipulate" time as easily. Conceptually, single processors can only execute one logical *process* at a time—despite being able to perform multiple atomic *operations* in parallel. Consequently, it's not possible for each object in the world to be simulated continuously. The closest the computer can get is an approximation; a portion of code determines what happened since the last update (for example, every 0.1 seconds). So despite being very precise, a floating-point number will not be entirely necessary to represent a value in time (see Figure 5.2).

Conversions

Fundamentally, because of the limitations of computers, each of these dimensions can be considered as discrete—although it does not *appear* that way. Regardless, these data types can be converted to one another by simple mapping; this involves scaling, converting to an integer by rounding, and rescaling back. Arbitrary discretizations can thereby be obtained.

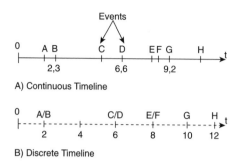

Figure 5.2   On the top, a continuous timeline with events happening at any point in time. On the bottom, the same timeline, but discrete. The time of each event is rounded to the closest mark every two seconds.

In practice, it's possible for the world to have one type of discretization and use a different discretization for the AI. For example, mapping continuous onto discrete domains enables us to exploit similarities in the AI design, and reuse existing AI routines (for instance, standard grid-based A* pathfinding). Of course, we may not necessarily want to perform the conversion for many reasons (for example, compromising behavior quality or sacrificing the complexity of environment). But at least AI engineers have the luxury to decide!

Handling Movement

The type of environment has a direct effect on the creatures that inhabit it. In fact, the type of movement is imposed upon the creatures by the environment.

Regardless of the dimensionality the environment, movement is handled in a similar fashion in both cases (2D or 3D). Although there are many possible ways of implementing this, a pattern arises in each of these designs: simulation loop, integration, and collision detection. The details classify as engine development rather than AI, but an overview of the principles will come in handy later.

The game engine has to take into account movement requests from all the players and creatures in the world. The physics system is in charge of resolving the collisions with the environment as well as with other entities. Each of the data structures representing in-game objects will then be updated accordingly, with new velocities, positions, and orientations.

To date, animation systems take care of low-level limb "control" as predefined animation cycles (for example, walk and run) are combined to move the player's entire body. Such animation cycles can be chosen based on the higher-level control of the players. Therefore, characters in the game are not actually walking (active behavior), they are merely animated (passive process). This animation system requires a minimal amount of coordination with the physics system to prevent breaking the illusion with inconsistencies (for instance, walking on the spot when stuck against walls, running in midair).

For all intent and purposes, the low-level aspects of movement are abstracted from the player—greatly simplifying the process. This underlying layer can be referred to as a *locomotion* layer. Computer-controlled characters can also rely on such locomotive capabilities. Indeed, handling the movement for AI and human players together is becoming commonplace in game development now; it's a good way to reduce the amount of code by inheriting AI classes from human-player classes (that is, with the same locomotive functions).

In the near future, there are prospects of the AI taking over low-level limb control, done in a fully dynamic fashion. For human players, controls are unlikely to change as they often prove complex enough. Humans will just have to adjust to having the AI control their character's legs in the game! For nonplayer characters (NPCs), the AI could theoretically control the entire body as a whole, dealing with locomotion at the same time as high-level requests. However, keeping the locomotion separate has many advantages (for example, simplicity and little redundancy), so it is advantageous to retain this distinction in the future.

Assumptions

Given knowledge from the game simulation, let's outline our assumptions. There is a physics system that takes care of applying the motor commands to the data structures representing each player. We'll suppose it is done with kinematics, in a physically plausible fashion. A physics system will also resolve any conflicts that happen within the simulation. This is the locomotion, which falls outside of the control of the AI.

We'll also assume that an animation system takes care of the low-level aspects of motion. Specifically, moving individual limbs and blending the appropriate animation cycles is handled transparently from the AI.

For the interface to be of any use to the animat, it's essential for the information returned to be consistent with the physics of the environment. Consequently, we'll assume the backend implementation of these interfaces rely on the movement simulation.

Testing Conditions

Because we are aiming for state-of-the-art NPC intelligence, nothing less than complex 3D worlds will be satisfactory—like those humans deal with. This needs to be an environment frequently used by human players, and not a simplified test bed for the sake of AI development. By keeping the experimentation process up to standard with the realism of actual game worlds, fewer problems will arise due to fundamentally flawed assumptions. Keeping the test "levels" and scenarios diverse will unconsciously prevent these problems. Such guidelines need to be followed throughout the development of the movement.

To be realistic, it should include doors and corridors, stairs and ladders, narrow ledges and dead ends, floors with gaps and irregular terrain, closed rooms and open spaces, jump pads and teleporters.

Now that the environments have been explained and defined, our focus can be set on the actual movement. As discussed, the world has a very important impact on the movement, but it takes certain capabilities from games characters to use it to their advantage.

Summary

The environment will play an important role when designing the AI. First and foremost, there are some additional restrictions that relate to the problem:

➤ The structure of the environment has a direct effect on the movement.

➤ Movement simulation is always handled discretely in time, so the AI gets limited opportunities to move.

➤ There is no way of gathering perfect information about the world.

We deliberated on some rough guidelines for the application stages:

➤ We can consider the world as "mostly" 2D thanks, to gravity.

➤ It's important to consider how to handle other characters in the environment.

➤ It's possible to use (seemingly) continuous movement in space, but discretization is a possible alternative.

Finally, we identified some assumptions about the platform to use in the specification phase:

➤ The low-level details of animation (for instance, locomotion) are abstracted out from the AI.

➤ The physics engine is in charge of conflict resolution between the players' movement and the environment.

➤ It's possible to extract information about the environment for the simulation.

After the practical interlude, the next chapter considers the art of navigation, and how it can be reproduced artificially.

Practical Demo

A small game level is sufficient to illustrate the ideas in this chapter. An example animat called *Dr. Spin* can be found on the web site at `http://AiGameDev.com/`, along with a guide to run the binary demo. *Dr. Spin*'s only behaviors are to move and turn, often bumping into walls and getting stuck in corners. These situations demonstrate the importance of the world simulation and the structure on the movement.

Chapter 6

Moving Abilities

Movement is an ability humans often take for granted. It is truly incredible how many different skills combine perfectly to create the smooth flow of a human body. One only appreciates the art when one studies it, practices it in extreme conditions, or tries to re-create it. Instead of attempting to practice it in extreme conditions, we'll take a less adventurous approach—which doesn't involve standing up. This chapter covers movement and shows how to re-create it instead!

To get an idea of the different ways of solving the problem of movement, this chapter will:

➤ Focus on understanding the ability of humans and animals to move around.

➤ Examine the approach of existing game bots, analyzing what they do particularly well—and badly.

➤ Discuss how animats deal with embodiment to tackle the some problem.

This general understanding identifies desirable properties of motion, later used as requirements applied to the AI. To finish the chapter, we'll propose a brief case study of the obstacle-avoidance behaviors we want to re-create.

The Art of Navigation

Navigation is the process of purposefully steering the course of an entity through a physical medium. Navigation is autonomous when a "system" can steer its own course unassisted (like most mammals). Navigation is one of the possible causes of movement. As a proactive behavior, navigation differs from plain movement, which is more of a passive consequence of the physical rules in the world (for instance, an object falling off a cliff).

To navigate, a human or animal must perform actions that produce movement. In biological creatures, the actions are executed by using combinations of muscles. This can result in walking, running, or crawling depending on the circumstances. The AI will generally not need the same precision in control as mammals, so we'll probably need simpler actions to emulate the important behaviors in nonplayer characters (NPCs).

Purposeful navigation in a cluttered world is not possible just by executing actions. Try walking through an unknown door without looking or feeling walls. In this case, reaching the other side is probably more a question of luck than intelligence. Information about the surroundings needs to be gathered beforehand.

In fact, most living creatures require spatial information to interpret, too, providing them with a sense of their surroundings. Being aware of the world helps the decision of what step to take next.

For biological creatures, much of the complexity of navigation arises from the acquisition of information. This may be done in a variety of ways, including the use of physical sensors (for example, feeling contact with the floor, collision with walls) or visual sensors (for instance, seeing a doorway, ledge, or obstacle). A rough description of space is encoded in these perceptions; both the empty areas as well as the solid ones can be picked out. Humans and animals must understand these before they can consider intelligent movement.

Evolution has allowed biological creatures to become particularly efficient at what they do. As AI engineers, it's much tougher for us to re-create this without billion years of survival of the fittest.

Game Bots and Movement

In most computer games, navigation is almost never achieved by sensing and interpreting the environment. As the world is virtual, it can be stored entirely in the computer's memory. Typically, an algorithm processes the world to extract the structural information from it. This can be done by dropping waypoints (as in Figure 6.1) or processing polygons. Once prepared, the bot receives compact knowledge of the terrain directly before the game starts.

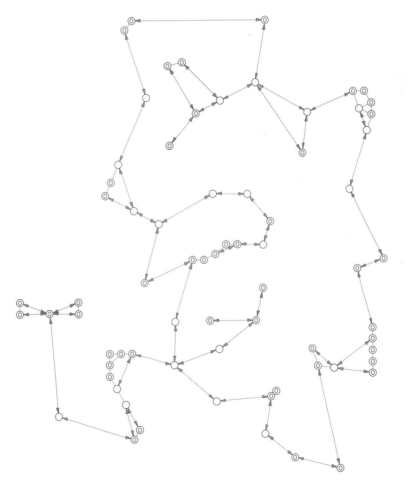

Figure 6.1   Description of the environment using a set of waypoints, known as a terrain model. These are generally placed manually by the designers during the development of the game.

Because the bot is part of the simulation of the world, its position is known perfectly. The AI code will know this position, too. This makes it possible for the AI to decide where to go next. For this reason, bots are particular good at *global* movement, such as crossing the entire terrain. Given the knowledge of the environment, standard pathfinding algorithms, such as A*, are particularly efficient.

> **THE A* PLANNING ALGORITHM**
>
> A* is a planning algorithm that searches through the terrain to find the shortest path to a single target. As a deliberative technique, A* is not discussed directly in this book. The web site at `http://AiGameDev.com/` has a list of online resources freely available on the subject.

However, bots do not "sense" the world like humans or animals. This goes a long way toward explaining the common problems with game AI, such as bots bumping into walls, getting stuck in doorways, or ignoring dynamic obstacles. The problem is that the bots rely only on preprocessed knowledge of the environment. First, the terrain model is often based on erroneous assumptions, and second, it does not remain up-to-date in dynamic environments.

Autonomous Navigation for Animats

The animat approach would physically simulate the body and give it the ability to sense the environment like animals do. Instead of passing data directly to the animats, active perception allows them to select the information they are interested in, which increases efficiency in dynamic situations.

This resolves most of the issues (faced by bots) by providing characters with fresh information about the local surroundings (see Figure 6.2). Dynamically moving obstacles are trivial to identify when the world is perceived continuously, and the characters act upon these perceptions.

When we get to the creation of movement in Chapter 10, "Steering Behaviors for Obstacle Avoidance," and Chapter 12, "Synthesizing Movement with Rule-Based Systems," we'll quickly realize that this approach is much easier too! Indeed, the problem can be interpreted as a reactive task—one of the many benefits of embodiment. This makes it particularly efficient, because no planning is required.

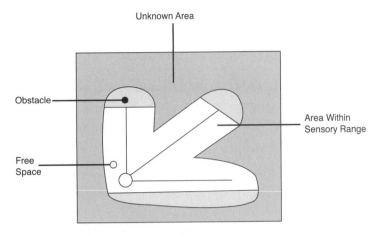

Figure 6.2   Using whisker-like sensors to perceive the environment. Areas of empty space are detected, as well as obstacles within range.

However, although many aspects of navigation are improved upon by this *nouvelle AI* approach, some aspects are not up to standard of the typical planning approaches. Notably, the reactive approach has trouble reaching particular points in space; it's good at the low-level details, but the higher levels can lack purpose.

Having analyzed different approaches to navigation, it's possible to decide what's expected from the NPC.

Criteria for Motion

The challenge of navigation is to generate a sequence of almost insignificant steps, which collectively form meaningful paths. Human navigation has many different properties that make it unique and desirable. Ideally, we would like to reproduce these with our AI system. The following list of properties for human-level movement can be taken as priorities for the development of the AI, and criteria for its evaluation:

➤ **Realistic**—Perhaps the most important facet of movement is producing human- or animal-like NPCs. Because movement is the most visible action, special care needs to be taken to increase realism.

➤ **Efficient**—Computer game programmers often pride themselves in saving processing time in critical sections of code. A system providing functionality as important and widespread as motion will need to be economical with processor cycles.

➤ **Reliable**—As discussed in the preceding section, there are many different kinds of situations that a game character could get into. The module taking care of movement must guarantee that nothing will go wrong in the various scenarios.

➤ **Purposeful**—Last but not least, movement is about the satisfaction of desires, the achievement of goals in space. An AI module that is not capable of fulfilling these requests is of little use!

As expected, these different properties may be in conflict with each other, making an AI navigation system even more challenging to develop. Things would be too easy otherwise, wouldn't they? During the design and implementation, issues will arise which compromise some of the requirements in favor of others. Therefore, it can be in a good idea to establish priorities.

Historically speaking, efficiency has been the primary concern of game developers. As better hardware implied more complex-level designs, the movement then needed to become reliable to handle these situations without any problems occurring. Not necessarily reaching the ultimate reliability, practice has shifted to now focus on realism. With regards to purposefulness, games have varying needs from cannon fodder to competent military units, making it hard to extract trends for this attribute.

Other applications of AI that require movement, such as robotics, have taken different approaches (mainly emphasizing reliability). Game developers can benefit from the experience accumulated in these fields over the years, so we'll make a point of looking into viable solutions when appropriate.

Case Study

An essential part of navigation is the ability to *avoid obstacles* successfully. This accounts for many of the properties previously described. It's also a good place to start learning about game AI development because obstacle avoidance is a relatively simple task.

To understand how obstacle avoidance works, it is worthwhile to analyze the behavior in different situations. The following list is a representative selection of all the possible states that the game character may encounter. For each scenario, the situation is briefly described and the desired outcome is explained (see Figure 6.3):

➤ When no obstacles are in proximity of the animat, it can move forward normally. This can be either *straight*, or a *wandering* behavior.

➤ In the case where walls are detected on one side, they should be turned away from slowly, in a preventive fashion.

➤ If there is an obstacle in front, a turn should be engaged to clear the danger on one side.

➤ For those situations where the animat is stuck in a corner, a more radical turn-around should be attempted.

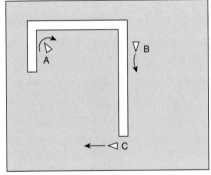

A) Complete Turn in Corner
B) Partial Turn Near Wall
C) No Obstacles, Forward Movement

Figure 6.3 Three different situations that require three different kinds of responses, ranging from quick turnaround to straight forward movement.

This list of expected actions, together with the four criteria of motion explained previously, forms the requirements for our obstacle-avoidance behavior.

Summary

What has this chapter introduced about movement, and notably the different approaches to re-creating it?

➤ Navigation is a skill that produces purposeful movement.

➤ Biological creatures do well at navigation because they continuously perceive their environment and act accordingly.

➤ Standard game bots generally use a static version of the world, often simplified. This can cause problems if the assumptions are erroneous, notably in dynamic environments.

➤ Animats can sense their environment, so they can navigate dynamically. However, this approach in itself doesn't perform as well as the nonembodied approach, because it lacks global knowledge of the world.

The next chapter steps back and focuses on game AI development in general. Before continuing with our quest for autonomous movement, we're going to examine the process we've just been through: analyzing and understanding the problem. This will enable us to draft requirements in other situations when designing different AI components.

Practical Demo

A quick demo is in order to build up motivation to go through the next chapter. On the web site at `http://AiGameDev.com/`, in the Demos section, there's an animat called *Bouncer*. Follow the online instructions to run the example. *Bouncer* runs around monitoring its own movement. When forward movement is not what was expected, a collision is assumed. *Bouncer* then turns around in a random direction until it can move again. The source code is very simple and can be found alongside the demo.

Chapter 7

Analysis and Understanding

In any serious AI engineering process, the two first phases are *analysis* and *understanding* (or equivalents). Here, we lay the foundations for the rest of the AI development by describing what we already have, what we're trying to do, and how it's generally done. This is good software engineering practice generally, but it's especially important for the AI as the creation of behaviors is not as easily managed as software.

The *analysis* phase aims to investigate the game environment, the engine, and existing software used for the development (a.k.a. the platform). When the game engine is being developed in parallel with the AI, the analysis takes into account its design document instead—with little impact on the AI analysis. The *understanding* phase uses the high-level requirements and goals to analyze of the problem at hand, irrespective of the game engine and for the sake of the AI development only. Both stages are relatively informal, because we deal with English descriptions.

It's vital to spend some time on this for all problems tackled. Already at this stage of the development, we should have such thoughts on paper—or even in digital form. It's imperative to write them down somewhere (for instance, along with the development log) because they'll undoubtedly come in handy, and prevent us from forgetting them later—thereby wasting time revisiting closed issues.

This chapter covers the following topics:

➤ A description of the big picture in the software, notably how the AI is split up; as well as the aspects of the AI dealt with by the first two software engineering phases

➤ An explanation of the analysis phase, examining the platform to determine assumptions, restrictions, and guidelines.

➤ A presentation of the understanding phase, describing the criteria (used to evaluate the desired outcome) and the definition of the problem using a case study

This chapter provides as much advice as possible to help deal with this informal process as rigorously as possible and to maximize its benefits.

The Big Picture

To better understand the purpose of software engineering processes in AI, and their link with the later stages of development, an abstract study of an AI component is necessary. Many concepts are involved in the development process, as shown in Figure 7.1.

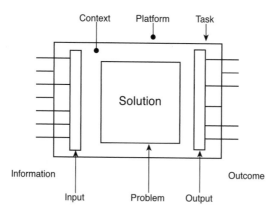

Figure 7.1   A diagram representing the role of the AI solution within the platform, notably emphasizing the different layers around the AI that it depends on.

In the case of navigation, the overall goal is a behavior. The following list explains the concepts one by one, using *obstacle avoidance* as an example:

➤ **Platform**—The software and hardware supporting the development, where the AI will have its effect (for instance, the game world and engine).

➤ **Task**—A conceptual explanation of the goals of the AI within the platform (for instance, understanding the local surroundings to prevent collision).

➤ **Information**—The collection of data available within the platform that may be used to achieve the task (for instance, the environment's structure and detail).

➤ **Outcome**—The results of the task within the platform, and possibly outside of this to (for instance, a collision-free trajectory).

➤ **Input**—A subset of the information available, converted into a suitable format (for instance, nearby obstacles). Together, the input and output form the *scaffolding* for the solution.

➤ **Output**—The possible actions that can be taken, combining together implicitly within the platform to generate the outcome (for instance, motor actions producing movement).

➤ **Context**—Implicit state that contains information about the task, defining the effect of the outputs and restricting the inputs (for instance, the player's physical properties: velocity, position).

➤ **Problem**—The description of an AI module capable of mapping the information from the input to the output (for instance, avoiding individual obstacles).

➤ **Solution**—A particular AI component that can resolve the problem, obtaining the desired outcome and respecting the requirements (for instance, steering behavior).

These concepts will come into play at different stages of the AI development pipeline. At first, finding the distinctions between the different concepts can be confusing. This will become easier with more experience, so we'll make a point of explaining all the concepts for each new problem in subsequent parts.

The Analysis Phase

The *analysis* phase does not focus on one particular scenario; instead, it tackles common principles. Analysis involves studying two things:

➤ **General task**—A universal ability that we want to provide using AI (for instance, navigation)

➤ **Platform**—Various aspects of the design (for instance, environment) and software (for instance, physics simulation) affecting the task

The idea is to quantify these two concepts to know what can be relied on during the AI development. The result of the analysis is split into three major parts: *assumptions*, *restrictions*, and *guidelines*—as shown in Figure 7.2. Each part is nothing more than a description in English (as detailed as necessary).

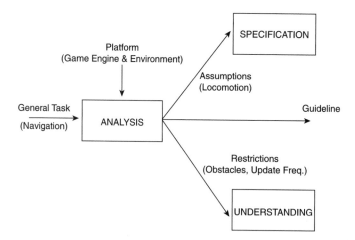

Figure 7.2   The analysis phase placed within the AI development process, used to explain the platform and the task by specifying a set of assumptions, guidelines, and restrictions.

Assumptions

The *assumptions* list the facilities of the platform that the AI can rely on. These are taken into account during the specification.

We can achieve this by explaining the environment in which the AI is to perform, as well as the relevant part of the game engine. In most cases, it's sufficient to enumerate and describe the interfaces provided for human players. Indeed, the AI will often be handled in a very similar fashion.

In the case of movement, for example, we assumed that there was a physics engine to apply the movement, and that it would resolve conflicts and collisions. We also relied on the animation system to provide low-level limb control, described as the *locomotion* system (used by human characters in the game, too).

Generally, little time is needed to draft the assumptions. At this stage, the design of the engine is usually already frozen. So, it isn't open to debate. The AI developer must decide how much of the platform to expose to the AI, and at what level it should be integrated. As a general rule of thumb, the maximum code should be reused, and the AI should rely on the human player interface as much as possible.

We should pay particular attention to troublesome aspects in the platform (for instance, clashes with the AI, temporary components that are not yet frozen). The description part of the assumptions should clarify the situation and help resolve the problems.

Restrictions

The *restrictions* are aspects of the design or software that affect the task at hand. The restrictions affect the problem itself, rather than its specification. As such, they are taken into account by the *understanding* phase later, which describes the problem.

Specifically, we need to describe the parts of the game engine that make the problem difficult to solve; these are restrictions. What aspect of the simulation has an affect on the way the problem is solved?

In the case of movement, the structure of the terrain is a restriction that prevents certain kinds of movement. There are also restrictions in model of the environment, notably our inability to gather perfect information. Also, the simulation itself can be restricting factor, as it implies that the AI can only get discrete opportunities to move around.

Guidelines

The *guidelines* are particular aspects of the design and platform that need to be taken into account during the application phase.

Guidelines take the form of various procedures that should be followed as closely as possible to assist the development. Often, developers have *general* guidelines that they follow throughout the process (for instance, document everything or at most 20 minutes per task). However, here we're talking about specific guidelines that focus on the particular task at hand. For this reason, it isn't possible to explain them generally, but once established, they should be followed all the same—as long as they improve the development process.

In the discussion about the environment, for example, a few paragraphs in Chapter 5, "Movement in Game Worlds," were spent describing the test bed. More specifically, suggestions are made about the use of normal game levels for development (not simplified ones), and making sure that many different levels are used to test the AI. These are examples of specific guidelines for the development of navigation behaviors.

Although there are guidelines that help developing AI behavior generally (for instance, diverse environments and time limits on experimentation), it's usually difficult to identify specific procedures before the development actually starts! Indeed, the best guidelines are based on practical experience. So, unless there is some existing wisdom that can be applied to this area, we're left with our theoretical insights as guidelines. That said, although it may be delicate to define good guidelines from the start, it's never too late to establish new ones and start following them—even far into the development; any form of structure is a good thing! Such practices, reminiscent of *agile development* (for instance, continuously upgrading to better methodologies) are particularly important for AI development because of the complexity of the task and its unpredictable nature.

The Understanding Phase

The *understanding* phase focuses on one particular task (for instance, obstacle avoidance). We attempt to understand how a solution works and describe it as best possible. The understanding phase relies on three different concepts:

➤ **Goals**—Description of what we want the AI to achieve. Goals can be understood as a very high-level explanation of the outcome.

➤ **Requirements**—A list of requests from various members of the development team that need to be taken into account when expressing the problem.

➤ **Restrictions**—Implicit aspects of the platform (its design or implementation) that also affect the solution to the problem.

The purpose of the *understanding* phase is to create the problem—or at least define it better. This involves translating the goals into a more explicit outcome, and then breaking that down into step-by-step actions—as shown in Figure 7.3.

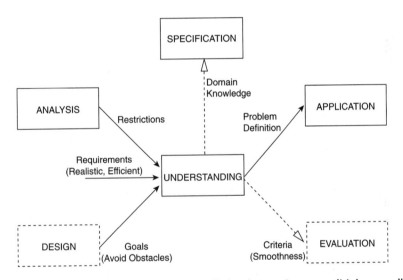

Figure 7.3   The understanding phase within the AI development process. It takes a collection of requests and attempts to specify the problem at different levels.

The *understanding* phase proceeds much like the *analysis*. We start with an overview of existing work to give us a feel for similar problems. Then, we can draft the criteria that will evaluate the outcome. Finally, a case study is used to split up the outcome into a combination of primitive actions.

Criteria and Desired Outcome

The first thing to describe is the resulting behavior. Ideally, we would like to have a well-defined outcome of the problem; the understanding phase makes sure of this! The goals we are given may be incomplete and somewhat inconsistent, unsuitable for engineering AI. Our aim is to interpret and understand what is implied and specify the outcome in a more precise fashion.

This generally takes the form of high-level criteria. We can draft a list of such criteria that will be used to evaluate the outcome of any solution. Because the list can be ordered, priorities between these criteria can be established. However, the ranking of criteria is not always obvious, as choosing between two of them is not always possible in the general case. In practice, the ranking becomes obvious when specific decisions must be made involving two factors. (The priorities are defined relatively to each other.)

The criteria are often problem specific, so they need to be described within the context of each problem. That said, some criteria appear regularly during AI development. These include reliability, efficiency, realism, flexibility, or even competence. Once again, we'll have to decide upon the list and priorities in each part separately.

For our obstacle-avoidance problem in Chapter 6, "Moving Abilities," properties are borrowed from human movement to serve as a reference for the AI behavior: realism, efficiency, reliability, and purposefulness. These take into account our goals for creating movement, overall requirements, and restrictions from the platform.

Being more specific, we could explain that animats should take no steps that cause a collision. Contact with obstacles is acceptable, as long as the animat is immobile or moving away from the contact point. A slightly more refined criterion would be to restrict the turns to a maximum of 20 degrees per second when no obstacles are within 4 steps, and no limits otherwise.

Problem Definition

When possible, the understanding phase must also decompose the outcome into a sequence of actions, those necessary to solve the problem. Breaking up the problem essentially makes it more explicit, thereby proving easier to solve.

Typically, it's possible to determine what should be done based on a case study (of human behavior, for example). Each of the situations is described, and assigned a particular result. Alternatively, a more implicit description would present key aspects of the behavior, using general examples and exceptions. So without listing scenarios one by one, we can describe what should happen and what should be avoided—in a much more convenient fashion.

For our reactive movement, we wrote down a brief list of situations along with the expected action (refer to Chapter 6). This didn't need to be exhaustive because the task is relatively simple; however, we still described the expected turns and speed controls. More complex problems need more time spent on this stage.

General Advice

While the role of the understanding phase is to describe the problem in a more explicit fashion, it should not attempt to explain the solution. The descriptions should be purposefully left informal (that is, in English) and high level, to influence the AI design decisions the *least* possible. Naturally, we will have some ideas while we describe the problem, but we should try to keep it unbiased; this is a good premise to help us come up with the best solution.

Another advantage of the intuitive nature of the understanding phase is that anyone can do it. All it takes is a bit of experience with computer games and some terminology to describe the situations. Then, all we need is a small amount of research to put us on the same page, and place these problems into context with respect to existing work. This is of the kind of understanding the previous two sections provide—although with a few more details than necessary. At this stage, we should be more than capable of communicating with other developers about technological requirements, and also dealing with vague requests from artists or designers.

Generally, the list of criteria will be relatively ambiguous—a curse associated with all natural languages. Ambiguity can be considered as an advantage because it translates into flexibility for the solution. However, misinterpretation is a nasty side effect of this flexibility, which may break assumptions with other aspects of the design. Pay particular attention to the criteria that have strong dependencies to other aspects of the design, removing ambiguity as much as possible.

Summary

The analysis of the overall task and platform is important in the short term, because it enables us to draft a few lists to be used in following stages of the development:

➤ Assumptions about the platform used by the specification phase to create a formal model

➤ Guidelines that will help the application phase make the most of the software

➤ Restrictions on the problem enforced by the design, and the environment itself

The understanding phase takes the restrictions, requirements from the rest of the team, and goals from the design and attempts to describe the problem:

➤ Problem definition takes the form of a case study that explains which actions should be taken in what circumstances. The application phase attempts to match this definition.

➤ Criteria are standard ways to judge the outcome of the simulation and used as the basis of the evaluation process.

Both these preliminary phases provide long-term benefits because they offer a way to check design ideas for consistency and allow empirical evaluation of the implementation. Revealing the criteria that are least satisfied is a good way to identify parts of the solution that need improving.

After another practical experiment, the next chapter defines an interface specification that provides the skeleton for the implementation of moving animats.

Practical Demo

Tobor is an animat that can obtain basic information from the environment. It has tactile sensors that detect physical contact with obstacles. *Tobor* has a robotic response to collisions, stopping immediately and turning around mechanically. The demo and documented code can be found on the web site at `http://AiGameDev.com/`.

Chapter 8

Formalizing Motion

KEY TOPICS

- Background Review
- Sketching Possible Options
- Rationalizing
- Proposed Specification

The preceding stages of the development are rather intuitive, providing a good base upon which to build. Before we can program an artifical intelligence (AI) component to perform navigation, however, we need to decide what this task consists of formally by designing an interface with the platform. This specification phase involves defining the animat, the information it receives about the environment, and how it can act upon that to achieve movement. To do this, we need to specify the *inputs*, *outputs*, and *context* of the problem.

Essentially, this chapter covers the following necessary steps:

➤ Briefly review existing approaches to navigation.

➤ Sketch all possible specifications in one creative burst!

➤ Discuss the options to pick out the best one.

➤ Establish a formal specification that describes everything involved.

➤ Select a representation for the inputs and the outputs.

After we have done this, we'll finally have a code skeleton ready for the AI solution to be inserted.

Background Review

Luckily, navigation is quite a common task. There are numerous existing projects on the topic, and plenty of experience to benefit from. In addition, because this is only the second part of the book, we would expect it to be a relatively straightforward task anyway:

➤ **Robotics** systems perceive their surroundings thanks to sonar or laser sensors, giving obstacles around them a sense of distance. Generally, this information is used directly—although more elaborate robots interpret the information with complex algorithms—to determine where to go next. Finally, navigation is performed by sending the chosen movement commands to the motors controlling the wheels (for instance, robots such as *AuRA*, *Rhino*, and *SSS*).

➤ **Artificial life** defines and studies the behavior of living synthetic creatures, usually as part of a group. A relatively important part of A-Life is movement, especially collective movement (for instance, flocking birds and swarming wasps). Some of this research—known as steering behavior [Reynolds89]—is applicable to individual creatures. Each agent is given artificial sensors, which can detect obstacles within range. This information is combined with the steering force using mathematical equations, and applied as linear and angular velocities.

➤ **Other academic projects** are too diverse to summarize briefly. Although most other academic (that is, not robotics) projects focus on 2D navigation as a practical application of an abstract algorithm (for instance, reinforcement problems), or small modular components of the whole system are developed (for instance, vision or localization).

➤ **Game AI** has historically simplified navigation as much as possible to reduce the computational overheads. This has involved precomputing the data structures necessary and passing them to the AI in the most optimal format possible. The position of each nonplayer character (NPC) can thereby be updated directly at runtime to achieve the illusion of conscious movement.

In the right circumstances, all of these approaches "work." It's just a matter of deciding which best matches our situation. Some of these methods disagree with our definition of embodiment listed in Chapter 2, "The Design of Intelligence." We'll need to decide which are convenient to develop game AI, and which have to be adapted.

Sketching Possible Options

Before continuing any further, it's necessary to brainstorm feasible options for all aspects of the problem, attempting to keep a wide range of choices. Each alternative need not be precisely defined; just a sketch will do.

Context

The main thing to consider is how to model the animat's state in space. Both position and orientation are important concepts when it comes to movement. Keep in mind, however, that neither may be explicitly required by the AI! The animat does not necessarily need to know its position or orientation to perform well, because it can rely on perceptions from the environment. Indeed, the context implicitly affects both the inputs and outputs provided to the animat encoded in a different format, as depicted in Figure 8.1.

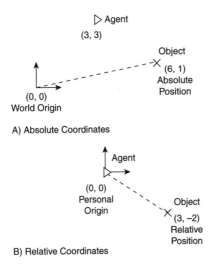

Figure 8.1   An agent and an object, represented with both absolute coordinates, where the world has the reference origin (top), and relative coordinates, where the agent is the reference origin (bottom).

Both position and orientation attributes can be encoded in a different fashion. This is purely an AI design issue, because the engine could store this information differently.

➤ **Absolute** vectors are expressed in terms of global coordinates, matching the axis of the world.

➤ **Relative** coordinate systems are based on each particular animat's experiences, and do not generally correspond together.

Additionally, different formats may be chosen to represent each of these quantities, as mentioned in Chapter 5, "Movement in Game Worlds":

➤ **Discrete** values can be used to represent the abstract quantities in a variably coarse fashion. For example, a north/south/east/west approach uses only four values for movement or turns.

➤ **Continuous** variables are not noticeably limited to finite values, and can accurately represent unrestricted domains.

Similar properties can be applied to the senses and actions (see Figure 8.2), as well as the underlying concepts.

Actions

The motor actions required for movement can be designed at different levels of abstraction; for example, does the AI request movement step by step, or as full paths? Lower levels of abstraction present simple commands such as "turn left" or "step forward." These may be provided explicitly as actual functions, or more implicitly by taking parameters. A high level of abstraction would offer actions such as "move to" and "turn toward."

It may be possible for the animat to do without the option of turning. This can either be implicit in the move functions (turn toward that direction automatically), or we can assume a constant orientation. This second option wouldn't be as realistic, but much simpler.

As you can see in Figure 8.2, discrete moves have limited directions and step sizes (top left), and discrete turns are restricted to 90-degree rotations (top right). Continuous steps instead have any magnitude or direction (bottom right), and continuous turns can rotate by arbitrary angles (bottom left).

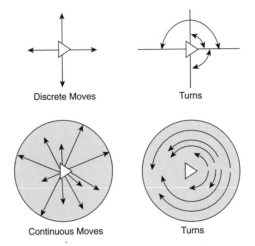

Figure 8.2   Different ways of modeling the actions.

Naturally, there is a trade-off between simplicity of implementation (on the engine side) and ease of use (by the AI)—so there may be more code on either side of the interface.

Choosing this level of abstraction is similar to the design decision about the commands given to human players. In first-person control, a balance between flexibility of control and intuitiveness is generally found. The movement interface between the engine and the AI can theoretically be handled in the same fashion as the human players, which actually reduces the work needed to integrate the AI into the game.

Senses

As previously emphasized, a sense of free space is needed for the animat to perform navigation. If a simplified version of the environment is not provided before the game starts, the animat can acquire it online with two different queries:

> ➤ **Point content** functions can return the type of matter at a specific location. It can be empty, solid, or contain some form of liquid, for example.

> ➤ **Line traces** can be used to find the first intersection of a segment with the structure world. This implicitly enables us to identify areas of free space.

The animat can decide where to go based on this information, but more elaborate queries of the environment can be devised to simplify its task (that is, ones based on the expected movement of the animat). On the other hand, much simpler sensors can be used instead, or even in conjunction with the ones just listed.

➤ **Collision** detectors can indicate when the animat has hit an obstacle of any description (walls, ledges, or other creatures).

➤ **Odometers** can be used to measure the distance travelled relatively to the current state.

➤ Other such **proprio-sensors** (based on the Latin *proprio*, the self; sensors that detect one's own state) allow relative angular movement to be monitored.

It is possible to understand the layout of the environment just using contact sensors and tracking the position (see Figure 8.3); terrain learning is required for collision prevention. However, this task is less realistic because it relies on trial and error rather than prediction, because the animat finds out about obstacles only when it is too late.

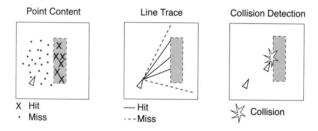

Figure 8.3   Three different kinds of sensors to allow the animats to sense their environment, using point and line queries or even collision indicators.

Historically, game AI developers just used relative movement to determine collisions; if the creature hasn't gone forward, an obstacle must have been hit. This is a consequence of poor interface design rather than efficiency; the physics engine already knows about collisions, but hacks have to be used by the AI to determine it again. A better interface would pass this existing information from the physics system to the AI.

Rationalizing

Many factors are involved in the decision of a particular model. Notably, it should correspond as closely as possible to the principles of embodiment explained in Chapter 2, allowing the AI to benefit from its advantages. The implication is that both senses and actions are relative to the body's position in space. This is not a hindrance because obstacle avoidance—as described in the requirements—can be performed locally; there is a direct mapping from the inputs to the outputs that produces satisfactory behavior.

The main concerns when selecting the right interface between the AI and the environment can be summarized in three points:

➤ **Consistency**—The information provided to the animat about its surroundings must be consistent with what really happens in the environment. If the divergence is too great, the resulting behaviors will be nonsensical (for instance, running into walls), or the AI will be too computationally expensive. Applying biologically inspired errors (for instance, errors in distance perception of obstacles) is a luxury we'll have once the system works.

➤ **Flexibility**—During the design, keeping the specification as customizable as possible ensures that similar problems (for instance, wall following) can be handled with the same interfaces, and that there is freedom in the choice of solutions.

➤ **Efficiency**—When it comes to movement, it is crucial for performance to be optimal. This implies keeping the exchange of data to a minimum (for instance, information about free space), and limiting the number of queries so that they can be highly optimized.

In the design of both inputs and outputs, compromises must be made regarding these issues. Often, there is a good balance to be found.

Proposed Specification

First, for motor control, two primitive actions are provided: Move and Turn. These actions provide a combination of simplicity and flexibility, because more complex actions (for instance, moving to, turning toward) can be trivially built thereupon. These actions are also left continuous, because this best matches the complexity of the environments we want to handle.

Second, for the sensors, we can provide multiple levels of information. On the lowest level, the animat receives physical feedback upon collision. In a more preventive fashion, the animat perceives visual information about the surroundings. To achieve this, we use line traces that return the first obstacle from the origin. This is a relatively flexible approach. In fact, if necessary, we can extend the line traces to perform a more accurate simulation of movement (for instance, detecting ledges too).

As for the mechanism for passing information, the AI is left to query the environment (information *pull*). This is preferable because the AI can lazily decide what part of the terrain structure it is interested in. When dealing with objects in the environment in Part V, it may be more efficient to broadcast minimal data from the environment (information *push*).

Interfaces

Rather than drown the issue in wads of mostly inconsequential source code, only the important parts are examined. The full documentation and interface headers are available online. The interfaces with the environment consist of three parts. These parts are conceptually different, but are also separated in the implementation. First, there's the output—as part of the *Motion* module:

```
void Move( const Vec3f& direction );
void Turn( const Vec3f& orientation );
```

The Move function attempts to step in a direction relative to the current state. Turn rotates the view to face a particular orientation, expressed relatively to the current one. Second, there is a physical interface—corresponding to the *Physics* module:

```
bool Collision();
```

This just returns true if the animat has bumped into something. An alternative—more efficient—approach is to define a simple callback function `OnCollision()` that gets notified in the same circumstances. Finally, a simulation of a visual interface is also provided so that predictive obstacle avoidance can be attempted. This is part of the *Vision* module:

```
float TraceWalk( const float angle, const float steps = 4.0f ) const;
```

This procedure tries to walk from the current origin at a particular angle, and returns how far it got without bumping into obstacles. We will improve the functionality of these separate modules in subsequent chapters, as we deem necessary.

Code Skeleton

To use these interfaces, it is just a matter of calling the relevant procedures. The particular AI solution used will decide how this is done in practice, but here is a minimal code skeleton containing each of these calls:

```
void Think()
{
        // check for contact
        bool col = physics->Collision();

        // locate any problems straight in front
        float front_obstacle = vision->TraceWalk( 0.0f );

        // decide what actions to call
        motion->Move( Forward );
        if (col || front_obstacle < 2.0f)
                motion->Turn( orientation );
}
```

The implementation will have to decide whether each of these functions is necessary, and how they fit in the relatively to the AI technique.

Summary

It took a few stages to get there, but we have a convenient interface with the game. We noticed a few important things along the way:

➤ There are many possible ways to define navigation formally.

➤ It's important to consider the definition the state of the animat in space (context).

➤ Inputs make the information about space explicitly available to the AI, although it doesn't have to use the information.

➤ Outputs allow the AI to control the resulting movement, and influence the outcome in a flexible fashion.

➤ We must take into account the high-level requirements to decide which model to pick.

➤ We've established a scaffolding for movement that's problem independent (can handle any type of movement).

This is an example of a *specification* process. It's a very important phase in AI development, because it defines the problem by exposing information to the AI. By doing this wrong, we can cripple the entire development. Conversely, selecting the right specification can make the AI very simple to develop. It's such an important concept—along with knowledge representation—that we'll dedicate the entire next chapter to it.

Practical Demo

Here's another chance to try out a quick demo before we discuss some concepts. Among the demos on the web site at `http://AiGameDev.com/`, there is one for Part II called *Pinbot*, along with source code. Follow the step-by-step procedures online to launch him into the game. *Pinbot* can actually detect the orientation of the wall when collisions occur. The direction of the collision allows *Pinbot* to ricochet off the wall in a direction that's very likely to be clear, like a pinball would! Once again, nothing complex, but it's something to distract us for a few moments before we discuss the importance of specifications and knowledge representation.

Chapter 9

Specifications and Knowledge Representation

The preceding chapter is an example of establishing a specification for movement. Because formalizing the problem in this fashion is so important, this process is discussed more in this chapter.

The *analysis* and *understanding* phases deal with intuitive descriptions. In contrast, the *specification* phase finds a way to represent the same concepts in either a formal notation or programming data structures. Most game programmers will deal with this phase subconsciously, but being aware of this will give us a huge advantage when AI development needs to scale up.

This chapter describes the specification process, as well as the theory behind knowledge representation and how it applies to game development. This chapter covers the following topics:

➤ What is meant by specifications in AI, using a procedural approach

➤ The importance of knowledge representation (KR) and its most important aspects

➤ The relevant *formalisms* (that is, KR languages) that AI research has invented

➤ An outline of each stage involved in the specification process and how KR fits in

➤ The benefits of the specification phase, and how it fits into the development process

Despite not being purely theoretical or practical, this lesson is one of the most important of this book. Insights into KR will not only make us better AI engineers, but also have direct implications into game programming.

Overview of Formal Specifications

Generally speaking, a specification describes the task at hand formally. A *specification* is a definition of the interface and data in a format the computer can understand. The fact that this description is *formal* means that it is officially agreed upon and consistent with other decisions made during the development.

The specification provides the bridge between an English description and the AI implementation. This phase is a final chance to think before the implementation starts, which will offer great assistance later.

Procedural View of AI

Taking a functional point of view can help explain the situation. Consider the AI as a single procedure, which needs to be passed information and return the results. In C++, the declaration of a function is known as a *prototype* (or *footprint*). After the prototype has been written, both the inputs and outputs have been formally specified—using C++ keywords to define the data structures.

Before we can implement a function, it's necessary to know about the relationship with external variables. Explaining the implicit behavior of the program outside the procedure is necessary to solve the problem. When we have the prototype, and the description of the context, programming the function is greatly simplified. This is exactly what we want to achieve for the AI solution: Make the implementation easier by formalizing the variables involved.

Aim of the Specification

At the end of the specification stage, the interface defines how the problem fits into the rest of the system. We call this the *scaffolding*. In a nutshell, there are three things to worry about formalizing: the context, the inputs, and outputs—as mentioned in Chapter 7, "Analysis and Understanding."

There are many design methodologies to handle this sort of programming conundrum, and developing AI can be similar in many ways. That said, there are numerous AI specific tips and tricks that we can use to customize this process to be more appropriate. The methodical routines described here—as well as knowledge representation theory—simplify the handling of complex problems.

Knowledge Representation

Knowledge representation (KR) is the theory for expressing information in computer systems. Fundamentally, the task of defining an interface is a matter of *knowledge representation*; how should the information passed to AI modules be encoded? Fortunately, beyond our experience with data structures, the theory of knowledge has been extensively studied within the field of AI [Davis93, Cawsey94, Yang01].

Fundamentally, a KR is a substitute for the real information (that is, it's a surrogate). Even with virtual worlds, we cannot provide the AI with the entire information available, so it often needs to be represented concisely.

KR *languages* are the means for formalizing the representation. The *expressiveness* of a language determines how well it represents knowledge in general. The information is partly in *notational* form (specified explicitly) and *inferential* form (deduced from existing knowledge).

The *efficiency* of the KR language is paramount for AI systems. Trade-offs apply when preferring a particular option; disk storage limits the notational aspect, whereas computational power prevents highly inferential approaches.

By supporting inference, a KR language is also a fragmentary theory for intelligent computing—with well-defined *syntax* (specifying the structure of sentences) and *semantics* (defining their meaning). A language should be *consistent*, guaranteeing that statements are valid and that conclusions drawn by the system are sound.

The *completeness* of a language is a measure of how well the required knowledge is expressed. The *extensibility* of a language determines how easy it is to customize to particular problems (either manually or automatically). Some languages are also more *natural* than others, easier to understand or write by humans wanting to communicate with the computer.

There is a very strong link between interface representation and reasoning. Choosing a representation is in fact an ontological commitment (that is, deals with the nature and relation of entities); these commitments accumulate in layers as the architecture is refined.

However, KR formalisms can almost always be roughly converted from one to another. This provides much more freedom during the interface design because we can specify a flexible representation, converting it internally to a format convenient for implementation.

Knowledge Representation Formalisms

Languages can be created to define knowledge representations in a high-level fashion. These are known as KR formalisms. There are different KR formalisms used to represent knowledge because there are various kinds of knowledge. Knowledge can range from simple statements to complex relationships, including natural-language sentences and mathematical formulas, not forgetting meta-knowledge (knowledge about knowledge) and compound associations, or even hierarchies of inheritance between classes.

KR formalisms are just concepts, and rely on lower-level programming details to be implemented. Many different C++ constructs can be used to express the following formalisms.

Symbols

Facts can be stored in a straightforward fashion as *symbols*. A symbol represents an object as a text string or number. Any primitive data type can be used (for instance, integers, floating-point numbers, Boolean, or character array):

```
[left_obstacle_distance 4.0]
[right_obstacle "unknown"]
```

In fact, it's believed humans store knowledge as symbols. The major problem with this approach is that each concept of the problem will need its own variable.

Object-Attribute–Value

The *object-attribute–value* paradigm resolves this problem by allowing objects or concepts to have multiple variables associated with them. If an object O has an attribute A with value V, this is generally noted A(O,V):

```
distance(left_obstacle,4.0)
presence(right_obstacle,"unknown")
```

This way, concepts can easily have multiple attributes, which limits the number of objects. C++ structures and classes are conceptually the same thing.

Frames

A *frame* defines an object by specifying its current state and relationship to other frames. This is achieved with *slots* containing attributes or references, often referred to as *fillers*:

```
frame-left-obstacle:
      distance:          (4.0)
      present:           (true)
      entity:            (frame-fred)
```

Accessing the information about any concept is made extremely easy with this method. On the other hand, modifying it can be slightly trickier, because consistency often needs to be maintained. In C++, this could be understood as pointers or references to other instances.

Semantic Network

A *semantic network* stores relationships between the objects in a graph-like structure. Nodes correspond to a single concept, and the links describe the relationship (see Figure 9.1).

Common relationships include is-a, has-a, and instance-of, although there are no formalized restrictions to the type of links. Concepts such as inheritance or dependencies in C++ can be understood with semantic networks.

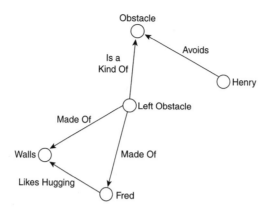

Figure 9.1   A semantic network that links symbols together. In this example, the symbols represent entities in the environment.

The Power of Introspection

The C++ language has analogous constructs for each of the formalisms presented. However, the C++ approach is generally static, so the higher-level knowledge is removed at compile time. For example, there's no way of knowing the name of a variable defined in the C++ code, or even query the inheritance tree between classes.

For the KR formalisms to have their maximal impact, they need to be implemented in a way that supports *introspection*—allowing the properties of the knowledge to be queried dynamically by the AI. This is possible with C++ by using additional variables to store the necessary information explicitly. When doing so, the KR formalisms previously described can be of great assistance.

Specification Procedure

Internally, the entire process of drafting a specification is repetitive, because it usually takes numerous iterations to find the flaws and iron them out. The preliminary brainstorming takes place during the *sketching* phase. Here, ideas are collected and described informally. Then, a *rationalization* phase can take place, to check for consistency—internally and with existing requirements. Each of the valid options can then be *formalized* as necessary by converting the sketch into a computer-friendly specification using a KR formalism. Another round of *rationalization* may optionally take place, because the choice of KR can affect the compliance of the model with requirements. We can repeat the process until we're happy with the results, and are ready to start the implementation.

Sketching

Generally, drafting a few options first is a good idea. These can be complete models, including ideas for inputs and outputs as well as the overall concept, or just ideas for one specific aspect. Initially, these ideas can remain vague—mainly because considering everything in detail is wasteful, but we should feel free to refine each sketch at this stage if it helps.

Role of Sketching

As mentioned, there are three different aspects of the problem we need to think about. Here are some practical tips to get us on the right track:

➤ **Context**—Deciding about the context of the problem is often dependent on the design and implementation of the surrounding software. What goes on behind the interfaces needs to be understood before the problem can be solved; because the design is hierarchical, we need to understand how the higher levels work. Which variables are involved directly, and how can their complexity be minimized to simplify the task?

➤ **Input**—This stage selects the relevant inputs. To pick appropriate information, thinking about this from a human point of view can be helpful; what information does a human use in this case? Alternatively, what variables are necessary for a programmer to solve this problem?

➤ **Output**—The output can be handled in a similar fashion to the input. However, this part is often much easier; it is usually obvious how a problem can be decomposed into a sequence of primitive actions. If it isn't clear, we need to do a little more research on the topic!

Although there is some dependency between these three components, we can treat them separately during this phase for additional simplicity.

Inspiration

Gathering ideas for sketches will become much easier as our experience grows, although initially inspiration can be harder to find. The following sources can help us get started, or find better approaches:

➤ Active **research** is the primary source of information. Look through academic journals or related conference proceedings. Check the web for related tutorials and articles.

➤ **Reading around** is one of the best alternatives. Keep an eye on the news for developer interviews and project postmortems, giving us a good idea of how colleagues handle the problem. Browsing the web can be "work"!

➤ **Related initiatives** often are great sources of help. By investigating related open source projects and reading through any code from SDK, we can find great reference implementations.

➤ **Borrowing ideas** from other domains is one of my personal favorites. This isn't always possible, but it is relatively satisfying when it works out.

Creating sketches can take time, because there are many things to consider. It can sometimes be best to leave the problem aside for some time, which provides extra clarity when returning to it later.

Formalizing

During the sketching phase, drafts, partial insights, and rough thoughts have been collected. From these, complete models can be formed. This can be achieved by combining our partial ideas if necessary (for instance, one possible input with this output). Now each part is ready to be formally specified. If this is the first model, we'll probably have to start from scratch; otherwise, we may reuse our previous work.

A complete formal model is a draft specification of the task that could become officially accepted. It consists of documented decisions about the KR and data formats of the inputs, outputs, and context. If it does become accepted, we can and should refine the documentation and polish it up; it will come in handy later.

Knowledge Representation and Data Structures

This phase involves selecting a KR language that is complete enough to represent the environment, flexible enough to extend, and efficient enough to manipulate.

However, this is only part of the formalization, because low-level C++ representations need to be considered, too. This problem falls into the category of data structure design. The data can be expressed with basic types `int`, `float`, `bool`, `char`; compound ones such as `std::vector`, `std::map`, `std::list`; and optionally exotic ones such as `boost::any`—see Table 9.1.

Table 9.1   Example Data Structures Chosen to Represent the Knowledge at the C++ Level

Knowledge Representation	Data Structure
Symbols	`bool` class members
Fuzzy symbols	`vector<float>`
Attribute/value	`map<string,boost::any>`

Modeling the more elaborate KR (frames or conceptual graphs) requires moderate C++ skills (that is, knowledge of object-oriented programming).

Formalization Process

Being simpler and limited in number, the outputs are often much simpler to formalize before the inputs. Despite their simplicity, the outputs offer great clarity to the problem. When formalizing the outputs first, we can assume all the inputs are valid and the AI is perfect.

By formalizing the inputs next, the rest of the specification quickly falls into place. Admittedly, the inputs are probably the trickiest aspect of the formalization process—and the primary cause of failure in the latter stages. Additional time and care is required for the inputs.

Finally, the supporting variables from the context can be modeled. These also implicitly affect the behavior of both inputs and outputs. However, the context is often defined abstractly rather than explicitly; this is often enough to complete the formalization, and allow the problem to be solved.

Rationalizing

The *rationalizing* stage involves consciously checking the options to see whether they fit with the requirements. Admittedly, we may constantly have the requirements in the back of our mind anyway, ruling out options as they come up. However, this generally limits our creativity of brainstorming and causes potentially great ideas to be discarded prematurely. Keeping this phase separate allows the *sketching* to completely fulfill its potential.

While rationalizing, we need to check a few things for each model, each of which is almost equally important:

➤ Does the model allow the case studies to be satisfied, and does it match the informal requirement of the solution?

➤ How does the model affect other requirements, such as hardware and software issues?

➤ Is the specification consistent with the rest of the design—via interfaces and hierarchical dependencies? If not, how is it affected?

➤ Are the interfaces flexible enough to handle a variety of implementations, and if not, does it at least match those that are applicable?

Once answered, each of these questions will either validate the specification, or not. In the latter case, the problem must be investigated further; if the cause is identified, the next design iteration can resolve it. Although keep in mind that imperfection is okay! The ideal model can be almost impossible to achieve, so don't hesitate to move on when our design is satisfactory; we will benefit more from the experience in the latter stages.

Discussion

Although it may seem wasteful to spend so much time on the specification, this phase is probably more important than design in software development! If handled incorrectly, the specification can become the bottleneck of the development.

A flexible interface has the advantage of simplifying the experimentation. If prototypes can be refined without changing the interface, the iterations are significantly reduced. As well as practical benefits, there are also design advantages:

➤ **High-level understanding**—The specification provides the blueprint for the AI as a black box, separating design from implementation. Not only does this place the task within a bigger picture (the entire architecture), but it also allows theoretical analysis of the process (for instance, can this problem be solved).

➤ **Abstraction**—If the input and outputs have been formally described, the entire problem may be classed as a particular variation of a more generic one (for instance, pattern recognition and function approximation). We can then use the expertise from this second domain to assist our development.

➤ **Comparison**—Given the same interface, different modular implementations can be easily integrated. Evaluating them together then becomes a much simpler task, which is an advantage when comparing prototypes.

These benefits very often outweigh the difficulty of establishing the specification—such as taking into account restrictions, comparing options, making compromises.

Summary

In brief, the purpose of the specification phase is to do the following:

➤ Describe the context of the problem.

➤ Formalize the inputs and the outputs.

This is done in three steps:

1. Sketching possible options in one creative burst.

2. Rationalizing to check for consistency internally and with requirements.

3. Formalizing the chosen model using knowledge representation and corresponding data structures.

The process of specification becomes easier with practice, but we can follow some rough guidelines:

➤ Starting with the outputs is often simpler. The rest of the solution can fall into place around them.

➤ Selecting the inputs is a matter of determining what information is required to solve the problem. Thinking about this as programmers helps; the AI will need similar information.

➤ It's a good idea to keep the specification very flexible to save us the hassle of having to update it during the application.

With a robust specification, all problems are easier to solve. The next chapter uses the specification for movement to create a simple working prototype that can navigate complex dynamic worlds using steering behaviors.

Practical Note

Diving back into developing movement behaviors, another animat demonstrates the flexibility of the specification. *Sir Tank* uses straightforward reactive behaviors to bounce off obstacles. This animat differs because its movement is dissociated from its orientation. This separates the movement capability from other capabilities, such as aiming, which will prove useful in the next parts. The demo and code is available online at `http://AiGameDev.com/`.

Chapter 10

Steering Behaviors for Obstacle Avoidance

KEY TOPICS

- Artificial Life Overview
- Algorithm
- Original Draft
- Evaluation

A world interface for movement allows any AI solution to be developed. It's generally a good idea to start with a simple solution for three main reasons. First, the validity of the interface specification in a practical fashion is checked. Second, it will provide a reference prototype in no time. Third, there will always be a working demo to show the producers and other team members.

Steering behaviors can be applied to solve the navigation problem reactively [Reynolds99]. A wide variety of different steering behaviors exist, capable of controlling creatures individually or as part of a group. Steering behaviors take the form of relatively simple equations, one of which we're particularly interested in: obstacle avoidance.

This chapter covers the following topics:

➤ The concepts behind steering behaviors, borrowed from artificial life

➤ A slight modification of the obstacle-avoidance algorithm to match our requirements and fit into the framework

➤ The solution in practice and theory, including a discussion of the pros and cons

This approach produces a surprisingly capable animat, which can avoid walls and steer around smoothly.

Artificial Life Overview

Artificial life (commonly termed *A-life*, or just *AL*) focuses on the behavior of individual creatures that combine into complex patterns, akin to life. The interaction of simple components can spawn incredibly sophisticated simulations.

Steering behaviors are a landmark example in the field, introduced by Craig Reynolds [Reynolds87]. By defining movements in terms of neighboring creatures or the nearby obstacles, we can model complex phenomena—including a flock of birds or even a herd of buffalo. To simulate crowds and realistic creatures in a complex environment, a combination of multiple *steering behaviors* are used.

The primary building blocks for steering behaviors are presented next; but first, it's important to explain a few lower-level details that the behaviors rely upon.

Assumptions

The steering behaviors assume that there is a lower-level of the engine that takes care of the simulation. This is known as the *locomotion* of the characters, which includes more than just animation. As expected, each character has a position and a velocity—both handled by the locomotion.

Usually in game environments, significant friction exists. This implies that the velocity diminishes very quickly when the player stops pressing a key. In fact, in many cases, the key presses control the velocity directly—rather than the acceleration.

In the model used by Craig Reynolds's autonomous characters [Reynolds99], the velocity instead persists. The steering forces adjust the velocity. A steering force can be seen as the acceleration applied by the AI. The simulation happens in a standard way for physics simulations (usually Euler integration), except the acceleration and velocity are clipped before they are added to the position. Listing 10.1 shows an algorithm used to update the velocity after a new steering force has been computed.

Listing 10.1   Algorithm to Update the Velocity When a New Steering Force Is Computed

```
# make sure the desired steering force isn't too big
truncate( steering_force, max_force )
# keep track of the velocity by adding the force
velocity += steering_force
# apply maximum velocity constraints
truncate( velocity, max_speed )
# and use our interfaces to create movement
Move( velocity )
```

From the point of view of the AI, to overcome the friction of the simulation with the existing world interface, we must keep track of the velocity in the AI. This desired velocity is different from the velocity in the physics engine, because it isn't subject to friction.

Another thing to note about the velocity is that it represents the direction of movement. If the characters can turn independently from the movement, their heading will be different from the velocity.

Seeking and Fleeing

Seeking and *fleeing* are steering behaviors that respectively move toward and away from target locations. If the targets are moving, the analogous behaviors are called *pursuit* and *evasion*. The only difference is that we use a prediction of the target position in the future to apply the seek behavior.

The seeking behavior is very simple. The idea is to find a steering force that turns toward the target. Ideally, we would use a velocity that heads straight for the target. By computing this ideal velocity (clipped by the maximum speed), the necessary adjustment is determined relative to the current velocity; this adjustment is used as the steering force. Listing 10.2 shows this computation. The flee behavior is the exact opposite; we just negate the desired velocity. This causes the animat actively to turn away from the target.

The ability to seek is the base of more sophisticated steering behaviors (for instance, path following and flocking). All that is required is a target point; if other behaviors can compute the desired target, seeking can be applied trivially.

Listing 10.2   Computing the Steering Force for the Seek Behavior

```
# compute the ideal velocity vector towards the target
desired_velocity = truncate( position-target, max_speed )
# the steering force is the difference with the current velocity
steering_force = desired_velocity-velocity
```

Because the speed is always set to full, the seek behavior will run through the target point, and oscillate around it. To slow the character down, we need to define a perimeter around the target; outside the perimeter, full speed is used; otherwise, we scale the speed down linearly. Reynolds calls this the *arrival* behavior.

Other Behaviors

Other steering behaviors deal with groups of characters. We do not really need the entire set of behaviors to satisfy our requirements. Besides, we're only interested in single animats!

The other steering components (such as *alignment* and *cohesion* for modeling flocks) also require a different kind of information; the position and orientation of neighboring creatures are required rather than surrounding obstacles. This implies we need to make small changes in the specification of the input before we can use these other steering behaviors.

Algorithm

Craig Reynolds's *obstacle avoidance* algorithm relies on the obstacles being a particular shape, namely circular. Other obstacle shapes are approximated with a circular bounding volume. The knowledge of the obstacle allows the AI to steer around it quite effectively. However, this is a significant assumption to make—especially in complex game environments. Using circles as an approximation can be particularly challenging (for instance, long and straight corridors).

The *generalized obstacle avoidance* is more desirable for this reason. Sadly, it too relies on some mathematical knowledge of the obstacles—notably the orientation of the obstacle surface (its normal). This is acceptable when the environments are simple, or when the world's structure is preprocessed for the AI. If this proves to be problem (when normals are not available or if they are misleading), the algorithm may require adapting. The original obstacle-avoidance algorithm is described first, and then the adapted version.

Original Draft

The type of behavior we're interested is *containment* [Reynolds99], although the algorithm in this section borrows ideas from specialized *obstacle avoidance,* which in turn is based on *seeking* (all from the same white paper). Listing 10.3 shows the pseudo-code for steering a creature within an arbitrarily complex environment. The algorithm uses the normal at the collision point to guess where free space is. A steering force is applied and turned toward that.

Listing 10.3   Generalized Obstacle-Avoidance Algorithm

```
function avoid_obstacles
      project the position in the future using the velocity
      if a collision is estimated
            find empty location by projecting away from collision
            point
            compute the desired turn to seek that free space
      end if
      if the obstacle is within a critical distance
            proportionally determine breaking force (slow down or
            stop)
      end if
      apply steering and breaking forces
end function
```

To implement this algorithm, we rely on the seek behavior—discussed in the previous section. In the preceding algorithm, we use seeking to steer toward free space when predicting a collision (see Figure 10.1).

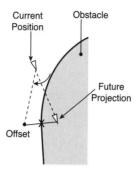

Figure 10.1 Generalized obstacle avoidance predicts the position in the future, and uses the normal of the obstacle to find an area in free space.

The application of steering and breaking forces is not problematic because our interface outputs (turn and move) support these actions. It's not entirely a pleasant coincidence, because such commands are commonplace, but some insight (and research) during the design always helps save time!

Instead, the challenge lies in the inputs, which must be used to determine future collisions. The algorithm relies on knowledge of the environment, performing intersection tests with the known obstacles. The normal at the collision point (that is, direction the obstacle is facing) is then required to find an empty spot in space nearby. In some cases, this is not suitable for the implementation and can lead to problems in the behaviors (for instance, turning in the wrong direction).

Updated Solution

For an embodied animat, the algorithm can be improved by gathering knowledge of the surroundings, which comes from its senses (instead of relying on normals). Fortunately, the AI can determine future collisions implicitly by scanning free space. Our existing specification allows this by tracing lines through empty space, as our animat would do if it were to move in that direction.

The normals returned by the queries are ignored, which can be an advantage; using the obstacles normals to find free space is a rough estimate, and the likelihood of success diminishes as the complexity of the environment increases. Instead, we can use the senses to find an alternative heading, from which a turning force can be derived.

In Reynolds's demo, random wandering behavior is engaged when no collisions need to be avoided. It might be interesting to include a more preventive course of action, whereby we step away from side obstacles. We can do this by checking the side sensors, and strafing laterally to shy away from potential problems (see Figure 10.2). Listing 10.4 shows the new algorithm.

Listing 10.4   Updated Obstacle Avoidance Algorithm That Can Deal with the Sensors Provided to the Animat

```
function avoid_obstacles2
        check the senses for free space in front, left and right
        if a frontal collision is projected
                find the furthest obstacle on left or right
                determine the best side to turn towards
                compute the desired turn to seek that free space
        end if
        if the front obstacle is within a critical distance
                proportionally determine breaking force (slow down or
                stop)
        end if
        if there is an obstacle on the left side
                proportionally adjust the steering force to step right
        end if
        if there is an obstacle on the right side
                proportionally adjust the steering force to step left
        end if
        apply steering and breaking forces
end function
```

Implementing this algorithm involves just translating the statements into C++ code. Suitable default values for each of the parameters need to be chosen (for instance, distances, weight coefficients). These will no doubt need to be fine-tuned in the short experimentation phase.

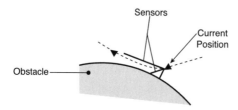

Figure 10.2   Avoiding obstacles using the sensors to detect areas of free space instead of relying on the normals of the obstacles.

Enhancements

A simple way to improve the behavior is to make it more purposeful. (It can be a problem with reactive AI.) The following behaviors may not be the epitome of purposefulness, but they are certainly a lot better than bouncing off walls!

Wandering

When there are no obstacles, the wandering behavior attempts to move around randomly. Because selecting a new steering force every frame leads to erratic behaviors, the AI need to maintain consistency in the steering forces over time.

One great way to maintain consistency is to use a deterministic—but almost unpredictable—function. There is one called *Perlin noise*, which is a combination of parametric noise functions at different frequencies [Elias98, Perlin99, Perlin01]. It's fully deterministic, so it can be smoothed, but is complex enough for the patterns to be unpredictable. We can use the noise function to determine the steering force as a function of time.

Alternatively, we can add random values to an accumulator variable (akin to Brownian motion). To determine the steering force, we can then use a sine function, so the turns will be both positive and negative at equal probabilities. The trends in the movement are no longer erratic, yet they are still random.

Forced Exploration

The problem with purely reactive steering behaviors—such as obstacle avoidance—is that they don't have much direction. It's desirable to prevent the animat from turning back on itself unless absolutely necessary.

A good way to do this is to keep track of a few past positions. A steering behavior can then actively flee away from them. To implement this with little memory, we can use only one vector. The idea is to use one orientation to points toward the area the animat just came from.

This can be implemented easily using a *moving average*. Assume that there's a vector pointing to many previous positions (*provenance*). We want to update the vector to take into account the last position:

```
provenance = previous * 0.1 + provenance * 0.9
```

The coefficients (a = 0.1 and b = 0.9) essentially affect how long we want to remember the past headings. These can be changed at will as long as a + b = 1. Small values of *a* mean the previous heading will be insignificant compared to the history, whereas large values of *a* mean we'll take the previous heading into account more than the provenance.

Projecting Targets

A final improvement tip involves randomly projecting targets as far ahead as possible. If we consider the animat as a dog, this would be like throwing a virtual ball. After the ball has been collected, it is thrown again.

This can be achieved by looking ahead in a random direction. When a good place to project the target is found (far enough), the animat seeks that point. This gives the movement a very strong sense of persistence and coherence, and works surprisingly well. However, the AI needs to watch out for inaccessible targets, and select new ones if obstacles are encountered along the way.

Evaluation

The evaluation of this animat involves observing the behaviors for a short period. Using insider knowledge and some constructive criticism enables us to identify both advantages and disadvantages of the solution.

Practical Demo

The animat demonstrating these principles is known as *Marvin*, and can be found on the web site at `http://AiGameDev.com/`—along with instructions to get the demo compiled. *Marvin* uses obstacle sensors and steering behaviors to prevent collisions in a reactive fashion. It can also wander around using the various enhancements described.

Advantages

The main benefits of this solution stem from its straightforward definition:

➤ **Simplicity**—From the case study to the actual implementation, the development is extremely straightforward. The pseudo-code is also self-explanatory. We'd be hard-pressed to find a simpler alternative.

➤ **Reliability**—Because of the simplicity of the task, we can identify most of the possible situations in the requirements. After we implement these within the system, it will prove capable of dealing with arbitrary environments.

➤ **Predictability**—A great advantage also lies in the predictable nature of the solution. First, as a reactive behavior, there is no possible ambiguity. Second, each rule is written explicitly, which means the developer can understand them.

➤ **Efficiency**—Thanks to the simplicity of the solution, it has a low computational overhead. For this reason, the sensor queries account for most of the time spent in the procedure. Even the use of the sensors can be minimized trivially; the front sensor can be ignored for a few frames when the animat is clear of danger, and the side sensors can be checked at even bigger intervals (if at all).

Disadvantages

On the other hand, the solution might be too simple, leading to the following pitfalls:

➤ **Local traps**—The layout of the environment can be quite intricate, so successfully avoiding obstacles can be tricky. In some cases, such as in a corner, the animat might get stuck (likewise when the sensors are not very accurate). This can be caused by the animat deciding to turn one way, and then realizing that the other way is potentially better. We must iron out such problems during the experimentation phase (for instance, including a turning momentum computed with a moving average).

➤ **Testing**—Local traps are one of many problems that arise during the experimentation. Despite the simplicity of the rules, there are many different parameters to tune and tweak. This generally increases the development time for the behavior.

➤ **Realism**—Because the system is based on rigid rules, we could have expected a similar "robotic" motion with jagged paths. However, it is not as bad as expected; using linear interpolation to blend the steering forces, and the underlying momentum applied by the locomotion combine together to form relatively convincing movement (though not ideally smooth). There is still also a problem linked with the reactivity of the task, which is not very humanlike (usually based on higher-level prediction and planning).

➤ **Scalability**—We modify the behavior by hacking extra lines into code. This has been manageable so far, but as complexity increases this task will become even more troublesome. For more complex behaviors for which 10 or even 20 different situations need to be encoded, this approach would be a struggle.

Summary

A-Life provides a good solution to the problem. It is obvious why the solution has been widely adopted—and we haven't even looked at all of the behaviors and their possibilities! Despite being a healthy compromise between simplicity and capability, however, there are a few issues with this particular solution to obstacle avoidance.

Some of the problems identified appear regardless of the solution, but one of them we can remedy: *scalability*. Artificial life, as implemented here, is essentially a collection of "if" statements, which are difficult to extend and manage. Such approaches have been the focus of another field of AI, namely rule-based systems. By looking into them further, we'll understand the fundamental ideas, enabling us to improve the solution and resolve its problems.

Chapter 11

Rule-Based Systems

Rule-based systems (RBSs) essentially consist in a collection of "if...then" statements. Such statements are particularly suited to encoding rules-of-thumb, similar to human expertise. Experts generally apply such knowledge mechanically to a problem to solve it. By transferring their experience into the computer, the same process can be done with similar reliability, but in a much more efficient and automated fashion.

In games, RBSs can be used in nonplayer characters (NPCs) for two distinct purposes: *problem solving* (reaching a single conclusion from initial facts) or *control* (producing a sequence of actions in a simulation). In problem solving, the rules explain the connection between different truths (for instance, "*If* an item is absent, *then* someone picked it up") so the system can reach the answer. As for control, the rules describe the action that should be taken in each situation (for instance, "*If* there's a wall ahead, *then* stop").

In practice, RBSs have the advantage of separating behaviors from the code. Of all the techniques that allow this data-driven approach, RBSs are the simplest to develop, extremely fast at runtime, very flexible, and easily extended.

This chapter covers the following topics:

➤ Rule-based systems within the context of AI, compared to other similar systems

➤ The different components in the system from a high-level point of view: the rulebase, the working memory, and the interpreter

➤ The methods commonly used with RBS, notably how the knowledge is acquired and modeled

➤ The different benefits and pitfalls of rule-based systems, and the typical approach taken by game developers

The next chapter covers the implementation and application of RBSs, but this chapter will provide a solid background to build upon.

Background

Rule-based systems (RBSs henceforth) are a simple but successful AI technique. This technology originates in the early days of AI (mid-twentieth century), when the intention was to create intelligent systems by manipulating information. One of the key issues encountered was *knowledge representation (KR)*, discussed in depth during Chapter 9, "Specifications and Knowledge Representation." How should facts about the world (or problem) be described to allow intelligent reasoning?

Inspired by work in psychology, human reasoning is understood as a characteristic behavior that can be modeled. Rule-based systems model human reasoning by solving problems step by step, as experts apply their experience. Knowledge is stored in a highly implicit representation. (That is, many facts need to be inferred.)

In practice, RBSs are extremely widespread. Many domains benefit from them, ranging from medicine to the manufacturing industry, including tech support. Many fields profit from deductive systems manipulating data according to simple rules. As such, they constitute one of the major successes of classical AI. There are literally tens of thousands of them, falling into various subcategories of knowledge-based systems, as shown in Figure 11.1.

RBSs are also known as *production systems*, but we'll avoid the term as it is less intuitive and often ambiguous within the industry domains it is applied to. Generally speaking, RBSs fall into the category of *knowledge-based systems*, dealing with the processing of information (for instance, sensory data in our case).

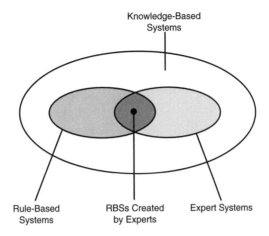

Figure 11.1   Venn diagram representing the different kinds of knowledge-based systems, and how RBSs relate to expert systems.

Specifically, the examples in this chapter as well as most other RBS—are *expert systems*. This means that the rules within the system have been crafted by a domain *expert*. This flattering word is used quite loosely; almost any solution where humans directly encode their wisdom and experience passes as an *expert system*.

Overview of Components

There is more to a *rule-based system* than a collection of "if...then" statements. Essentially, we need to know about three different components [Sharples96]: the working memory, the rulebase, and the interpreter (see Figure 11.2).

Working Memory

The *working memory* is a collection of facts about the world (or the current problem), known as the *internal representation*. Generally, the working memory contains few symbols; human reasoning inspires RBSs, so short-term memory is relatively small.

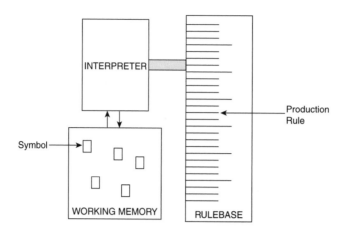

Figure 11.2 The architecture of an RBS, composed of three interacting components.

Here's an example of a working memory for the task of obstacle avoidance. There are two symbols present, implying they are true and all the others are false (for instance, there is no `obstacle_right`). Discarding symbols that aren't applicable is often easier and more efficient:

```
[obstacle_left]
[obstacle_front]
```

Typically, RBSs are applied to problem solving, so there is a starting configuration and a particular desired result; these are both states of the working memory. In the case of control problems, however, we are just interested in the simulation itself, so there is no goal state per se; the symbols are updated repeatedly.

The working memory defines the base of the system's architecture. This can be just an array of symbols, or something slightly more elaborate—such as a database. Extensions to the working memory are quite common, although the underlying concepts remain the same (that is, storage of facts).

Rulebase

The second of three RBS components is the database of production rules stored by the system.

Single Rules

The database contains a collection of rules, also sometimes called *operators*. They all have the following form:

```
IF <condition> THEN <action>
```

The first part of the rule is a collection of Boolean statements. It is also known as the *head* of the rule, or *antecedent clause*. The second part of the rule is a set of actions that manipulate symbols within the working memory. This part is also known as the *body*, or *consequent clause*. Both clauses are generally represented as combination of simple symbols (for instance, A and B, C or D).

Data Structure

A major aspect of the rulebase is the data structure chosen for internal storage. If a procedural approach is used, the production rules cannot be automatically reorganized for efficiency; this requires the programmer to edit the code and recompile.

Instead, if the rules are stored separately from the system, in a *declarative* fashion, they must be loaded at runtime (that is, data driven). When implemented with a simple array of rules, a linear scan of the rulebase is needed to find conditions that are true.

By organizing the rules further, the relationships between their conditions can be modeled with a tree-like data structure (see Figure 11.3). This splits the production rules into logical blocks, and proves more efficient when checking for applicable rules. Testing all the rules is done by a traversal of the tree. Each node corresponds to a single symbol test, and a match has been found once a leaf is reached.

This tree is built in two phases; one identifies the common truth tests and organizes them into a tree, and the other merges common branches together. This procedure is extremely similar to building a decision tree, which Chapter 26, "Classification and Regression Trees," discusses in depth. In the meantime, see [Forgy82] for the details.

This is a significant optimization of the time required to find matching rules. The computational power no longer scales linearly with the number of rules, which allows large systems to be treated efficiently.

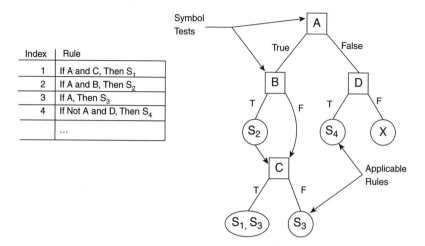

Index	Rule
1	If A and C, Then S_1
2	If A and B, Then S_2
3	If A, Then S_3
4	If Not A and D, Then S_4
	...

Figure 11.3   A linear data structure for storing rules, compared with a tree of hierarchical symbol tests.

Extensions

RBSs often interface with an external system. This can be a machine, a simulation of a problem, or—in our case—a synthetic body interacting with a virtual world. In many cases, it's necessary to communicate data with this system, for the RBS to work with up-to-date information and then act on the system. Standard declarative rules support sensors (inputs) and effectors (outputs) indirectly; sensors set corresponding symbols before they are used, and effectors test the working memory to see whether they should execute afterward. This approach is acceptable, although with the inconvenience of a pre- and postprocess.

This problem has been the focus of practical research. The answer is to borrow the advantages of the procedural approach, only for sensors and effectors (allowing function calls in both clauses). This is a known extension to RBSs typically based on declarations. A compromise is also possible, and seems appropriate in our case; motor commands are procedural action, whereas symbols are automatically set according to the senses—as shown in Figure 11.4. This prevents the procedural sensors from being checked multiple times by the RBS, and allows the tree-based storage of the rules to work without modifications.

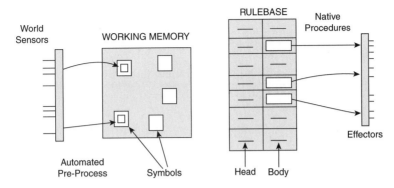

Figure 11.4   The rule-based system interacts with the environment using a combination of declarative and procedural approaches.

Supporting partial matching of rules can simplify the rulebase; the entire condition does not need to be true for a rule to fire. Formally, this can be understood as a condition with an OR operator. Standard systems using only conjunctions (AND) can handle this by splitting up the disjunction and duplicating the rule's body:

```
IF <condition1> OR <condition2> THEN <action>
IF <condition1> THEN <action>
IF <condition2> THEN <action>
```

However, this approach is cumbersome because of the duplication of the rule's body. If partial matching is an important feature, the system should be extended to support it, either allowing OR operations or supporting references to actions (to prevent duplicating them).

Interpreter

The *interpreter* is the part of the program that controls the RBS, interacting with the database of rules and the working memory. It decides which rules match the current state and how to execute them. This last component of RBS is also known as an *inference engine*, because it allows knowledge to be inferred from the declarations.

For an RBS, there are two different kinds of inference mechanisms: *forward* and *backward* chaining. This describes how rules can be applied to the working memory to solve problems.

Forward Chaining

A *forward-chaining system* starts with a set of assertions, and repeatedly attempts to apply rules until the desired result is reached. This is known as a *data-driven* method, because facts and rules are combined to derive new facts. For example, given assertions about the situation, determine what weapon to use.

A single cycle of the forward-chaining interpreter happens as follows. It is known as a *recognize-act* cycle:

➤ **Matching**—This stage identifies all the rules for which the condition is true, given the state of the rulebase.

➤ **Conflict resolution**—If multiple rules are applicable, only one must be chosen out of the entire set.

➤ **Execution**—The body of the rule chosen is now executed, generally entailing a change in the working memory (directly or indirectly).

In a simulation (that is, a control problem), these rules are applied repeatedly as necessary, whereas for deductive problem solving a specific condition terminates the loop upon success—as shown in Figure 11.5. There are occasional problems with the interpreter getting stuck in infinite loops or in dead ends. We'll discuss solutions to these problems in the upcoming section, "Control Strategies."

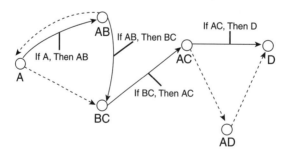

Figure 11.5 Result of a forward-chaining execution toward a goal. The discarded rules are drawn as dashed arrows.

FORWARD-CHAINING EXTENSIONS

There are simple implementations for each of the three steps in the cycle, but it is possible to develop more elaborate strategies. These can provide more flexibility (for instance, partial matching), different forms of control (for instance, sensors and effectors), or just more efficiency as required (for instance, tree-based storage). This depends heavily on other parts of the system, so a good overall understanding of RBSs is required.

Backward Chaining

In contrast, a *backward-chaining system* starts with the hypothesis and attempts to verify it by returning to the current state. This is known as *goal-directed* inference, because consequent clauses are matched to attempt to prove antecedent clauses recursively. For example, estimate the status of enemies based on their behavior.

A cycle of this interpreter works in a similar fashion. It is known as a *hypothesize-test* cycle. The hypothesis about the solution is built step by step starting from the end—as shown in Figure 11.6:

➤ **Matching**—This stage identifies all the rules whose *body* match the current state (the rules that could have led to here).

➤ **Conflict resolution**—Again, if more than one production rule is applicable, all but one must be discarded.

➤ **Update**—The working memory can now be changed to reflect the hypothesis. We need to determine what the previous state would be for this rule's condition to be applicable.

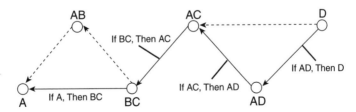

Figure 11.6   Result of a backward-chaining execution moving from the goal toward the start state. The discarded rules are drawn as dashed arrows.

Backward inference is more challenging to implement correctly, because the interpreter must keep track of the rules applied from the end to rebuild the solution from the start state. There are also more possibilities of finding dead ends (no applicable rules), and infinite loops are more likely too (same sequence of rules firing repeatedly). The solution to both these problem lies in the understanding of control strategies.

Control Strategies

One part of each cycle (forward and backward) requires a decision from the interpreter: conflict resolution. Different methods can be applied to select the rule; these are known as *control strategies*. The following ideas can be combined to produce custom selection processes:

➤ Select the **first** production rule found during matching.

➤ Pick the **best** option available, where expert indicates a priority for each rule.

➤ The **most specific** rule can be applied. This is the one with the most statements as a matching condition (A&B&C is more specific than C&D).

➤ The system can keep track of previous matching operations. **History** can be used to prevent a rule from firing twice in a row.

➤ **Random** selections also can be made, which proves surprisingly effective.

When a decision is made as to which rule to pick, other alternatives are thereby not chosen. The control strategy affects what happens to the unchosen rules. The process of the interpreter was described in three steps as a "cycle." This cycle can be either iterative (that is, keep looping and ignore the alternatives) or recursive (that is, call another function for each of the options). With recursion, each alternative is kept in a stack, so it's possible to backtrack if something goes wrong. This allows all the options need to be *searched* exhaustively, guaranteeing the solution will be found if it exists.

This process of going through all the options is known as a *search*, and can be done in many different ways. There is much to say about the search process itself, how it can be controlled and implemented, and even what can make it more efficient. However, such advanced control strategies are not commonly used in RBSs, and fall beyond the scope of reactive techniques.

Further Information

As well as in the Bibliography at the back of this book, there's a page on the web site providing links to material about search in RBSs. It can be found under Online References for Chapter 11. This includes pointers to tutorials and academic publications.

Hybrid Interpreters

Bidirectional strategies have the option of supporting either type of inference separately. Combining forward and backward chaining prevents the interpreter from getting stuck, without using search mechanisms. Instead, both forward and backward rules can be chosen randomly until a solution is found! Backward chaining takes care of avoiding "dead ends" when moving forward, and vice versa. Search mechanisms are generally more robust and efficient at avoiding such traps, but bidirectional interpreters are appropriate for the simplest cases.

Theory and Knowledge

This section looks at the theory behind RBSs generally, instead of focusing on the algorithmic details. The key concept is the underlying knowledge representation. We'll look at how expertise is acquired, and how RBSs fit in with existing representation languages.

This will give us additional understanding beyond the mechanical processing of the system. On one hand, we'll get an idea of the potential of such systems, along with their possible applications, but on the other hand, their problems will also be revealed.

Knowledge Elicitation

Despite being extremely powerful and flexible in theory, RBSs need to be provided with problem-specific expertise. (For instance, the RBS needs rules to be able to avoid obstacles.) The main question is how should this knowledge be acquired? Unfortunately, this is a problem with AI solutions in general, but it is particularly serious with knowledge-based systems. This process is known in lingo as *knowledge elicitation* (that is, acquisition) to those in the field.

RBSs rely on human-like rules-of-thumb, which makes it slightly easier to convert expert knowledge into production rules. However, this task is surprisingly complex, and has become a problem known as the *knowledge acquisition bottleneck*. Researchers in the field have attempted to improve this phase by developing tools and methodologies for creating expert systems, but the bottleneck still remains.

The first kind of KBS (pre-1980s) relied on domain experts encoding their knowledge procedurally within the system—as programmers would. Especially obvious in large-scale systems, this development lacked structure, exposing brittleness and many maintenance difficulties. This led to an initiative in 1983 to separate the system from the knowledge by encoding it in a declarative form. This emphasized the distinction between the knowledge and its application (see Figure 11.7). Such systems fall under the category of *second-generation expert systems*.

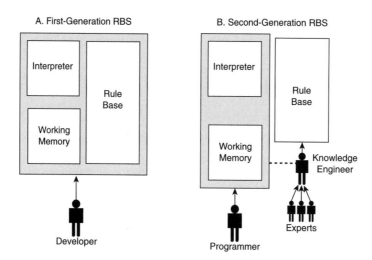

Figure 11.7 Knowledge elicitation in RBSs. Comparison of procedural and declarative approaches, and the people involved.

Nowadays, it is the job of the *knowledge engineer* to act as an intermediate between the human experts and the computer system. Such is the complexity of the task that it often requires a dedicated person, assisted by a set of tools. The job of the *knowledge engineer* can be summarized as follows:

➤ Read literature about the targeted domain to understand the fundamental concepts and the terminology.

➤ Schedule interviews with experts in the field to "extract" their knowledge of the problem.

➤ Summarize the information collected, organize the facts, and enter them into a computer system after an appropriate format has been chosen. Common decisions that have to be made at this stage are discussed in the next few sections.

This combination of expert and knowledge engineer is the most widespread method for providing the system with knowledge, and has proven itself extremely successful in numerous domains. Game AI development can also benefit from this approach.

Further Information

There are automated knowledge-discovery techniques that can be used to extract rules from data. In this book, we'll cover two other techniques suitable for learning such rules. One approach is *decision tree* induction covered in Chapter 26, and the other technique is known as *classifier systems*, as explained in Chapter 33, "Learning Classifier Systems." In many cases, learning approaches are not as high quality as expert solutions, but they can simplify the development significantly.

Knowledge Representation

Production rules are fundamentally part of a knowledge representation language: RBSs themselves. However, they can be enhanced with other KR formalisms. Because RBSs are defined as a set of "if...then" statements, they are extremely flexible. The formats of both the head and the body can be chosen to match the problem at hand.

Symbols are the most widely used KR paradigm, but they require as many symbols as concepts. The object/attribute/value paradigm can be used to structure the information in a more convenient fashion (for instance, member variables). Frames are useful for describing relationships between objects (for instance, pointers), and semantic networks express higher-level concepts (for instance, inheritance)—reducing the number of rules needed for complex problems. All these KR formalisms are common in everyday object-oriented programming; the difference here is that they need to be made explicit for the RBS to understand them (that is, allowing introspection).

> **Further Information**
>
> RBSs can also be extended to deal with uncertainty, using concepts such as confidence or certainty factors. When the facts are associated with a degree of truth, the RBS becomes a *fuzzy expert system*. The theory and practice behind this technique is discussed extensively in Chapter 30, "Fuzzy Logic."

Discussion

At this stage, we can identify some of the primary benefits of RBSs as well as their pitfalls. Additional experience will help us easily decide when RBSs are appropriate for game AI problems. Until then, to assist our decisions, here is a list of characteristics.

Advantages

It is not a coincidence that RBSs are one of the most successful AI techniques ever. Here are the main reasons they are a tremendous benefit in game development:

➤ **Simplicity**—Individual rules have simple syntax and express knowledge in a natural fashion. Rule-based systems are based on human reasoning, which implies it is straightforward for experts to understand their functioning. The knowledge is also defined in an implicit fashion, saving much time and effort.

➤ **Modularity**—Production rules capture knowledge in a relatively atomic fashion. Statements can be combined and edited independently from each other. This makes RBSs simple to extend.

➤ **Flexibility**—By specifying knowledge in a relatively informal fashion (not as logic), the data can be manipulated to provide the desired results. It is also easy to add more symbols in the working memory, or even improve the knowledge representation used.

➤ **Applicability**—Because most problems can be formalized in a compatible way (for instance, symbols), RBSs will often be a possible solution—and one that works! The scope of applicable domains ranges far, from simulation to problem solving.

Naturally, there are some trade-offs to be made, taking into account the possible problems.

Disadvantages

Rule-based systems are no miracle solution. The following points will help us decide whether to use them, and help identify the pitfalls if we do choose them:

➤ **Expressiveness**—As a knowledge representation language, RBSs aren't very expressive; little knowledge is in notational form and inference plays an important role to extract information. This implies it can be difficult to predict the behavior of an RBS just by looking at the rules.

➤ **Power**—Although single-production rules are quite flexible, their body is often restricted by the syntax of the representation (for instance, set symbol to value). The body can also be limited to one statement, especially in backward-chaining systems. This doesn't come close to the power of modern programming languages such as Java or C++.

➤ **Efficiency**—In simple systems, the computational power required scales linearly with the number of rules. This is the typical cost of the condition matching phase. Although it can be optimized for processing speed, memory usage cannot be decreased as easily. In addition, in systems where exhaustive search is required to solve the problem, RBSs can be fairly slow.

➤ **Suitability**—Although the technique can be applied to many domains, it is not always the best option. Symbols aren't suited to modeling some problems (for instance, smooth control or sequences of actions), and expert knowledge is just not always available.

Most of these disadvantages can be resolved in one way or another, although it often depends on the problem itself.

Game Developer's Approach

This section presents pertinent insights into RBSs for computer games and explains the game developer's attitude toward them.

Design and Development

A professional game AI developer will most likely be expected to be the *programmer*, the *knowledge engineer*, and the *domain expert*. It is a good idea to separate these three jobs even if only one person does the work. This can be achieved by splitting content and code. The implementation of the knowledge-based system comes first, and the declaration of the expert rules will follow later in the game development cycle. Generally, development is an iterative process of writing code and testing it. The distinction between mechanical reasoning and knowledge declaration splits this process into two, making it easier for one person to handle.

This has many additional advantages in game production, as well as those advantages associated with such second-generation expert systems:

➤ **Reusability**—Having the RBS as a separate module enables you to apply it to different problems. This would not be possible with procedurally encoded knowledge, but with declarative knowledge it can be loaded from a file at runtime.

➤ **Debugging**—If the RBS is performing a behavioral simulation (rather than solving problems), the results will be visible to the rest of the team. When a bug is encountered, a report can be filed describing the exact situation. To do this, a procedure can be written to save the working memory's current state to disk. Then, adding an extra rule to correct the behavior is trivial. A simple user interface could potentially allow almost anyone to update the rulebase!

There is a small drawback in developing a flexible system such as this: execution speed. This warrants looking into further.

Efficiency

It's the processing of rules that is going to be the most computationally expensive in knowledge-based system. Let's analyze both aspects of these rules—the conditions and the actions—in terms of both procedural (hard-coded) and declarative (data-driven) approaches:

```
Procedural code:    if (a && b && c) { d = true; }
Declarative file:   IF a AND b AND c THEN d
```

In terms of raw execution speed, a condition that is hard-coded will beat any other approach (for instance, scripted and interpreted dynamically). However, this is no reason to discard the declarative approach; with a procedural approach, the system has no chance of acquiring high-level understanding of the conditions. On the other hand, when handling the rules separately to the code, the system will be given the opportunity to read and analyze the conditions. This allows the RBS module to reorganize declared production rules in convenient form (that is, a tree or graph). So, the system will minimize the number of tests required to match each rule with the current state. Such an approach will outperform the procedural alternative on large data sets.

As for the body of the rules, the problem is similar. Hard-coded actions provide more efficiency and power (thanks to native languages such as C++). The declarative alternatives are slightly more flexible at runtime, but incur a speed hit and more syntactic restrictions—usually limited to setting symbols in the working memory. This will be necessary if you require backward chaining. However, for forward chaining there is a compromise to be made. A set of default actions can be hard-coded and referenced inside a small database. Then, the declarative rules can refer to these, and the simple lookup can call the native actions at a runtime. This provides the best of both worlds!

Suitable Problems

Because of the knowledge acquisition bottleneck, we must make sure that any problem we tackle will have sufficient expert knowledge available, or that can be easily acquired. If this is not the case, it will be extremely tedious to develop a working RBS. We also rely on the domain to be represented with symbols—which RBSs are particularly suited to.

In some problems, we may find ourselves writing long sequences of if statements in C++ (for instance, defining a reactive behavior for movement). RBSs are extremely well-suited to handling of this type of problem in a flexible and extendable fashion. Often, this can be done much more efficiently, too!

RBSs strive on *solving problems*. The solution will be found efficiently as long as there are many alternatives to reach the goal state (that is, with no traps). In this case, the choice of the rules during conflict resolution will only be moderately important, and the complexity of a search process will not be required.

Rule-based systems do very well as a *control technique*, as long as the behavior is purely reactive. When the RBS need an additional internal symbol to support non-determinism, things can get problematic. (We'll see this with wall following in the next chapter.) In fact, the problem is worse when well-defined sequences of actions are required. A finite-state machine, as discussed in Chapter 38, "Finite-State Machines," would be better suited to these problems.

Summary

To recapitulate, RBSs are split into three components:

➤ The *rulebase* is a big database storing all the rules.

➤ The *working memory* keeps track of the symbols representing the problem.

➤ The *interpreter* uses the rules to manipulate the symbols.

Interpreters can have three different inference mechanisms:

➤ *Forward chaining* works on a recognize-act cycle starting from the current state. This is a simpler and more common approach.

➤ *Backward chaining* works with a hypothesize–test cycle, starting from the theoretical end state. This is not quite as common, and slightly trickier to implement.

➤ *Bidirectional* approaches combine both forms of chaining together.

The biggest problem with RBSs is the acquisition of knowledge; experts are needed to create the rules. The process can be simplified with these policies:

➤ Separate the rulebase from the interpreting code, using a declarative approach.

➤ Allow the rules to interact with the system using procedural effectors and sensors.

RBSs are particularly well-suited to deductive problem solving. They can also handle reactive control very well, but tend to suffer in complexity when internal symbols are required—or when sequences of outputs need to be supported. In the next chapter, we'll apply RBSs in practice to create a wall-following behavior.

Practical Demo

There's an example that bridges the gap between RBS theory in this chapter and the next on movement. *Brutus* is an animat with dog-like activities, capable of following players or stopping at their feet among others (a combination of steering behaviors). Each action is expressed as a C++ `if()` `then` statement, essentially a first-generation procedural expert system. *Brutus* can be found on the web site at `http://AiGameDev.com/` with the other animats, in binary and source form.

Chapter 12

Synthesizing Movement with Rule-Based Systems

Now that we have learned about rule-based systems (RBSs) in theory, this chapter focuses on a practical problem still related to movement. Because the *obstacle-avoidance* problem was solved comfortably, this time a *wall-following* behavior is attempted instead to diversify the experience.

The RBS provides the advantage of separating the behaviors from the AI system, so they are intuitive to edit. The format of production rules is very straightforward and easy to understand at a glance. This helps the development of non-player character (NPC) behaviors in general as well as wall following.

This chapter covers the following topics:

➤ The obligatory *understanding* phase, including a quick case study of wall-following behaviors

➤ The integration of the technology, including deciding on design details of the RBS

➤ The development of a modular RBS, describing its runtime interfaces and data storage

➤ The implementation of the module and the data structures used internally

➤ Applying the RBS module into the code skeleton to synthesize wall-following behaviors

➤ The solution and various aspects of the behavior, and the success of the RBS at this particular task

At the end of the chapter, the RBS should resolve some of the issues encountered with standard steering behaviors in Chapter 10, "Steering Behaviors for Obstacle Avoidance."

Case Study

Instead of continuing to study obstacle avoidance, this time we attempt *wall following*. These problems are very similar in nature, and most of our existing work still applies to wall following. Notably, the targeted environments remain the same, as do the rest of the requirements and interface specification.

Only the behavioral outcome differs. This requires a new case study. Essentially, the animat must first find a wall, and then follow outward and inward corners:

1. If no wall is present and the animat is not already following one, a random move forward should be made.

2. If there is a wall in front, the animat should turn away from it, regardless of the presence of a wall on the side.

3. If there is a wall to the side and not in front, it should be followed by moving forward.

4. If no wall is present and one was being followed, the animat should turn toward the side where the wall last was.

Conceptually, the main difference with obstacle avoidance is the need for context-sensitive action. Indeed, the lack of obstacles means two different things, depending on whether a wall was previously being followed (cases 1 and 4). The mapping from senses to actions is thereby ambiguous, so a reactive system would have to pick the same rule in both these cases. If the animat deterministically selects the "turn" action, it will spin around in uncluttered areas; whereas always selecting the "move forward" action will make the animat lose contact with walls that turn away.

Luckily, nondeterminism is not a problem for RBSs, because we can add an internal symbol to distinguish the context. This "already following wall" symbol allows the system to be aware of the necessary behavior—which makes wall following possible (see Figure 12.1).

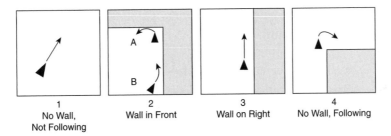

Figure 12.1   The four different cases that arise in wall following, and what actions are required.

Rationale

Before diving straight down into the low-level details of the implementation, we need to consider the previous research or design decisions to determine how it all fits together.

Rule-Based System or Not?

The main concern during development is a trade-off between work and results. How much time are we willing to invest in developing an RBS? A fully fledged system might take weeks to develop and may be overkill for this relatively simple problem. On the other hand, a simpler alternative (such as steering behaviors) will be much quicker to implement but might not be suited to other problems.

In this chapter, we *will* actually design a modular RBS. However, efficiency remains of prime importance because of the nature of the application; when targeting other problems than fundamental behaviors (such as motion), flexibility and extensibility are often the main requirements.

Type of Chaining

As far as the type of RBS is concerned, we'll stick to a forward-chaining system (explained in Chapter 11, "Rule-Based Systems") for two main reasons:

➤ **Behavioral simulation**—Because we're simulating reactive *control* behaviors rather than problem solving, backward chaining is not a feasible option.

➤ **Procedural actions**—With forward chaining, the body of each rule does not need to be in declarative form; the RBS executes it without knowing about it. This enables us to hard-code some of the actions. The major benefits lie in expressive power and efficiency (thanks to C++).

The intention is to allow direct support for hard-coded effectors (which perform actions in the environment), but also allow declarative conditions (loaded from a file). We'll support sensor indirectly by using preprocessing to gather information from the surroundings.

Precautions to Simplify Rules

Even though rules are conceptually simple, ideally we want to keep their complexity down to a minimum (both head and body). We also want to reduce the number of rules as much as possible. This will undoubtedly simplify the knowledge acquisition greatly.

Each of the rules is implicitly ranked, which hints to the interpreter which rules to pick first. When the processing starts with the higher priorities, latter rules can assume that the conditions of previous rules are true. This simplifies the conditions of rules lower down the ranks.

In addition, symbols are often set to the same values in the body of rules. For example, all but one rule may set symbol A to true. Explicitly including this action in every rule is highly redundant. Instead, we can use default values to set A to true unless it's overridden.

To reduce the number of rules, we'll allow for multiple actions in the rule body. This avoids the duplication of rules, and supports atomic operation; in some cases, we must set two symbols at the same time, instead of waiting for the next cycle of the interpreter to do so.

RBS Module Design

This section explains how an RBS module can be initialized from a data file, and how the main AI program should interface with it.

Initialization

The setup of FEAR modules is done with XML (as discussed in Chapter 4, "FEAR: A Platform for Experimentation"). In the case of RBSs, this makes it easy to describe the system in a flexible and extendable fashion. Going through the document specification will give us a good understanding of how to implement the system.

Working Memory

As discussed in Chapter 11, the working memory can be described by the symbols it contains. Its initial state consists of each symbol set to its default values, unless initial values are actually provided. Listing 12.1 is an example with two symbols indicating the presence of a wall on the side, and another to keep track of the context.

Listing 12.1   XML Code Describing a Simple Working Memory with Two Example Symbols in It
(The symbols have default values and initial values.)

```
<memory>
        <Symbol name="sideWall" />
        <Symbol name="following" initial="true" default="false" />
</memory>
```

Although symbols are all declared in the same way, there are two different types. *Internal* symbols are used by the RBS only (for instance, the `"following"` symbol). *Native* symbols correspond to sensors or effectors outside of the RBS (for instance, `"leftWall"`), while the others are purely internally. This enables us to handle functional extensions indirectly; the native symbols will be set automatically before the interpreter cycle starts.

Rulebase

The rulebase just contains a set of production rules, specified as condition/action pairs (see Listing 12.2). Conditions need to correspond with the symbols in working memory. Actions can also set symbols, although the system supports procedural sensors that don't rely on being declared explicitly.

Listing 12.2   A Simple Rulebase Expressed in XML, Containing Only One Rule
(The rule is split into conditions and the action.)

```
<rulebase>
     <Rule>
          <conditions>
               <Symbol name="sideWall" value="true" />
               <Symbol name="frontWall" value="false" />
          </conditions>
          <action>
               <Symbol name="moveForwards" value="true" />
          </action>
     </Rule>
</rulebase>
```

The condition for a rule is a conjunction between the atomic statements: *AND* operations combine the individual symbol matches together implicitly. This is the most common type of condition. In our case, there is no need to worry about *OR* operations. All our conditions are conjunctions (AND), and sentences with disjunctions (OR) can just be split into two. Either the *knowledge engineer* can do this, or a simple tool can make sure of it.

Interface

The interface must allow data to be passed to the module at runtime. This mainly involves telling the system the location of native symbols and how to execute native actions. Runtime data is thereby synchronized with static declarations. Dynamic extensions can also be provided for advanced uses, such as setting/getting the value of symbols or adding new rules.

Synchronization

Variables can be registered with the module by passing pointers to their locations (first parameter) along with their name (second parameter). The name is needed to achieve correspondence with the XML declarations:

```
SetSensor( &SensorSideWall, "sideWall" );
```

The procedural actions will be implemented as functors (that is, classes that store functions [Haendel02]), which are a good way of implementing callbacks in C++. We could implement each action in its own class, overriding a method called Step(), for example. The RBS would just make this virtual call when the action needs to be applied. Instead, with functors each action can be a method in the same class. We also can place the native variables in there for a convenient implementation. See the source code with the demo for practical insights.

Dynamic Extensions

The accessor methods for each of the internal symbols are fairly trivial to define for Boolean values. The first function Set() can be overridden to handle different types (that is, duplicating it and changing the type of the last parameter); the second must be renamed to prevent clashes (for instance, GetBool). Indeed, type safety would not otherwise be guaranteed because the functions differ only by their return type. (The compiler will complain.)

```
void Set( const string& symbol, const bool value );
bool Get( const string& symbol ) const;
```

Adding rules dynamically to the system is not something we'll typically have to do, but it can be done as follows:

```
void AddCondition( const string& symbol, const bool value );
void SetAction( const string& action );
```

The first method can be called repeatedly to set up the conjunction, and the second method validates the condition sentence and assigns it a specific action.

Implementation

Having defined a formal interface, the implementation of the RBS is abstracted out. By reusing containers from the standard template library to store both the rulebase and the working memory, the reference implementation remains simple, too. Using a flexible file format (as described in the preceding section) means most of the preparations can be left to the developer. Notably, thanks to the rule priorities, the interpreter can perform a simple traversal of the rules—as suggested by the knowledge engineer.

All the implementation is transparent from the interface, so extending it would usually not break the system. If we want to optimize the rules, for example, we can build a tree internally after the rules are loaded (although this would involve discarding the priorities).

> **Source Code**
>
> The C++ module that implements the RBS is available on the web site at `http://AiGameDev.com/`. There's also a high-level walkthrough of the implementation available, and the source code has extensive comments on the lower-level details.

Data Structures

One of the essential concepts for maintaining an efficient implementation is to represent the symbols as integers rather than strings. Because all the interfaces deal with strings (for intuitiveness during initialization), we need an internal map to convert the strings to integer symbols.

After this is done, the working memory can be a simple array, with the integer symbols used directly as the index in the working memory. The effectors and sensors are stored in two containers associating integer symbols with native functions passed by the interface.

Interpreter

The main loop of the interpreter is split into three steps conceptually. First, `CheckSensors()` calls the native functions to set the appropriate symbols. Doing this before the matching phase guarantees the function is only called once. However, we could sacrifice a small amount of memory and opt for lazy evaluation instead (for instance, a "gathered" bit). The native functions are checked as they are needed by the rules, only if the symbol value is not up-to-date.

Then, `ApplyRules()` scans through each of the rules in the order they were specified. Each condition in the rule head is checked. If one condition doesn't match, the rest are skipped and the next rule is used. If all the conditions match, the default values are applied. Only then is the rule body executed to override the defaults and set other symbols as appropriate. If no rules match, the defaults are set.

Finally, `CheckEffectors()` scans only the effector symbols in the working memory and calls the native functions if any of them are true. Because we're using the RBS for control, it's more appropriate for the effectors to be checked every iteration—rather than when a rule is executed. This reduces the number of rules required.

Application

Given the case study of a wall-following behavior, the module design, its implementation, an interface with the environment, and an empty skeleton, the application phase is surprisingly straightforward!

The application process is iterative. We implement a prototype that we believe will work and try it in the game. If it fails, the problem is identified (that is, visually or with debugging tools) and fixed for the next iteration.

Working Memory

First, it's important to decide what symbols are contained within the working memory. Assuming that wall following is only done on one side, this reduces the number of symbols required.

First, a symbol needs to indicate whether the AI is currently following the wall (see Table 12.1). This is defined as *false* initially, but it's *true* by default because we're optimistic; the animat should follow the wall most of the time!

Table 12.1 The List of Symbols Used for Wall-Following Behavior, Along with Their Default Values and the Initial Status

Symbol	Default	Initial
Sidewall	(sensor)	
frontWall	(sensor)	-
Following	true	false
moveForwards	true	-
turnAway	false	-
turnTowards	false	-

We also need two symbols for sensing obstacles: one ahead and one on the side. Symbols corresponding to sensors need no default values because they are updated continuously; default values are also intended to simplify the actions, not the sensors. Then, we need three actions symbols: one to turn toward the wall, one to turn away from it, and, of course, we need the ability to move forward. In fact, that's done by default!

Rulebase

Defining the rules for the system is just a matter of expressing the case study as a set of rules. Consider the rules of Listing 12.3.

The actual rulebase used by the system is stored in XML format, but the conversion from this intuitive form to XML is just an exercise in syntax.

Until the animat has found a wall, it keeps looking for one by setting the symbol for following to false, using the default forward move. If there is a front wall, the animat turns away and overrides the default forward move to slow down. If there is no side wall, the animat stops and turns toward the previous location of the wall. Implicitly, there is a fourth rule that orders a move forward in all other cases (done by default).

Listing 12.3 The Rules Applied on the Working Memory to Define the Wall-Following Behavior (The latter rules can assume that the conditions of the previous rules are false.)

```
IF NOT following AND NOT frontWall AND NOT sidewall
     THEN following = false
IF frontWall
```

```
        THEN turnAway = true AND moveForwards = false
IF NOT sideWall
        THEN turnTowards = true AND moveForwards = false
```

From the description, we realize the importance of default symbols. The rulebase would be much more complex without them; a) there would be a fourth rule, b) each rule body to set the unused effectors to false, and c) all but the first rule would have to set the `following` symbol to true.

The priorities in the rules enable us to process the "looking for wall" behavior first, so the "following-wall" behavior (rules 2 and 3) can assume the wall has been found. The multiple actions in the rule body prevent rule duplication.

Sensors and Effectors

Both the sensors and effectors are very similar to the ones used for obstacle avoidance. They are coded as member methods in the *Brain* class, and passed to the RBS as function pointers—but with a pointer to the class. This implies that we can legally access member variables from the *Brain* in the callback.

The sensors are placed at 0 degrees (in front) and 45 degrees (to the side), with the same length only of a few steps. A value of true is returned if an obstacle is detected within that range, and false otherwise.

The effectors were originally implemented as direct calls to the `Move()` and `Turn()` interface functions. However, this produces very jerky movement, so instead we can use a smoothed version of the RBS output as actions (a moving average is ideal). This was particularly important for the movement, less so for turning.

Evaluation

The solution doesn't perform as fast as humans. The rules tell the animat to slow down at corners, to prevent getting lost. Humans with the same sensors as the animats would struggle, too. That said, increasing the length of the whiskers helps the animats detect walls better, at the cost of more computation.

In some rare cases, the animats lose track of the wall. When they do this, they go into an endless spin, trying to find the wall! This is particularly problematic, because it really shatters any sense of realism. To solve this, we can use a counter that resets every time the animat moves forward. If it gets stuck in a spin, the counter starts to increase. When the counter reaches a certain value, we have detected a spin. In this case, we reset the `"following"` symbol in the working memory to start looking for walls again. By using the right value of the counter, we can time the release from the spin so that it happens at 180 degrees. When the bot has turned around fully, it's more likely to find the wall it lost track of.

The implementation of the sensors in FEAR detects obstacles and ledges. However, at the bottom of the stairs, for example, there is a blurry zone with neither (not a bug). The animats can get lost there because the ledge is not high and the wall is too low. These spots are particularly problematic for spins, but the U-turn release strategy is fairly good at getting the animat back on track.

Some tweaking is required to get smooth behaviors. The RBS needs to be executed relatively often; the default of every 0.1 seconds produces smooth results. However, it's the moving average on the forward movement request that really helps the most. Using this averaging mechanism, the frequency of updates can be decreased.

Practical Demo

The animat demonstrating the ideas in this chapter is known as *Stalker*, available in both source and binary formats. *Stalker* uses a combination of simple rules driven by an RBS interpreter to follow walls. This animat is also capable of finding walls if it gets lost and preventing spinning motion.

Summary

Using an RBS to express the rules in reactive behaviors certainly has its benefits; the resulting wall-following capability has turned out efficient and realistic in the end, but at what cost?

It undoubtedly took more time to develop the RBS module than writing a script with steering behaviors would have required. In this case, there are mixed benefits of RBS over scripts:

➤ The performance of this RBS is slightly worse, because the sensors are checked automatically by the RBS upon every execution.

➤ The memory consumption of the system is slightly less than a scripting environment would have required.

➤ Conceptually, the rules are simpler, but they need to be translated into a format accepted by the module (XML).

There are also pros and cons compared with a native implementation:

➤ A native implementation is much faster than declarative rules.

➤ The programmer gets more control over the C++, so it can be optimized and customized.

➤ The RBS has the advantage of separating the knowledge from the implementation.

On the bright side, we also have a good feel for the development of AI using an existing module. There are some good lessons to extract from this, including the following:

➤ The RBSs are more appropriate at higher-level control (decision making) than motor control.

➤ Using an RBS for a simulation takes a bit more effort than just problem solving! More actions (or default values) are required to keep the working memory in the right state.

➤ Many of the benefits of RBSs are no longer applicable in simulations. The rules may be modular, but they are so interdependent that either may break the behavior when removed or added!

➤ Custom extensions to RBS are necessary for problems to be solved in an elegant fashion.

Although wall following wasn't the best of problems for RBSs, they actually worked and didn't take too much effort (revealing their flexibility). As an exercise, we will use them again later at a higher level of control to get a better feel for the wide capabilities of this AI technique as a problem-solving mechanism.

Part II

Conclusion

In this part of the book, we created competent animats with realistic moving behaviors, such as obstacle avoidance and wall following. Both reactive techniques that we used successfully solved the problem, each with its own set of advantages. This gives us a solid base upon which to build better behaviors.

Retrospective Overview

Because the big picture is now much clearer, it's a good time to perform a retrospective overview of all the knowledge and experience we've acquired.

Movement

The motion of the animats is relatively simple because it does not use any global knowledge of the terrain. For this reason, such reactive movement does not seem as purposeful as movement with planning, although many tricks can make the characters' behaviors more persistent.

This kind of movement is often satisfactory, because a majority of AI characters do not actually need to move far—especially in single-player games. Efficiency, reliability, and realism are the major advantages of this solution. The illusion of intelligence is unlikely to be shattered by careless maneuvers (for instance, getting stuck in doors) in the presence of human players. That said, it's a good idea to assume that things may go wrong with the behaviors and plan accordingly to attempt to recover from them (for instance, preventing spinning during wall following).

Techniques

The steering behaviors shine with their simplicity. They can be applied within a few minutes to a problem that has been prepared in advance. However, one problem that remains is fine-tuning the parameters during the experimentation phase, and dealing with more complex behaviors.

Rule-base systems come to the rescue for larger problems (and more general ones), providing a flexible and modular approach—at a relatively small development cost. However, the acquisition of knowledge still proves to be a huge problem that cannot be circumvented. It also seems that rule-based systems are not particularly suited to low-level control, because it can be a challenge to get the smooth output with a manageable number of rules.

Outlook

Rule-base systems are very useful; in fact, we'll be using them again as an exercise (see the web site at http://AiGameDev.com/). That said, rule-based systems have their flaws. Many alternative approaches are appropriate in games, but none are further away on the spectrum of AI techniques than neural networks. They do extremely well at solving the problems of rule-based systems, but they fail to provide some of their advantages. The two most popular kinds of neural network are investigated in Part III.

In the next part, we expand the behaviors of the animats. Indeed, they are taught how to shoot at moving things. This proves an extremely good way of testing the learning capabilities of the AI characters.

Part III

Learn to Shoot!

In this part, the animats learn how to shoot—as true action game bots should. The shooting behaviors are split up into subtasks that can be handled independently. A combination of physics and neural network technology produces the ideal balance between effectiveness and realism. This proves to be a surprisingly challenging problem (although equally entertaining).

Motivation

Given a satisfactory solution for movement, the next step to building up a deathmatch bot is to give it weapon skills. The nonplayer character (NPC) can handle a variety of lethal weapons, ranging from slow rockets to instantaneous railguns.

After forward and side movement, turning is the most primitive capability of animats. Turning has already been put to use for movement, but tight control wasn't necessary. Shooting, on the other hand, emphasizes the capability to turn precisely. Together with other simple actions to control the weapon, this will provide an interesting challenge for the AI.

The shooting behavior can be split up into different tasks, including anticipation, prediction, target selection, aiming, and firing. Unlike the previous examples, the shooting behavior requires more than just one function. This behavior will give us a feel for simple architectures using a single-level decomposition.

Outline

The process of development is covered in order through the chapters. Theory is split into two chapters, with a welcome practical interlude!

Chapter 13, "Combat Settings." The platform for the AI is analyzed, with a description of both the game engine and the environment. We're particularly interested in how they affect the task of shooting.

Chapter 14, "Player Shooting Skills." The problem itself is analyzed (and understood) thanks to a case study of human players. We discuss the information required to shoot and discuss criteria to evaluate the outcome.

Chapter 15, "Shooting, Formally." The specification of world interfaces is established to provide a hook for our AI. The world interfaces allow the animats to interact with the environment in terms of sensors and effectors.

Chapter 16, "Physics for Prediction." As a first prototype, an AI capable of predicting the movement of enemies is implemented. Both a mathematical solution and one based on physical simulation is demonstrated.

Chapter 17, "Perceptrons." We tackle some theory, covering perceptrons, one of the first types of neural networks. Simple technology is the focus, including an explanation about how the algorithms manage to solve problems.

Chapter 18, "Dealing with Aiming Errors." This chapter provides a practical interlude in which perceptrons are applied to aiming. Neural networks learn to shoot smoothly and to compensate for error—combining efficiency and realism.

Chapter 19, "Multilayer Perceptrons." After that practical break in the preceding chapter, this chapter continues the theory behind neural networks with a discussion of multilayer perceptrons, which is a generic form of perceptron. This chapter explains the crucial improvements that allow perceptrons to solve arbitrarily complex problems.

Chapter 20, "Selecting the Target." In this chapter, multilayer perceptrons are applied to target selection. The neural networks learn to estimate the damage inflicted by the rockets so that the AI can pick spots with high chances of damaging the enemy.

Chapter 21, "Knowledge of the Problem." Finally, we investigate the elusive skill of understanding a problem. These concepts shed light on the application phase of development.

Assumptions

Naturally, the same fundamental requirements as in Part II are assumed. Specifically, we need a game engine and a framework for the AI. To develop shooting behaviors, there are a few more prerequisites:

➤ **Support for weapons** in the game, including many different environments with weapons and ammunition.

➤ The ability to **respawn bots** back into the game no matter what they do! Moving around was fairly simple; there were few opportunities for dying. With shooting, we must expect the worst.

➤ **Independent movement behaviors** that can explore the terrain without needing assistance.

This should be more than enough to get us started. We'll develop the rest as we progress through this part! Be sure to check the web site at `http://AiGameDev.com/` for the corresponding source code and demos.

Chapter 13

Combat Settings

KEY TOPICS

- In the Armory
- Weapon Requirements
- Environment Conditions
- Training Zone

When designing animats to deal with combat, it's essential to analyze what's involved in the task generally. Moreover, it's crucial for the developer to have a solid grasp of the game design and its consequences on the AI.

No matter how great the battle, warfare takes place at an individual level. This chapter provides an informal description of the concept of combat on a personal level, where the objective is to inflict the most possible damage upon the opponent. AI design ideas are built by looking into challenges faced by soldiers throughout the centuries, and investigating the approach taken within existing computer games to model these activities.

This chapter covers the following topics:

➤ The varieties of weapons used in warfare

➤ Different weapon types (to abstract out the essence of combat: shooting skill)

➤ The role of the environment in individual fights, revealing its importance

➤ Design of a test bed where we can train and evaluate animats at one-on-one combat

As game players, principles of combat in games are familiar to us. As game developers, it's important to understand the dynamics of the design well enough to implement the AI.

In the Armory

There are two fundamentally different types of weapons: *melee* (or *contact*) weapons and *range* (or *projectile*) weapons. They are generally designed for only one of these purposes—but sometimes both, such as the spear or even the musket and bayonet. Of course, one can physically use any type of weapon outside of its intended purpose, but it will not be too effective!

Instead of discussing the abilities required to use such weapons, this chapter focuses on the physical requirements for them to serve their purpose—and hence what the AI needs for shooting. This section discusses existing computer games and how they model weapons as objects. Different levels of weapon modeling are presented, including conceptual and physical levels.

Melee Weapons

Hand weapons, such as axes and swords, have the advantage of being reusable, a logical progress from throwing rocks or bits of tree. The important aspect of such weapons is the physical contact (naturally)—the impact of the weapon on its target causes harm. Therefore, any concepts that affect this collision (such as velocity, momentum, or pressure) need to be understood by the AI, too.

Computer games can capture the complexity of such contact weapons relatively well, although low-level details of limb control are often abstracted out for playability. This means the player cannot manipulate the weapon freely. Select attacking behaviors are instead provided; clicking the mouse is a poke action, and mouse movement is a slash of the sword—as in role-playing games or first-person adventures (for instance, *Jedi Knight 2* and *Die by the Sword*). The alternative is to press combinations of buttons to control the weapon behavior, as in popular beat 'em up games (for instance, *Soul Blade* and *Caliber*). These design decisions can be reused directly to create interfaces to the AI.

Such games require a good model of weapons, because the gameplay relies on them heavily. Generally, however, contact weapons in first-person games do give the impression of desperate fighting, as a last measure before the fatal fall. Because sophisticated combinations of key presses reminiscent of beat 'em ups are quite rare, the skill often boils down to raw clicking speed or unpredictable slashes.

The modeling of the weapon itself is always simplified in games, because full physical simulations are rarely performed in great detail. This is typically just an animation of a weapon moving. The collision detection between the weapon and the target remains crude, for efficiency and simplicity purposes. Some games handle the contact as a Boolean fact; if the weapon hit the bounding box around a character, reduce its health. Simpler models such as these require lower levels of understanding from the AI, resulting in simpler behaviors.

Range Weapons

Rocks and sticks are often popular choices, although technology can significantly improve projectiles. The properties of projectiles (materials, shape) and the way they are thrown affect their trajectory the most. Therein lies the key concept: The object's flight through the air determines its impact on the target.

Fundamentally, all the computer model needs to do is simulate the trajectory of the projectile. When checking the targets, a simple Boolean hit test is enough, although variable injury models (where individual limbs can get hurt) are becoming increasingly popular (for instance, *Soldier of Fortune*). The AI needs to be aware of such concepts to perform realistically.

Fairly simple models of projectile weapons tend to work very well (that is, linear flight with no gravity). It's easier to develop nonplayer characters (NPCs) with an understanding of projectiles—or *ballistics*. Parameters are easy to tweak for playability by the designer (for instance, precision and velocity). As such, range weapons often prove much more fun than melee weapons. The process of aiming at a distance is both challenging and rewarding, and therefore interesting from the AI's perspective, too.

As for the process of aiming and firing, the simulation also contains different levels of realism. Depending on the weapon, the player's view can include wobble or angle restrictions. The timing for the release the projectile can also influence power and accuracy (for instance, arrows or grenades). Finally, the player may have to reload manually. The combination of these properties can contribute to the immersiveness of the game, but conversely can steepen the learning curve. Games tend to handle this very differently, so various restrictions may be imposed on the AI, too.

Weapon Requirements

Modern first-person games usually include many different kinds of weapons. This adds to the players' entertainment by varying their experience, providing them with more challenges. Different weapons require different abilities from the players—whether human or AI. Obviously, contact weapons require movement abilities to get into proximity of the target, but direct control of the weapon is also required to inflict the damage. On the other hand, projectiles require being fired from a distance while aiming for the target.

Beyond these rough categorizations, each variety of weapon requires different skills— each of which may need handling separately by the AI. For example, a weapon with fast projectiles behaves very differently from a slow one. Each alternate firing mode also requires different abilities. The essence of the combat is the common denominator: the ability to damage the enemy by shooting. This basic ability may be modeled as a reusable component in the AI, from which specific skills are derived.

Other tactical decisions, such as weapon selections (covered in Part IV) and combat strategies (from Part VII), just attempt to make the most of these shooting behaviors.

Environment Conditions

Skill with the weapon itself is only part of the story. The layout of the environment significantly influences close combat. Not only does it constrain player movement, but also the weapons and the blast resulting from the explosion (a.k.a. splash damage). Both participants in the fight have to deal with the environment. It affects the attacker and the defender in different ways:

➤ The **defender** can exploit the layout of the environment to hide temporarily, or secure an escape. In general, however, defenders have little room for error; they depend on the terrain, which can make them vulnerable if a wrong decision is made.

➤ The **attackers** are in the favorable position, because the traps of the environment play in their favor. Attackers can take advantage of splash damage by aiming for nearby walls, and constrain enemy movement with targeted fire (for instance, in dead ends).

Interestingly, the roles are almost never as clear-cut. Firing often happens simultaneously, which means each player is partially an attacker and a defender. That said, there is usually a dominant party, so the descriptions apply as trends.

This can be especially challenging when the parties involved are in close proximity. Local fire is both very important and extremely dangerous. Both players therefore have to look out for backfire. It can be quite damaging—and embarrassing—to accidentally shoot into a nearby wall. Such pitfalls are quite common in close combat, and need to be prevented by the AI, too.

Training Zone

Having described the important aspects of combat such as the weapons and conditions, we can now define a test bed to develop the AI behaviors. The chosen environment needs to be representative of real in-game situations, because skills developed and learned here should be transferable. By making the training zone a real game level, the chances of this happening successfully are significantly increased.

The focus of the training zone will be medium-range combat, emphasizing aiming skills, weapon handling, and immediate decisions. To improve these conditions, the environment needs to be designed with care:

➤ **Frequent targets**—The bots learning to aim need to find cannon fodder as often as possible, which will speed up the training process.

➤ **Variety of weapons**—To offer opportunities for more than one weapon, they need to be scattered throughout the training zone.

➤ **Abundance of ammo**—In addition, so as not to limit the bot to particular weapons, ammunition needs to be provided at regular intervals in space.

Also, paying attention to such little details will improve the development process and the learning of computer agents. For this, we'll use a fairly small deathmatch level, with good connectivity and plenty of weapons.

Summary

First, we made some assumptions about the underlying model of the weapons in games:

➤ Contact weapons need close proximity to be effective!

➤ Simulation of contact weapons is not very detailed in most games.

➤ The control is mostly high level, with one click (or press) corresponding to a compound weapon behavior.

➤ The properties of projectile weapons affect their trajectories (for instance, speed and weight).

➤ Projectiles are easy to simulate accurately, but often simplified instead (that is, no gravity).

We noticed some restrictions of the game design that affect how the problem is solved:

➤ By their very nature, different weapons require different skills.

➤ The raw ability to handle these weapons is the essence of combat.

➤ The environment has a very important effect on the fight, constraining both weapons and players.

Finally, we drafted some guidelines to assist the rest of the practical development:

➤ We need to test the AI in real game environments so that the skills transfer (especially when learning).

➤ The level needs to have plenty of diversity in combat settings (that is, weapons, ammo, players).

After a brief practical interlude, the next chapter continues by covering the skills required to manipulate weapons and perform well in combat.

Practical Demo

Some concepts in this chapter are illustrated by the animat called *Rampage*. Although the source code is explained in subsequent chapters, there's a guide on the web site to insert the compiled animat within the game. This procedure will remain the same for the rest of this part. *Rampage* has no particular shooting skills, but can fire repeatedly regardless of the weapon. This demonstrates the properties of each projectile and the effect of the environment (on explosions, for example).

Chapter 14

Player Shooting Skills

Now that we've covered the settings for combat, including the different kinds of weapons and the role of the environment, we're ready to start understanding the problem of shooting. Specific examples will aid in the development of the AI, notably how the shooting behaviors are split into abilities.

This chapter covers the following topics:

➤ How humans perform this aggressive task and what skills are needed

➤ Based on this knowledge, how players shoot in computer games

➤ Draft criteria to evaluate our animats with regard to their shooting behaviors

➤ A case study of the different scenarios the AI should handle

The information from this phase will enable us to reproduce the shooting skills artificially.

The Art of Combat

A successful human combatant has many skills, ranging from strategic planning to power and raw shooting skill. Clearly, each has an important effect on others, but when the person is involved in a fight, tactics often take a much lower priority. As such, we'll focus on the combat skills here, first looking at melee and then range weapons.

Close Fights

Manipulating a sword or axe requires dexterity and some strength. Most importantly, the target needs to be within reach before contact can even be considered, so there's a certain amount of movement involved, too. This requires simple locomotive abilities to approach the enemies and keep in touch with them. Luckily, these abilities have been covered in the previous part.

The behaviors used to handle the weapon are acquired through heavy training, so they become almost instinctive maneuvers. Training consists a significant aspects of contact fighting (for instance, sword duels), although reaction times and good reflexes also help.

Distant Battles

Training is also a distinctive advantage for range weapons, although the skills are quite different. Here, accuracy and composure are the key advantages. These skills are gained via target practice to improve aiming or possibly other training missions to gain more experience—whenever possible.

Even static targets can be tricky to hit. Moving targets present even more of a challenge. Depending on the speed of the projectile, judging the shot can be extremely difficult; this is manageable when the projectiles are quasi-instantaneous (for instance, bullets), but can get tricky with slower distance weapons (for instance, arrows or water bombs).

Accurate shooting is a consequence of many skills: anticipating enemy movement, understanding ballistics, predicting trajectories, selecting the appropriate target, aiming for the location, and knowing when to fire. Figure 14.1 shows this set of skills. Combined together, these determine where best to shoot, and when.

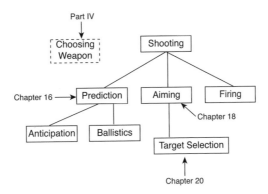

Figure 14.1   The hierarchy of skills required to successfully shoot down a moving enemy with distance weapons.

Gaming Skills

In principle, high-level skills in real life transfer into computer games (for instance, prediction and ballistics), although there are differences in the manipulation of the mouse (hand/eye coordination). The gameplay itself is usually significantly different; the speed of deathmatch games is much faster than real life, and one-on-one situations are extremely rare in real war.

The shooting skills are very specific actions, particularly those discussed in this part (for instance, turning to aim, firing). However, these low-level actions bring out trends in the game. (For instance, one player starts dominating and chasing the other.) These high-level trends in turn affect the use of weapons, notably changing the criteria for shooting.

This section covers the low-level skills, but also discusses the effect of higher-level trends on these skills.

Break It Down!

Understanding the combination of abilities helps developers with the design of the AI architecture for shooting (what composition pattern to use).

Anticipation

Anticipation of enemy movement is one of the most important abilities to hit moving targets. Because projectiles do not travel instantaneously, it's necessary to think in the future and estimate the enemy's position.

Ballistics

The trajectories of projectiles are relatively complex in some cases, notably when gravity is taken into account. Even in simple cases, it's necessary to determine where the projectile will collide with the terrain.

Prediction

With the ability to estimate the trajectories of enemies and projectiles, they can be combined to predict the outcome of a situation. Given firing parameters, the flight time and position of the enemy are taken into account to compute the likelihood of damage.

Target Selection

Given the power to predict the future (inaccurately), it's possible to decide the most appropriate place to shoot. Usually, the potential damage is maximized.

Aiming

After a spot has been chosen, the weapon must be prepared to release a projectile. This often needs to be done quickly and accurately for the projectile to reach the desired destination.

Firing

Often, these different abilities are continuously working to determine the best target and aim toward it. It's therefore necessary to decide when to actually release the trigger—to inflict most damage.

Combat Trends

In games close to real life (for instance, *Rogue Spear* and *Hidden & Dangerous*), one of the participants would bite the bullet. But game designers in other first-person shooters prefer to reduce the damage to prolong the duels. Fights in some computer games last long enough for trends to arise (for instance, *Quake 3* and *Unreal Tournament*). Such trends enable us to distinguish the two players—in deathmatch situations again.

➤ The **defender's** chances of survival can be enhanced by retaliating fire, buying extra time for the escape. It does not have to be extremely precise, just well placed to force the assaulter to withdraw temporarily. This can be seen as self-covering fire, which should be rapid above all.

➤ **Attackers** on the other hand have the advantage, which gives them more options. The aim is to keep the pressure on! This involves shooting to maximize the chances of damage, either directly or not. In this respect, the layout of the environment can be of great help; the movement of the player can be predicted, and the potential for splash damage can be assessed, too. Aiming for the floor or wall can therefore prove a valuable policy.

In games, humans tend to behave differently depending on the type of situation they are in. So, once again, these are rough categories that nobody belongs to fully; however, identifiable patterns do arise during the fight.

Criteria for Shooting

There are different qualities to expect from human combatants using real projectile weapons. These characteristics generally apply to game players, too, and become restrictions on the AI:

➤ **Reliable**—Firing a weapon should be done in such a way to prevent self-injury. Constant measures should be taken to avoid this.

➤ **Smooth**—When aiming for a target, adjustments are done in a realistic fashion, as you would expect from humans (a.k.a. leading). This contrasts with the mechanical step-by-step aiming.

➤ **Effective**—People do generally prove accurate at aiming, especially with training. Although even when humans miss a target, they do so in a justifiable way (when longer predictions are required).

These can serve as a set of criteria for the evaluation of AI nonplayer characters (NPCs).

Case Study

The AI should be able to handle some situations easily, while others demonstrate more advanced shooting capabilities. We'll assume the use of range weapons with relatively slow projectiles (for instance, rockets or blaster). In this case, there's less worry about the AI being too perfect because the task is not straightforward.

Considering each scenario, starting with the easiest, the following apply:

➤ The AI should be able to hit still targets.

➤ Targets moving at constant speed should be anticipated and intercepted with projectiles.

➤ Targets accelerating and then breaking, turning arbitrarily to dodge fire should also be hit when their movement averages out to a constant vector (see Figure 14.2).

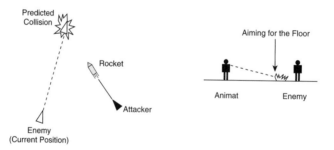

Figure 14.2   Two scenarios showing prediction abilities. On the left, a player uses a rocket to intercept the target. On the right, the plan is to aim for the floor where the enemy is predicted.

The following situations assume that a projectile with splash damage is used:

➤ When the fight happens on the same level and there are few walls around, the AI should decide to aim for the feet of the enemy.

➤ When the NPC is on the floor below the enemy, it should attempt to hit a nearby wall—also to maximize splash damage.

Gamers have developed these tactics notably for deathmatch games. If the design of the AI is successful, we expect it would use similar tactics.

Summary

This chapter discussed the different skills required for shooting and the different situations in which these skills are used:

➤ Close combat requires mostly movement abilities!

➤ Range combat involves a combination of skills: prediction, target selection, aiming, and firing.

➤ The player must estimate the trajectories of the enemy and projectiles to determine the possible damage.

➤ Different situations require different types of shooting (for instance, cover fire or containing fire).

We also described what we would expect from the AI:

➤ The criteria we'll use to evaluate the AI are reliability, smoothness, and effectiveness.

➤ The AI should be able to do straightforward prediction.

➤ Animats should also be able to use the environment to maximize splash damage.

The next chapter formalizes an interface with the environment, allowing the animats to accomplish these tasks. We'll also increase the level of difficulty by adding biologically plausible errors to the actions.

Practical Demo

An animat called *Rookie* demonstrates concepts in this chapter. *Rookie* has virtually no skills, just aiming in random directions while shooting. The web site contains the demo and source, but most importantly, the description of the architecture. *Rookie* has shooting skills that are based on the simplest abilities discussed in this chapter (for instance, prediction or firing), forming a functional AI architecture.

Chapter 15

Shooting, Formally

KEY TOPICS

- Background
- Sketching Possible Options
- Rationalizing
- Proposed Specification

Taking a gun out of a wooden box, turning one's back to the opponent, walking 20 paces before turning and opening fire can be seen as a formalization of the shooting process. However, this is not quite what's in store for this chapter, which focuses on a mathematical definition of shooting upon which to build the AI. Then, the animats could handle duels if so desired!

The preceding chapter investigated some of the principles behind combat—notably prediction, aiming, and firing. The main concern is not directly to satisfy the requirements given, but to make a solution possible by extending the framework. A flexible interface is ideal, supporting a wide variety of possible solutions.

This chapter covers the following topics:

➤ The general task at hand and ideas about how to formalize interfaces

➤ Possible specifications for the inputs and outputs of the problem

➤ Rationalization of these options, notably with criteria for the decision

➤ A formal specification using C++ data structures

At the end of this chapter, we'll have an understanding of what information the shooting behavior has to deal with. A code skeleton will also be ready for our first prototype.

Background

In most realistic first-person games, the AI doesn't need to do any prediction because the bullets fly almost instantaneously. This implies that aiming is the only aspect of the nonplayer character (NPC) that requires thought. There is an extremely simple solution to aiming, which involves nothing more than vector algebra. When the enemy is located, a bullet is spawned traveling toward that position.

The simplicity of this solution implies that there is little documentation on the subject—compared to movement at least. When more complex projectiles are used, AI developers tend to borrow solutions from physics manuals for the prediction. In fact, the problem of *fire control* is not as simple as it seems when different constraints are applied to the projectile (for instance, wind or spin).

A few recent articles focus on different aspects of range combat, mostly on the aiming problem:

➤ [Tozour02] provides a great overview of the tips and tricks used to fake ranged combat. This includes firing bullets that are almost aligned with the gun barrel, determining when to hit or miss, and tips on how to miss in the best possible way!

➤ [Alexander02] discusses response curves, and investigates their applicability to faking the aiming of humans. By using a sine function together with response curves of different slopes, varying degrees of accuracy can be obtained.

➤ [Sterren01] focuses on more advanced weapon strategies, which involve knowledge of the terrain to determine the ideal place to fire a grenade. This illustrates the need to gather information about the environment, even if we need a simpler solution (without planning).

Generally, game developers seem content to just add a random noise to the bullet's initial orientation, which results in a spread fire. Considering the big picture and the seeming unimportance of shooting details, the quick solution is often a good compromise.

As far as developing genuine behaviors for shooting is concerned, the documentation is quite rare. The same applies for formal interfaces. Not to worry, it's beneficial from an educational point of view. It provides us the opportunity to try our skills at designing a specification unassisted.

Sketching Possible Options

At this stage, we're interested in collecting and sketching rough ideas about how to handle ranged combat. Specifically, the inputs (that is, information needed from the weapon and environment), the outputs (that is, the possible ways to control the weapon), and the context (that is, how the weapon and projectiles behave, how the animat holds the gun) need to be modeled.

In this case, the options possible are mostly borrowed from existing game designs—or at least the aspects that are obvious from playing the games. This explains why some of the drafts seem familiar. However, other ideas are not as obvious, but are still worth exploring for potential options.

Context

The model of the weapons, projectiles, and the animat itself are part of the context.

Weapons and Projectiles

One of the most important questions is how to model the weapon itself. Although the weapons could be represented as a 3D mesh, fewer details are exposed within the game logic to the AI. A relatively low-level model could be used, with physical properties of the weapons exposed to the AI (for instance, using a bow and arrow). In this case, the loading of projectiles and handling of the weapon's behavior when it fires is left to the player. This would require particularly precise limb control, allowing the body to deal with the weapon in all its detail (for instance, to load the arrow, arc, and release).

On the other hand, the design can use ideas similar to the handling of movement; the low-level details can be abstracted out of the model. Weapons can be considered as an entity on which actions can be performed conceptually (that is, reload and fire). Much of the capabilities of the weapons can be exposed this way, while still retaining a simple high-level approach.

As for the projectiles, they will generally fly in a straight line. Most popular first-person shooters add gravity only to a few projectiles, such as grenades.

Animat

How does the animat hold the weapon? This could be linked to the body itself, so the animat has to look in the direction it wants to shoot at. This is a popular option in first-person shooter games.

This seems fairly restrictive, but there is a surprising amount of flexibility because the animat can move in any direction independently for its orientation.

It would be possible to handle the weapons independently from the body. This is generally not done in most games, undoubtedly because of the challenges of the animation and the control issues for human players.

Senses

The information required by an animat can be split into three categories: weapons and projectiles, target, and environment.

Weapon and Projectiles

Some sense of the current weapon is needed to maximize its use. How is it possible to fire a projectile without knowing what kind of weapon it is, or whether it's loaded and ready to go? Such information may be provided in a conceptual way (for instance, symbols indicating the weapon "isReady"), or in a more implicit fashion. (For instance, if the weapon doesn't fire, it wasn't ready.) Using this second approach, the animat would require learning the reload times.

The information about projectiles is not directly needed by the AI to perform aiming. Only understanding of how the projectile reaches the target is necessary to shoot. This can be assumed by the AI, or potentially learned within the game. Alternatively, projectiles can be represented explicitly and perceived as entities, or they can be tracked implicitly given their effect on the environment (for instance, explosions or damage).

Target

To engage combat with a particular target, an animat needs to perceive it first! Unlike the projectiles, this requires explicit sensing, allowing direct action can be undertaken. One option is to consider the enemies as an entity, and communicate that to the animat as a symbol. Alternatively, the enemy can be perceived visually as a human would see the game environment and isolate the target—although this is unlikely to be feasible technically and computationally. (We're aiming for biological plausibility not accuracy.)

Environment

As mentioned in Chapter 14, "Player Shooting Skills," a player requires knowledge of the environment to optimize the aiming performance. This knowledge can be acquired by perceiving the structure of the terrain surrounding the target. Specifically, the distance from the attacker to points around the desired impact point can help reveal the gross structure of the terrain, improving the decisions about where to shoot.

Tracing the path of the projectile is also useful, because it may prevent embarrassing shots into close obstacles, or shots that are blocked before reaching their intended target.

Actions

The actions provide a way to control the weapon as needed. Depending on how the weapon is modeled, this can be achieved as high-level actions, or on a much lower level via the control of limbs. Either way, this needs to indirectly allow firing and, potentially, reloading.

The aiming is a similar process to turning the body of the animat (defined for movement). It's possible to lock the body and the weapon's orientation together, so aiming is done by turning. Alternatively, the two can be handled separately, providing more control but increased complexity.

Rationalizing

One common design principle is to put the AI on the same terms as human players. As such, whichever option is chosen should be kept compatible with the handling of player weapons. This makes implementing the interfaces much easier, and has most of the advantages of embodiment.

Deciding Factors

Aside from these primary concerns, the model chosen must exhibit the following properties:

➤ **Realism**—Shooting is an obvious behavior, visible from a long distance. Although it may not be as important as movement, it can still give away the illusion of intelligence. Therefore, we should strive to reach a convincing level of realism when designing these abilities.

➤ **Efficiency**—Aiming and firing are not required as regularly as other abilities; their use is limited to combat situations. Therefore, it is not feasible to dedicate a lot of time to these abilities because many other processes may require attention (whether AI or not).

➤ **Capabilities**—Ideally, our animats should be capable of outperforming humans so that the pressure can be increased if the game gets too easy for the player. The interfaces should allow this.

As well as maintaining compatibility with the handling of human weapons, our decisions will need to promote these properties.

Assumptions

Throughout Part III of this book, we'll assume that the weapon itself is mostly autonomous. This means that it can deal with reloading without the AI having to worry about it. It would be fairly trivial for the AI to check the state of the weapon and reload if necessary. This would probably be our approach if the game design allowed this.

The AI can focus on aiming and firing it without concern. This makes it more convenient to focus on the difficult part of the task and not worry about the little details.

Projectiles are assumed to be governed by well-determined rules, such as the physics applied to the game entities. This helps devising an AI that does not need to deal with arbitrary projectiles. Specifically, the development focuses on the ones that fly in a straight line (such as bullets or rockets).

Proposed Specification

The enemies will be perceived as tuples containing a symbol (stored as a `string` or `int`) and a position (three floating-point numbers, one for each dimension X/Y/Z). This is done relatively to the current position and orientation, in the spirit of embodiment. It makes the AI easier to program in this case anyway.

The weapon is fired by calling a simple fire method. The projectile is launched automatically, and there is no need to reload. The projectile itself may be returned as an entity, depending on its type and speed. (For instance, bullets are too fast and are not perceived, whereas slower rockets may be followed.)

The aiming is done with the body turns, as defined for the movement. Because the direction of travel is independent from the orientation, this will prove satisfactory. This is the method used by human players, and proves relatively simple to master.

Because we may have AI that is too good at shooting, we'll probably need to add some noise to some of the functions. This will enable us to vary the skill of the AI implicitly.

Interfaces

The *Weapon* interface has two functions we are interested in. Firing launches the projectile, and weapon selection is handled by a requesting symbol (`string` or `int`). False is returned if something goes wrong.

```
void Fire();
boor Select(const Symbol& weapon);
```

Next, the *Vision* interface is extended to handle tracing projectiles. (It was used for finding obstacles.) The vector given is relative to the current view. The return value is the distance to the first obstacle.

```
float TraceProjectile(const Vec3f& orientation);
```

Finally, a query is used to gather the visible entities as an array. This is also part of the *Vision* module. The second parameter is used to filter the entities that the animat is interested in. (Only those that unify are returned.)

```
void VisibleEntities(vector<Entity>& visible, const Entity::Type&
unifier = 0 );
```

Letting the brain gather the entities manually provides it with the most flexibility to handle different situations (for instance, multiple different players). If only one enemy is present, a message-passing approach may be more suitable.

Code Skeleton

A successful implementation will involve more than just using all these interface calls, but here's a simple example nonetheless:

```
void Think()
{
    // query the visual interface for an array of players
        vision->VisibleEntities( players );
    // scan the nearby players to find an enemy
        for (int i=0; i<players.size(); ++i)
        {
            // remember target
        }
    // turn the view and launch a projectile
        motion->Turn( target.GetPosition() );
        weapon->Fire();
}
```

This book does not cover the weapon selection until Part IV; a randomly selected weapon is assumed. The implementation of the different brains in the next few chapters will be split into parts, roughly corresponding to each of the skills discussed (that is, prediction, targeting, and aiming).

Summary

This chapter covered the specification of interfaces to allow shooting behaviors:

➤ The standard approach to aiming involves omniscient control, deciding when to hit or miss, and which point to target.

➤ There are many ways to define an interface to expose such data to NPCs, allowing them to shoot (for instance, high level, or implicit model of projectile).

➤ An interface in chosen to match the human controls, allowing animats to be realistic while maximizing their capabilities.

➤ Most importantly, the visual capabilities of the system are extended to deal with projectile traces and gathering visible entities.

➤ The weapons are made autonomous with automatic reloading. The weapon selection too is left aside until later.

In the next chapter, a "standard" approach based on physics predicts the trajectory of enemies. There are two approaches presented, either using simulation or equation solvers.

Practical Demo

There's an animat called *Salty* demonstrating the use of the new interfaces, downloadable in binary and source formats from `http://AiGameDev.com/`. *Salty* selects the closest player as its enemy, and points directly toward that location. Projectiles are fired during combat only.

Chapter 16

Physics for Prediction

KEY TOPICS

- Foundations
- The Perfect Intersection
- Predicting Behavior
- Simulation Algorithm
- Experimentation
- Evaluation

Accurate shooting can be understood as a combination of many skills. One of these is the ability to predict what's going to happen in the near future. This involves anticipating player movement, as well as understanding the ballistics of the projectile. We'll focus on this aspect of shooting in this chapter.

Throughout the explanations, we'll assume that the aiming can be done satisfactorily by just turning toward the estimated target. (Matching pitch and yaw angles is often good enough.) The weapon is fired whenever it's ready—with an enemy present of course! The target selection itself is done implicitly as part of the prediction; the predicted outcome becomes the target.

In the quest to find the best place to launch a projectile at an enemy, this chapter covers the following topics:

➤ Theory from Newtonian physics such as integration, used to simulate movement

➤ A solution purely based on physics that solves an equation to find the target

➤ A more practical approach to predicting movement using an iterative approach

➤ The conditions for experimentation with predicting movement of other players

➤ An analysis of the quality of the behaviors in the game, as well as the development process

By the end of the chapter, we'll have an animat capable of firing a weapon (with slow projectiles) to intercept a moving enemy.

Foundations

Successful prediction of movement requires a minimal understanding of Newtonian physics. No need to worry; we'll keep it down to accessible concepts. This approach is at the foundation of physics engines—although it is very simplified here.

Physical State

All objects have a set of properties that define them as physical things: shape, size, or weight. These properties combine to determine the movement of objects. To understand the behavior of objects, their properties are modeled—including velocity, acceleration, and center of mass.

Physicists have been able to express relationships between these variables, so they can be used to solve problems. For example, the velocity is the derivative of the position x (that is, the position changes based on the velocity) and the acceleration a is the derivative of the velocity v. (That is, the velocity changes based on the acceleration.) In physics, dots are the preferred notation for derivatives with respect to time (they both are):

$$v = \dot{x}$$
$$a = \dot{v}$$

The laws of Newtonian physics enable us to determine some of these values (for instance, the acceleration based on force and mass). However, we need calculus to compute the other values indirectly. This allows problems to be solved or simulations to be performed—both involving the movement of objects.

Numeric Integration

The biggest problem in physics implementations is generally to keep track of the position over time. We know the velocity is the *derivative* (that is, rate of change) of the position, so the position is the *integral* (that is, the accumulation) of the velocity. Essentially, it's often difficult to exactly determine the position.

The algorithms used to compute values that change over time are known as *numeric integrators*. Integrators compute the values of the position $x(t)$ and velocity $v(t)$ as a function of time t, generally in terms of previous values.

One of the first and simplest solutions to do this is Euler integration [Bourg01] (referred to as *kinematics*). The idea is to estimates the next values (with time step Δt), based on the derivative and the current value:

$$v(t+\Delta t) = v(t) + a(t)\Delta t$$

$$x(t+\Delta t) = x(t) + v(t)\Delta t$$

This means that we compute the next value of the velocity by adding the acceleration, and add the velocity to the position to get the next position. This is known as *explicit integration*, which involves barely more than vector algebra.

Sadly, Euler integration has many problems in practice. Indeed, the acceleration often changes between the time steps Δt, and there are collisions to deal with. Many better solutions for numeric integration have been developed, which work very well on both solid objects and elastic ones. Although these are of great benefit to applications in physics, AI rarely requires more sophisticated solutions.

The Perfect Intersection

It is possible to use physics to predict the collision of two moving points. Suppose there's a player, for example, defined as a position in 3D space $p = [p_x, p_y, p_z]$ and a corresponding velocity $v = [v_x, v_y, v_z]$. In t seconds, the position of the player will be $p(t) = p + vt$ (vector scaling and addition). There is no need for integrators if we assume the velocity is constant; the estimate is exact.

To simplify the proof, assume that the weapon is fired from the origin of the world at [0,0,0]. We don't know where to fire the weapon yet (unknown direction), so the exact velocity of the projectile is not known. We do, however, know the speed s of the projectile.

At time t in the future, the projectile will be at a distance of st from the origin (distance is speed multiplied by time). For the projectile to hit, the player must be in the same position at any t. So the distance of $p(t)$ to the origin (denoted $|p(t)|$) will be the identical to the projectile's distance to the origin:

$$|p(t)| = |p + vt| = st$$

This equation is sufficient to enable us to compute the time of collision. To make it easier to extract t, we can use the square of these values. The second equation here expands the vector algebra into real numbers:

$$|p + vt|^2 = s^2t^2$$

$$(p_x + v_xt)^2 + (p_y + v_yt)^2 + (p_z + v_zt)^2 = s^2t^2$$

Using a sum Σ to simplify the notation, then developing the inner square:

$$\sum_{i=[x, y, z]} (p_i + v_it)^2 = s^2t^2$$

$$\sum_{i=[x, y, z]} (p_i^2 + 2p_iv_it + v_i^2t^2) = s^2t^2$$

We would like to compute the collision time t from these equations. Factorizing to expose t, we get a quadratic equation in the form $at^2+bt^2+c=0$ (second order polynomial). The symbols a, b, and c are arbitrary variables used to simplify the equations and the implementation. They are defined as follows:

$$a = -s^2 + \sum_{i=0}^{2} v_i^2 \quad b = 2\sum_{i=0}^{2} v_ip_i \quad c = \sum_{i=0}^{2} p_i^2$$

Computing the time of collision involves first calculating these values for a, b, and c. Then, we plug them into the miracle solution for quadratic equations to get the result:

$$t = \frac{-b - \sqrt{b^2 - 4ac}}{2a}$$

The result is defined as long as the statement in the square root is positive. (That is, the speed of the bullet must allow it to hit the moving target.) Theoretically, there is actually another solution to the polynomial using the positive square root. However, this predicts negative values of t (in the past).

Given t, we can compute the estimated point of collision with $p(t) = p + vt$. So that's the place the animat aims for the bullet to hit the enemy!

Predicting Behavior

When it comes to predicting the movement of living things, it doesn't really matter how precise the equation is, or how well the integrator performs. Indeed, creatures are not passive objects that obey rules; there is much uncertainty in the forces they can apply, so the acceleration itself can vary. As such, better integrators can be discarded, because the underlying assumptions about the acceleration will often lead to the wrong result anyway. So, we might as well keep it simple!

Unlike the physics engine, human and AI players have no insider knowledge about the state of objects. They can only make deductions by observing objects and monitoring their position (embodiment). With this approach, the velocity can be estimated only between two observations; the velocity is the change of position.

For additional precision, monitoring the change in velocity allows the AI to determine the acceleration. The entire process requires three observations at different times: first, monitor the position; second, understand velocity; and third, extract the acceleration.

Because each of these quantities (velocity, acceleration) can vary quickly from one second to the next, it can be beneficial to average them over a short period of time. This cancels out part of the *noise* caused by errors in the observation or unpredictable behaviors. However, the problem with averages is that they lag behind the actual value (because past values are taken into account). In games, it might be better to predict the velocity on a stopped/running basis, because these are the two most common states.

Many minor decisions about the model must be made, because many parameters can be adjusted according to observations, or to match particular requirements. These values can be chosen and tweaked during the experimentation phase, using empirical judgment to decide what works best.

Simulation Algorithm

Instead of using a miracle equation to find the target collision point, a simulation can predict the outcome. In this case, an algorithm based on successive iterations finds a good estimate of the intersection. This is based on forward integration, applying Euler's equations to the position of the enemy and projectile—as shown in Figure 16.1.

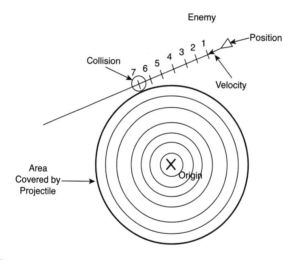

Figure 16.1 Simulating the trajectory of the enemy with forward integration, comparing it to the distance traveled by the projectile. During the simulation, the position of the enemy moves along the line, and the potential area covered by the projectiles increases as circles.

Essentially, the iteration starts at the current time and steps through time, predicting the position of the enemy along the way. When the projectile can reach the position of the enemy in the same amount of time, we've found the intersection. Listing 16.1 has more details.

Listing 16.1   Using Forward Integration to Find the Point of Collision Between the Enemy and the Projectile

```
repeat
        # update the position of the enemy for this time step
        enemy.position += enemy.velocity * delta
        # add the step to the current time
        time += delta
        # determine time taken by projectile to reach enemy
        flight_time = length(enemy.position—origin) / projectile.speed
        # compute time difference for enemy and projectile reaching
        difference = abs(time - flight_time)
# stop if the projectile is very close, or too many iterations
until difference < threshold or time > max_time
```

Notice that this iteration is done step by step, which might seem somewhat inefficient. In most cases, however, only a few iterations will actually be needed, because of the speed of the projectiles.

A different kind of integration could resolve this problem, performing in log(n) average time. The idea is to use a much larger step. Then, if the simulation goes too far, we negate the step and reduce its size. This will narrow the exact solution much quicker, and with greater precision. The additional code in the loop is shown in Listing 16.2. A suitable delta to start with is the time taken by the projectile to reach the original position of the enemy.

Listing 16.2   Update to the Forward Integration Algorithm That Adjusts the Delta

```
# if the sign changes, the simulation has gone too far
if sign XOR time < time_flight then
        # reduce the step size and reverse direction
             delta = -delta / 2
end if
# remember if the enemy is further away than the projectile
sign = time < time_flight
```

There are few cases where this updated version of the algorithm should be preferred. Indeed, it essentially computes the result of the previous equation, most likely in a slower fashion. So, if such precision is required, the mathematical approach should be chosen.

On the other hand, there are other advantages to the plain forward iteration algorithm. Indeed, at each time step, it is possible for the artificial intelligence (AI) to anticipate the velocity of the enemy. So, for example, if there were an obstacle in the way, the velocity of the enemy would be adjusted. This would lead to the prediction of paths that are not linear.

Practical Demo

Colin is an animat that attempts to anticipate the enemy based on what it can see. During the prediction, it tries to check whether there is a wall in the way of the enemy. If the wall can be side-stepped, the velocity will be adjusted slightly by guessing. If the wall is a major block, the simulation stops and that point is used as a target. You can find the source code as well as a step-by-step guide to launching *Colin* on the web site at `http://AiGameDev.com/`.

Experimentation

To emphasize the benefits of prediction, the animats use the blaster—which fires fairly slow projectiles. Rockets are an option, but they reduce fight time and increase self-damage. We'll use rocket launchers in Chapter 20, "Selecting the Target," when the animats can prevent blowing themselves up. Naturally, making each of the animats invulnerable is an option for development, too. However, using the blaster instead means fights in fact finish, still lasting long enough for us to get a feel for the abilities of the animats.

It's also more interesting to force the animats to shoot from a distance, which really emphasizes their prediction skills. This is done by declaring a truce at short distances. When the animats are in proximity, they'll stare at each other, and eventually walk away. After ten paces, they can open fire, like in a duel. This is a gimmick in many ways, but it serves a valid purpose!

Very simple movement code can be used to test the prediction. In fact, a slightly modified version of *Pinbot* is used. The only additions were to allow the animats to look somewhere other than the direction of travel. This is important during fights because the attention is focused toward the enemy rather than in the direction of movement.

To handle movement without always seeing the obstacles, physical contact is used for the animats to bounce of walls. The steering behaviors perform well when the animats can see where they are going. During the fight, however, it's not always possible to look for walls (when traveling backward, for example). Bouncing off walls is also very predictable in nature, so it's a great test for the prediction.

Evaluation

In many cases, shooting without prediction is satisfactory. This is the case when the animats are close by, or running directly in the line of fire (forward or backward). The prediction works very well for these cases.

At a distance, the prediction skills are surprisingly good—particularly on the other bots. Prediction is particularly good in large areas, where few turns are necessary to move around. Estimating the velocity of enemies using a moving average gives good results. However, this needs to be biased toward the most recent velocity observations (that is, 80% / 20%).

When two animats are on the same level, the prediction of the movement is essentially one dimensional, because only left and right turns are needed. When the animats are on different levels, this becomes 2D prediction because the view needs to be tilted up and down. Naturally, this is not as effective. For example, running toward a staircase will cause *Predictor* to shoot on the same level, not taking into account the stairs. *Colin* does a bit better from this respect, because it won't actually shoot when the enemy is heading toward a wall. However, the assumptions made to correct the velocity when enemies encounter walls are often just as wrong as the naive estimates!

That said, the prediction is also conceptually limited to reactive patterns. Using dodging tactics (for instance, keeping mostly still, but staffing back and forth only to avoid incoming projectiles) proves very effective at avoiding damage from blaster shots. Having higher-level understanding of the situation (both spatially and temporally), humans can break such patterns by shooting at the same spot.

Summary

In this chapter, we developed animats capable of predicting enemy movement:

➤ A physical solution can compute the intersection of any projectile with a moving object.

➤ It's necessary for animats to observe the players to determine their velocity and possibly their acceleration.

➤ Using a simulation of the enemy with forward integration, we can predict nonlinear trajectories.

➤ The bots perform relatively well, although they lack the higher-level capability to predict patterns over time.

The flaws pointed out in the evaluation could be resolved by giving the animats better temporal and spatial understanding. In the heat of the battle, however, these details will often not be obvious, and the inabilities of the animats will be compensated for by other skills.

The other skills involved in shooting are covered in two chapters. Learning can solve a few difficult problems and improve the weapon skills of animats. However, some theory is necessary before moving on to discussing other shooting skills.

Chapter 17

Perceptrons

Perceptrons are one of the simplest kinds of artificial neural networks. They consist of parallel processing units—inspired by biological neurons. The units are linked together with weighted connections. The term *perceptron* generally refers to networks with a single layer of processing units. Therefore, their computational complexity is relatively low; perceptrons solve linear problems or approximate complex solutions linearly.

Applying the perceptron to a problem requires a simulation algorithm, filtering the input data through this network to produce an output. In games, the output can be used as a prediction of a situation (for example, win or loss), classifying patterns (for instance, identifying friends or enemies), and controlling the body of animats (for instance, turning left or right).

This chapter covers the following topics:

➤ The history of connectionism: the field of artificial models of brains

➤ The representation used for perceptrons, including how the network is formed between inputs and outputs

➤ The simulation algorithm used to process the information and obtain a result

➤ An overview of optimization techniques (using mathematics to find a better representation) from a general perspective

➤ How to adjust the weights of a perceptron as an optimization problem, so the neural network can be changed to produce the right output

➤ Perceptron training algorithms that allow a system to learn from multiple examples of correct inputs/outputs

➤ The role of a perceptron in graphical terms, to provide a more intuitive understanding

The next chapter applies perceptrons to multiple problems in a much more practical fashion. The next few pages cover the theory, using simple game examples when appropriate.

History of Perceptrons

Although much of the artificial intelligence (AI) community focused on symbolic reasoning, a few researchers around the mid-twentieth century were investigating parallel distributed computing, and notably models inspired by the nervous activity in biological brains. In 1943, McCulloch and Pitts started experimenting with simple simulations of the nervous system [McCulloch43].

Rosenblatt's Perceptron

It wasn't until 1959 that a neural system caught the attention of the AI community. This was Rosenblatt's perceptron [Rosenblatt59], modeling the human visual system—hence the name.

The perceptron is capable of extracting visual patterns from images (a popular problem at the time). From the bitmap, random weighted connections provide a set of features to the actual perceptron. In turn, these features are connected with weights to the output, which provide interpretations of the image. By training the perceptron on a collection of sample bitmaps with their corresponding outputs, the system could learn to classify the images (see Figure 17.1).

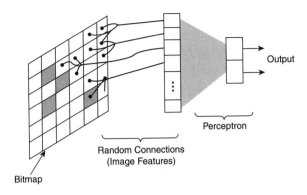

Figure 17.1   Rosenblatt's perceptron connected to a bitmap image, capable of recognizing some of its features.

For the AI community, one of the most interesting aspects of this perceptron was the proof of convergence established by Rosenblatt. This proved that if a possible solution for the perceptron existed, the training algorithm would find it. This generated quite a bit of interest!

Widrow and Hoff's Adaline

Widrow and Hoff took a hardware-based approach, presenting many useful improvements on the perceptron. Notably, the signals used within the neural network take the values [−1,1], rather than the common [0,1]. This allows more interesting computational properties in each of the processing units; there's always an input signal, positive or negative, so the role of the weights is more important.

However, the major contribution of the *Adaline* was the training rule. Based on the more robust mathematical power of the "delta rule" (explained later in the chapter), these networks can be trained to find the best possible approximation of the problem, and not just a solution. This rule is now used most commonly in neural network learning, rather than the original perceptron training algorithm.

Biological Inspiration

Most of these neural networks tend to be introduced as a biologically inspired model of the human brain. Although the initial inspiration is undoubtedly neurobiological, presenting them as a small "brain" with "neurons" raises many unfounded and often irrational assumptions. The capabilities of such techniques therefore become somewhat uncertain, turning would-be developers into dreamers.

Instead, we'll study the computer representation of perceptrons, rather than the biological neurons it's supposed to model. We'll then demonstrate the problem perceptrons try to solve, explaining how they manage to do it, and analyzing how well it works. This is the kind of scientific knowledge we would expect from AI engineers and game programmers (and is more intuitive).

Model Overview

Perceptrons essentially consist in a layer of weights, mapping a set of inputs $\vec{x} = [x_1,\ldots, x_n]$ onto a single output y. The arrow above the $\vec{x}$ denotes this is a vector consisting of multiple numbers. The mapping from input to output is achieved with a set of linear weights connecting the function inputs directly to the output (see Figure 17.2).

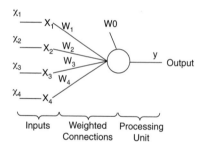

Figure 17.2   A perceptron with four inputs and a single output.

Multiple outputs $\vec{y} = [y_1,\ldots, y_n]$ can be handled by using the same principle again; another set of weights can connect all the inputs to a different output. All the outputs and weights should be considered—and actually are—independent. (This, in fact, is one limitation of the perceptron.) For this reason, we will focus on networks with a single output y, which will simplify the explanations.

The weights are denoted $\vec{w} = [w_0, w_1 \ldots w_n]$; weights 1 through n are connected to the inputs, and the 0th weight $w_0 = b$ is unconnected and represents a bias (that is, a constant offset). The bias can also be interpreted as a threshold; if you add the bias, the threshold is 0; otherwise, it's $-b$.

Practical Note

The bias represents a constant offset. As such, we can treat it as a separate value that is not connected to any inputs. In practice, however, it's often easier to include an additional input that remains constant at $x_0 = 1$, connected to the bias w_0. This way, the bias can be treated as a normal weight, which simplifies the code slightly!

The choice of data type for the inputs, outputs, and weights has changed over the years, depending on the models and the applications. The options are binary values or continuous numbers. The perceptron initially used binary values (0, 1) for the inputs and outputs, whereas the *Adaline* allowed inputs to be negative and used continuous outputs. The weights have mostly been continuous (that is, real numbers), although various degrees of precision are used. There is a strong case to use continuous values throughout, as they have many advantages without drawbacks.

As for the data type, we'll be using 32-bit floating-point numbers—at the risk of offending some neural network purists. Indeed, 64 bits is a "standard" policy, but in games, this is rarely worth double the memory and computational power; single precision floats perform just fine! We can do more important things to improve the quality of our perceptrons, instead of increasing the precision of the weights (for instance, revise the input/output specification, adjust the training procedure, and so forth).

The next few pages rely on mathematics to explain the processing inside perceptrons, but it is kept accessible. (The text around the equations explains them.) The practical approach in the next chapter serves as an ideal complement for this theoretical foundation.

Simulation

Perceptrons are in fact function approximators, denoted $y = f(\vec{x})$. The process of simulation—or computing the function f—involves filtering an input pattern $\vec{x}$

through the network to get the corresponding output y. This is done in two stages: computing the net sum and applying the activation function.

The Net Sum

The first part involves determining the net sum, denoted with the Greek zeta ζ. This is the addition (denoted by the Greek sigma Σ) of all the inputs multiplied by their weights $(x_i w_i)$:

$$\zeta = \sum_{i=0}^{n} w_i x_i = w_0 + \sum_{i=1}^{n} w_i x_i$$

The first statement equivalent to ζ assumes the first input is grounded at $x_0 = 1$ to represent the bias. The second statement shows the offset w_0 explicitly (see Figure 17.3). This is to remind ourselves that it's there and should not be forgotten!

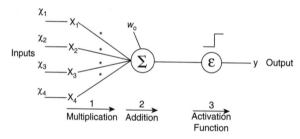

Figure 17.3 Outline of the operations used for computing the output of a perceptron, based on the input pattern.

Generally speaking, the process that combines all the weighted inputs is called a *combination function*. In theory, this can be almost any function, but in practice, a sum is used most often. This has many advantages for the learning by keeping the model simple.

Activation

After the net sum ζ has been computed, it can be used to determine the output y. The only thing left to do is to pass the result through an *activation function*, usually noted σ (lowercase Greek sigma):

$$y = \sigma(\zeta)$$

In the original perceptron, this activation function outputs a result based on the sign of the net sum ζ. If it is positive, the output is set to 1, and 0 corresponds to a negative net sum:

$$\sigma(x) = \begin{cases} 1 \text{ if } x > 0 \\ 0 \text{ otherwise} \end{cases}$$

Generally, it's beneficial to keep the result as a continuous value rather than restrict it to two discrete values. This mainly allows continuous numbers to be used in the problem at hand (for instance, smooth movement control), but can also be easier to deal with during training. It's also feasible to have both; a binary output is computed, and training is based on the net sum ζ. Early variations of the *Adaline* did this.

Further Information

Many other smooth functions are used for activation. These are generally nonlinear functions corresponding to a smooth curve within [0,1]. Such functions have little benefit for single-layer perceptrons, but prove essential when multiple perceptrons are cascaded. Chapter 19, "Multilayer Perceptrons," discusses these in depth.

Algorithm Outline

Listing 17.1 shows an outline of the algorithm in pseudo-code—almost as long as the actual implementation! It assumes that there are two initialized arrays (`input` and `weight`) and an `activation` function.

Listing 17.1   Computing the Output of a Single Perceptron

```
net_sum = 0
for all i
    net_sum += input[i] * weight[i]
end for
output = activation( net_sum )
```

The output is often used as the prediction of an arbitrary function of the inputs. For example, the output may evaluate the suitability of a behavior or determine whether a situation is dangerous. We'll discuss in much more detail how to use this result, and show how to it can be applied in practice later. For the moment, we need to know how to train the perceptron to approximate a function correctly—regardless of its use. This is done by optimizing each of the weights in the network.

Introduction to Optimization

Optimization techniques lead to the best solution for a problem.

An Example

Suppose, for instance, that there's a way to determine how much damage is inflicted based on where the animat shoots. This is done by a simulation on a case-by-case basis, changing the orientation of the weapon and checking how much health the enemy loses. This corresponds to one single point on the 2D graph.

By doing this regularly for many orientations, we could get a relatively smooth curve linking all the points together—assuming there are no errors or noise. This curve represents our best knowledge of a mathematical concept of the problem: a *function*, which links damage with orientation. We say that damage d is a function of orientation o, for some unknown function f. This is written $d = f(o)$ (see Figure 17.4).

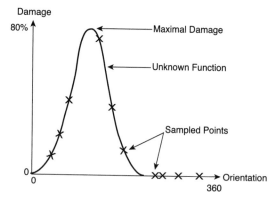

Figure 17.4   Samples of damage inflicted based on the orientation, along with the curve modeling the concept.

Now this function is just a concept, and only specific orientations (o_1, o_2) can be checked. However, we are really interested in this function because it can help the animats perform better! By knowing the orientation that inflicts the most damage, the effectiveness of the behaviors can be improved. This is known as a *maximization problem*: Find the orientation ô for which the damage is highest:

$$ô | \forall o \; f(ô) \geq f(o)$$

This equation means that the optimal orientation ô is defined such that (|) for all orientations o ($\forall o$) the damage of ô (that is, $f(ô)$) is above or equal to the damage of o (that is, $f(o)$). Finding the solution to this equation, however, is not quite as straightforward. The major problem is that only specific points on the curve are known, namely those where the damage has been computed by simulation.

Brute-Force Optimization

Generally, the notation used is $y = f(x)$ (similar to the definition of the perceptron). The function is sometimes called an energy function (denoted E), which expresses the energy cost of a particular value of x. This originates mainly from physics backgrounds, where many problems require finding the *minimal* energy instead.

To find the optimal value of x, we could use brute force by checking all its values and finding the corresponding y, as illustrated in Figure 17.5. However, there are two problems:

➤ This approach is often too computationally intensive, especially when the function is complex.

➤ Only discrete points can be checked on the curve (for instance, every 0.01 units), so the best solution may be missed out (for instance, 0.005).

Instead, more efficient methodologies can be borrowed from mathematics, physics, or even biology.

Generally, examples demonstrate optimization based on single continuous numbers. However, it is also possible to optimize vectors (denoted $\vec{x}$) of variable dimensionality with the exact same theory. So despite all the examples focusing on cases where $\vec{x} = [x]$, any arbitrary set of numbers can be substituted such that $\vec{x} = [x_0 ... x_n]$.

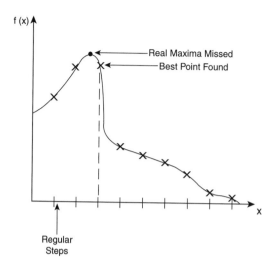

Figure 17.5 Brute-force optimization checking the values of the function at regular intervals. The maximal value is missed.

Numeric Optimization

We can use a wide variety of techniques to solve these problems, including differential calculus, numeric analysis, and stochastic approaches. Most operate as best-guess techniques, which iteratively improve an estimate. Some of these techniques are easy to understand and implement, whereas others rely on a significant knowledge of calculus. In many cases, the simplest approach is often used—and usually proves satisfactory for game development. The following sections review some of the most popular techniques used.

The methods described next can be used to find optimal configurations, whether minimal or maximal. The theory is the same in both cases, although existing terminology focused on minimization. This type of problem is generally known as an *optimization problem*. In some cases, this optimization is constrained, meaning we need to maintain a condition for the parameters (for instance, *x* or *y* within some range). However, we'll focus on problems that have no such constraints because they are more common and appropriate for training perceptrons.

Steepest Descent

The *steepest descent* technique uses information about the slope of a function to find a solution x such that $f(x)$ is a global minimum (that is, the absolute lowest point of the curve). Fundamentally, steepest descent is an iterative process; estimates of the current value x are corrected incrementally.

We start with the first estimate x_0 and continue until the $n + 1^{th}$ prediction x_n is good enough. Deciding when to stop the iteration can be done quantitatively by measuring the change in the estimate: $|x_{i+1} - x_i| \le \varepsilon$. The Greek epsilon ε is a small quantity used as a threshold to compare the difference in successive estimates. The process is said to have *converged* when this inequation is verified.

The first guess x_0 is generally made randomly. To improve any estimate x_i and get a new one x_{i+1}, we take a step Δx_i, which is added to the current value (Δ is pronounced delta—another Greek letter, of course).

$$x_{i+1} = x_i + \Delta x_i$$

The gradient of the function is needed to determine the value of this step. Visually, the gradient corresponds to the slope of the curve of f at x_i, as shown in Figure 17.6. It is written $\nabla f(x_i)$ in mathematical notation.

So why is the gradient needed? The assumption is that the slope of the curve can lead toward a lower point, and eventually the lowest one—where the iteration converges. Basically, the gradient of the function a particular point x_i is used to adjust the estimate in the appropriate direction to get x_{i+1}.

$$x_{i+1} \leftarrow x_i - \eta \nabla f(x_i)$$

The second factor $\eta \nabla f(x_i)$ is subtracted from the first because we want to move against the gradient, namely down toward the minimum. The only unexplained factor in this equation is the Greek letter eta η. In AI, this is called a *learning rate*, which is used to scale the step taken at each iteration. Confusingly, the learning rate parameter has no relation with how quickly the result is found! Large values of η imply that large steps are taken each time, which works for simple functions—and tends to converge fast. Small values of η mean that smaller steps are taken, so the solution is less likely to be missed, but it will take more iterations to converge.

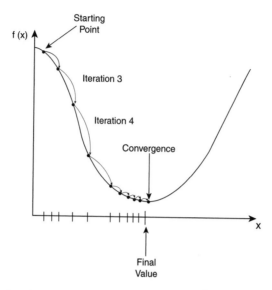

Figure 17.6   Successive steepest descent iterations showing the improvement in the estimates until the process converges at the global minimum.

The graphs in Figure 17.7 reveal the importance of the step. Selecting a learning rate that is too large or too small will lead to two different kinds of problems: oscillation and slow convergence, respectively. Both of these are undesirable because they prevent us from finding the optimal value quickly.

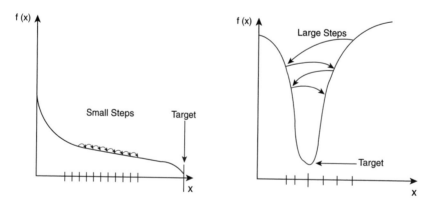

Figure 17.7   Problems with the learning rate. On the left, slow convergence, and oscillation on the right.

As such, the adjustment of the *learning rate* η can play an extremely important role in the whole process. What's more, there is no ideal value for every problem; the learning rate must be chosen on a case-by-case basis, depending on the nature of the function. This unfortunately requires time-consuming experimentation, or setting up a script to gather results.

Local Minima

There's another twist in the plot: Minimal values are not always what they seem; some are imposters! Indeed, there are *local* minima and *global* ones. A local minimum is the lowest value in its surrounding neighborhood, but there can exist a lower value elsewhere—the *global minimum*. This is like the Holy Grail for optimization algorithms, and often takes nothing short of a crusade to find (and guarantee this is the right one).

Why can't gradient descent realize that this is the local minimum, and keep descending further? The problem is that the two cannot be distinguished. The process will converge in the local minima as well as global minimum, which means successive estimates will be similar (that is, within ε of each other), hence triggering the halting condition (see Figure 17.8). We don't know this solution is not the right one until a better one is found. It is just the best we've found so far.

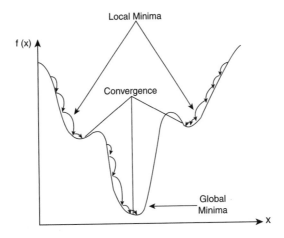

Figure 17.8   A more complex function with multiple local minima, but only one global minimum. The process converges in each case.

Generally, functions are even more complex than the ones depicted here (with one or two minima), so things are worse for real problems. Taking into account oscillation problems and slow convergence reveals an even tougher dilemma. Naturally, AI algorithms prefer near-optimal solutions, which explains the need for more powerful and reliable methods. As we'll see, even more elaborate processes have their problems.

Adding Momentum

The optimization algorithms need a simple technique to prevent premature convergence and reduce the likelihood of finding local minima. The concept of *momentum* comes to the rescue. Momentum decreases the likelihood of premature convergence by providing a sense of short-term history when deciding the next step. Essentially, the value of the previous step Δx_{i-1} is scaled by α (the Greek alpha) and added to the step normally used in steepest descent (opposite to the gradient with learning rate: $-\eta \nabla f(x_i)$).

$$\Delta x_i \leftarrow \alpha \Delta x_{i-1} - \eta \nabla f(x_i)$$

The key observation leading to this approach is that the steps taken from iteration to iteration can be extremely erratic. This is caused by the gradients changing often, especially when the steps are large or the function is complex. The addition of momentum can help smooth things out and use previous trends to help choose the next step (see Figure 17.9).

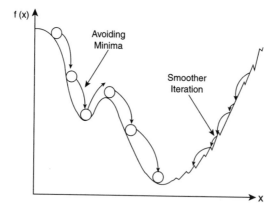

Figure 17.9   Using momentum to overcome local minima and smooth out the steps to prevent oscillation in areas with high variations.

Metaphorically, a process with momentum can be understood as a ball rolling around a landscape. The speed of the ball will build up on the way down toward the valley, and its physical momentum will carry it quite far up the other side. If this peak is relatively low (local minimum), the momentum will push the ball straight over into a larger valley (global minimum). This can lead to better solutions being discovered.

Simulated Annealing

Simulated annealing is another simple and relatively efficient solution to the optimization problem. Unlike the previous methods, this is not gradient based, although in practice, information about the slope can be used to assist the process.

Simulated annealing is modeled on the physical process that happens to the atomic structure of a metal while it cools down, as it settles into a configuration that minimizes energy. This process is known as *annealing*, and can be simulated to solve optimization problems—hence the name *simulated annealing*.

Conceptually, the method is based on chaos. No matter how much we know about the function already, the estimate of the next iteration is always a guess (the global minima is unknown). So why not voluntarily introduce a bit of randomness into the process to get around the problems of selecting the step's value? In simulated annealing, this is done by a *generation mechanism*, which stochastically picks a new estimate in the neighborhood of the current estimate. The generation mechanism depends on the type of variables being optimized; generating neighboring estimates requires knowledge of the representation. For real numbers, this can be done with random offsetting (that is, addition of a small value).

Just like for the metals cooling, simulated annealing is based on the concept of temperature. If the new estimate is better, it is always used rather than the current one. On the other hand, when the new estimate is worse, we decide whether to accept it based on the temperature. Temperature is a value denoted T that controls the probability p of accepting a positive change Δf in the function f when a new estimate is made:

$$p = \exp(-\frac{\Delta f}{kT})$$

This equation is known as a *Boltzmann distribution*. k is a constant used to scale the temperature. The procedure for decreasing the temperature is known as a *cooling schedule.* In practice, temperature starts very high and decreases in stages. The theory behind simulated annealing is that the optimization will settle into a global minimum as the temperature decreases (see Figure 17.10).

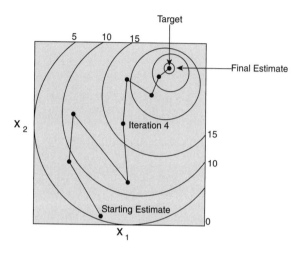

Figure 17.10   Optimization in a 2D plane using simulated annealing. Large steps are taken at first, and then smaller ones as the temperature cools.

This method has variable benefits; in some cases, it can work nicely to optimize functions, but in others, it can be extremely slow because of its stochastic nature. One of the major criticisms is that simulated annealing is just greedy hill-climbing when the probability $p = 0$. (That is, better neighbors are always selected.) This reveals the importance of the cooling schedule, and explains why simulated annealing can be such a dark art.

Optimization of Perceptron Weights

How it is possible to apply these techniques to teach a perceptron, and specifically train the weights to produce the right results? This is done on a case-per-case basis. Given specific inputs ${}^{\mu}x_{(k)}$, the corresponding desired output $y_{(k)} = t$ is needed; this is the target for the optimization.

In computer games, the desired output can be obtained in many ways. It can be designed by an expert (training), copied from human behavior (imitation), computed by another AI component (automated learning), or based on a previous result (bootstrapping). This process is discussed further in Chapter 35, "Designing Learning AI."

Optimization of perceptrons is also a best-guess process. In this case, the estimate is a set of weights. The output of the perceptron can be evaluated with these weights. Comparing the actual output to the desired output gives us an error. Then, given the current network, we compute a new estimate of the weights that generate fewer errors. Correcting the weights is done by the delta rule.

The Delta Rule Explained

The delta rule is used the most often to adjust the weights. The key observations are as follows:

➤ Each weight contributes a variable amount to the output.

➤ The scale of the contribution depends on the input.

➤ The error in the output can be "blamed" on the weights.

Reducing the error requires adjusting the output toward its ideal value. To do this, we use multiple small adjustments in the weights instead (because only they can change). The adjustments can be distributed proportionally to the contribution of the weights; the bigger the contribution to an error, the bigger the adjustment!

With the intuitive explanation covered, let's move into a more practical mode. First, relative error E is computed using the difference between the actual output y and the desired output t. This is known as an *error function*, which usually takes the form of $E = \frac{1}{2}(t-y)^2$. This is known as a *least mean square error* (LMS). Using the square of the difference $t-y$ implies that the error has the same magnitude whether the output is too high or too low. Ideally, this error should be zero and the purpose of the training algorithm is to get it as low as possible.

Technical Fact

The LMS error has a few other useful properties, including the fact it can be easily derived (that is, finding its rate of growth). This is extremely useful, because we can find the gradient of the error function. Indeed, this implies that optimization techniques based on gradient methods will be applicable.

It's now possible to compute the gradient of the error in each of the weights. This is denoted $\partial E/\partial w_i$, which can be read "gradient of the error E relative to weight w_i." The ∂ symbol is not Greek, but is used to denote a partial derivative (that is, a derivative of a variable in terms of another). In this case, the partial derivative simplifies the signed error $t{-}y$ scaled by the input x_i, but negated (see Figure 17.11):

$$\frac{\partial E}{\partial w_i} = -x_i(t{-}y)$$

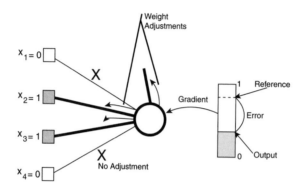

Figure 17.11 Correcting the weights of the perceptron based on the output error, proportionally to the input values.

Then, to adjust the weights, we can use any gradient method: steepest descent, for example. The step Δw_i, which is used to adjust each weight, is the difference between the desired output and the actual output $(t{-}y)$ multiplied by the input x_i:

$$\Delta w_i = -\eta\frac{\partial E}{\partial w_i} = \eta x_i(t{-}y)$$

Again, eta η is a small constant known as the learning rate.

Formal Proof

This part of the chapter provides proof of how to compute the gradient $\partial E/\partial w_i$ for each weight. Those with little interest in the proof should skip a page to the last paragraph in this subsection. However, understanding this outline really opens the doors to more advanced optimization techniques (in academic papers), but isn't really necessary to implement the code! The proof relies on differential calculus.

Noting that the error only depends on the net sum ζ, the chain rule can be applied:

$$\frac{\partial E}{\partial w_i} = \frac{\partial E}{\partial \zeta}\frac{\partial \zeta}{\partial w_i}$$

This expresses the gradient of the error in each weight as the gradient of the error relative to the net sum $\partial E/\partial \zeta$, multiplied by the gradient of the net sum relative to the weight $\partial \zeta/\partial w_i$. Noting that $\zeta = \sum_i w_i x_i$, the second right-side term can be simplified greatly. (Weights are independent from each other.)

$$\frac{\partial \zeta}{\partial w_i} = \frac{\partial \sum_i w_i x_i}{\partial w_i} = x_i$$

Now for the first right-side term. The net sum is the output y before the activation function σ, so the gradient can be re-expressed (using the derivative of the error function):

$$\frac{\partial E}{\partial \zeta} = \frac{\partial E}{\partial y}\frac{\partial y}{\partial \zeta} = -(t-y)\sigma'(\zeta)$$

Because most perceptrons since the *Adaline* use an identity activation function as $\sigma(\zeta) = \zeta$, $\sigma'(\zeta) = 1$ holds. This implies the following:

$$\frac{\partial E}{\partial w_i} = -x_i(t-y)$$

There we have it. The gradient of the error for each weight is just the negated input multiplied by the relative error $-x_i(t-y)$. This can be used to adjust the weights by one of the many gradient methods previously presented (usually stepping opposite to the gradient).

This result is surprisingly intuitive. When we want to adjust the output for a given input, all we have to play with is the weights. Each weight could be adjusted to contribute toward the target using $(t-y)$. However, the contribution of the weight depends on the value of the input, so this step $(t-y)$ can be scaled by x_i to influence only the relevant weights. Scaling that by the learning rate between $[0,1]$ will allow for better learning.

Training Procedure

Training procedure uses weight optimization to produce the desired neural network. Effectively, the aim of the training procedure is to satisfy an *objective function*. The objective function determines the quality of a network, based on a high-level metric: Measure the performance for numerous examples, or just compare the total weight adjustments to a threshold. The objective function mainly determines when the training process is complete.

Data Sets

The training of a perceptron requires example data, namely an existing collection of input data with the desired output. Each of these input/output pairs is known as a sample, a single training case. Together, these samples form the data set.

Typically, not all the data set is used for training; it is split into two or three different subsets. Only one of these is used for *training*. The other two can be potentially used for *validation* (checking the results of the training to improve it), and *testing* (the final performance analysis of the network). Because of the simplicity of single-layer perceptrons, this is not always necessary, but this method comes in handy for more complex problems.

Further Information

The management of data sets is generally an extremely common problem in pattern recognition. Perceptrons also can be used for classification and feature recognition, but do not require any measures to split the data set (because it always converges). Chapter 26, "Classification and Regression Trees," covers the handling of data sets in more detail.

Training Algorithms

Training a perceptron usually adjusts the weights together using the optimization techniques presented. The key difference between training algorithms is how to process the samples, and there are two different approaches:

➤ Each case can be treated individually, in an **incremental** fashion. The weights of the network are updated every time a sample is processed.

➤ All the samples can be treated as a **batch**. The weights are updated only after the entire set has been processed. This is known as an *epoch*. (It's a reference to measure the performance-learning algorithms.)

Regardless of the approach used, the aim of the training process is to adjust the weights into a near optimal configuration, which will allow the network to perform well when evaluated.

Perceptron Training

The perceptron training algorithm is an incremental approach, but makes use of gradient information for better convergence (see Listing 17.2). This is done using the steepest descent technique, which computes the necessary adjustment Δw_i for each weight w_i:

$$\Delta w_i = -\eta \frac{\partial E}{\partial w_i} = \eta(t-y)x_i$$

$$w_i \leftarrow w_i + \Delta w_i$$

This equation expresses the necessary change to a weight in terms of the learning rate η, the output difference between the actual output y and the desired target t, and the current value of the input x_i. The learning rate η is a small constant, usually chosen by the AI engineer, as discussed for the gradient methods. Formally, this is gradient descent on the error surface.

Listing 17.2   The Perceptron Training Algorithm

```
initialize weights randomly
while the objective function is unsatisfied
      for each sample
            simulate the perceptron
            if result is invalid
                  for all inputs i
                        delta = desired-output
                        weights[i] += learning_rate * delta *
                        inputs[i]
                  end for
            end if
      end for
end while
```

Testing of the result's validity is usually based on Boolean logic. The inputs and outputs are also usually set to 0 or 1. The interesting point to notice is that only the misclassified patterns are used to update the weights of the network.

Delta Rule

The *delta rule* is the equation expressing the gradient of the error in each weight, but it has also given its name to a training algorithm (see Listing 17.3). (It is also the basis of preceding solution.) A batch approach processes all the training samples before updating the weights.

Listing 17.3   The Delta Rule Applied as a Batch Learning Algorithm

```
while termination condition is not verified
      reset steps array to 0
      for each training sample
            compute the output of the perceptron
            for each weight i
                  delta = desired—output
                  steps[i] += delta * inputs[i]
            end for
      end for
      for each weight i
            weights[i] += learning_rate * steps[i]
      end for
end while
```

Mathematically, this corresponds to gradient descent on the quadratic error surface. In practice, it means the error is minimized globally for the entire data set, and provably so! The best result is always reached, so no validation is needed.

Synopsis

Perceptrons are an incredibly simple model providing a solution to linear problems. As such, there are very straightforward and efficient ways to teach it. The main decision is between the perceptron training algorithm and a batched delta rule.

Both methods are proven to find solutions if they exist, given a small enough learning rate η. The perceptron training will just make sure that all the outputs are correct in binary terms. On the other hand, the delta rule will minimize the error over all the training samples in continuous space. This guarantees that there is one single global minimum, and that the learning will converge (given a suitable η). This has many advantages, including the ability to deal with noise and provide a good approximation for nonlinear functions.

As such, the delta rule used in batch mode should be chosen whenever possible. The main requirement for this is to have all the data sets available for training (for instance, a log of wins and losses from the game). If this is not the case, and the perceptron needs to be learned using a stream of incoming data samples, the only option is an incremental one (for instance, learning tactics from experience during the game). Once again, just a simple application of the delta rules suffices; discarding samples classified correctly as in perceptron training can be useful in this case to prevent favoring recently learned samples.

Graphical Interpretation

A concrete example will give us a better understanding of what's going on internally. A linear function in 2D is just a line. In fact, the equation of the perceptron has the same format as a line ($a+bx_1+cx_2$). When the weights are multiplied with the input, this is reminiscent of a dot product. In 2D, the dot product enables us to determine the "signed distance" to the line; taking the sign of the result determines the side of the line, and the absolute value represents the distance (see Figure 17.12).

What does it mean for function prediction? The output of perceptrons is the signed distance from the input to the line. If a binary output is used, the perceptron indicates on which side of the line the input sample lies.

The training process is all about finding the right position for the line in space. To achieve this, the delta rule adjusts the weight coefficients of the lines (that is, orientation). The bias is necessary to change the position relative to the origin. If all the data can be plotted in two dimensions, it is possible to visually find a solution; this is the line that minimizes the errors in classification.

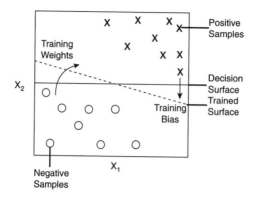

Figure 17.12   Visualization of the perceptron's decision surface on a 2D example.

In 2D, understanding the perceptron as a line is quite straightforward. In 3D, this corresponds to a plane, separating the patterns in a volume. For *n* dimensions, this theory generalizes to a "hyperplane." It can be difficult to imagine any more than three dimensions, but the process is just as simple.

Summary

In practice, perceptrons prove amazingly simple to implement and train:

➤ Perceptrons consist in an array of floating point numbers representing the weights of the inputs.

➤ To compute the output, the inputs are scaled by the weights and the sum is passed through an activation function.

➤ Learning is achieved by adjusting the weights, choosing a step that minimizes the error.

➤ The model has some serious limitations, notably only being able to handle linear problems. However, this can be more than suitable in many cases where the approximation is satisfactory.

➤ The delta rule in batch mode is proven to converge to the global minimum, and the incremental perceptron training finds a correct solution if it exists.

➤ The ideal learning rate depends on the problem, but a small value is a safe guess (for instance, 0.1).

➤ Given the possibility of using perceptrons rather than more complex neural networks—even if this involves simplifying the model—we should consider doing so. Perceptrons are incredibly good at what they do best: linear approximations.

The next chapter applies perceptrons to improve aiming abilities. The neural networks allow smoother movement, and prevent over- and under-aiming errors. Expanding on the theory in this chapter, Chapter 19 covers perceptrons with multiple layers, which potentially have better capabilities—at the cost of complexity.

Practical Demo

Major Pain is an animat that uses a very simple perceptron to learn when to fire. It's okay to fire when there's an enemy and the weapon is ready. The perceptron learns a simple AND operation on two inputs (which is a linear problem). The demo and overview of the AI architecture are available at `http://AiGameDev.com/`. The source is available and commented, although the next chapter explains the design of the perceptron module in greater depth.

Chapter 18

Dealing with Aiming Errors

KEY TOPICS

- Momentum and Friction
- Dealing with Errors

The preceding chapter covered a specific kind of neural network known as perceptrons. These are capable of solving simple problems using linear approximations. To help demonstrate the theory, the next few pages apply perceptrons to improve shooting capabilities. Many problems could be adapted for this purpose, but this chapter focuses on creating realistic yet efficient aiming, which involves problems that are linearly approximable by design.

The sections in this chapter cover one problem each, dealing with realism and then effectiveness:

➤ One perceptron improves the aiming realism by smoothing the actions. The friction and momentum (in the mouse) is modeled. A perceptron provides a fast linear approximation of these aiming errors for the animat.

➤ To deal with these imprecisions, another perceptron solves the inverse problem by trial and error. The artificial intelligence (AI) collects information online and retrains the perceptron accordingly.

At the end of this chapter, the animats will make plausible aiming errors, but also correct the turning angles to take them into account. This provides an ideal compromise between realism and effectiveness at shooting (with adjustable skill settings).

Momentum and Friction

When human players aim with their mouse, momentum generally turns the view further than they expect for large angles. Conversely, the friction also slows down the turn for small angles. Therefore, when either small or large adjustments in the view are necessary, human players can lose accuracy. The trade-off is between finding the target quickly and overshooting or taking more time to reach the target with higher precision.

For the AI, it's often a matter of specifying the exact target and firing the weapon. Because bots with perfect accuracy aren't as fun to play against, physically plausible turning errors could be added to the animats (see Figure 18.1). This increases the difficulty of the task and puts the animats on par with human players.

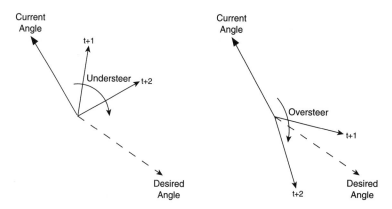

Figure 18.1   Two examples of errors that commonly affect the aiming process.

Explicit Model

A mathematical function is used to model these kinds of errors, expressing the actual angle in terms of the desired angle and the previous angle. This feedback loop represents momentum carried over from frame to frame, and scaling the desired angle adjustment represents the friction.

The function itself is defined over the desired angle and the previous output. We also include a parametric error in terms of the desired angle; the noise() function returns a value between −1 and 1:

Equation 18.1

$\beta = 1.0 + 0.1 * noise(angle)$

$output(t) = (angle * \beta) * \alpha + output(t-1) * (1-\alpha)$

➤ α (alpha in Greek) is a scaling parameter used to blend the previous output with the angle request. This factor can take into account different properties that affect the accuracy: movement, angular velocity, fatigue, and so on. The designer can set the parameter to be within the range [0.3,0.5].

➤ β (beta) is effectively initialized randomly within [0.9,1.1]. It can be seen as a parametric error factor for the angle request. It's multiplied to the angle because we don't want small errors when no movement is requested. (That is, the error is proportional to the angle.)

➤ The `noise()` function is defined arbitrarily as long as it returns a value within [–1,1]. For example, the function $cos(angle^2 * 0.217 + 342 / angle)$ oscillates almost unpredictably within that range.

This makes the aiming more realistic, because the AI will also be subject to under- and overshooting and aiming errors.

Linear Approximation

A *perceptron* is used to approximate the function illustrated in Equation 18.1. This can be understood as the animat learning to turn in a smoother fashion. Alternatively, it can be seen as a way of learning a faster approximation of an expensive function in the interface's implementation (inaccessible from the animat). In fact, after the function is learned, it could be moved to the interface—hidden from the AI code. The aiming errors would then become a constraint.

The equation is well-suited to being approximated linearly. In fact, it becomes a moving average; the previous angle requests and the current request are weighted together. The major task of the learning will be to understand the α parameter, approximate β, and adjust the weights accordingly (see Figure 18.2).

To be able to approximate the equation, we need the previous output to be explicit. We'll have to plug it into the input ourselves so it seems like a direct mapping for the perceptron (reactive).

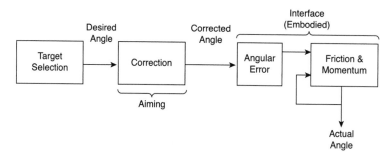

Figure 18.2 Flow chart representation of the processing of the angles before they are passed to the engine.

Methodology

We'll compute the approximation by training the network iteratively. Random inputs are chosen, and then the desired output is computed with Equation 18.1. By grouping these results all together, a batch training algorithm can be applied to find the desired values for each of the weights and biases. This can be done during the initialization or, better still, offline.

The perceptron itself will be modular: A large perceptron does not compute all the angles together (that is, yaw and pitch); instead, a smaller perceptron is applied twice (for both angles). This reduces the memory used to store the perceptron, but requires slightly more programming.

Evaluation

This is not an especially difficult problem. Even if it is not linear by nature, the linear approximation is close. The behaviors generated by the perceptron are more realistic, because the turning is much smoother (visibly subject to friction and momentum).

When the perceptron learns a function with a lot momentum, there's a certain feeling of motion sickness. That said, beginners often have this problem, too, and the problem can be just as unstable.

As for the training, this is done very quickly. Few samples (for instance, 10) are required for the weights to be adjusted suitably. The iterations required vary greatly depending on the initial random weights.

Practical Demo

The example animat demonstrating this problem is known as *Missy*, which can be found online at `http://AiGameDev.com/` in source and binary formats among the other demos. See the attached guide to get the animat running in the game. A perceptron is used to approximate the aiming error function, learned using a batch algorithm during the initialization.

Dealing with Errors

The model of momentum and friction is an error that accumulates over sequences of turns. Additional errors for single angles can be included, too. The idea is to complicate this nonlinear problem to reveal how well a perceptron approximates the solution.

These errors can be seen as a constraint to get the animat to perform realistically. The AI should take these errors into account so that the animats can still be effective at aiming—but realistic at the same time.

Ignoring the variations in aiming would be error prone, causing the AI to under- and overshoot. Such errors are acceptable when the animats are playing against beginners. However, we want a top-quality AI that can deal with aiming errors so that expert human players feel challenged, too.

Inverse Problem

To compensate for errors, we could model the inverse of the error function (see Figure 18.3), so that the perfect corrected aiming angle is suggested. However, mathematical understanding of the problem is required and the inverse of a function does not always exist (like the one equation in Chapter 16, "Physics for Prediction").

Ideally, the AI needs a simple math-free way of approximating a function that will serve as the inverse of the aiming error. This approach would allow the animats to learn to perform better as they practice—without a model of the error.

In the simulation, the AI can compare the desired angle (action) with the actual angle (observation). Given enough trial and error, it's possible to predict which corrected angles are required to obtain the desired angles. This approach gathers input/output pairs from the simulation, and learns the inverse relationship by flipping the pairs.

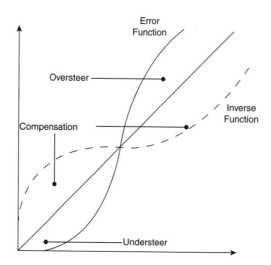

Figure 18.3 An error function over an angle, and the inverse function that satisfies f(g(x)) = x.

Further Information

The AI manages to deal with aiming errors by learning the inverse error function. However, this problem is particularly suited to reinforcement learning. In these types of problems, each action gets *evaluative feedback* based on how close the result is to the desired output. By using the feedback, the AI can adapt itself incrementally to perform the task better. This technique is covered in Chapter 46, "Learning Reactive Strategies," and aiming could be re-attempted later as an exercise.

Implementation

The AI uses sensors to regularly check the actual angles by which the body has turned since the last update. This allows the AI to compare what actually happened with what was requested in the previous update. However, the result must be flipped around; the AI needs to know what angle to specify based on the desired turn. Because the system now knows which angle to request to get the result that was observed, this preprocess provides a training sample for the perceptron. The neural network can be trained incrementally to learn these patterns.

The information gathered does not help solve the same problem next time around. Consider, for instance, that we are trying to get the desired angle d_1. If we try angle a_1 as an action and observe an angle of d_2, we still don't know how to get d_1! All we know is how to get d_2. Given enough samples, we'll eventually discover the angle that produces d_1.

For this problem, an online learning approach is used. The obvious benefit is for the animats to learn to improve their aiming during the game. This sounds more impressive than it is, but it's still fun to watch the animats improve their skills.

One important thing to remember is that the perceptrons may have to deal with input and output values that are not within the unit vector. This is the case for angles in degrees, for example. For this reason, we'll use rescaling on both the input and output. On the output, it's absolutely necessary to rescale for the perceptron to learn—or the output unit couldn't produce all the possible results. Scaling is also applied to the input because it learns faster empirically. In theory, this is not necessary, but we can use suitable default parameters (for instance, a learning rate of 0.1) and get good results.

Evaluation

Because turns are required for movement too, the animat has the opportunity to learn to correct the aiming while moving around. Perceptrons can thereby learn to aim much faster as more training samples are presented. When it comes to aiming for targets, the neural network should already be familiar with the basic concepts.

The animats are three-dimensional entities, but can control their view along two angles: the pitch and the yaw. The perceptron controls and corrects the angles for both of these dimensions. However, controlling the pitch raises many problems during the learning. Only when the pitch is near horizontal is movement possible; when looking fully up or down, there is no forward movement (as defined by the player physics). In these cases, the yaw is constrained as well, which prevents the AI from learning altogether. To prevent such learning traps, we only allow the perceptron to control the yaw until satisfactory results are obtained. When these precautions are taken, the worse that can happen is the animat spinning around while learning. To the untrained eye, this often seems like the animats are ballroom dancing!

On a more technical note, giving the perceptron full control can lead to other learning traps. The way the yaw is chosen determines all the examples that are available for learning (that is, requested angles and observed angles). So, by allowing the perceptron to determine the yaw fully, it also has the full capability to affect what it learns. In these cases, it can converge into a configuration that always suggests the same turn. To solve this, the AI needs to force the situation by generating a variety of angle suggestions (for instance, by generating random angles or adding noise to the actions). This implies the perceptron always gets a representative sample of the input/output patterns, and forces it to learn balanced knowledge.

> **Practical Demo**
>
> On the web site, among the other examples, there's an animat called *Aimy*, which demonstrates these issues. A perceptron is used to learn the corrected angles to prevent under- and overshooting. *Aimy* gathers the data by its sensors to determine how far its body turned based on each angle request. Incremental training can then approximate the inverse of this function to prevent aiming errors. See `http://AiGameDev.com/` for more information.

Summary

This chapter used two perceptrons to increase the realism of the aiming in animats, but also to allow them to deal with these errors effectively—as human players do:

➤ To improve the realism of the aiming, a perceptron learns to turn smoothly by approximating a more extensive model of aiming errors. This is learned offline using a batch training algorithm.

➤ To increase the effectiveness of the aiming, but still behaving realistically, another perceptron approximates a solution that compensates for the aiming errors. This is learned online by gathering training examples.

Because of the simple nature of the problems (easily approximable and tolerating suboptimality), the limitations of the perceptrons are not exposed. In many cases, it's preferable to spend additional time in AI design to be able to apply single-layer perceptrons. In some cases, however, this is not possible; the additional power of multilayer perceptrons is necessary—accompanied by the extra complexity. The next chapter covers the theory behind multilayer perceptrons, paving the way for a problem in Chapter 20, "Selecting the Target," that requires better capabilities to recognize patterns.

Chapter 19

Multilayer Perceptrons

Multilayer perceptrons (MLPs) are another kind of artificial neural network, with layers of weighted connections between the inputs and outputs. The structure of MLP essentially resembles a set of cascaded perceptrons. Each processing unit has a relatively complex output function, which increases the capabilities of the network.

This chapter builds upon the information in Chapter 17, "Perceptrons," which covered single-layer perceptrons. This chapter covers the following topics:

➤ The history behind perceptrons, notably why multiple-layered models are necessary

➤ The representation of MLP, introducing the concept of topology and nonlinear activation

➤ The simulation of multiple layers of processing units, and how it differs from the single-layer variant

➤ The parallels between perceptrons with their biological counterparts: neural networks

➤ Methods for training MLP based on the concept of back-propagation of error

➤ Practical issues behind the training process, and the problems that occur with multiple layers

➤ The major advantages and disadvantages of perceptrons for game development

Perceptrons with multiple layers can recognize patterns in the gameplay, predict the outcome of a fight, and control the nonplayer character (NPC) movement. These tasks can be learned from a set of examples, and with potentially better performance than single-layer perceptrons.

History of Perceptrons

Perceptrons with a single layer of weights can only cope with linear problems. Complex problems are approximated in a rough fashion. These are known as nonlinear problems and can be too difficult for perceptrons to deal with altogether; even the linear approximation is little use sometimes.

The problems with perceptrons were partly acknowledged by the original authors, but Minsky and Papert shed light on the limitations of the technique in their 1969 book *Perceptrons* [Minsky69]. They showed that perceptrons have trouble dealing with higher-order problems. Specifically, they cannot cope with orders above 1 (linear problems).

Perceptrons showed that to handle problems of higher order, at least one partial predicate must be supported by the whole space. Intuitively, this means that at least one intermediate unit must be connected to all the inputs. Perceptrons violate this "limited order" constraint, which explains their inability to cope with nonlinear patterns.

Minsky and Papert subsequently argued that even multiple layers of weights connected together (or cascaded linear networks for that matter) could not cope with high-order patterns, although they could not prove it. Indeed, as long as the activation function is linear, nonlinear problems are still not possible.

Rosenblatt touched upon this in his initial perceptron with Boolean activation functions (they are nonlinear), but could not find a way to train the whole system. This dried up funding in the area, and many researchers moved to symbolic AI as an alternative.

Model Overview

Multilayer perceptrons are based on their older sibling with one single layer. There are two major differences between these models:

> ➤ The first difference is straightforward: There are extra middle layers. They increase the power of approximation of the perceptron.

> ➤ The second difference is not quite so obvious, but is necessary for the middle layer to have any benefit on the system. This involves using more sophisticated activation functions.

The next section looks at each of these differences separately.

Topology

The topology is the layout of the processing units inside a neural network, and how they are connected together. The topology of an MLP is said to be *feed forward* (as in Figure 19.1); there are no backward connections—also called *recurrent* connections. The information flows directly from the inputs to the outputs. The important structural improvement of MLP is the middle layer.

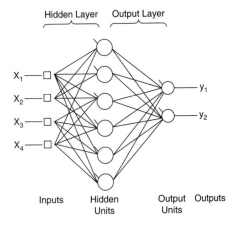

Figure 19.1 Topology of an MLP, including inputs, middle layer, and output.

Middle Layers

There can be an arbitrary number of middle layers, although one is most common. These middle layers are sometimes referred to as *hidden*—because of the fact that these are not directly connected to the output. From the user's perspective, they could not be there! Another historical reason for calling them "hidden" is that they could not be directly trained according to the error. So once initialized (usually randomly), they were no longer touched.

Because including more hidden layers increases the computational complexity of the network, why not have more? There are many factors to take into account (for instance, memory), but essentially one middle layer is almost always enough. One hidden layer enables us to get a universal approximator, capable in theory of modeling any continuous function (given a suitable activation function). So for most kinds of nonlinear problems (as in games), one hidden layer is enough.

In some cases, however, there is much interdependency between the input variables, and the complexity of the problem is high. Here, an extra layer can help reduce the total number of weights needed for a suitable approximation. In practice, rarely more than two hidden layers are used in any topology. Perceptrons with two middle layers can approximate any function—even noncontinuous ones.

Hidden Units

Choosing the number of units in the hidden layer is also a decision linked with the topology. Unlike for the *output* layer, the number of hidden units is not bound to any explicit characteristic of the problem; it's the AI engineer's responsibility to decide about this magical number. This can have a great effect on the performance of the network generally, so it's quite an important decision. What's more, there is no analytical way (that is, a miracle formula) for determining the number of hidden units required, so no wonder this seems like a black art!

Multilayer perceptrons require hidden units to represent their knowledge of the problem internally. These hidden units provide coverage of the input space, forming a decision surface. Each input pattern can be evaluated compared to this decision surface. For complex problems—with complex decision surfaces—the number of hidden units required can grow faster than exponentially! Certain properties of functions are just not *suited* to perceptrons (for instance, discontinuous functions, sharp and jagged variations), requiring too much memory and computation.

Technical Fact

For perceptrons with two inputs, the decision surface is a 2D line. For MLPs, the decision surface is more precise than a straight line, and can be understood as a curve separating the input patterns; the output value is positive on one side of the curve and negative on the other. For larger problems, this curve lies in n dimensions, where n is the number of input variables.

As the number of dimensions grows (more inputs), the complexity of the desired decision surface increases, too. Again, this can require the number of hidden neurons to grow exponentially, a predicament known as the *curse of dimensionality*. It's one interpretation of why neural networks do not scale well, and why they have trouble coping with huge problems. It's a good idea to keep problems small for this reason. For example, aiming and target selection are handled separately in this part, but modeling them all together with prediction requires many neurons and layers.

Much of the topology depends on the complexity of the decision surface. Therefore, we should expect to be confronted with these issues on a case-per-case basis. We'll take a practical approach to this problem in the next chapter.

Connections

A final property of the topology resides in the connections between the units. In many cases, the units are all connected from one layer to another. However, this can be customized and individual connections can be removed arbitrarily. This is the difference between a *fully connected* network and a *sparse* one.

Together with this, connections can be established that skip layers. For example, one connection could be established straight from the input to the output, ignoring the middle layer.

These "exotic" configurations are extremely rare compared to fully connected MLPs. Although it is possible to create a simulator that can deal with arbitrary topologies, there is a large overhead in doing so. Indeed, the connections will have to be stored explicitly as pointers. The connections are implicit with fully connected perceptrons and only arrays of weights need storing. However, arbitrary topologies can have their uses given insider knowledge about the problem (that is, the engineer knows exactly what the topology should be, which rarely happens).

Activation Functions

The activation function computes the output based on the net sum of each unit. Different types of functions are applicable. However, *linear* activation functions in the middle layers are no use at all! The MLP would have the same power as a plain perceptron, because combining two linear functions gives another linear one. For the hidden layers to have any effect on the computational capabilities of the MLP, a nonlinear activation function is necessary.

Properties

We need to watch out for a few things when selecting an activation function. It needs to have the following properties:

➤ **Derivable**—The activation function needs to have a known derivative easily computable. This allows gradient descent on the error.

➤ **Continuity**—A continuous function (that is, with no breaks in the curve) would make the derivative easier to find and defined for all points.

➤ **Complexity**—The function must be nonlinear for higher-order problems to be feasible for an MLP.

➤ **Monotonous**—A monotonously increasing function ensures that the derivative is not zero or negative, and makes gradient descent useful (and going in the right direction).

We also may desire optional properties of the activation function for a particular implementation:

➤ **Boundedness**—This guarantees that both the activation output and its derivative are finite. This can make interpreting the result of the MLP more convenient.

➤ **Polarity**—The polarity corresponds to the function's sign. Some are only positive, whereas others are symmetrical—becoming negative at certain intervals (bipolar).

These last two options are linked to practical issues during the development. We'll look at them in more detail in the discussion, and during the application.

Possible Activation Functions

In general, activation functions are selected from a commonly used set, as shown in Figure 19.2. Some of the choices we discussed for the standard perceptron are also used in MLP. These include step functions (allowing binary output) and linear activation functions (identity transformation). A combination of the two is known as *threshold logic*, where the linear output is clamped to a certain range.

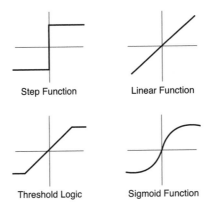

Step Function   Linear Function

Threshold Logic   Sigmoid Function

Figure 19.2   Graph of functions that are used as activation functions in the output layer.

These functions make suitable choices for the output layer, but not for the hidden layer (because not all the required properties are satisfied). Instead, so-called *sigmoid* functions are a popular choice. One of these is known as a *logistic* function.

$$sig(x) = \frac{1}{1+e^{-\beta x}}$$

$$sig'(x) = x\beta(1-x)$$

β (Greek beta) is a value that controls the smoothness of the curve. For large values, the sigmoid can become close to a step function. This is useful because it has all the right properties as well! Another choice is the *tanh* function, but it is slightly more expensive computationally. This has the property of being negative and positive:

$$\tanh(x) = \frac{e^{\beta x}+e^{-\beta x}}{e^{-\beta x}-e^{\beta x}}$$

$$\tanh'(x) = \frac{2}{(e^x+e^{-x})}$$

Instead of this, a *bipolar sigmoid* can be a more efficient alternative, giving the same features:

$$\text{sig}_b(x) = \frac{2}{1+e^{-\beta x}} - 1$$

$$\text{sig}'_b(x) = \frac{\beta}{2}(1+x)(1-x)$$

The choice of a bipolar or positive sigmoid is often dependent on the problem (negative output values), but the bipolar option should be preferred because it seems to provide better precision for training with floating-point values.

Simulation

As mentioned, the main differences with MLPs are the extra hidden units. The intermediate layer implies that the information required to compute the output is not immediately available. Instead, the first layer must be processed before the second one. Its output then serves as the input for the next, and so forth until the final result is determined. This is a simple iterative process that goes through the entire network.

This process emphasizes the feed-forward structure of perceptrons, and especially MLP. Hidden layers do not affect this property. Listing 19.1 shows some pseudo-code to compute the output for an arbitrary number of layers.

Listing 19.1   Feed-Forward Simulation Algorithm Used to Filter the Inputs Through the MLP

```
# the first layer processes the input array
current = input
for layer from first to last
# compute the output of each neuron
for each i in [1..neurons] from layer
        # multiply arrays together and add up the result
```

```
      s = NetSum( neuron[i].weights, current )
      # store the post-processed result
      output[i] = Activate( s )
   end for
   # the next layer uses this layer's output as input
current = output
end for
```

In practice, this procedure can be used in the same fashion as plain perceptrons; we provide input patterns and collect the corresponding result. The output can be applied to approximate functions, classify patterns, or even control actuators (that is, artificial muscles). The next chapter demonstrates perceptrons in a game situation using function approximation.

Biological Parallels

With the definition from artificial intelligence covered, it may finally be time to explain the biological analogy. This is not important—one might even say unnecessary—to understand neural networks, but it explains the terminology used and puts current research into perspective.

Original inspiration was drawn from the visual cortex, forming the frontal part of the brain. Rosenblatt's perceptron in fact modeled the connections right from the retina to the brain. The simulation was oversimplified from the neurobiological knowledge at the time, and since then, it has proven even more inaccurate.

MLPs have been significantly enhanced over the years by mathematically convenient techniques (for instance, sigmoid activation functions). Although some claim that such aspects are "biologically plausible," these are clearly hacks to get perceptrons to work at all. Today, all that's left of biology in MLP is a metaphor, a crude approximation, but more prominently, the trace of shattered dreams and illusions.

Perceptrons and MLPs no longer form the bulk of neural network research for this reason. They are classed as *old connectionism*; and despite the success and popularity of their applications, they do not generate the same hope and enthusiasm that they once did.

Neurons

The main parallel with biology takes place at a cellular level. The processing units of perceptrons and MLPs can be compared to individual neurons, from which the inspiration for the model was drawn (see Figure 19.3).

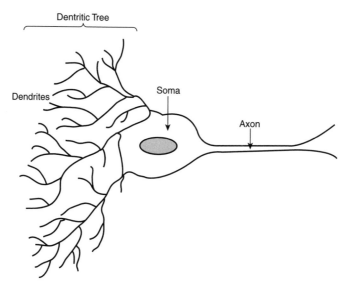

Figure 19.3 A single biological neuron with a soma, a dendritic tree, and an axon.

A *neuron* is a single cell in the brain. It consists of a main body (soma). The main function of the soma is that it fires a signal when it has been stimulated enough. Many dendrites lead into the body forming a tree-like structure. The role of the dendrites is to collect surrounding information: stimuli of preceding neurons. The dendrites transmit two kinds of signals: *inhibitory* ones (which prevent the body from being stimulated), and *excitatory* ones (which contribute to stimulating the body). Finally, there is usually one axon, which projects out of the main body.

When the body *fires*, it releases an electromagnetic impulse down the axon. There are indications that many other things happen when a neuron fires (for instance, release of gases), but some of these still remain to be investigated—and even revealed.

Conceptually, there are some parallels to be made with processing units. The inputs can be compared to the dendrites, the soma represents the actual processing unit, and finally the axon is analogous to the output.

The perceptrons model is extremely simplified. Known properties of neurons are not modeled; there are regular spikes of activity released by the body, and neurons are also susceptible to be triggered by gases. Some of these ideas are modeled in other kinds of neural networks, but not perceptrons. There are undoubtedly many other unknown properties about neurons that perceptrons fail to capture as well.

Brains

The complexity in a biological brain arises from the combined power of individual neurons working in parallel. These are connected by *synapses*, linking the axon of previous neurons to dendrites of the next. The underlying functioning of a synapse is extremely complex, but conceptually, this mechanism essentially transmits the electromagnetic impulses between neurons. This is one way neurons communicate, as shown in Figure 19.4.

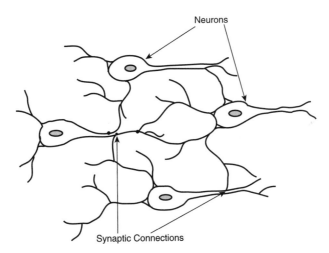

Figure 19.4   A set of interconnected neurons, similar to those found in biological brains.

This brain structure can be compared to an MLP—using a bit of imagination. The processing units are reminiscent of interconnected neurons. However, few of the abilities of biological brains can be seen in perceptrons. The reason for this once again is oversimplification. Scientific knowledge about the brain has improved, but this increased knowledge is not reflected in such old connectionist models.

The main limitations lie in the feed-forward restrictions. Arbitrary connections and sparse networks can be used, but the lack of efficient automated methods to establish these exotic topologies seriously reduce their appeal. Finally, the perceptrons have no spatial structure, and remain virtual weights stored in memory. Using an organization in 3D space would allow the propagation of gases to be simulated, for example.

Summary

The important aspect of MLPs does not lie in their biological inspiration. This is merely good for marketing purposes, because neural networks undeniably have a certain aura associated with them! The important property of MLP lies in their mathematical foundations, which have been thoroughly researched and proven over the years. Such understanding has been emphasized in this chapter; as AI engineers, we should make the effort to see beyond the biological metaphors.

Training Algorithms

The mathematical background in MLPs does provide one advantage: They can be trained. Just like for perceptrons with single layers, the task of training an MLP is fundamentally about numeric optimization. The ideal value of each weight must be found to minimize the output error. This is slightly more challenging because it's harder to determine the necessary adjustment to correct the weights (because the gradient of the error cannot be computed directly). This explains the additional complexity of the training algorithms.

Back Propagation

Backprop is the process of filtering the error from the output layer through the preceding layers. This was developed because of problems with the original perceptron training algorithms: They were unable to train the hidden layers. Back propagation is the essence of most MLP learning algorithms, because it allows the gradient to be determined in each weight (so they can be optimized).

Informal Explanation

For the last layer, the error of the output is immediately available, computed as the difference between the actual output and the desired output. Using the exact same principles as for the perceptron, the gradient of the error in each weight can be found. The gradient descent algorithms can use the slope of the error to adjust the weights in the last layer.

For hidden layers, the error is not immediately available because there is no reference to compare the output to! Instead, we notice that some hidden neurons are connected to output neurons whose error is known. The error in the output must partly originate from the hidden neurons. By propagating the error backward through the neural network, it's essentially possible to distribute the blame for the error on predecessor neurons.

This back-propagation process, shown in Figure 19.5, propagates the error *gradient*. The error gradient of a hidden unit is the weighted sum of the error gradients in the output units. The weights of the connections determine hidden error gradient from known processing units.

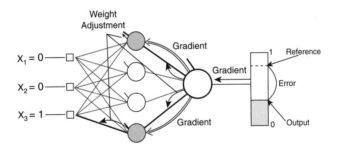

Figure 19.5   Backward propagation of the error throughout the layers, distributed from the output via the weighted connections.

This can be understood as a recursive definition of the error gradient. No matter how many layers are present, we can work backward from the outputs and compute all the error gradients in the processing units. Then, using the same technique as for perceptrons, we can compute the gradient in each of the individual weights. Steepest descent—or any other gradient based optimization—is then applied to the weights to adjust them accordingly.

Formal Proof

This section is only intended for those with an interest in the underlying details of training. We're trying to find the derivative of the error with respect to the weight connecting unit i to unit j, denoted $\partial E/\partial w_{ij}$. This can be split into three parts using the chain rule (as done implicitly for the proof on the perceptron):

$$\frac{\partial E}{\partial w_{ij}} = \frac{\partial E}{\partial y_j} \frac{\partial y_j}{\partial \zeta_j} \frac{\partial \zeta_j}{\partial w_{ij}}$$

We start with the third term on the right, the derivative of the net sum of unit j with respect to the weight $\partial \zeta_j/\partial w_{ij}$. This turns out to be the output y_i of the previous unit i (or the network input for the first layer):

$$\frac{\partial \zeta_j}{\partial w_{ij}} = y_i$$

The second term $\partial y/\partial \zeta_j$ expresses the gradient of unit j's output with respect to the net sum. This is defined by the activation function, so its derivative needs to be taken:

$$\frac{\partial y_j}{\partial \zeta_j} = \sigma'(\zeta_j)$$

Finally, the first right-side term is left $\partial E/\partial y_j$, representing the gradient of the error in terms of the unit's output. This is straightforward for those units in the output layer (as with standard perceptrons):

$$\frac{\partial E}{\partial y_j} = -(t_i - y_i)$$

For those units j that are not connected straight to the MLP's output, the term is computed recursively in terms of the units k that are along the connection toward the output. It's the sum (Σ) of the error gradient relative to the output of k $\partial E/\partial y_k$, multiplied by the gradient output relative to the net sum $\partial y_k/\partial \zeta_k$, and the weight between j and k w_{jk}.

$$\frac{\partial E}{\partial y_j} = \sum_k \frac{\partial E}{\partial y_k} \frac{\partial y_k}{\partial \zeta_k} w_{jk}$$

In general, it is useful to use an easier notation to implement the algorithm. If we define the following

$$\delta_j = -\frac{\partial E}{\partial y_j}\frac{\partial y_j}{\partial \zeta_j}$$

Then the gradient of the error relatively to the net sum δ_j can be computed depending on its position in the network:

$$\delta_j = \begin{cases} \sigma'(\zeta_j)(t_j - y_j) & \text{if j is an output unit} \\ \sigma'(\zeta_j)\sum_k \delta_k w_{jk} & \text{if j is a hidden unit} \end{cases}$$

This emphasizes the need for a backward-propagation process, where δ_j is computed for each unit of each layer depending on the previous unit's k.

Backprop Algorithm

There is a simple training algorithm based on the application of these equations; incremental training is applied to a set of examples. The method is known as *backprop*, but in fact the actual backward propagation is only one part of the process. Back propagation is the first stage of the algorithm, used to compute the gradients in each of the neurons (and then the weights later).

The outline in Listing 19.2 is at the core of all the gradient-based techniques, because it actually computes the gradient. Now the second stage of the *backprop* algorithm performs steepest descent to the weights (see Listing 19.3). (This is where learning happens.)

Listing 19.2   Backward-Propagation Algorithm Used to Compute the Gradient of the Error in Each of the Units

```
# compute the gradient in the units of the first layer
for each unit j in the last layer
delta[j] = deriv_activate(net_sum)
       * (desired[j] - output[j])
end for
# process the layers backwards and propagate the error gradient
for each layer from last-1 down to first
      for each unit j in layer
            total = 0
            # add up the weighted error gradient from next layer
            for each unit k in layer+1
```

```
                    total += delta[k] * weights[j][k]
            end for
        delta[j] = deriv_activate(net_sum) * total
        end for
end for
```

Listing 19.3   Steepest Descent on the Error Gradient in Each of the Weights

```
for each unit j
    for each input i
        # adjust the weights using the error gradient computed
        weight[j][i] += learning_rate * delta[j] * output[i]
    end for
end for
```

The rule used to compute the step for each weight Δw_{ij} is known as the *generalized delta rule*, an extension of the delta rule used to train standard perceptrons. The learning rate η is a small constant set by the engineer. δ_j is the gradient of the error of unit j relative to the net sum ζ_j. This is used to compute the necessary change in the weights to perform gradient descent.

Quick Propagation

Quickprop is a batch technique based on a combination of ideas. First, it exploits the advantages of locally adaptive techniques that adjust the magnitude of the steps based on local parameters (for instance, the nonglobal learning rate). Second, knowledge about the higher-order derivative is used (such as Newton's mathematical methods). In general, this allows a better prediction of the slope of the curve and where the minima lies. (This assumption is satisfactory in most cases.)

Quickprop Theory

The procedure to update the weights is very similar to the standard backprop algorithm. The gradient of the error in each weight is needed, denoted $\nabla E(t)$. This is the gradient for all the training samples because quickprop is a batch update algorithm:

$$\nabla E(t) = \frac{\partial E}{\partial w_{ij}} = -\delta_j y_i$$

This value is necessary for the current epoch t (a learning period) and the previous one t-1 denoted $\nabla E(t-1)$. The same applies for the weight update step $\nabla w_{ij}(t)$ and $\nabla w_{ij}(t-1)$. Then, the weight update can be determined as follows:

$$\nabla w_{ij}(t) = \frac{\nabla E(t)}{\nabla E(t-1)-\nabla E(t)}\nabla w_{ij}(t-1)$$

In practice, this proves much more efficient than the standard backprop on many problems. However, some of the assumptions about the nature of the slope can prove problematic in other cases. This really depends on each problem, and can be tested by comparing this algorithm's performance with the two others.

Implementing Quickprop

To implement this, two more arrays are needed for the step and the gradient, remembering values from the previous iteration. Because it's a batch algorithm, all the gradients for each training sample are added together. The backprop algorithm can achieve this by accumulating δ_j at each iteration. These values will get reset only when a new epoch starts (that is, when the iteration over all the samples restarts).

The second part of the backprop algorithm is replaced; we use the new weight update rule rather than steepest descent (see Listing 19.4).

Listing 19.4   The Weight Update Procedure as Used by the Quick-Propagation Algorithm

```
for each unit j
     for each input i
            # compute gradient and step for each weight
            new_gradient[j][i] = -delta[j] * input[i]
            new_step[j][i] = new_gradient[j][i] /
(old_gradient[j][i]-new_gradient[j][i])
                   * old_step[j][i]
            # adjust the weight
            weight[j][i] += new_step[j][i]
            # store values for the next computation
            old_step[j][i] = new_step[j][i]
            old_gradient[j][i] = new_gradient[j][i]
        end for
end for
```

Given a working backprop algorithm, the quickprop variation does not take long to implement and test.

Resilient Propagation

RProp is another batch algorithm that updates the weights only after all the training samples have been seen [Riedmiller93]. The key idea is that the size of the step used to update the weights is not determined by the gradient itself, which removes the major problems associated with steepest descent techniques.

RProp Theory

The algorithm introduces the concept of update value Δ_{ij}, which is used to determine the step Δw_{ij}. It's important not to confuse the two, and the notation chosen by Riedmiller and Braun does not help. The update value is used to determine the step:

$$\Delta w_{ij} = \begin{cases} -\Delta_{ij}(t) & \text{if } \nabla E(t) > 0 \\ +\Delta_{ij}(t) & \text{if } \nabla E(t) < 0 \\ 0 & \text{otherwise} \end{cases}$$

This is relatively intuitive to understand. If the slope goes up, we adjust the weight downward (first case). Conversely, the weight is adjusted upward if the gradient is negative (second case). If there is no slope, we must be in a minima, so no step is necessary (third case). This equation is needed to compute the new update value:

$$\Delta_{ij} = \begin{cases} \eta^+ * \Delta_{ij}(t-1) & \text{if } \nabla E(t) * \nabla E(t-1) > 0 \\ \eta^- * \Delta_{ij}(t-1) & \text{if } \nabla E(t) * \nabla E(t-1) < 0 \\ \Delta_{ij}(t-1) & \text{otherwise} \end{cases}$$

η^+ and η^- are constants defined such that $0 < \eta^- < 1 < \eta^+$. Informally, the size of the step is increased (multiplied by η^+) if the gradient maintains the same direction (first case). The step size is decreased (multiplied by η^-) if the gradient changes sign (second case). Otherwise, the step size is left untouched if the gradient is 0.

Implementing RProp

Once again, we need extra arrays with the previous error gradients as well as the previous update value for each weight. As a batch algorithm too, the first loop to compute the sum of the gradients is the same as quickprop's. Then, the second stage of the algorithm is applied to update the weights, as shown in Listing 19.5.

Listing 19.5 The Weight Update Procedure Behind the Resilient-Propagation Algorithm

```
for each unit j
    for each input i
        # first determine the gradient in the neuron
        new_gradient[j] =-delta[j] * input[i]
        # analyze gradient change to determine size of update
        if new_gradient[j] * old_gradient[j] > 0 then
            new_update[j][i] = nplus * old_update[j][i]
        else if new_gradient[j] * old_gradient[j] < 0 then
            new_update[j][i] = nminus * old_update[j][i]
        else
            new_update[j][i] = old_update[j][i]
        # determine which direction to step in
        if new_gradient[j] > 0 then
            step[j][i] = -new_update[j][i]
        else if new_gradient[j] < 0 then
            step[j][i] = new_update[j][i]
        else step[j][i] = 0
        # adjust weight and store values for next iteration
        weight[j][i] += step[j][i]
        old_update[j][i] = new_update[j][i]
        old_gradient[j][i] = new_gradient[j][i]
    end for
end for
```

This is slightly trickier to implement, but is still classified as a simple task after backprop has been written!

Practical Issues

The theory covered so far has practical repercussions, as the additional hidden layers make perceptrons tricky to apply. It's essential to monitor the quality of the learning.

Generalization

The learning phase is responsible for optimizing the weights for the examples provided. However, a secondary purpose of the training is to make sure that the multilayer performs well for other unseen examples (the objective function). This is known as *generalization*: the capability to learn a general policy from the examples.

Generalization can be understood as finding a suitable decision surface. The problem is that if we learn the decision surface based on a particular set of examples, the result may not match the general decision surface. If we fit the examples too closely, the neural network may not perform well on other unseen examples. This predicament is known as *overfitting*—depicted in Figure 19.6.

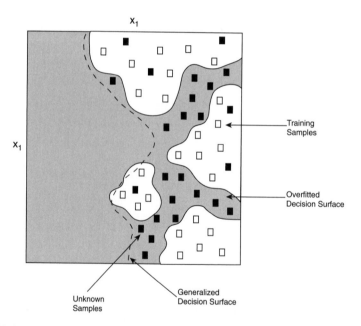

Figure 19.6   Example of overfitting where the learned decision surface fits the training samples too closely and generalizes poorly to other examples.

For single-layer perceptrons, generalization is not a problem because the decision surface is always linear! In MLPs, the number of hidden units affects the complexity of the decision surface, so this parameter plays an important role in the generalization capability. We need to find the trade-off between the number of hidden units and the apparent quality of results.

Incorrect or incomplete data does not help generalization. If the learning doesn't produce the right result, the training examples are usually to blame (for instance, too few samples, examples not representative).

One way to improve generalization is to gather *all* the data of the problem—or as close as possible to everything. Then, it's a matter finding a compromise between the number of hidden units and the quality of the results, which can be done by validation.

Testing and Validation

There is a method to deal with the data, to improve changes of successful generalization. It essentially involves splitting the training data into three different sets:

> ➤ **Training** sets train the perceptron directly. The algorithms optimize the weights to their best capability given a set of parameters.

> ➤ **Validation** sets check the quality of the training. As the parameters of the training are being changed, the validation set is used to find the best combination.

> ➤ **Testing** sets check the final quality of trained and validated perceptrons. No information from the testing set is used to improve the perceptron.

Essentially, the procedure to find the best model involves training many perceptrons, each with different parameters. Using the validation set, the best perceptron is identified. This is the final solution, and it can be optionally checked with the test.

Incremental Versus Batch

As a general rule, batch training should be preferred whenever possible. Batch algorithms converge to the right result faster and with greater accuracy. Specifically, if RProp can't solve the problem, there's little hope for other methods. Even when a batch algorithm is not directly applicable, the problem should be changed to a batch prototype. The idea is to validate the design by using an algorithm with the highest chances of success. If necessary, incremental data can be gathered together for batch processing. Then, if the first test proves successful, incremental learning can be attempted.

Incremental approaches are especially suited to online problems (learning within the game itself), because they require less memory. Indeed, the idea is to let the perceptron learn the examples as they are encountered, and discard them immediately. However, this runs the risk of "forgetting" early knowledge in favor of more recent examples.

Dealing with Incremental Learning

There are general ways of dealing with adaptive behaviors. We'll discuss these in Chapter 48, "Dealing with Adaptive Behaviors." For perceptrons specifically, there is a common trick to acquire knowledge online—without forgetting it.

One possible approach is to slow down the learning as time goes by. There's little risk of forgetting earlier experience when later training examples have a lesser importance. In practice, you do this by decreasing the learning rate over time. The adjustments made to the weights by steepest descent will thereby diminish over time.

There's no formal approach to decreasing the learning rate over time, because it really depends on the problem itself. Generally, a linear or slow exponential decay over time often appears as successful strategies.

Sadly, this also implies that the learning is effectively frozen as time passes. This is beneficial in some cases for preventing problems with incremental learning, but it can also cause problem where learning is actually necessary. As such, we need to pay special attention as to when to use this method.

Discussion

Perceptrons—and neural networks generally—are an extremely controversial technique, especially with game AI programmers. On one hand, MLPs solve specific problems extremely well and surprisingly efficiently. On the other hand, there are undeniable problems that hamper perceptrons during game development, which partly explains why they aren't applied more often in games.

Advantages

Perceptrons have a consequential mathematical foundation. Recent techniques (such as RProp) prove very robust at finding solutions when there is one. For well-defined problems, perceptrons will often surface as one of the best choices. On the other hand, if something goes wrong, we know it's a problem with some of the parameters—or even the design.

Another advantage of perceptrons is the wide variety of training algorithms available. These enable us to exploit MLP in many different settings, under various constraints; this provides amazing flexibility. As such, it's the actual nature of perceptrons that come into consideration when choosing whether to apply MLP.

Finally, MLPs work natively with continuous values. They can also deal with noise extremely well, and take various different data types on the inputs and outputs.

Disadvantages

Neural networks are not very expressive when it comes to their knowledge; we can print out the values of the weights, but they'll mean nothing unless we spend hours analyzing the results. This also implies that perceptrons depend fully on the algorithms that are used to create them. We can't manually modify the weights without understanding what they mean!

Once learned, the representation of MLP is fixed. This means that updating it will either involve starting again or retraining it. When retrained, there's no guarantee that it'll conserve the knowledge it learned previously. This means that all efforts done to test and debug the perceptrons will have to be duplicated.

There is a lot of experimentation involved in developing a successful MLP. The number of processing units and even the layer count are both parameters that require exploration. The design of the inputs and outputs also needs special care, because they have an incredible impact on the problem. In addition, MLPs often require scaffolding: pre- and postprocessing to expose the true nature of the problem (which neural networks often cannot understand alone).

Finally, MLPs have real problems with scalability. It's quite difficult for them to cope with complex decision surfaces, or those of high dimensionality. (Memory and computation grow exponentially.)

Summary

The representation of MLP is an extended version of single-layer perceptrons:

➤ MLPs have middle layers of processing units, with weighted connections between them.

➤ The activation function of hidden units needs to be nonlinear (a *sigmoid* function ideally).

➤ The output is computed by propagating the inputs through the layers one after the other.

➤ Because of the additional complexities of the middle layer, training is harder to achieve.

➤ Backprop computes the error gradient in the last layer, and then filters the error in reverse through the layers.

➤ Both batch and incremental algorithms can be applied to this representation, including delta rule solutions or adaptive weight adjustment strategies.

The result is an AI technique that can learn to approximate functions. In practice, this can be used by game AI programmer to make decisions, predict an outcome, or recognize a pattern in the current situation. The next chapter applies MLPs to target selection, estimating the benefit of aiming for a point in space.

Practical Demo

Onno is an animat that uses a large neural network to handle shooting in general, including prediction, target selection, and aiming. The information provided to the perceptron is the combination of the features used in the previous chapters. Although the results are moderate, *Onno* demonstrates the versatility of MLP and the benefits of decomposing the behaviors. The documented source code is available on the web site at `http://AiGameDev.com/`.

Chapter 20

Selecting the Target

KEY TOPICS

- Case Study
- Rationale
- Module Design
- Implementation
- Application
- Evaluation

This chapter applies multilayer perceptrons (MLPs) to a difficult problem. Animats are going to learn to estimate the damage of a rocket on the enemy. This capability enables them to pick targets that are most likely to injure the opponent—either directly or via splash damage. Better target selection also prevents the animats from blowing themselves up.

The next few pages cover all aspects of the problem, from an informal description to the implementation and evaluation.

This chapter covers the following topics:

- ➤ A case study of the target-selection problem, explaining what properties of the situation affect the decision of where to shoot

- ➤ A few ideas for the development, notably to tackle the experimentations if things go wrong

- ➤ The interfaces to the multilayer perceptron, both for runtime and initialization

- ➤ The implementation and how the data structures and algorithms come together

- ➤ How the application phase tackles the problem, what issues arise, and how the perceptron fits into it

- ➤ The resulting animat and the target-selection behaviors

At the end of this chapter, the animats will be capable of handling rocket launchers as lethal weapons—without hurting themselves too much.

Case Study

A few points made in the previous chapters need expanding to more fully explain how they affect the target selection. We'd like to determine what properties of the situation affect the likelihood of damage, and the benefit of particular targets.

First, certain features affect the problem directly. Figure 20.1 shows the four points in space involved in the problem, with five key features:

➤ The distance from the origin to the target; the closer the target, the higher the probability of hitting it.

➤ The distance between the enemy's position and the target; the further the enemies, the less likely they are of ending up at the target.

➤ The distance between the selected target and the estimated enemy position (because this is a relatively accurate prediction).

➤ The relative angle between the trajectory of the projectile and the velocity of the enemy.

➤ The relative angle between the velocity of the enemy and the vector from the target to the estimated position.

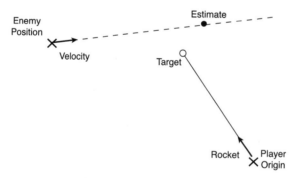

Figure 20.1 Possible scenario with one selected target, close to the predicted position of the enemy.

Second, some properties of the animat may influence the choice of targets:

➤ The angular divergence from the heading of the animat to the target, as well as the angular velocity; some targets will be easier to aim at.

➤ Both the speed of travel and the direction of the movement can affect the ability to hit particular targets.

Given these key factors, it may be possible to guess how much damage the projectile will inflict upon the enemy. Because manually designing a system that can predict the damage is complex enough, a perceptron is used to learn this task.

Rationale

As far as the multilayer perceptron is concerned, there is little room for artistic interpretation. With the rule-based system, we had to customize it to our problem. Perceptrons, on the other hand, are pretty much standard, and only the underlying implementation of the training algorithm changes. So, there's little need to worry about the design of the neural network; a standard fully connected feed-forward module will do fine.

As far as the behaviors are concerned, it would be ideal for the animats to learn about target selection online. However, this may not be directly possible because of the complexity of the data or the unpredictability of the problem. For this reason, if problems are encountered, data can be gathered in the game but learned offline. This will also give us the opportunity to analyze the data ourselves to check that there is actually something to learn. We can thereby determine whether the features discussed in previous chapters (and in the case study) are relevant. Having knowledge of relevant features improves the prediction, reduces the size of the MLP, and speeds up the learning.

Gathering vast quantities of data is a good idea regardless, because we can investigate how strong the noise is (and whether preventive measures are necessary). Because of the unpredictability of games, the outcome of two similar fights will be different. As such, the noise is expected to be very high, which often makes learning the data directly more difficult. In this case, statistical analysis may be required first, using the MLP to learn from those intermediate results.

Module Design

This section discusses the design of the MLP module, notably how it can be initialized from data and its runtime C++ interface.

Initialization

The initialization is left very high level; only the topology of the MLP is specified. This includes the number of inputs and the description of each layer with its number of units. In XML, this could look a bit like this:

```
<layer inputs="4" units="8"/>
<layer units="1"/>
```

The number of inputs for the layers is only specified once, because only the inputs for the first layer are unknown; these are the inputs to the perceptron. The inputs to the other layers are the outputs of the previous layers, so they can be assumed. If specified, the other input values need to be internally consistent.

The perceptron module also has the capability to save itself to disk. Because developers do not need to (and often cannot) manipulate the data manually, there is no need to describe the format. We can just assume that the implementation of the saving and the loading are internally consistent.

Interfaces

There are two kinds of interfaces: those expected to read the perceptron's data (simulation), and those intended to update the perceptron's data (training). Separating these two interfaces means the implementation can be made lighter when only simulation is required—a popular feature for game developers.

The interface for *simulation* consists of only one function. This takes the network's inputs and produces the outputs. The interfaces use the STL for simplicity and safety, but this can be modified trivially if it is a problem:

```
void Run(const vector< float >& input, vector< float >& output);
```

Two kinds of interfaces update the data: incremental training and batch learning. The *incremental learning interface* consists of two functions. One function deals with individual samples, defined much like the simulation function, but provided with a variety of default parameters (for instance, a learning rate of 0.1, momentum of 0). The other function randomizes the network:

```
float Sample(const vector<float>& input, const vector<float>& output);
void Randomize();
```

In contrast, *batch algorithms* tend to use more memory than incremental learning techniques, so they are kept separate in the implementation; more memory will be used only if batch training is required.

The batch training procedure actually takes entire arrays of input and output patterns. These are provided along with default number of iterations and error threshold:

```
float Batch(const vector<Pattern>& inputs, const vector<Pattern>&
outputs);
```

The perceptron can be implemented transparently behind these interfaces.

Implementation

The implementation itself is entirely abstracted out from the interfaces. This gives us the luxury of implementing different techniques as appropriate, without breaking compatibility.

Data Structures

The fundamental data structure is an array of layers, each containing a set of neurons and the layer's output. The output is an array stored in each layer rather than per neuron because such storage simplifies the filtering of information through the neural network.

The training data is stored separately so that it can be used only when required. The training data has the same structure as the data used for simulation. For the layers, the module stores the derivative of the activation function for the output, as well as the gradient of the error in the neuron. The layers also store the weight deltas, which are used to remember the gradient descent step. This allows momentum to be applied to the steepest descent algorithm.

Simulation and Learning

The simulation is essentially a set of nested loops. The outer loop processes the layers, propagating the information from the inputs to the outputs. The middle layer handles each of the neurons in the layers, and the inner loop actually computes the net sum of the neuron. Each loop is located in its own function to simplify the code and prevent redundancy. The inner loop is inlined for efficiency.

The learning algorithms first perform a forward simulation to determine the derivatives and gradients. Then, the error is propagated backward to determine the gradients in each of the neurons. Any algorithm can then be applied onto the gradients to adjust the weights. For batch processing, the gradients are summed together, and those are used by other gradient optimization techniques.

Application

Now it's possible to apply this perceptron to target selection. Our primary objective is to analyze the effectiveness of each rocket based on the situation. Then, theoretically, it should be possible to learn to predict the effectiveness of any shot before it happens.

The AI code combines many of the techniques covered previously discussed. For navigation, a solution that provides good coverage of the terrain is essential. Tracking of enemy movement and estimating the velocity is also necessary. Then, the AI can launch a rocket around that target and see what happens.

Algorithm

The algorithm that selects the target is an iterative process. This is not done all at once; the decision can easily be split over multiple frames of the AI processing.

Essentially, a generation mechanism creates new random points around the estimated position of the enemy. The animat checks for the first obstacle along that line (floor, wall), and uses that as the target. Then, the perceptron is called to evaluate the potential for damage at that point. Only when the damage is good enough is a target returned. Listing 20.1 shows this. The `randvec()` function returns a random offset, and the perceptron is called by the `estimate_damage()` function to assess the value of a target.

Listing 20.1   The Iteration That Selects the Best Nearby Target by Predicting the Damage and Comparing the Probability to a Threshold Set by the Designer

```
function select_target
     repeat
            # pick a candidate target point near the enemy
            target = position + randvec()
            # use the perceptron to predict the hit probability
            value = estimate_damage( target )
       # stop if the probability is high enough
until value > threshold
return target
end function
```

This reveals how the neural network is put to use. However, some programming is required to teach it.

Tracking Rockets

Keeping track of the situation proves the most problematic. Most of the programming involves gathering and interpreting the information about the shot. The AI must be capable of answering the following questions:

➤ Did a projectile explode nearby?

➤ Was it someone else's projectile?

➤ Was there any damage attributed to the projectile?

➤ What were the conditions when the shot was fired?

To prevent any misinterpretations, each animat tries to have only one rocket in the air at any one time. It's then easier to attribute damage to that rocket. Embodiment actually helps this process, because all the rocket explosions that are invisible to an animat are unlikely to belong to it.

There are four different stages for gathering this information. The major part of this problem is solved using events and callbacks (steps 2 and 3):

1. When a rocket is fired, start tracking the situation and remember the initial conditions.

2. Upon perceiving a sound of pain (or visual cue, such as blood), determine whether it was caused by the rocket by checking the origin of the sound. Take note of it.

3. If a rocket explosion is detected, set the target to the point of collision, and set the expected time of collision to the current time.

4. When the expected time of collision is past (given a small margin), use the information gathered to train the neural network.

All four stages follow the life cycle of a rocket. After it has exploded, the AI has a unique data sample to train the perceptron.

Dealing with Noise

Despite all these precautions, there is a lot of noise in the data. This means that two similar situations may have different outcomes. This is due to many things:

➤ The representation of each situation is simplified, so there are many unknown parameters that vary.

➤ The features gathered from each situation are even more limited (by design).

➤ The environment is in itself unpredictable, as many animats autonomously behaving cohabit together.

There are large variations in the training samples, making it very difficult to learn a good prediction of the outcome. The task is even tougher online, because the noise really takes its toll when learning incrementally. Instead, working with entire data sets really helps, so the noise averages out to suitable values.

To gather the data, a number of animats (around five of them) store all their experience of different shots in logs. We can therefore acquire more information and process it manually to see whether the data indicates trends—thus confirming the design decisions. In Figure 20.2, for example, analyzing the hit ratio in terms of the distance between the player and the target reveals an interesting trend: Targets close to the estimate are likelier to cause more damage (this is accidental damage because the animats do not voluntarily shoot at close targets), but the damage is maximal at around 15 steps away (between distance 180 and 324). This curve reveals the strength of the prediction skills, which the perceptron for target selection will learn. (Manual design would no doubt ignore such factors.)

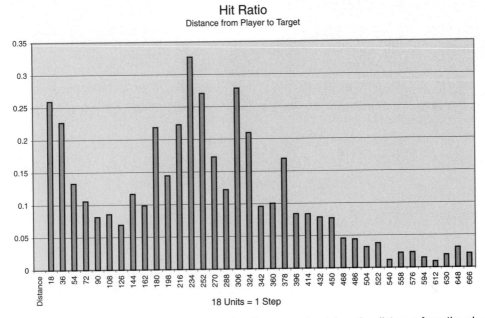

Figure 20.2   The likelihood of a rocket damaging the enemy based on the distance from the player.

Inputs and Outputs

The inputs are chosen from among distances and dot products using combinations of the four points in space (that is, player origin, enemy position, estimated position, and chosen target):

➤ **Dot products** are plugged straight in to the perceptron, as they have suitable range (always [−1,1]). Their absolute value can be taken if the sign is not an important feature.

➤ **Distances** are rescaled slightly to be more convenient. This is not necessary, but rescaling works best with the initial random weight values (chosen with a uniform random distribution). The input distance is divided by the maximum distance if known (for instance, between estimate and target), or a suitable guess.

Three primary distances between the four 3D points of the problem are the most useful as inputs (see Figure 20.3). There are trends in the dot products, too, but these are not as obvious. We could use further preprocessing to extract the relevant information out of the situation, but in a more generic fashion. For example, the dot product between the projectile and enemy velocities is 0 when the enemy is still; this situation would seem the same to the perceptron as a side-on shot. Returning a value of 1—similar to a full-on shot—would prove more consistent.

The unique output corresponds to the damage inflicted. Because the damage is very often zero, and we want to emphasize any damage at all, we use a Boolean output that indicates injury.

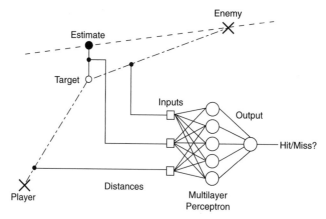

Figure 20.3   Graphical representation of the inputs to the perceptron. The three primary features are the distances between the origin, enemy, and target.

Training Procedure

During the training, the bots are not given unlimited rockets; they have to pick up the rocket launcher along with ammunition. In the test level, the rockets are easily available, and even the simplest-movement AI has no trouble picking them up accidentally. Animats without ammunition actually serve as good target practice for others with the rocket launchers (without causing chaos).

To reduce the time taken by the simulation to gather the same data, the game can be accelerated. For example, this can be done by running the *Quake 2* game in server mode and disabling the graphics. By default, these servers will only use necessary processing power to maintain the simulation real time. FEAR has an option to enable acceleration so the simulation runs at full speed, taking up as much processor time as possible. This is a great feature and saves a lot of development time.

Practical Demo

The animat used to illustrate this chapter is called *Splash* and can be found on the web site at `http://AiGameDev.com/`. Both the source code and the binaries are available and ready to run. *Splash* predicts the enemy position, and then generates a random target around it, using a perceptron to evaluate its likelihood of success. If the changes of success are acceptable, a rocket is fired. Training data is gathered when the expected time of collision is past.

Evaluation

Even with all the precautions, the example data collected is indeed very noisy. In most situations, an average error is as high as 25 percent (the best being 17 percent). This takes the batch algorithms hundreds of training periods (epoch), depending on the random weights. Experiments show there is no miracle number of hidden weights; low values, such as 4/5, seem to work as well as others. Still, the perceptrons manage to learn some trends, notably using the distances.

Despite the relatively low precision of the learning, the perceptron still proves a valuable help in optimizing the target selection. The neural network visibly increases the effectiveness of the animat's shooting capabilities. The perceptron tends to favor spots that are close to the estimate, close to the enemy's current position, and closer to the origin of the rocket. Targets near the enemy on the floor are often chosen as targets (good compromises). Generally, the perceptron is also very good at finding flaws in suggestions made by the target-generation mechanism, which prevents the animat from blowing itself up! Manually enforcing a minimal distance to engage an enemy prevents such kamikaze shots.

Note that a suitable default generation mechanism could be developed relatively easily without learning technology. For example, a suitable policy is to generate a random point near the estimate and drop it to the floor to find a target. However, the perceptron learns to find trends in a complex problem (which increases performance generally), and manages to optimize target selection according to individual skills.

Combining this generation mechanism with a perceptron allows the animats to appear realistic while learning. This design means that the perceptron only improves the target selection according to experience; there's no risk of learning "stupid" behaviors.

Summary

In this chapter, we developed a generic MLP module, using formalized interfaces:

➤ The perceptron simulation interfaces are left separate from the training interfaces so that there is minimal overhead for nonlearning neural networks.

➤ The batch training algorithms also require more memory, and are separated.

We designed an animat capable of gathering information from the environment to extract facts about its rocket shots. This enabled us to learn to predict the damage of each rocket. The animat can therefore select random targets, and use the perceptron to estimate the best:

➤ Gathering the information from the environment to monitor the rockets was the biggest challenge.

➤ To deal with the noise in the data, the examples were stored in a common file.

➤ Plotting graphs and histograms of the different features revealed that the distances are the most reliable inputs.

➤ The target selection is best learned offline by a batch algorithm.

Thanks to the perceptron, the AI developer spends less time solving a relatively complex problem. The perceptron exploits learning technology to improve the aiming capabilities beyond hand-crafted solutions. The MPL has the advantage of being easily adapted to the skills of different animats, too.

The next chapter presents an important concept: understanding the problem. This is an essential skill for AI developers because understanding the problem always drives AI system design.

Chapter 21

Knowledge of the Problem

This chapter describes a fundamental principle of AI development in general: knowledge of the problem. Part II covered the early stages of AI development—namely the *analysis*, *understanding*, and *specification* phases. These provide valuable insights into the problem; however, this knowledge only falls into place during the *application* phase.

During development, the *application* phase is indirectly about refining knowledge of the problem using experience from the prototypes. The next few pages discuss the different levels of knowledge and how they can be acquired using practical examples.

Knowing the problem may seem trivial compared to understanding the solution. However, it's arguably more important. By emphasizing the general principles in this chapter, we'll quickly realize that we have the power to do the following:

➤ Analyze complex problems

➤ Design efficient systems

➤ Find issues with broken solutions

➤ Improve existing behaviors

Spending time understanding the problem is justified because such understanding enhances our ability to manipulate the problem into a convenient form. Notably, the problem can be refined into one that's efficient to solve, or divided into manageable parts.

This chapter covers the following topics:

➤ Informal and theoretical understanding of the problem and indications of its complexity

➤ A more refined way to understand the problem using data analysis with statistics

➤ The analytical understanding of a problem, used to extract complex properties of the problem

➤ How the developer can apply these levels of knowledge, notably for refining problems

➤ A few guidelines to using and refining our knowledge when solving the problem

High-level knowledge of the problem is covered first, progressing toward the gory details.

Black Box Understanding

Considering the problem from an external point of view, it can be understood as a *black box* in two ways: as a behavior trying to accomplish a task, or as a software component processing information.

Informal Knowledge

Informally, the problem can be understood in terms of the *task* it must accomplish. We can consider the task as a behavior interacting with the environment (shooting), requiring information (enemy position and terrain), and producing an outcome (targeted projectile). See Figure 21.1.

Such knowledge of the task is refined in the *understanding* phase of the AI development (see Chapter 7, "Analysis and Understanding"). You can further this informal black box knowledge by establishing the correspondence between the situation and the outcome—generally with a case study. In addition, the criteria used to evaluate the behaviors provide an informal indication of the task's complexity. (The description of wall following is longer than obstacle avoidance, for instance.)

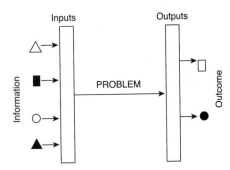

Figure 21.1 Graphical representation of the task; the information is used to produce an outcome. The problem involves mapping inputs to outputs.

Software Specification

Informal knowledge of the *task* (high level) is often combined with a more formal approach to specify the *problem* as a software component (low level). The *specification* phase aims to describe the interfaces with other components (and the platform) by formalizing the data representation (see Chapter 9, "Specifications and Knowledge Representation").

Initial understanding of the problem as a software component is often refined during the *application* phase with observations made from prototypes. For example, providing the target selection with knowledge of the terrain as well as the enemy is a refinement. A stable formal interface enables developers to analyze the problem theoretically.

Theoretical Analysis

The benefit of the specification is that we can rationalize over the inputs and outputs (the variables of the problem). Indeed, from the representation of the variables, we can deduce the theoretical complexity of the problem—which affects the capabilities of the AI and our ability to design a solution (see Figure 21.2).

The size of the problem essentially depends on the number of input and output *configurations*. As a reminder, each possible parameter combination forms one configuration. The set of all input configurations is known as the *domain*, and the output is the *codomain*.

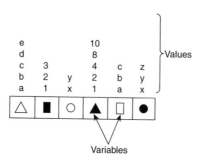

Figure 21.2 Example problem with six variables, each with two to five values. Both inputs and outputs are treated identically.

The magnitude of these domains can be measured by two factors:

➤ **Dimensions**—The number of parameters in the problem, including input and output variables

➤ **Size**—The number of different values for each of the parameters

The total number of configurations for the problem is calculated by multiplying the size of each dimension (see Figure 21.3). As more parameters are introduced to the problem, the total number of configurations grows exponentially, because we take the product of these values. This is known as the *curse of dimensionality*.

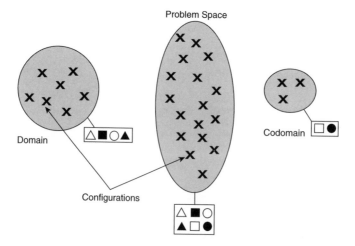

Figure 21.3 The set of configurations representing the inputs (left), the problem (middle), and the output (right). The size of the problem is the product of the input and output sizes.

Table 21.1 shows an example domain size for a simple problem: deciding whether to attack based on the identity of the enemy, his distance, and the health. This simple problem has total number of *1,656,400* configurations. Adding another parameter, such as enemy health, would increase this size to *167,296,400!*

Table 21.1 The Size of a Simple Problem: Deciding Whether to Attack Based on the Identity of the Enemy, Distance, and Health

Parameter	Type	Range	Size
Health	Integer	[0..100]	101
Distance	Integer	[0..1024]	1025
Enemy	Enumeration	[fred,...,jim]	8
Attack	Boolean	[true,false]	2
		Problem size	1,656,400

The theoretical analysis reveals the worst-case scenario. In practice, however, problems are often simpler.

Underlying Knowledge

The black box view is limited to rough knowledge: intuitions and theory. Obtaining a better understanding involves trying out the problem in practice. To do this, a solution—any solution—is required. It can be a simple prototype, a random solution, or even a human controlling the game character.

Trying the problem in practice reveals usage of input and output values. It's possible to gather lots of example configurations (for instance, by logging network games among the development team), and analyze the data empirically. In this section, the understanding is mainly statistical, explaining different trends in the problem data.

Usage Analysis

Given the data gathered by random solutions to the problem, we can use different statistical techniques to provide a deeper insight into the problem. The simplest form of analysis identifies the frequency at which the values are used for each variable (see Figure 21.4, which shows the usage analysis of the problem in Figure 21.2).

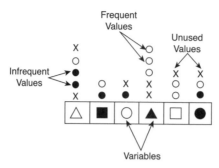

Figure 21.4   Statistics collected about the usage of the values for the problem from Figure 21.2.

Given this knowledge about relevance of the values, we can determine the best representation, focusing on the important aspects and ignoring the less-relevant ones. In weapon selection, for example, a more precise representation can be used if there are large variations in the distance, or the discretization for the health parameter can be decreased if enemies have mostly full health.

Variables and Covariance

In practice, most of the *values* are used for each variable. However, not all the possible *configurations* are used for many problems. This happens particularly when input parameters are interdependent. In this case, there are commonly used input and output combinations.

For example, the rules of the game or properties of the environment limit the number of situations (for instance, players mostly touch the floor, damage is linked with sounds of pain). The inputs are affected by external constraints (game logic and rules of the simulation), but the outputs are subject to internal constraints (requirements for realistic and intelligent behaviors).

Formally speaking, this can be measured by the *covariance* between two parameters (see Figure 21.5). Intuitively, if one parameter can be fully determined from another, their covariance will be high (for instance, damage probability and likelihood of hitting the enemy). Conversely, if two parameters are unrelated to each other, their covariance will be near zero (for instance, the presence of a side obstacle and the amount of ammunition held by the enemy).

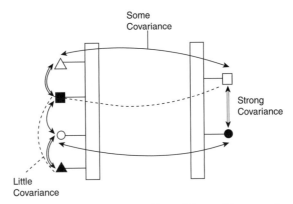

Figure 21.5   The dependencies between the variables of the problem are denoted as arrows. Strong covariance makes the problem easier to solve.

> **NOTE**
>
> Conditional independence implies that two parameters vary freely of each other. Covariance can only measure dependencies between two variables, so a value of 0 is not sufficient to guarantee conditional independence. Indeed, there may be higher-order dependencies involving many parameters, which covariance does not identify.

In practice, high covariance between two input parameters indicates redundant information. The lower the covariance, the more information is encoded in those inputs. As for the covariance between inputs and outputs, a high value indicates this is an extremely simple problem (for instance, obstacle avoidance). A covariance near zero implies the problem is not easy to solve (for instance, target selection by predicting damage). Finally, high covariance between the outputs is a good thing because it indicates that they are related. (Computing all the outputs is easier.)

Effective Domain

Both the usage and the covariance statistics imply that different parts of the domain are used less often than others (see Figure 21.6). In fact, for most problems, the domain is rarely used entirely. We can therefore modify the representation to cover only the relevant part of the domain. This is a good way to optimize the problem.

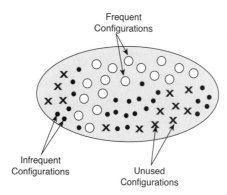

Figure 21.6 Statistics on the use of individual configurations in the problem. This emphasizes the relevant parts of the domain, as well as less-important ones.

However, optimizations need to be done with care. Removing or simplifying the variables from the problem reduces the flexibility of the interface, so the solutions are more limited. There also may be flaws in the statistical analysis, particularly when insufficient data has been gathered. So it's best to simplify the representation later after everything works, and optimizations can be validated by comparison and testing.

Until then, knowledge of the effective domain is useful for developing a solution that is tailored to the problem, which reduces the complexity of the AI required to solve it.

Fundamental Understanding

Statistics certainly provide an improvement over the purely theoretical approach, but there is still room for even further understanding. In many cases, the inputs and outputs exhibit more than statistical relationships. This knowledge of the problem domain is acquired in a more analytical fashion.

Properties of the Problem

Statistics reveal the big picture, but particular subareas of the problem domain exhibit patterns of their own.

Symmetry in the Domain

The different configurations of the variables may be indirectly related. In a certain part of the domain, for example, the values may be identical to another part (or even the opposite values). This is the case for navigation; turning left is the opposite of turning right.

This implies there is duplicate information, which the solution can take advantage of. Large problems will very often exhibit a certain level of redundancy. To extract this information, we need to make use of our own abstract thought and pattern-recognition abilities.

Tightness of the Solution

In the problem domain, particular combinations of inputs and outputs are classified as "valid" solutions (see Figure 21.7). For simple problems, the ratio of valid configurations over the total number will be very large (for instance, obstacle avoidance has much freedom in open space). With tougher problems, there will be significantly fewer valid solutions. (For instance, wall following required precise actions in each case.)

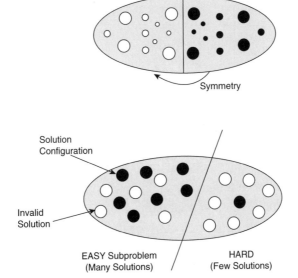

Figure 21.7 Two example problem domains. Above, the configurations are symmetrical. Below, different areas of the domain have different complexity.

Variable Complexity of Subdomains

The solution may also vary in complexity in certain parts of the domain. The inter-dependency of the parameters may depend on other parameters.

In open space, for example, obstacle avoidance is pretty simple because almost any behavior is acceptable. The required output is restricted when the obstacles are nearby.

Nature of the Problem

Analysis of the problem parameters can reveal indirect dependencies involving more than just two variables (for instance, symmetry and conditional dependence). Conceptually, we can understand this as a direct dependency with hidden parameters. Expressing these parameters explicitly can help us understand the true nature of the problem (see Figure 21.8).

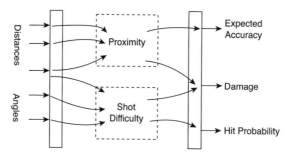

Figure 21.8   The problem has hidden parameters (shot difficulty and proximity) that are mostly independent from each other, but establish dependencies between the inputs and outputs.

This isn't straightforward to understand, so let's use target selection as an example. It's possible to learn to estimate the potential damage of a targeted rocket based on the state of the enemy. However, there's a hidden concept there: the prediction of the enemy's future position. Indeed, the damage estimate depends on this prediction. So, internally, the problem can be split up to expose the prediction aspect. Alternatively, we can use a rough prediction as an additional input to assist the solution.

Refining the Problem

This section discusses how to apply knowledge of the problem as development practices. Specifically, problems are simplified so that common AI techniques can solve them, or split recursively into manageable subproblems.

Simplification

Generally, the inputs and outputs are defined in a flexible fashion to prevent us from having to change the interfaces for each of the prototypes. It's often necessary to refine these interfaces before developing the solution (see Figure 21.9).

AI techniques generally rely on getting concise data represented in a convenient format. The raw information available from the interfaces is often unsuitable or partly irrelevant, so the AI techniques often need help to solve the problem.

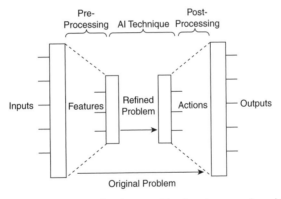

Figure 21.9 Refining the problem into a simpler one. The inputs are reduced into important features, and the actions set the outputs.

For the AI to perform well, we provide it with *features* and *actions*. As far as data flow is concerned, features and actions are still considered as inputs and outputs, although they are usually highly relevant to the solution. The AI engineer generally selects these features by refining the inputs in a concise fashion. For example, the target selection is provided with features about the disposition of players in space (instead of the raw vectors), and the output is used to evaluate the benefit (instead of providing the point in space directly).

We can understand this refinement as an additional layer of pre- and post-processing used to simplify the information. In essence, this reduces the domain (input) and divides the codomain (output). The size of the refined domain is also thereby decreased.

Divide and Conquer

Understanding the domain in depth makes it more obvious how to decompose the problem. This is particularly appropriate if there are dependencies between certain inputs and outputs, or if the outcome has distinguishable patterns.

Finding the right decomposition is a matter of identifying the aspects of the problem that can be dissociated, and then creating a component to handle it separately. In this case, the input and output domains are divided into multiple subdomains. The input domains of the subproblems will almost always overlap. However, the outputs can be handled independently (see Figure 21.10).

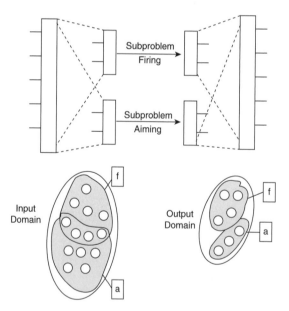

Figure 21.10   Splitting up the problem of shooting into multiple subproblems of aiming and firing. The input domains are often similar, but the outputs domains can be independent.

The problems can be refined recursively at will until they reach a manageable level that can be solved with a simple AI technique (a process much like software design).

Combining the subproblems is then a matter of organizing the components together. The flow of data between these components needs to be managed using the architectural patterns discussed in Chapter 3, "Reactive Approach." For example, the outputs can be combined by suppression or combination; the components can be assembled sequentially or distributed.

Methodology

So, specifically how do game AI developers proceed when refining the problem and trying to understand the data? Basically, there's wisdom, experimentation, and analysis!

Expert Features

Essentially, as AI engineers, we can have an effect on both the size of the problem and its complexity. We can do this primarily by selecting the right *features* as inputs to the problem. A good place to start for finding features is to use the case studies, and combine the inputs to more relevant problem variables:

➤ **Compound features** are made up of combined multiple inputs. This is generally achieved by a mathematical function combining multiple parameters into one value.

➤ **Pre-processing** allows the results of algorithms to be used as inputs. This can be considered as a compound feature over many variables.

These are often called *expert features* because the engineers use their knowledge of the problem to extract meaningful information for the AI. The outputs also can be defined as higher-level actions to further simplify the problem.

Identifying Features Empirically

As programmers, we generally have a good feel for solving problems. We can identify important points and exploit them. AI engineers use a similar methodology. They use their experience to identify the relevant data and put it to use.

Essentially, wisdom is used to assign preliminary priorities to the features. Then they can be ordered by importance. Correcting these estimates is a matter of experimentation by trying out lots of different examples with different features. There are two methodologies to find good features:

➤ The **incremental** approach starts with a few features, adding or improving inputs as needed to get a working model.

➤ The **decremental** approach removes inputs from working models to simplify them as much as possible.

The incremental approach is used for obstacle avoidance; one front whisker is used by default, but side whiskers are added to provide guidance when turning. The decremental approach is used for target selection; three angles and three distances are the inputs at first, but only the last three are reliable features.

With a bit of experience, the first set of chosen features can become quite accurate. Then, if it works, the model can be simplified. If it doesn't work, more features can be added until the problem is solvable. There is no algorithmic solution, so expert design and testing is unavoidable. Other automated solutions will most likely follow this approach (for instance, using genetic algorithms).

Data Analysis

Experimentation relies on the intuition of the AI engineer. Understanding the problem in practical terms can become a formal process thanks to data analysis. This topic in itself deserves more than a subsection, but these few hints should be enough to get us started.

In classical game development, it's quite rare that statistical analysis is necessary; A* pathfinding and finite-state machines certainly don't need it! With techniques based on learning, however, this is very important. As AI becomes more complex, the chances of getting the model right will diminish drastically when only experimentation is used.

Data analysis does incur a certain time investment (overhead), notably to gather the data (or even to get comfortable with the analysis tools). However, the insights provided by statistics more than make up for lost time, and can even improve the quality of the behaviors. Reliable adaptation is arguably only possible with these methods.

The Right Tools

Many packages, both commercial and freely available, can perform statistical analysis. These include Mathlab, GnuPlot, Mathematica, and Excel. It can take a while to get comfortable with these, but most of them are easy to use for simple tasks.

These tools provide ways to manipulate data, as well as visualize it. We need both these operations to extract trends out of the data. Let's cover visualization and then basic manipulation with statistics.

Visualizing Data

Most data samples are multidimensional. When there are only two parameters, it's easy to visualize the values using a 2D plot. We can easily extract trends from this data by looking for patterns; X/Y scatter plots, line graphs, box-whisker diagrams, bar charts, and histograms are all good choices. Chapter 20, "Selecting the Target," did this to analyze the effectiveness of the target selection, plotting the hit ratio in terms of the distance.

With three dimensions, data is already much harder to observe. Some visualization tools can handle arbitrary dimensions (for instance, self-organizing feature maps). Such techniques work by organizing the data into groups that can be visualized in 2D. Patterns become obvious with this approach, but it's harder to understand *where* the patterns are!

The alternative is to manually select pairs of parameters, and plot them together using 2D techniques. Sadly, this only reveals "first-order" patterns. *Projections* can also be used to convert *n* variables into one dimension (to reduce the dimensionality by combining parameters). The projections take the shape of user-defined equations that take *n* parameters and produce one result. Projections can be difficult to understand, but provide a viable solution to visualize multidimensional data.

Relevant Metrics

When trying to understand data, it often helps to extract relevant information from the data. Various statistical metrics can provide great assistance.

The *mean* μ (Greek mu) is the sum off all the data samples X divided by the number of samples. The *median* is the data sample right in the middle of the sorted array. It's also useful to find *percentiles*; for example, the first *quartile* is the sample 25 percent of the way through the sorted data, and the third quartile is at 75 percent. These metrics describe the body of the data, so we can understand which part of parameter space it occupies.

The *variance* (denoted σ^2) is a measure of the spread of the data. It is computed using the sum of square distances of each sample X to the mean, divided by the number of samples N:

$$\sigma^2 = \frac{\sum (X - \mu)^2}{N}$$

Most statistical packages provide this equation. The more commonly used *standard deviation* σ is computed by the square root of the variance.

Covariance measures the amount of correlation between two random variables. This enables us to identify dependencies between parameters of the problem (and potentially causal links). Covariance is computed much like variance, but using two parameters, i and j, for each sample X:

$$\mathrm{cov}(i, j) = \frac{\sum (X_i - \mu_i)(X_j - \mu_j)}{N}$$

This really brief crash course in statistics should be enough for most game AI developers. See [Weisstein03] or [Kachigan91] for more information.

Summary

There are different levels of understanding of the problem: informal, theoretical, statistical, and analytical. These provide a good combination of experience:

➤ The description of the task provides an indication of the complexity.

➤ By multiplying the size of the problem parameters together, we obtain the total number of configurations in the domain.

➤ Gathering arbitrary data about the problem enables us to establish usage of values and configurations.

➤ Some parameters depend on each other; this can usually be identified in pairs using covariance.

➤ More complex relationships between variables need to be established analytically.

This understanding enables us to manipulate the problem in two ways:

➤ Refining the problem into a simpler one that can be handled by standard technique

➤ Splitting the problem into manageable subproblems that can be divided recursively

The AI engineer plays a crucial role in acquiring this understanding and applying it:

➤ Expert features can be ranked by priority, and they can be added or removed as necessary.

➤ Experimentation reveals the importance of features.

➤ Statistical metrics also provide essential hints to the quality of inputs.

This chapter discussed knowledge of the problem in conceptual terms. More than half a dozen problems have already been solved using most of these concepts. These ideas will also enlighten the design of remaining prototypes. The methodology for solving complex problems will become more obvious with further practice.

Practical Demo

You can download an animat from `http://AiGameDev.com/` that facilitates data collection and analysis. *Lumberjack* logs everything: most details from the senses and each action executed. The log file can be processed by standard packages or custom scripts when necessary. *Lumberjack* provides a good framework for putting the ideas in this chapter into practice.

Part III
Conclusion

This part had everything to keep a modern AI game developer happy: rockets, neural networks, and many different prototypes. We also discussed a very important aspect of the application phase: how to understand the problem and manipulate it so that we can solve it easily.

Retrospective Overview

With a bit more distance, let's go over the various behaviors and techniques to extract key lessons.

Behaviors

This part showed us how to split a problem into manageable parts. We were then able to implement each of the solutions separately.

The prediction of enemy movement is very efficient—in both computation and quality. However, the physics-based approach is fundamentally limited to linear trajectories; this can be error prone for large distances. Improving upon this requires getting into the mind of the enemies and simulating their movement, which requires different assumptions. The linear guess is the best compromise of quality/cost, without going into the full probabilistic analysis!

There were few problems applying the standard perceptrons to aiming. However, the problems were simple and the results were predictable. Although learning that task with a perceptron was somewhat unnecessary, it remains a good example to demonstrate online learning. It also provides a unique way of learning to cope with complex errors; in this case, an analytical approach would have been more difficult.

The target-selection behavior provided a great example of applying a neural network. The learning component itself is not particularly effective, reaching 25 percent error in many cases. However, the behaviors are realistic and the system benefits from the experience of the perceptron (thanks to the quality of the design). This reveals the kind of problem to which neural networks should be applied: ones that don't require too much precision and where the learning can only improve the model. In this case, the generation mechanism allowed realistic results regardless of the neural network's performance.

Techniques

The first technique used was based on physics. Although other solutions with predictive capabilities could be used, the hard-coded approach turned out to be the base of the other tasks. To reiterate, it's fine to use "standard" programming to solve problems when necessary. After all, a significant proportion of the system is always customized anyway. Trying to apply modern AI techniques to each problem will slow progress.

Another technique we used was neural networks. Whenever possible, we should try to use the single-layer perceptron. They are limited, but they have far fewer issues. (For instance, they are easy to understand and always provide the best approximation.)

Multilayer perceptrons are very good at solving problems, as long as they are applied correctly. Data preparation, feature selection, and topological choices are all parameters that the AI engineer has control of, so these neural networks can be applied to anything. However, this level of control leaves room for the solution to go wrong, and it can be hard to find problems in game AI that actually *need* multilayer perceptrons.

Outlook

Throughout the rest of this book, there are many opportunities to apply neural networks. They can be applied to most pattern-recognition or function-approximation problems. They'll be particularly welcome as an exercise in Part VII, because they prove to be a convenient way to approximate experience learned about the problem.

Part IV builds on the shooting capabilities of the animats. By learning the success rate of different weapons in various situations, it's possible to estimate the best weapon to use in the current scenario. Such weapon selection plays to the strengths of the weapon skills of our animats.

The next part also looks into decision trees. They combine similar capabilities of neural networks with regard to pattern recognition, but also provide the readability and intuitiveness of rule-based systems.

Choose Your Weapon

Numerous different scenarios can arise in combat: stealth missions or ambushes, frontal attacks and flanking, mobile warfare and entrenched battles, and so on. When soldiers find themselves in particular situations, they undeniably want the best tools for the job to increase the likelihood of success, or just the chances of survival. This part covers weapon selection, allowing the animats to prepare for each situation. We'll discuss both a voting system created directly by experts, as well as a decision tree that can learn with less supervision.

Motivation

In the previous part, when considering the shooting behaviors alone, higher-level abilities are disregarded completely. The importance of shooting is undeniable; however, tactics can often make the most out of any situation. As a complement to weapon skills, the choice of weapon falls into the category of higher-level strategies. This seems to be the next step in developing a competent animat for deathmatch.

The problem of weapon selection itself is very interesting; it provides a problem where there is more variation within the game. With shooting, often one good behavior works fine regardless of the context. However, for weapon handling, the animat must take more factors into account dynamically. The scope of weapon-selection behaviors is also much larger, taking into account most of the local surroundings. Even though it's not rocket science, the problem of choosing a weapon is certainly an increase in complexity; therefore, this problem seems an ideal next move.

Using learning to deal with weapons reveals interesting trends in the design of the game, or even the AI. For example, we can determine whether weapons are well balanced, and modify the game logic if necessary. In our case, the weapon design is already frozen, so we can identify strengths and weaknesses in the AI and spend more time working on shooting abilities.

Outline

Many of the following chapters extend their counterparts in Part III. Indeed, many of the software, interfaces, and behaviors used in weapon selection partly depend on shooting abilities. We'll make a point of emphasizing higher-level behaviors in the next few pages, relying on the lower-level details of the previous part when necessary.

Chapter 22, "Fighting Conditions." We start by analyzing the platform for the AI. Specifically, the different conditions of the environment that affect the choice of weapons are discussed (that is, layout of the terrain, location of the enemy).

Chapter 23, "Weapon Selection." The understanding phase explains the different methods humans use to make decisions. Specifically, we'll investigate deduction- and experience-based approaches applied to weapon selection.

Chapter 24, "Formalizing Weapon Choice." The interfaces used for choosing weapons can be formalized. This involves extending the inventory interfaces and weapon interfaces.

Chapter 25, "Scripting Tactical Decisions." This chapter is a practical one, using a scripting language to implement such tactical decisions. After covering the basics of scripting, we explain voting systems and how they can be used to solve this decision-making problem. These ideas are implemented with a simple script.

Chapter 26, "Classification and Regression Trees." After identifying a few problems with the scripting solution, we look at the theory behind decision trees—both the classification and regression variants. We show how these are particularly well suited to learning patterns in data to predict unknown values.

Chapter 27, "Learning to Assess Weapons." Decision trees are applied to assess weapons, learning from experience how well weapons perform in the game. We notice the importance of having highly plausible errors, and identify the additional code required to collect the data and compute the training pattern.

Chapter 28, "Understanding the Solution." Finally, we cover a lesson about knowing the solution in general, and thereby gain an understanding the complexity of the solution in theory and practice. These concepts provide developers with more control over the AI techniques during the application phase.

Assumptions

Naturally, all the software used so far is required for weapon selection. The essential parts are as follows:

➤ We need **animats capable of shooting.** They don't need to have perfect behaviors; in fact, any kind of aiming mistakes will make this part more interesting.

➤ The **support for multiple weapons** in the game is an absolute necessity for weapon selection! As usual, this needs to be handled by the game engine.

➤ We assume that the environment has a **wide diversity of locations** that lead to many different combat situations.

Now we're finally ready to get involved with the design of the AI, starting with the first analytical stages of the development. Be sure to visit the web site at http:// AiGameDev.com/ for the digital complements to each chapter.

Chapter 22

Fighting Conditions

KEY TOPICS

- Weapon Properties
- Applicability of Weapons
- Training Zone

Games are often designed to provide a diverse experience for the player. When it comes down to first-person shooters, diversity implies myriad combat situations. Implicitly, each of these situations may suit different weapons. The next few pages investigate how the different elements of the design come together to influence the task of weapon selection.

This chapter has much in common with its counterpart in Chapter 13, "Combat Settings," introducing the low-level details about combat with a particular slant toward shooting capabilities. The next few pages only emphasize and expand the concepts appropriate for weapon selection.

This chapter covers the following topics:

➤ The different attributes of weapons (for instance, projectile speed and rate of fire), showing how they affect the weapon's behavior

➤ The different aspects of the design and simulation that affect the applicability of weapons

➤ An ideal test bed that we can use later

The information in this chapter will help us analyze the role of the platform (that is, the environment and engine) for the AI and understand how it must be taken into account in the later stages of the development.

Weapon Properties

The variety of weaponry goes way beyond of the two classes that we identified in the previous part, namely *melee* and *range* weapons. Both of these categories are refined according to many parameters, affecting the precision of the weapon, types of ammunition, speed of fire, reload times, and so on. Some of these properties are explicitly designed (for instance, bullet speed), whereas others are indirect consequences (for instance, damage per second).

All these different properties implicitly affect the behavior of the weapon itself. For example, a heavy-contact weapon is likely to be very damaging but also slow to maneuver. A light-projectile weapon will often not carry much ammunition, and have a slower firing rate (for instance, a handgun or crossbow). The capability to inflict damage in different ways is an indirect consequence of these weapon properties. Table 22.1 shows some commonly known properties of weapons in computer games, along with their unit of measurement. The properties in italic are consequences of other properties and can be computed indirectly.

Table 22.1   Some Commonly Known Properties of Weapons in Computer Games, Along with Their Unit of Measurement

Property	Unit
Projectile speed	Meters per second
Rate of fire	Seconds per shots
Damage	Health units per shot
Spread angle	Degrees
Damage rate	Health units per second

Because of these different attributes, each weapon will usually perform the same task in a very different fashion. For example, a rocket launcher can take out a tank in a destructive fashion, whereas a small grenade can deal only with the crew onboard. Both accomplish the same goal of disabling the vehicle, but in different manners because of their properties.

In computer games, the contrast between weapons is amplified by the creativity of the designers; in a game world, technological and physical constraints are secondary to entertainment value. Freezeguns or portable railguns may not be far away, but still remain science fiction. Game developers have the freedom to include them in the design. Therefore, the spectrum of possible weapon properties is much wider, which obviously means more variety in the weapon behavior (and even more ways to accomplish the task).

Applicability of Weapons

Certain weapons are suited to different situations. Although ubiquitous weapons have been developed to handle many of these combat situations, it's often the case that different weapons perform better in particular situations. As the saying goes, an infinite number of monkeys with rocket launchers will have more success in some cases. This is because of aspects of the design combining implicitly via the game simulation. Weapons are therefore variably effective, mostly regardless of the player's abilities.

Situation of Participants

The disposition of players in space is one of the most important factors on the applicability of a weapon. Clearly, the relative position of the enemy affects the efficiency of any particular weapon (depending on its precision).

When the battle is up close and personal, a weapon requiring high precision with a low firing rate will not prove too efficient. Conversely, a weapon that can spit out bullets at a fast rate will have the advantage, even if it is less accurate.

For long distances, projectile weapons with high damage may be preferred, rather than a multitude of smaller ones. Fast-traveling projectiles may also have an advantage, because they are generally more accurate on moving targets (reaching the destination quicker).

Figure 22.1 shows the effectiveness of the super shotgun and railgun. The spread of the super shotgun makes it suitable for very close fights, whereas the railgun is equally effective at a distance.

These are two of many examples showing the importance of distance—and the position generally—in the equation. To a lesser extent, factors such as relative height and orientation to the target also affect the effectiveness of a weapon.

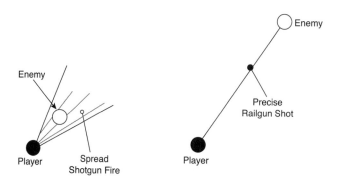

Figure 22.1   Demonstrating the effectiveness of the super shotgun and the railgun at different distances.

Fight Progression

The dynamic nature of the fight can also have an impact on the effectiveness of a weapon. This includes the relative movement of the players as well as the evolution of the fight over time. Stages of engagement (for instance, observation, opening fire, retaliation, and full exchanges) and changes in dominance are some examples.

When the player is trying to ambush another, the most effective weapon is a powerful one—capable of delivering a lethal blow without the opponent being able to react. On the other hand, when a player is running around expecting to be ambushed, or suddenly ending up face to face with the enemy, a weapon allowing fast retaliation will be instantly effective.

When a player is fleeing, a weapon with rapid fire ensures that pressure is kept on the attacker. The person playing the predator will want to finish off the prey as soon as possible using big and clumsy weapons, although this example depends more on player style.

Player and Enemy Status

Different targets may be variably receptive to weapons. For example, an electromagnetic shield may successfully block electromagnetic pulses, but have no protective effect against the good old axe. To this extent, the effectiveness of a weapon depends on the state of the opponent's weapon, and how they are equipped to reduce damage.

On the other hand, personal modifiers can enhance the damage inflicted. This isn't so much applicable in real life, but things such as *quad-damage* (the enemy suffers four times the damage) and *haste* (the rate of fire is accelerated) can have a dramatic impact on the gameplay. Selecting a powerful weapon and one with rapid fire (respectively) will generally pay off.

In some cases, the applicability of weapons is independent from power-ups, but instead influenced by other state variables. For example, a player with low health will be more desperate and keen to inflict much damage in the short term. Conversely, a well-armed and protected player may have more freedom of choice, and the luxury to take a less-effective weapon (but with higher consistency).

Finally, other little details about the state have an important effect on the benefit of changing weapons. The warning of low ammunition is a strong factor, because changing weapons before the fight will save valuable firing time during the fight. Similarly, if a player has just changed weapons, even if there are compelling reasons to switch again, the benefits will be lessened; more time will pass before a shot can be fired.

Environment Layout

The environment itself influences the effectiveness of a weapon. Because weapon-selection behavior operates on a broader scale than shooting skills, the layout of the environment is much more important to them. Specifically, the AI needs to take into account the effect of the environment on itself, the enemy, and the weapons—in the medium-term future.

Factors such as the openness of the terrain or its closed nature will have a huge effect on the value of a weapon. These characteristics of indoor and outdoor environments invite different weapons.

For example, some obstacles may impede the trajectory of projectiles, making them less effective. On the other hand, the layout of the terrain can also constrain the splash damage and cause the player to suffer more harm.

Secondary properties of the world such as contraptions (for instance, ladders and platforms) or detail (for instance, foliage or cluttering objects) also determine how efficient weapons are. As game players, we can understand these properties of the environment. We'll have to make sure the AI can acquire or learn this information.

Figure 22.2 shows an example. Note in the figure that players standing near walls are more likely to get hit indirectly. The floor can also be a risk for the same reason, but is not taken into account in these top-down views.

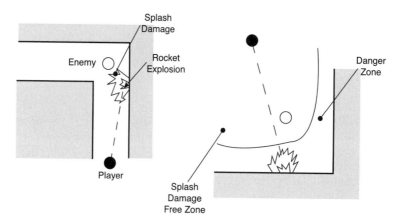

Figure 22.2   Example of the importance of radius (or splash) damage.

Arms Race

Of all the different weapon properties discussed, some can be identified as weaknesses (for instance, slow to reload, slow projectile). It's safe to say that no weapon is perfect. For entertainment value, the design emphasizes the different properties of the weapons (for instance, speed or power). This implies that strengths and weaknesses are also enhanced.

An implicit consequence of this is weapon balance. Vulnerabilities can be emphasized by complementary properties of another weapon. This implies one weapon will be particularly suited to counter another.

Player Skill

So far, the criteria for the applicability of weapons have been implicit consequences of the design. However, the players themselves have an important role in determining the effectiveness of a weapon. This is the link with the previous part, focusing on weapon skill.

A player with bad weapon skills will not have the option of using it efficiently. On the other hand, good shooting abilities will open up additional options for the weapon selection. All the other conditions will kick in to determine the effectiveness of the weapons (for instance, restrictions of the environment, state of the player, and so on).

Training Zone

Given all these factors that influence the weapon selection, we need to agree on a terrain that will be representative of the ones we're interested in, and that will allow easy development of the AI.

We need a terrain where a lot of ammunition and weaponry are available. This will enable us to not cheat by giving the bots all the weapons to play with. More than just a principle, this has the advantage of forcing the bots to use all the weapons (as they pick them up).

Alternatively, we could enforce the use of specific weapons during different stages of the game. This would allow the animats to get to grips with each of the weapons without any bias. Either option seems feasible for learning about all the weapons, so we can use whichever approach suits our training zone best.

Ideally, when developing the AI, we would also like as many scenarios as possible occur. This is also for the sake of diversity. Most game levels will have a good blend of architectural styles. However, we should not feel limited to any one level during the development. This will allow the animats to acquire the most experience with the weapons.

Summary

In this chapter, we've briefly covered most of the aspects of the game design that affect weapon selection (implicitly). As discussed, some assumptions will influence the specification:

➤ Weapons have certain properties such as projectile speed and reload times.

➤ The various weapons behave differently when performing similar tasks.

Some environmental restrictions also affect the weapon-selection process:

➤ Aspects of the environment's design combine together to determine the applicability of a weapon (for instance, obstacles).

➤ There are characteristics of the combat itself that make particular weapons suitable (for instance, distance and movement).

➤ The skill of the players is an important restriction on the effectiveness of weapons.

Finally, we drafted some guidelines to assist the testing and experimentation:

➤ We need to maximize the variety of weapon use—either explicitly or not (for instance, good weapon availability).

➤ It's important to emphasize the diversity of terrains by using many different levels.

The next chapter investigates the problem of decision making and how human players perform the task.

Practical Demo

The demo animat is known as *Mr. Versatility*—partly as an example of the ideas in this chapter, and partly as an extension of the capabilities of the previous part. *Mr. Versatility* is capable of using all the weapons in the game, and has shooting skills for each of them. Most importantly, a description of the AI architecture is available online at `http://AiGameDev.com/` along with the source code and demo, as usual.

Chapter 23

Weapon Selection

KEY TOPICS

- Appealing Choices
- Evaluation Process in Practice
- Criteria for Weapon Selection
- Case Study

Selecting the best weapon is a matter of decision making. The preceding chapter covered all the information that is taken into account in the process. This chapter analyzes the role of decision making and how it can be achieved, specifically in the context of weapon selection. Notably, we'll discover how the benefit of a weapon can be determined from properties of the situation and attributes of the weapon.

This chapter covers the following topics:

➤ A theoretical approach to decision making, covering the evaluation of weapons and the methodology for picking them

➤ Two opposite solutions to this problem in practice (deduction and experience), and how the human approach to decision making is balanced between these two extremes

➤ The criteria used to evaluate the weapon-selection behaviors of animats

➤ A brief case study that describes the expected reactions in different situations

By the end of this chapter, the foundations will be set for solving the problem of weapon selection using AI techniques. In fact, the following pages describe a variety of different implementations.

Appealing Choices

Weapon selection is about choosing the most appropriate weapon for the job. This much is obvious, but it raises two questions: How do you define "appropriate," and how do you pick the best weapon? Let's elaborate on these issues in turn, looking at the concepts at the base of the problem.

A Theory for Weapon Evaluation

First, we need to understand how the properties of the environment are taken into account, and then discuss the essence of weapon evaluation.

Features and Criteria

As discussed in the preceding chapter, many features of the environment, enemy player, or spatial configuration can be taken into account. These features can be modeled as a set of features $[f_1, f_2, \ldots f_n]$, either symbols or numeric values (that is, heterogeneous).

Each person may have different goals and motivations, so these features will be taken into account differently according to a set of criteria $[c_1, c_2, \ldots c_m]$. For example, these may represent the desire to limit self-injury, inflict maximum damage, or alert the enemy. For those players with better skills, criteria can correspond to other measurable benefits, such as minimizing fight time and judicious use of ammo.

In games, players may increasingly select weapons for entertainment purposes, or to encourage diversity in the gameplay. As such, the set criteria may include different goals in practice, but these can be applied in the same fashion—theoretically speaking.

Weapon Fitness

Whether a complex system of desires and motivations drives the selection process, or a unique goal instead, the problem can be simplified to a fundamental level. All the details about the situation, the state of the player, or even the properties of the weapon can be abstracted out.

Only a single number is needed to indicate the benefit of weapon; in the current situation, how good is this weapon? This is a single continuous value, which we'll call the *fitness* of a weapon.

The process of determining the applicability of a weapon can be seen as a *fitness function*. The idea is that an unknown function encodes all the decision criteria or features that are taken into account in the decision. This function *f* can be applied to each weapon considered as a choice, resulting in a scalar value *k* (not necessarily limited to a discrete range):

$$f(w) = k$$

In the case of weapon selection, the scalar value *k* would indicate how "fit" the weapon $w \in W$ is (on any scale). For a simple game, the set of all weapons may be defined as W = {rocket launcher, chaingun, blaster}. The fitness function can be can be modeled formally, expressing the mapping from the set of weapons W to the set of real numbers $\mathbb{R}$:

$$f: W \rightarrow \mathbb{R}$$

By understanding the features and criteria, the problem can be modeled in more detail. Specifically, instead of seeing *f* as a mystery function, we can express it in terms of the features and criteria:

$$g:[f_1,f_2,\ldots,f_n]\times[c_1,c_2,\ldots,c_m]\rightarrow(W\rightarrow\mathbb{R})$$

This equation describes a function g, which can map the features and criteria onto another function (denoted $W\rightarrow\mathbb{R}$). For future reference, this is the notation used in *functional programming*, a type of language that allows functions to return functions. Essentially in this case, it's possible to build a fitness function for evaluating weapons from sets of criteria and features.

These criteria can be taken into account in different ways, some more intricate than others. For example, a linear model is probably the simplest: 65 percent f_1 and 35 percent c_2. This corresponds to weighted contributions in the final fitness value. Nonlinear functions would be more appropriate, allowing criteria to rank the importance of features.

Selection Methodology

The concept of fitness to allow weapons to be selected is this: If someone makes a decision to pick a weapon *w*, and claims it's his best choice, the weapon will certainly maximize some unknown fitness function f (that is, w has the largest value of k). All weapons x ($\forall x$) except w ($x \in W - \{w\}$) would presumably have lower fitness:

$$\forall x \quad f(x) \leq f(w) \quad x \in W - \{w\}$$

So, a considered decision would go through all the choices and compare their fitness—explicitly ranking them. By discarding the worst option at each comparison, the best choice will remain in the end. This is an expensive procedure of complexity $O(n)$; the AI needs n comparisons to guarantee it has the best choice.

When humans make a choice, they go through a similar process, although often not consciously. It's rarely important, and the process is rushed for practical reasons (for instance, picking vegetables at the store).

It seems obvious that the essence of the decision lies in the unknown fitness function, which evaluates the benefit of each alternative. Some understanding of the animat's motives is needed to design the AI; therefore, a fitness function can be implemented, which is used to evaluate a decision. This is the tricky part; the rest is just methodology.

Evaluation Process in Practice

The process of choosing is mostly based on evaluating the benefit of an object. The theory behind evaluating fitness values has already been considered. However, things are much different in practice. Providing a good estimate of fitness for any object is extremely difficult.

Fundamentally, the process is about mapping features onto possible choices according to criteria. To make this easier, humans use two different techniques: one based on logical reasoning, and the other based on experience.

Deduction

It's certainly possible to perform critical analysis of any situation. This process breaks down the decision into smaller parts that can be understood easily.

The first step of this process involves extracting key features of the situation (for instance, low health, constrained environment, and being chased). From these facts, it is possible to induce what weapon properties are necessary. This requires a simple form of knowledge in the form of statements (for instance, if being chased, use a weapon with a fast firing rate)—very similar to the production rules covered in Chapter 11, "Rule-Based Systems." Finally, it's possible to select the most suitable weapon by finding one that matches the induced properties.

This approach assumes that it's possible to model this knowledge and decision process. It certainly is feasible to do so in many cases, although it's questionable whether humans do. When applying the rigorous method, we can only take into account features that we are aware of. It's quite easy to overlook secondary features and criteria when evaluating a choice! Often, a simpler empirical approach is favored.

Experience

Humans have the gift of memory, which can save them from countless deliberations. With memory, the history of fights can be drawn upon to estimate the benefits of weapons; "I was shot from behind last time here, I have a bad feeling … I'll prepare my weapon for ambush!"

Certainly, when using an approach based on experience, it is essential to have history in combat—at least if the decisions are expected to be any good! This is where games (and simulations generally) have the advantage; it's possible for players to run through different scenarios quickly, without running as many risks. So, with simulation, it's eventually feasible to try every scenario. For each specific situation, it's possible to know how well the weapon performs.

Humans can get close to this kind of knowledge by sharing their experience with each other and training extensively. Therefore, this approach is highly applicable to people as well.

Even if the outcome of individual situations is unpredictable, with experience, it's possible to extract a trend from the outcome (like gathering statistics). This is sufficient to estimate the effectiveness of a weapon.

Hybrid Approaches

Both alternatives—whether based on deduction or experience—have their advantages and disadvantages. The first uses heavy reasoning based on simple knowledge, whereas the second uses no reasoning but assumes extensive experience. Both approaches prove useful, but an option somewhere down the middle may be more applicable.

Humans use a combination of reasoning and experience. Using past experience improves the estimates, whereas deduction enables us to apply the knowledge to new situations; "I won the duel in a similar situation with this weapon, so I'll try it again."

There is a clever balance in gathering knowledge by experience, and using logical reasoning to manipulate this knowledge further. Such a compromise is beneficial for simulations, too, because there is a trade-off between the time needed to acquire data and the accuracy of the estimates.

Criteria for Weapon Selection

There are two ways of selecting weapons in common first-person shooters; the players can select their weapons before the game starts, and during the game, they get the opportunity to switch weapons. The theory is similar for both scenarios, but we'll cover the harder option of in-game weapon selection.

Two essential qualities are expected from the weapon-selection behavior, both contributing to the illusion of realism.

Decisiveness

Humans can make many wrong choices during combat. Even if the weapon selection isn't ideal, however, a human player will generally stick with it. The last thing we want from the AI is to repeatedly change weapons, thinking it would provide slightly more optimization.

Changing weapons is quite visible externally, because the weapon is visible. One also really notices the *change of projectiles* more than anything. If the weapon selection is not working well, it will be noticed almost immediately from a distance. This really needs attention to maintain the illusion of realism.

Justifiability

What is a justifiable weapon choice? It seems intuitive but the concept is difficult to express formally. Ideally, we want human players to empathize with the AI and approve its decision.

This is essential to maintain the illusion of intelligence. It's a safe choice if the player can claim, "He had no other weapons, so he used the machine gun," or, "She used the blaster to fool me into believing she was out of ammo!" With the AI being constantly under focus, there is very little leeway. With one stupid decision (for instance, using an axe at a distance), or an exotic one, the credibility is lost. Advanced tactics can also attract unnecessary attention, so keeping it "standard" can help.

Case Study

Look at the kind of weapons that are expected to be used at various ranges:

➤ At **long distance**, precise weapons are preferred because they increase the likelihood of hitting the target (for instance, a railgun).

➤ At **medium range**, projectiles with high splash damage should be used to increase indirect damage (for instance, a rocket launcher).

➤ At **close distance** scrappy fights, weapons with a high spread of fast projectiles may be used (for instance, a chaingun or hyperblaster).

The flow of control during the fight is also likely to affect the weapon selection. Notably, powerful weapons could be used when the NPC is desperate, and a more precise weapon when the player is in control.

Weapon changes should to be limited to just five seconds during combat (approximately), but with fewer restrictions when wandering around.

Summary

This chapter started by discussing the theory behind weapon selection:

➤ The fitness of weapons is determined by mapping features and criteria onto a single value.

➤ By comparing the fitness, we get an indication of the best weapons.

In practice, two fundamental ways to evaluate the weapons prove effective, and humans use a combination of the two:

➤ Deduction uses existing facts to come to a conclusion about a weapon. Deductive reasoning can be used to extract better trends from experience.

➤ Experience learns about the benefits of weapons in each situation.

Any of these three approaches may be used by the AI, as long as the approach fulfils its expectations, which we covered toward the end of this chapter:

➤ As high-level criteria for the evaluation, we expect the behaviors to be justifiable and decisive.

➤ The problem definition itself consists of a recommendation for types of weapons in certain situations, as well as restrictions.

The next chapter specifies the world interface used by the animats to perform weapon selection by interacting with their environment.

Practical Demo

A simple implementation of the selection method demonstrates the ideas in this chapter. The animat named *Joyce* has a weapon-selection component in the architecture. When called, this component scans through all the possible weapons and calls an unknown evaluation function to compute their fitness. The evaluation is done with a rule-based system, transparently from the weapon selection, and returns the best weapon. The demo and source for *Joyce* is available online at `http://AiGameDev.com/`.

Chapter 24

Formalizing Weapon Choice

KEY TOPICS

- Sketching Possible Options

- Rationalizing

- Proposal

Having analyzed the software platform and developed a good understanding of the problem of weapon selection, the specification of the world interface can now be established. Additional information from the environment is required for the task of weapon selection, but many of the existing interfaces can be reused.

This chapter covers the following topics:

➤ Options to model the inputs, outputs, and context of the problem

➤ How to make the final decision

➤ Using data types to formalize the chosen option and the functionality of each interface function

At the end of this chapter, the animats will be capable of handling weapon selection, thanks to extended interfaces.

Sketching Possible Options

This chapter complements the work done to specify the weapon handling in the previous part. Although both relate to combat, Chapter 15, "Shooting, Formally," focused on aiming and firing, whereas this part focuses on weapon selection. Some overlap certainly exists in the specification, so incompatibilities must be reduced by reusing the existing model wherever possible.

The next few pages discuss the three aspects of the task that need to be specified: the inputs (that is, information required), the outputs (that is, possible actions), and the context (implicit variables that affect the problem).

Context

The weapon model is the most important aspect of the context. How detailed must the design of each weapon be for the artificial intelligence (AI) to be able to choose one? Once again, instead of exposing the complexity of the 3D model to the AI, a more abstract alternative is suitable: The weapon is considered as a symbol.

The most straightforward approach is to represent the weapon *type* as a symbol. The AI would include references such as "machine gun," or "rocket launcher." Using the type of weapons is generally not a problem in first-person shooters; either the inventories contain only one weapon of each type, or it doesn't matter which instance is used.

This is unlikely to be a problem, but it's easy to disambiguate them; each weapon instance can have a distinct symbol, such as "blaster1" and "blaster2." This may be appropriate in role-playing games, where the inventory is more important.

When using this symbolic approach to deal with the weapons, the 3D models will still be animated. A lower layer is relied upon to translate from our abstract representation (that is, perform gestures). This is done commonly when human players request weapon changes, too.

Senses

Three different aspects of the environment are required to select weapons, each with multiple possible models.

Environment

When selecting a weapon instead of just shooting, more information is required about the situation. Indeed, only localized terrain information is required when predicting movement, because the direction of travel is usually obvious. This means it's possible to focus on a small part of the environment. Weapon selection is a higher-level process; the decision lasts longer and has repercussions on the shooting behavior. To this extent, a broader view of the environment is required.

As well as the line-of-sight queries used to create the shooting capability, properties such as spatial constriction (that is, how much room there is to maneuver) around the player and the enemy are important factors. Letting the AI know these important factors will allow it to make more informed decisions.

To model the interface, we can use a direct approach, offering a function such as `GetSpatialRestriction()` to the animats. This function would return a high value for highly restricted areas, and a lower value in open environments. Alternatively, the result of the function could be simpler to understand as the average distance to an obstacle.

In contrast, we could let the animat sense the spatial restriction using visual queries: Line sensors can already return distances (like precise lasers). Estimating the amount of restriction may be less efficient using line traces, so a hybrid combination with the previous high-level approach may be more appropriate.

Player State

The personal state is more obvious to handle. All we need is a query for health, armor, and the current weapon. This information is typically displayed to the human player by a head-up display (HUD), so it's readily available in the engine for the AI to query.

However, it isn't as easy to determine the health of enemies (or at least shouldn't be). Conceptually, directly querying information about other players violates the principles of embodiment; most players would call it "cheating." As game AI developers, the interest in embodiment is due to the emergent behaviors and weapon decisions that arise from not knowing the enemy's state.

It is possible to monitor the state of other players in various indirect ways, some of which benefit from being biologically plausible. One of the simplest, and arguably the most efficient, is an event-driven approach. When a projectile is fired, the players nearby perceive a sound. Therefore, the animat knows which weapon the enemy used. Likewise, when a sound of pain is emitted or blood splashes, the event can be used to decrease the health estimate.

It's also interesting to note that an animat keeping track of the enemy's state needs internal variables and is no longer truly reactive—although sensing and acting upon personal state is still reactive. Although this is not a problem because simple enemy models are easily dealt with, it's still important to be aware of this.

Weapon Properties

The properties of a weapon (for instance, reload times and firing rate) can be used in the decision, too. There are three different ways of handling them:

➤ **Declarative**—Each of the characteristics of the weapons can be stored as a set of rules and accessed by the brain of the animat. The benefit is separation of data and code. The rules used by the AI may be independent from the game logic, although the AI often benefits from having accurate facts.

➤ **Implicit**—The easiest way to handle the properties of a weapon (from the specification's point of view) is not to mention them. Each weapon property has an implicit effect on the environment, so each property can be induced relatively easily (for instance, monitoring weapon readiness as the reload time and counting projectiles per second as the rate of fire).

➤ **Query**—Finally, a dedicated interface to the game logic could be devised, which returns the precise weapon properties at runtime.

If any, human players use the implicit approach, because they are rarely told about weapon statistics before the game (or they don't pay attention). Humans can learn the behavior of weapons with practice.

Actions

An interface is necessary to apply the weapon choice. Specifically, the weapon must be ready to use soon after the decision is executed.

The action for selecting a weapon can be a direct selection, using only one procedure call. The model is similar to human players pressing the keys bound to specific weapons (usually the number keys on the top row).

Alternatively, weapons can be selected by cycling through all the items in the inventory. This is a sequence of commands, analogous to using the mouse wheel to select weapons. The advantage is that no direct knowledge of the current weapons is needed; the AI can just cycle through the current inventory, regardless of its content.

Rationalizing

Before scanning through each of these sketches to find the right specification, we need to identify its objectives!

Deciding Factors

Modeling the actions seems relatively straightforward, although the sensors may prove more challenging. We need to adhere to two main principles for this specification—somewhat different to the previous ones:

➤ **Compatibility**—The interfaces need to remain compatible with all the previous ones. All the extensions should ideally be consistent (for instance, with regard to information and format).

➤ **Simplicity**—Conceptually, the interface is actually not too complex, although the implementation needed to gather the information may be more of a challenge. We would like to keep the AI simple regardless of this.

As well as adhering to these two principles, we also must formalize the assumptions of the game engine.

Assumptions

As usual, the AI assumes that a lower level is handling the animation. This will take care of selecting the appropriate keyframe cycle for the weapon preparation. After the weapon has been selected, a short delay may occur before the weapon is available for use. This delay corresponds to the time needed to find and prepare the weapon. However, the AI can assume that after the weapon has been selected, it will always become available automatically, with an acceptable delay. This same policy applies to human players.

Proposed Specification

The more abstract approach is preferred, modeling the weapon as a symbol. A lower-level approach exposing a detailed model to the AI would be unnecessary and complex to handle. It would be trivial to use static definitions (such as a C++ enum) to inform the AI about the types of weapons at compile time. However, this enumeration approach implies the AI is dependent on the engine's implementation. Instead, we'll define symbols that are numerically independent for each of the ten weapons.

We can let the AI know about the weapons available through a specific function of a new inventory interface. This could be extended for generic use later, but leaving the weapon queries separate seems more appropriate—both for the AI and the implementation of the back-end of the interface. The properties (for instance, speed and reload times) of the weapon will not be exposed by a runtime interface; this information has to be innate to the animats (provided by design) or induced online.

Maintaining consistency with the interface for human players also seems worthwhile because it reduces the code required. Players press a key or move the mouse wheel to select a weapon. Cycling through the weapons could be supported by the interface specification indirectly, but direct selection will prove sufficient for the AI.

As for the terrain layout, a high-level query returns a single value as an indication of constriction. This can transparently be implemented using the existing line traces to determine the average distance of nearby obstacles. A more elaborate implementation would cache the resulting values in a spatial data structure so that it does have to be computed every time.

Interfaces

All that's needed in the *weapon* interface is the capability to execute the decision. This is done via one additional function that takes a symbol and returns a Boolean indication of success:

```
bool Select(const Symbol& weapon);
```

Ideally, an inventory is necessary to determine which weapons the animat can use. The *personal* interface can be extended to support other inventory items, but keeping this separate is more convenient:

```
void WeaponsAvailable(vector<Symbol>& weapons);
```

To query the animat's health, we'll use a simple extension to the personal interface:

```
int Health();
```

A visual query to determine the level of constriction of the surroundings is also necessary for weapon selection. A high-level query was chosen, easily integrated into the *vision* interface—allowing it to be implemented within the engine. This function could be kept separate if the implementation needs to be extended:

```
float GetSpatialRestriction();
```

This function returns the average distance to an obstacle in any direction from the current position.

Finally, the AI needs a way to determine the amount of damage taken by other players. This takes the shape of an event callback:

```
void OnDamage( const Event_Damage& e );
```

The event itself will contain information about the location, an estimate of the amount of damage, and, potentially, a symbol for the player who took damage.

Code Skeleton

So, putting all these different bits together, we get a rough outline of what we need to do to implement our animats:

```
void Think()
{
        // determine what weapons are available
        vector<Symbol>& weapons;
        personal->WeaponsAvailable( weapons );

        // extract properties from the situation
        float f = vision->SpatialRestriction();
        int h = personal->Health();

        // make the weapon decision
        weapon->Select( weapons[i] );
}
```

The callback `OnDamage()` must be a separate function for C++ function pointers to be usable. The rest of the code will be split, too, but this is a stylistic issue (not a requirement).

Summary

This chapter discussed the interaction between the weapon-selection capability and the game engine, used to gather information and perform the weapon changes:

➤ The weapons are modeled as symbols; their properties need to be learned or included into the AI.

➤ The interfaces with the environment are extended to provide queries for spatial restriction.

➤ Queries to the personal state and inventory are also provided, allowing the animat to determine health and weapons available.

➤ Information about enemy damage is handled indirectly, thanks to callbacks and events sent by the environment.

➤ All the interfaces were chosen to be compatible with the existing ones and are simple to use.

The next chapter provides a simple prototype for weapon selection using scripting facilities and a voting system.

Practical Demo

Sir Obvious is an animat that makes use of the interfaces defined in this chapter. It checks the inventory to find the weapons and corresponding ammo available and prints the result to a debug console. Health changes and the constriction of the terrain are also worthy of *Sir Obvious*'s comments. The source and demo is available online at `http://AiGameDev.com/`.

Chapter 25

Scripting Tactical Decisions

The previous chapters prepared the way for a preliminary implementation by analyzing the platform, defining (providing an understanding of) the problem, and providing a specification to interact with the world. The first prototype performs weapon selection using a voting system, implemented in a scripting language.

This chapter covers the following topics:

➤ An overview of scripting languages, from a very high-level point of view. The focus is drawn to the advantages of scripting as an essential tool in our reactive architectures, complementing the generic AI techniques discussed throughout this book. This discussion covers typical features of scripting environments, the languages, and how scripts can be considered as other components in the AI system.

➤ The principles behind voting systems, notably how they can achieve weapon selection. A script is used to implement the voting system.

➤ An evaluation of the system, and a description of the experimentation procedure used to set up the voting system in practice. Some of the problems with adjusting votes are resolved by suggesting a learning approach.

At the end of this chapter, the strengths and weaknesses with scripted voting systems will be more obvious, particularly as a solution to weapon selection. Analysis points in the direction of hybrid approaches, including a learning component, will be discussed. But first, let's take a deeper look at scripting languages in game AI.

Foundations in Scripting

Although scripting is not a product of AI research, it's certainly very commonly used in AI—and particularly in computer games. The need for convenient scripting languages extends beyond traditional game AI approaches; scripting will not die out as AI improves; it will serve a different purpose (other than behaviors). Systems with modern AI techniques benefit from scripting languages providing the glue between basic components.

This section briefly covers scripting languages, without focusing on any one solution in particular. Much of the lower-level details of each language (for instance, Python or Lua) can be found in their thorough documentation.

Scripting Languages

Scripts are generally much simpler to write than standard programs. Thanks to loosely typed—or even typeless—syntax (variable types do not always need to be declared explicitly), more flexibility is immediately available to the programmer. Scripting languages also benefit from dynamic typing; the type-checking only happens during execution of the instructions. For these reasons, fewer lines are generally required to implement the same algorithms.

Scripting languages are often ideal complements to standard programming languages. For example, C++ is a compile-time, statically typed language that offers the *potential* for amazing performance. Scripting languages are usually interpreted at runtime and dynamically typed, implying they are very flexible, albeit slower. Scripts allow easy modification and reduce the need for compiling and hard-linked code (builds are expensive), customization is much easier, and prototyping is faster.

Script Environments

The major advantage of scripts is that they can be loaded and executed at runtime without a *separate* compilation phase. There generally is a compilation phase, but this is often done dynamically—at the same time the script is loaded. For efficiency, the precompiled code can often be saved for later as bytecode (that is, sequences of instructions as platform-independent binary code).

Then, the bytecode is processed thanks to an *interpreter*, or virtual machine. The interpreter executes each of the statements in the script as operations (for instance, to modify variables, or call core functions). This results in the capability of scripts to provide the same functionality as normal programs.

The scripting environment is the area of memory where all the necessary variables reside, as well as each of the functions defined by the script. This is the core of the scripting system, and the main part of the code required to support the scripting language.

Integration as a Component

Most other AI techniques can be considered as black box components with well-defined interfaces exposing their functionality. Scripting environments are no different. This is one of the reasons we can provide a high-level overview without going into any details of specific languages.

Integrating the scripting environment into the application is called *embedding* it. Conversely, integrating the native language into a scripting environment is known as *extending* it. After that's done, the AI engine has the capability to load and run any script, combined with native code. There are two ways to weave these scripts into the architecture, described in the next two sections.

Exporting Interfaces

Components higher up in the architecture hierarchy that include the scripting language often need to interact with it. Just like other AI components, this is done by exporting interfaces. Third-party components can then easily call the underlying functions.

Using a high-level interface, it's possible to pass all the data to the script before it runs. This means the script is fully isolated, and can only deal with the information it is provided. In Figure 25.1, on the left, only a high-level interface is exported, allowing the parent component to interact with the script. On the right, the scripting environment imports the input and output interfaces, so the script can interact directly with the world.

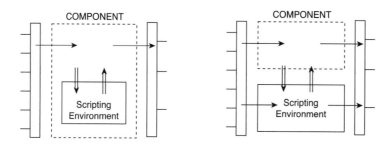

Figure 25.1 Integrating the scripting environment with the AI architecture.

Importing Interfaces

On the other hand, the scripting module can also import interfaces from other components. This allows scripts to gather the data themselves, without relying on being passed information.

Conceptually, the interface components are nested within the scripting environment, because the script depends on them. In the architecture, the script is a higher level in the hierarchy.

A Scripting Module

The scripting environment can be accessed by an interface that fits into our AI framework. All we really need is the ability to call functions and query the scripting environment. The interface in Listing 25.1 is not directly reflected in the scripts; it merely interacts with the *interpreter*.

Listing 25.1 Simple Python Function to Evaluate the Benefit of Weapons

```
def EvaluateWeapon(type,ammo):
    if ammo > 0:
        if type == "railgun": return 2
        return 1
    return 0
```

Function calls are relatively simple to handle because we can refer to the function by name:

```
bool Run( const string& function );
```

In some cases, parameters are required and the result must be queried (for example, in the Python snippet shown in Listing 25.1). Supporting such arbitrary function prototypes is quite difficult because the interface needs to handle any parameter types. Providing two overloaded functions, `Param` and `Result` achieves this in a flexible fashion; only floating-point numbers are shown here, but integers and strings could be handled just as easily:

```
void Param( const float f );
```

```
void Result( const float& f );
```

Finally, generic functions for querying and modifying the scripting environment are sometimes necessary. These overloaded functions set and retrieve the content of global variables of arbitrary types:

```
void Set( const string& name, const float f );
bool Get( const string& name, const float& f );
```

The process of importing interfaces into the scripting environment is handled differently because there is no need for a runtime interface for this. Instead, this will generally be handled during initialization time. The idea is to convert the existing C++ interfaces (for instance, vision or motion) into Python code, using an automated interface wrapper.

Scripted Weapon Selection

A script handles most of the little details mentioned in the past few chapters (for instance, extracting features, analyzing weapon properties, and dealing with timing). Scripts are very good at providing custom solutions to exotic problems, so this approach makes the most of them. The AI techniques used later in this part (such as decision trees) are great at handling general-purpose solutions to generic problems. The script in this section is not discarded because it can help manage and train the decision tree.

Overview

Along with the scripting approach, the following ideas are used (as discussed in the preceding three chapters):

➤ **Deductive reasoning.** Decisions can be deduced from initial facts. We'll use the properties of weapons (for instance, damage and rate of fire) to select the most appropriate.

➤ **Declarative approach to specify weapon properties.** The AI will know about the firing rates and expected damage.

A voting system determines how to rank each of the properties of the weapons. Essentially, many different features are taken into account, and a vote for the most important weapon property occurs. Then, each weapon is evaluated according to the vote, and the best weapon is returned. This works well because there are often more than two candidates, and most of them are legitimate choices.

This section examines each aspect of the solution in more detail: defining weapon properties, the voting system, collecting the votes, defining the features, and dealing with simple restrictions.

Weapon Properties

A quick search on the World Wide Web saves us the hassle of looking through the game source code for the information about weapons. The following statistics can be found in the *Quake 2* Weapons and Combat FAQ [Quake2FAQ]. The speed of the projectiles had to be found in the *Quake 2* game source code, and are shown in Table 25.1.

Table 25.1 Statistics for Most of the Weapons in Quake 2

Weapon	Rate	Damage	DPS	Speed	Spread
Blaster	0.5	20	40	1000	0
Shotgun	1	48	40	∞	500/500
Super shotgun	1	120	120	∞	500/1000
Machine gun	0.1	8	80	∞	300/500
Chaingun	0.05 and 0.025	6	120 and 240	∞	300/500

Table 25.1 Statistics for Most of the Weapons in Quake 2

Weapon	Rate	Damage	DPS	Speed	Spread
Grenade launcher	1	120*	120	400 to 800	0
Rocket launcher	1.25	120*	96	650	0
Hyperblaster	0.1	20	200	1000	0
Railgun	1.5	100	67	∞	0

The properties of weapons, in the order of Table 25.1, are as follows:

➤ The rate of fire

➤ The damage per shot

➤ Damage per second

➤ Speed of the projectile

➤ Precision

Time units are in seconds, and distances are in *Quake 2* units (18 = 1 step). There is radius damage (marked *) around the explosion points of rockets and grenades, as well as damage for a direct hit. The BFG is not included because it is very random (and rarely used). These properties will be declared in a separate file so that they are easy to modify. The script will include this file so that it can be taken into account in the deductions.

Voting System

Given these facts, the AI must decide how appropriate a weapon is for the current situation. Chapter 23, "Weapon Selection," discussed the concept of a fitness function, combining the features of the current situation with the decision criteria. The result of the fitness function is a single value representing the suitability of a weapon.

Here, the features consist in the layout of the environment, the distance between players, current health, and so forth. The criteria for deciding which weapon to use are actually combinations of these features.

The idea behind a voting system is that the features decide which weapon property they require most, and vote for it (see Figure 25.2). Unlike a democracy, it can be easier to allow more than one vote, and it's even possible to use partial votes (that is, floating-point numbers less than one). The votes are then used to scale the properties of the weapons. Many votes mean that a property is important, so multiply the value by a large number; conversely, few votes mean that the property is not very significant.

$$f(w) = P_i(w)*V_i + P_n(w)*V_n$$

Where $f(w)$ is the fitness of weapon w, $P_i(w)$ is the ith property of that weapon (for instance, speed or damage per shot), and V_i is the total number of votes for that property.

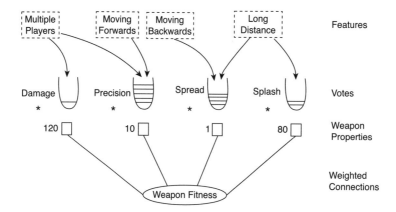

Figure 25.2   Overview of the voting system, with the features contributing to the votes. The votes are multiplied by the weapon property, and the weighted sum determines the fitness of the weapon.

Collecting Votes from Features

The first thing to do is to get an expert to determine the importance of properties in different situations. Before the voting begins, the candidates need to be identified. We'll use all the weapon properties that were listed in Table 25.1, as well as two more:

➤ **Precision** is defined as the opposite of spread.

➤ **Potential** is defined as the maximum damage per shot, but a different weighting is used to make it less important.

As a reminder, the *splash* property is the splash damage, denoted by an asterisk in Table 25.1. The *DPS* property stands for damage per second.

Now, the features of the situation that are involved in the voting must be chosen. Deciding upon these features is a matter of intuition, and their balance no doubt will need to be tweaked during the experimentation phase. As shown in Table 25.2, some features have votes of strength of greater than one, and other features vote for multiple features. The last row is applied independently of any feature, and uses a vote proportional to the ammunition.

Table 25.2   A List of Features Along with Their Corresponding Votes

Feature	Votes
Multiple players	Damage +4
Long distance	Precision +2
Medium distance	DPS +1, precision +1
Short distance	DPS +2
Moving forward	Precision +1
Moving backward	Spread +1
Restricted movement	Splash +3
Ambush mode	Precision +2
Seek mode	Damage +1
Fleeing mode	DPS +1
	Potential +ammo

After all the votes have been collected, they are multiplied by the value of each weapon property. The sum of the weighted properties gives us the final weapon fitness. The weapon with the highest fitness is selected as the best weapon.

Timing Restrictions

We're going to apply a few restrictions to the timing of the weapon selection manually. We'll apply the following two restrictions:

➤ Prevent changing weapons when the last change occurred only a few seconds before.

➤ No weapon switching while firing at the enemies that have ammunition remaining; we wait until they are temporarily out of view, or until they stop firing.

This completes the description of the weapon-selection script. We'll actually implement this in Python because it's the language of preference of the FEAR developers. However, a Lua module and script could easily be substituted.

Practical Demo

There is an animat that demonstrates these principles, known as *Picky*. You can find it on the web site at `http://AiGameDev.com/` under the demos. A small script implements a voting system, used to decide about the best weapon. The script can query the world interfaces directly to gather the necessary information. The selected weapon is returned via a higher-level interface.

Evaluation

The experimentation phase requires a fair amount of tweaking. Both the values of the votes and the weights of the weapon properties need to be adjusted. Both these values could be handled together, because there is no need for weights if the votes are floating-point numbers. But keeping them separate makes it easier to achieve the correct output by incremental adjustment. Therefore, we can consider the votes as integers, worrying only about their relative importance. Then, the weights are tuned independently of the weapon properties.

The experimentation phase involves observing the weapon choices during the play. When a decision is dubious, the voting is broken down to see what went wrong. It's possible to see which weapon property had too many votes and isolate the features that contributed most. The feature is adjusted until the total votes are reasonable. Then, when the votes seem balanced, it's a matter of adjusting the weights for each weapon property. These values can be adjusted by identifying the property that contributes too strongly to the final fitness and reducing its weight as appropriate.

This methodology makes it somewhat easier to adjust all the values involved. The voting system also has the advantage of being easy to extend. New features can be added easily, and mostly independent from other existing features. The resulting system does relatively well at selecting weapons; although the behavior is no doubt suboptimal, it's practically indistinguishable from human behavior.

On the downside, setting up a voting system often requires this kind of experimentation because the results of the votes are not necessarily known. In this case, it's not possible to use supervised learning techniques. There's also a problem with the assumptions made; indeed, rarely do player skills match the exact statistics of the weapons. This implies the behaviors are not customized to individual player abilities.

Summary

This chapter discussed the importance of scripting, even when modern AI techniques are used:

➤ Scripts are easy to modify; there is no separate compilation phase.

➤ The syntax is simple, flexible, and high-level, which leads to less coding.

➤ Scripts are separated from the code and are handled in a data-driven fashion.

➤ As customizable glue between generic components, scripts provide the ideal complement to native code.

The idea of a voting system was also presented in detail. In the case of weapon selection, the following concepts apply:

➤ Candidates are the weapon properties.

➤ The features of the situation are the voters.

➤ The votes can be cast with different weights and for multiple candidates.

The solution works very well, and matches our requirements for justifiability and decisiveness. This requires a certain amount of experimentation and adjusting by the developer. However, sometimes the assumptions do not lead to the best decision, and the system is not tailored to individual skills.

The next chapter covers the theory behind decision trees, an AI technique that can be used to make decisions by evaluating the benefit of a choice. The advantage is that the weapon selection can be learned from examples, and the application of this theory is covered in Chapter 27, "Learning to Assess Weapons."

Chapter 26

Classification and Regression Trees

Regression and classification trees—also known collectively as *decision trees* (DTs)—are data structures that can interpret patterns in data in order to recognize them. They are organized as hierarchical decisions over certain variables to predict a result value. With classification trees, the result is a symbolic class, whereas regression trees return continuous values.

Decision trees must be learned from example data, so it's necessary to create or gather it beforehand. An expert can prepare the data, or a collection of facts from the problems can be accumulated. Many tasks, including simulating intelligence, can be seen as just interpreting—or classifying—such data. In practice, each problem can be encoded as a set of attributes and the DT can predict an unknown attribute (the solution).

This chapter discusses the following topics:

➤ The concept of a data sample, with predictor and response variables

➤ The representation of decision trees, with decision nodes and branches

➤ The process of classifying and regressing based on an existing tree

➤ How trees are learned—or *induced*—from data sets, using recursive partitioning

➤ The training procedure from a wider perspective, aiming to find the best DT for the problem

These items can become the decision-making component in game characters. Each situation is represented as a set of attributes, so the DT can suggest the best course of action in a certain situation. Also, it's possible to use regression trees to evaluate the benefit of an object (or predict an outcome, both positive and negative). The next chapter does this in the context of weapon selection.

Representation of Decision Trees

Before looking into what a DT can do, or even how we can build one, we need to understand the basic concepts behind the data structure.

A DT outputs a prediction based on some input attributes. There are two different kinds of DTs: classification and regression trees. There are no differences in the types of inputs; both can take continuous or symbolic values. It's the output that determines the type of tree. A DT with continuous outputs is known as a regression tree, and classification trees output categorical values instead—as summarized in Table 26.1.

Table 26.1   Two Different Varieties of DTs Distinguished by the Type of Result Returned

Tree Type	Prediction	Data Type
Classification	Categorical	Symbol
Regression	Continuous	Real number

The first subsection explains data samples and their relevance. These are processed by DTs and often serve as the input/output format, too. Then we investigate the representation of the tree, revealing what makes them so simple and fast. Finally, the important parts of the tree—such as the decision nodes and leaves—are examined further.

Data Samples

Data is a fundamental requirement of pattern recognition, and even machine learning generally. Data is often expressed as individual *samples*—also known as *cases*, *instances*, *patterns*, and, no doubt, many other things.

Essentially, a data sample is a set of *attributes*, a.k.a. *predictor variables*. Each attribute can be a continuous value (that is, floating-point number) or a symbol (that is, unordered discrete values). These attributes can represent just about anything conceptually; in the context of weapons, properties such as weight, firing rate, and maximum ammo would be attributes.

There is an additional attribute with a special meaning, known as a *response variable* (or *dependent variable*). It can be a symbol representing discrete categories (for classification) or a continuous value (for regression). This is the criteria for making decisions on each of the samples for both classification and regression problems.

Table 26.2 shows the problem of predicting the total damage inflicted based on the properties of the weapon. Damage is used as the response variable, so the others are predictor variables. Weight and type are categorical, whereas the rest are continuous.

Table 26.2 Four Data Samples with Multiple Attributes

Weight	RPM	Capacity	Range	Type	Damage
Light	47	10	40m	Handgun	5%
Heavy	200	500	100m	Machine gun	10%
Very light	6	6	25m	Handgun	4%
Very heavy	280	1000	200m	Machine gun	13%

There is no difference between the predictor and response variables; almost any attribute can be a response. The variable used as a basis for the classification process will be chosen depending on each problem. To classify weapon *types*, for example, we could choose the attribute for damage or capacity (among others).

NOTE

Data samples are commonly used throughout the fields of AI, including for other techniques that can be used for pattern recognition and prediction. This notably includes neural networks. We sidestepped the problem of classification during Chapter 17, "Perceptrons," and Chapter 19, "Multilayer Perceptrons" (focusing mostly on function approximation), but a majority of the concepts throughout this chapter can be applied directly to neural networks.

Decision Tree

A DT is basically a tree, in the standard computer science meaning of the word. The data structure is formed of *nodes* joined together by *branches* (see Figure 26.1). These branches are not allowed to form cycles, or the tree would become a graph (difficult to use for decision making).

One special node is known as the *root*. This is conceptually the base of the tree, and it's possible to traverse the tree from any node to the root. Another particular kind of node forms the end of each branch: *leaf* nodes.

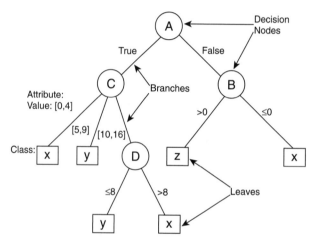

Figure 26.1 A simple DT with the root node at the top, and each decision node as a circle. The leaves are represented as boxes.

This is a very broad description of a tree data structure. Anyone with reasonable experience of programming languages should be familiar with this. However, for DTs in AI, there are particular meanings associated with each of these concepts.

Each level in the tree can be considered as a decision; a node is a conditional test, and each branch is one of the possible options. More formally, the nodes contain a selection criterion, and the branches express the mutually exclusive results of the test.

Fundamentally, each conditional test sorts the data samples so that each corresponds to only one branch. If we consider all the samples as one large data set, the decisions split this set into distinct subsets—as depicted in Figure 26.2. Combining these tests into a hierarchy actually splits the data into even smaller parts until the leaf is reached. Each leaf corresponds to a small but exclusive part of the initial set.

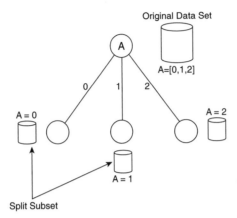

Figure 26.2 Splitting the DT into mutually exclusive subsets using the decision nodes.

Conditional Tests

Naturally, there are many possible ways to represent the decisions. These depend on the type of the attribute as well as the operation used in the conditional test. Because the attributes can be symbols and continuous values, the tests can be Boolean conditions as well as continuous relations. The number of possible results to the test corresponds to the number of branches starting at this node. Common conditional tests include the following:

➤ **Boolean**—Is the statement true or not? Possible results are obviously true and false.

➤ **Sign**—What is the sign of this expression? The results can be either positive or negative. This can be seen as a special case of the *Boolean* test.

➤ **Class**—What class does the symbol belong to? The outcome is one of the possible classes (arbitrary number).

➤ **Range**—In what range does a value lie? Possible results are each of the ranges that divide the domain of the value. This can be understood as a *class* test.

Typically, a unique conditional test over only one attribute is used (for instance, B==true). This often suffices because decisions can be combined hierarchically in the tree to form more complex decisions. As an extension to DT, however, some conditional tests involve more attributes (for instance, testing A==1 and B<0), which can improve the accuracy of the tests—at the cost of simplicity. In this case, there are more combinations of possible results, so there are more branches. See Table 26.3.

Table 26.3   Four Examples of Simple Conditional Tests, as Well as a Decision Over Multiple Attributes

Conditional Test	Possible Results
A (Boolean)	true false
B (sign)	$B > 0$ $B \leq 0$
C (range)	C in [0..4] C in [5..9] C in [10..14]
A, B	A == true and $B > 0$ A == false and $B > 0$ A == true and $B \leq 0$ A == false and $B \leq 0$

Generally, more predictor variables used in a test imply more branches. However, it's possible to use an arbitrary number of attributes and map them to a single Boolean decision. This would require evaluating expressions such as (A and B) or C. Similar equations can be used to convert continuous values to a single number. The problem with such complex expressions is that they are harder to learn!

Leaves and Response Variables

There is a single response variable associated with leaves of the tree only. These response values also can be either discrete or continuous.

Each of the leaves corresponds to a particular subset of the data samples (see Figure 26.3). For classification trees, the response variable matches the estimated category for all the samples in this leaf. On the other hand, in regression trees, continuous response variables generally indicate the average of all the samples corresponding to the leaf.

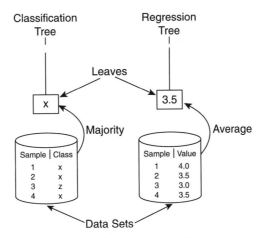

Figure 26.3 The value stored in each leaf corresponds to the response variables of the samples.

The type of response variable does not affect the structure of the tree, although a different data type container is needed in the leaves—obviously! There are also key differences in the way the tree is built, but we'll get to that after we know how to use it.

Classifying and Regressing

Given an existing DT, we can estimate the response variable for unknown data samples, based on the value of the attributes only. This is done sample per sample, allowing entire data sets to be filtered and evaluated.

How is each data sample processed? Specifically how do we determine the class/value of a sample? This is done by a *traversal* of the tree, starting from the root toward the leaves. The traversal is based on the result of the conditional tests, guided by the predictor variables (see Figure 26.4).

At each level of the tree, a decision is made based on the value of the attributes. The conditional test in each node is used to evaluate predictor variables. One unique branch from the node will match the result of this evaluation. There is always *one* applicable branch because the conditions are complete (that is, minimum one option) and mutually exclusive (that is, one option only). The traversal will follow that branch to the next decision node where the process repeats.

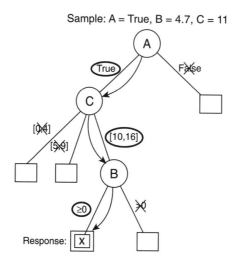

Figure 26.4 Using a data sample to guide the traversal of the DT.

The traversal of the tree terminates when the end of the branching is reached (see Listing 26.1). Each leaf in the tree corresponds to a class (or value); the data sample that was used to traverse the tree must therefore belong to this class (or have this value). There is a guarantee that each sample will correspond to one and only one leaf—hence, one category or one estimate.

Listing 26.1 Algorithm Used to Traverse a DT, Based on the Value of a Data Sample

```
node = root
repeat
      result = node.evaluate( sample )
      for each branch from node
            if branch.match( result )
                  node = branch.child
            end if
      end for
until node is a leaf
return leaf class or value
```

This is an extremely simple process conceptually, which explains its efficiency. The biggest challenges lie in designing the software capable of simulating this in a flexible fashion.

Tree Induction

Most DTs are quite simple, and in practice don't get very big either—especially in computer games. It is feasible to build these trees by hand. However, such an approach is similar to creating an expert system hierarchically—but ignores the major advantages of DTs: They can be learned automatically.

Numerous learning schemes have been applied to learning DTs. These algorithms generally build up DTs based on assumptions from sample data; this is known as *inducing* a DT. Each method has its own set of benefits and pitfalls. However, one approach has become the basis of most other solutions—proving very fast and simple to implement. This algorithm is known as *recursive partitioning*. Essentially, a tree is created incrementally by batch processing the data set. Statistics are used to create decision nodes and the corresponding conditional tests, in an attempt to find efficient and compact trees.

Recursive Partitioning Outline

Quinlan's original algorithm works by recursively partitioning the data set, building up the tree incrementally [Quinlan93]. Many other algorithms are based on the same template, so we'll look at the outline before analyzing the details.

The concept at the core of the algorithm is *divide and conquer*. The goal is to build a tree for categorizing data samples; we split the data set into roughly classified subsets, and try again until the classification is perfect—or good enough. This is a recursive process, building up the tree of decisions during the process.

The algorithm starts with an empty tree and a full data set. First, we must find a good split point to divide the original set into subsets. Generally, a heuristic picks an attribute (or a few of them), which is used to partition the data. It's not important for the algorithm to know how the attribute is picked, as long as a decision node can be created, and the data set can be partitioned. The first node in the tree can thereby be created, corresponding to this conditional test.

Now we have a tree with one node, splitting the data set into two (or more) subsets. This process can be repeated on all the subsets to create a subtree. It terminates when there's no need to split the data set any further. The decision to stop splitting can be handled by the same procedure that creates the decision nodes, as shown in Listing 26.2.

Listing 26.2 Outline of the Recursive Partitioning Algorithm, Attempting to Create a New Decision and Then Splitting the Data Set Accordingly

```
function partition( dataset, node )
     if not create_decision( dataset, node )
                return
     end if
     for each sample in dataset
                result = node.evaluate( sample )
                subset[result].add( sample )
     end for
     for each result in subset
                partition( subset, child )
                node.add( branch, result )
                branch.add( child )
     end for
end function
```

This is intrinsically a recursive process, but rarely reaches depths beyond single digits. Indeed, the amount of recursion is primarily determined by the complexity of the problem. The function terminates quickly for simple data sets. A secondary factor in the recursion is the number of attributes; one level in the tree is a decision, so the more attributes can split the data the more recursion may happen. If this proved problematic, it would be possible to unroll the recursion into a stack-based iteration, although it seems unlikely computers will have any trouble with most data sets (because the algorithm was designed for scalability).

The same *conditional test* is never used twice in the tree; it will have no affect in splitting the data set (a redundant node). All algorithms avoid this problem implicitly as all the other options will appear better! However, a particular *attribute* may easily be used again to split the data set. This may be the case if the attribute is continuous, or has many possible symbolic values. For some data sets, it can be beneficial to split twice along the same dimension, but in different places.

Splitting Data Sets

The only part of the algorithm that requires more thought is the creation of decision nodes. Given a data set, what should be the criteria for partitioning the set?

The attributes are generally chosen in a greedy fashion. Statistical analysis can reveal the attribute that does the best split. Splitting along this attribute generates subsets of minimal error. This doesn't guarantee, however, that the entire tree will be optimal. Indeed, the greedy choices are by definition shortsighted, so generally suboptimal. But trees built greedily get reasonable results nonetheless. See Figure 26.5.

In practice, batch processing identifies the best way to partition. All the samples are scanned, and the *impurity* of the data set is measured for each attribute. An "impure" set means that it contains a wide variety of response variables. We want to identify the impure attributes to make them pure, specifically to reduce the variety of response variables. This will improve the results of the classification and regression. We can improve purity greedily by partitioning the set along the most impure attribute.

Impurity is measured by computing *entropy*. It means almost the same as impurity, and can be substituted to impress/confuse management if necessary! There is a common definition of impurity for Boolean/binary values from a set S:

$$\text{Entropy}(S) = -p_+ \log_2(p_+) - p_- \log_2(p_-)$$

Here, p_+ is the ratio of true values, and p_- is the ratio of false ones. The entropy will be 0 if all the examples are in the same category, and 1 if there is a 50%/50% mix of values. More generally, for sets with c number classes:

$$\text{Entropy}(S) = \sum_{i=1}^{c} -p_i \log_2(p_i) \quad \text{where} \quad p_i = \frac{|S_i|}{|S|}$$

The entropy is defined as the sum of the weighted logarithms for each class i. p_i is defined as the proportion of samples of class i. (That is, the number of samples $|S_i|$ over the total size of the data set $|S|$.)

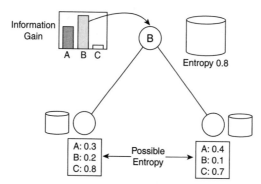

Figure 26.5 Recursive partitioning at one node, splitting the data set into mutually exclusive subsets.

Entropy is not sufficient to determine the best attribute to pick for partitioning. *Information gain* measures the expected decrease in entropy if an attribute is used for the split:

$$\text{Gain}(S, A) = \text{Entropy}(S) - \sum_{i=1}^{c} p_i \text{Entropy}(S_i)$$

This expresses the information gain as the total entropy of a set, but subtracting the entropy of the subsets that are created during the split. Putting this into procedural form gives us the pseudo-code shown in Listing 26.3.

Listing 26.3 Function Used to Find the Best Attribute for Partitioning a Data Set, If Any

```
function create_decision( dataset, node )
    max = 0
    # find the impurity for the entire training data
    entropy = compute_entropy( dataset )
    for each attribute in dataset
        # split and compute total entropy of subsets
        e = entropy-compute_entropy_split( attribute, dataset )
        # find the best positive gain
        if e > max
            max = e
            best = attribute
        end if
    end for
    # create the test if there's a good attribute
```

```
    if best
            node.evaluation = create_test( attribute )
    # otherwise find the value of leaf node
    else
            node.class = find_class( dataset )
    end if
end function
```

Training Procedure

When creating a DT, the data set itself will greatly influence the final result. This is not particularly desirable because we want the result to reflect the problem itself, not the data used.

Data Set Management

Data set management is particularly important for creating DTs and preventing the algorithms from learning too specific models. Just like for multilayer perceptrons, this symptom is known as *overfitting* and can prevent DTs from *generalizing* to other data.

Many improvements to DTs actually involve simple tricks to manipulate the data sets. The fundamental concepts remain the same as for perceptrons. We need to keep three different sets:

➤ The **training** set is used for the recursive partitioning algorithm.

➤ A **validation** set then assists the process of tweaking the learned DT (notably pruning).

➤ The **testing** set finally checks the results of the learning as an indication of performance.

Dividing the entire data set can be done as equal parts: randomly picking a third of the samples. This somewhat depends on the total data available, because a minimal amount is needed for training. Validation works best with a much greater quantity of samples, and testing can optionally be skipped if there's a shortage of data!

Pruning Branches

The pruning of DTs is generally done as a postprocessing after learning. It's important to use a different data set for pruning, because using the training data set would not suggest any changes! Pruning uses the validation set. Intuitively, if the results of the classification are better when a branch is pruned, we prune it.

To do this comparison, each node needs to know the response variable it would have if it were a leaf. Computing this class (or value) can be done in the same way as for the leaf; the class with the most instances (or the average value) is used.

Then, we run a test of the entire data set. In each node, we count the number of successful classifications (or the total regression error). When finished, we can perform a simple check: Does any node have a better score than all its children put together? If this is the case, the children are in fact unnecessary, so we prune the tree at that node (see Figure 26.6).

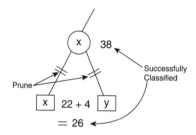

Figure 26.6 Pruning a branch by counting the number of successfully classified examples in each node.

Bagging and Boosting

The idea behind *bagging and boosting* is that poor classifiers can be combined to form better ones. We can use many different parameters and training sets to generate a collection of DTs. For example, bagging arbitrarily selects different samples from the training set, and boosting assigns them weights to influence the learning. Then, two different policies can be used to combine the different decisions:

➤ **Bagging** works like a democracy. The class with the most votes by individual classification trees becomes the output of the combined classifier.

➤ **Boosting** instead assigns weights to each of the trees, based on their success at classifying the validation set. The sum of weighted votes is used as the output for the combined classifiers.

The advantage of these techniques is that the quality of the final classifier is usually improved. However, the results are purely empirical. There's no guarantee that the combined classifiers will perform better on the entire problem, although there's proof for closed sets that the results will not be worse.

The cost of combining classifiers scales linearly with the number of DTs used. Additional memory is needed to store the data structures in memory, and for each decision, there is a cost for traversing each of the trees.

Discussion

Decision trees are extremely efficient at computing estimates for unknown samples. The data structure is simple and small, and requires little effort to traverse. DTs are particularly suited to data-mining problems, so mass processing of information in real time is not a problem.

In addition, due to the small amounts of information needed, the footprint for storing DTs in memory is very small. After the knowledge has been encoded in the tree, there is often little need to keep the data samples.

Finally, DTs are relatively flexible. They can be used on continuous and symbolic predictor variables. The response variables can also be used for regression or classification, which makes them easy to apply to a wide variety of problems.

However, some disadvantages are worth noting. Decision trees are well suited to batch processing data sets. When it comes to learning them online, however, existing algorithms can be somewhat clumsy (both memory intensive and tricky to implement). Everything considered, gathering the samples incrementally and then applying batch learning seems the easiest approach—which usually results in the same behavior.

The recursive partitioning algorithm is greedy in nature. This performs relatively well, but it is usually suboptimal in both the quality of the results and the size of the tree. This is the case for surprisingly many trees, although the quality is good enough for game development.

Last but not least, there can be problems dealing with overfitting. Secondary pruning phases can be used to remedy the problem, but this requires additional computation and additional data to validate the result. Integrated algorithms, sadly, loose the benefit of simplicity.

Summary

There are two kinds of decisions trees: Classification trees result in categorical responses, and regression trees return continuous values. The representation of DTs is very intuitive, and almost identical in both cases:

➤ Each decision node has a conditional test over predictor variables.

➤ The branches correspond to the possible results of the test (mutually exclusive).

➤ Layers of the tree can be combined hierarchically.

➤ The leaves store the response—either categorical or continuous.

The simulation algorithm uses a data sample to traverse the tree according to the results of each conditional test. The training—or *induction*—algorithm operates with recursive partitioning:

➤ The data set is partitioned according to the best variable, resulting in the purest subsets.

➤ The corresponding decision node is created in the tree, and the process continues recursively.

The best way to improve the training is to manage the data set, using additional validation and testing sets. Pruning also is a very effective option in computer games, but other techniques such as bagging and boosting are not very suited to game development.

Because DTs are capable of finding patterns in data, and learning to recognize them, the next chapter applies them to weapon selection. Based on the situation, the DT will learn to evaluate the fitness of each weapon.

Practical Demo

Detox is an animat using an architecture rooted with a DT. The decision controls all the actions specified until now (for instance, movement, aiming, selection) and the corresponding senses. *Detox* is taught by imitation, collecting data from human players. The performance is relatively poor, because every action being handled homogenously (that is, no decomposition based on behaviors or capabilities). Source code and demo are available online at `http://AiGameDev.com/`.

Chapter 27

Learning to Assess Weapons

Now that we've investigated different varieties of decision trees (DTs), we can use them to improve the weapon-selection behaviors. The main problem with the voting system is that it was tedious to set up and used theoretical assumptions to derive the weapon choice.

In this chapter, we focus the power of DT learning algorithms to resolve these problems. Notably, we'll be able to learn about the weapons by experience during the game, which prevents making unfounded assumptions. The learning may also reduce the effort needed to get a working behavior. Because we already have a voting system, however, we could take advantage of it.

This chapter covers the following topics:

➤ A description of the four different ways we can use the DTs to learn weapon selection

➤ An analysis of the options and how to pick out the most suitable one, which actually assesses weapons as a whole—as hinted by the chapter's title

➤ The design of some interfaces to interact with the DT as a modular component

➤ The implementation of the algorithms discussed in the previous chapter

➤ The application phase, applying the DT to weapon selection

➤ A swift evaluation of the system and potential improvements

At the end of the chapter, we'll have a fully working deathmatch bot that's not only capable of moving and shooting, but capable of making tactical decisions about what weapon to use.

Four Different Approaches

The great thing about DTs is that they are very generic. There are also numerous ways to tackle weapon selection. As expected, there are even more ways to combine the two together. In fact, there are four options, as shown in Figure 27.1:

1. Learning the appropriate weapon

2. Learning the fitness of weapons

3. Learning properties of weapons

4. Learning the importance of properties

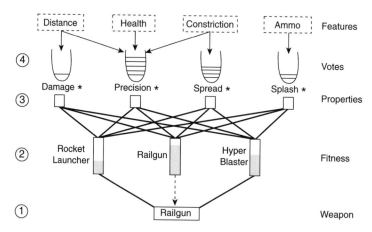

Figure 27.1 The different concepts and processes involved in the decision of selecting a weapon.

In each of these cases, the DTs use features of the current situation as predictor variables (for instance, distance, health, and terrain constriction)—as discussed in Chapter 23, "Weapon Selection." However, the four different models optionally use additional predictor variables and different response variables.

Learning the Appropriate Weapon

The first approach is to use a DT to return the most appropriate weapon for each situation. This corresponds to a mapping from a set of environment features to a weapon type. In theory, this approach summarizes what weapon selection is all about. Sadly, using a single AI component to determine only the best weapon has many problems in practice:

➤ Because the DT returns only one weapon suggestion, it doesn't work when that weapon is not available.

➤ By returning a unique choice, the DT provides little insight into the selection process.

➤ The AI somehow needs to determine the best weapon manually to supervise the DT learning.

There are three obvious ways to fix these problems—in a more or less improvised fashion. First, we could duplicate the DTs, so different trees would be used depending on the weapons available; this requires more memory and is slower to learn. Second, we could specify the weapons available as additional inputs, but this leads to a combinatorial explosion of the problem space, and the approximation of the DT would be error prone. Third, we could have the result of the DT as a list of weapons ranked by preference. However, this requires adapting the DT to deal with multidimensional responses.

In brief, it's possible, but not ideal. A more appropriate approach would be to learn the fitness of weapons in each situation, as described in the next section.

Learning Weapon Fitness

In the second model, the DT maps the features of the situation onto a single fitness value (see Figure 27.2). Then, a small script (or a native C++ function) finds the highest fitness and selects the corresponding weapon.

Each weapon could have its own DT to evaluate its fitness based on the current situation. This requires nine DTs for *Quake 2* (excluding the default weapon). This approach organizes the selection skills by weapon, so they can easily be learned modularly. However, this dissociation has the cost of using additional memory and code.

Instead, the weapon type could be used as a predictor variable in the DT, so only one large tree is needed to evaluate the fitness of all weapons. This option is more convenient because only one tree is needed, and the tree may be more compact.

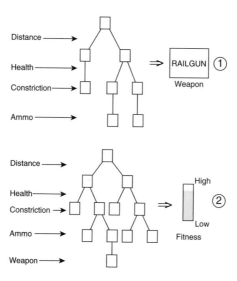

Figure 27.2 On the top, the DT that learns the right weapon directly. On the bottom, it estimates the fitness.

The biggest problem is computing the fitness values in some situations to supervise the learning. In essence, the problem must be solved in some cases, allowing the DT to induce the general behavior. An easy way of doing this is to reuse the voting system we developed in Chapter 25, "Scripting Tactical Decisions." The DT is based on the exact same features as the voting system. Then, the final result of the voting is used to induce the DT. The learned DT would be capable of approximating the result of the voting efficiently, without having to go through the whole process.

Learning Weapon Properties

Working on a lower level, the DT can learn the different weapon properties based on the features of the current situation. Naturally, rate of fire and speed of projectiles don't need learning—or at least, not with DTs—because they are constant values. On the other hand, characteristics such as maximum damage and estimated damage per second are very much dependent on the current situation (as discussed for the shooting skills).

The advantage of this approach is that it results in accurate measurements for the weapon properties that were relied upon in Chapter 25. Thanks to the DTs, the statistics are dependent on the skill of the animat, and even the different situations. On the other hand, the DT is not a self-standing solution, and still relies on other aspects of the AI. If we opt for this approach, we'll be able to reuse the entire voting system—which will be enhanced by learning.

Learning Votes for Properties

The final approach learns the votes for the weapon properties based on the features. This model avoids using a voting system, replacing it with a hierarchy of decisions that would be more efficient but approximate. The voting system is still required during learning to provide the DT with some examples, but it can be removed in the final architecture. The fitness of the weapon is then the sum of the fitness of its characteristics.

Rationale

Of the designs previously listed, the second option is chosen; the fitness of each weapon as a whole is predicted from the features of the situation, instead of breaking down the decision into attributes. This keeps the number of required DTs to a manageable level, which increases the efficiency of the AI (low memory usage and only querying a few DTs). Also, it makes for a more challenging application that deals with more data.

Methodology

The fitness of weapons is learned within the game. The benefit of each weapon is learned separately first, induced online using an incremental regression tree. The tree learns to estimate the average damage inflicted on targets based on features of the current situation.

Necessary information is gathered using the usual interfaces for predictor variables (for instance, enemy position, health, terrain constriction). For the response variable, a combination of information from the game is gathered by events to determine the damage (for instance, sounds or explosions)—as in Part III.

The simulation allows the AI to learn the trends associated with the weapons. Given enough accelerated time, good patterns should arise in each of the regression trees. Then, it'll be possible to query these trees for the best weapon for action; out of all the damage estimates, which is the highest?

Then, if necessary, the regression trees could be processed to build a near-optimal single classification tree (first option discussed). This final classifier would take the same attributes as each of the regression trees, but return the most appropriate class of weapons, factoring out the fitness estimates. As discussed, this wouldn't work in all cases—although it's an interesting problem.

Discussion

As it stands, the regression tree is a substitute for most stages of the voting system. Using a regression tree instead has many advantages:

➤ The decision process is less complex (only two stages).

➤ The representation is compact and very efficient to query.

➤ The AI learns to deals with unforeseen situations by generalizing.

➤ It is possible to induce the weapon selection from expert advice, instead of the voting system.

Thanks to their expressiveness, the induced trees are easy to modify if the learned behaviors are not appropriate. This will be useful for the designer to override the behavior with an explicit design.

Module Design

Before starting the implementation, it's worth spending some time on the design of a DT. DTs are used ubiquitously in game AI development, so a generic and flexible interface is worthwhile.

The implementation is covered in the next section. It supports both categorical and continuous variables (that is, `bool`, `int`, and `float`). An unlimited number of predictor variables are possible (decided at initialization), but only one response variable.

Initialization

The main purpose of the initialization is to describe what kind of data the DT has to deal with. The module requires the types of each of the variables expected. The range of continuous variables may also be greatly appreciated by the underlying algorithm, as well as suggested discretization:

```
<predictor name="health" type="integer" min="0" max="100" />
<predictor name="distance" type="real" min="0" step="36" />
<predictor name="visible" type="boolean" />
<response name="fitness" type="real" min="0" max="1" step="0.1" />
```

This information allows the DT to prepare its internal representation as much as possible before the data is provided by a runtime interface.

The DT itself will undoubtedly need to be saved to disk, and then reloaded later. Because DTs have a relatively intuitive representation, we may want to modify it manually—which requires explaining the storage format. The structure of DTs is well-suited to be represented in XML, because hierarchies of nodes are simple to express. The basic outline of a DT is shown in Listing 27.1. The DT is built up by a recursive definition of all the nodes. The `decision` tag specifies the criteria for choosing the `branch`, and the `match` tag explains the required result of the evaluation for this node to be chosen.

Listing 27.1   The XML Structure of a Single Node of a DT

```
<Node>
      <decision> ... </decision>
      <branch>
            <match> ... </match>
            <Node> ... </Node>
      </branch>
</Node>
```

However, defining the decisions and branches requires fundamental assumptions about the nature of the implementation. For example, is there a limit to the number of attributes? Are there restrictions on possible branches? Does the implementation use other pattern-recognition techniques to perform individual decisions?

Interface

Supporting different types of predictor variables makes the interface tricky to specify.
Indeed, one generic interface for all the possible types is ideal, but this requires some
form of polymorphism. To specify the interface in a flexible fashion, we assume a new
data type called any is specified:

```
any Predict(const vector< any >& inputs);
```

This function is the main entry point of the DT module. It takes a set of values (for
each of the predictor variables), and produces a response on the output. The data types
will be agreed upon during initialization. The any needs to be capable of representing
different types, such as int, bool, and float. To do this, we can either use a C union,
void pointers, or inheritance. A safe existing approach is to use the boost::any facil-
ity, which also handles conversions in an elegant fashion. The other solutions could be
interchangeably used without modifying the code, as long as assignment and type cast-
ing operators are available.

For the learning, two different interfaces are defined for batch and incremental learning. Using the same approach as for perceptrons, different implementations require
varying amounts of persistent memory, so keeping them separate reduces consumption. The developer will then have memory costs depending on the interfaces chosen
(rather than the same overhead upfront):

```
float Increment(const Sample& sample);
float Batch(const vector< Sample >& samples);
```

The two functions return the floating-point error for learning the training samples provided. A Sample is a simple data-structure that stores a vector of any values for the
predictors, and the desired any response value.

Implementation

Implementing the interfaces in a generic way is actually slightly more challenging than one would expect, particularly dealing with the different possible types of the any values.

Data Structures

Three essential data structures are used in the implementation. The first is obviously a node in the tree, the other is a decision, and the third represents an attribute.

Tree Nodes

The nodes in the tree contain three different elements: children, a decision, and the response. The children are basically stored as an array of nodes. The response is an any variable that's most representative of the subset of data corresponding to this node, and the decision is a criterion used to evaluate each sample.

Decision

A decision is a base virtual class that needs to be inherited from. This allows any kind of decision to be implemented in the system, regardless of the number of attributes or their type.

Boolean decisions, for example, check the value of a particular predictor variable, and suggest one of the two branches. Numeric decisions split the attribute up into ranges, one for each branch. The most common decision is based on one single attribute, which is directly referenced.

Attributes

Attributes represent both the predictor variables and the response variable. These store important information, such as the name, range, or type—allowing the learning algorithms to find out more about the attributes relatively easily.

Tree Induction Algorithm

The algorithm used for both incremental and batch learning is based on recursive partitioning, explained in Chapter 26, "Classification and Regression Trees." The algorithm is the same, but the online learning approach tries to minimize changes to the tree by only relearning it when necessary. We could implement other incremental learning algorithms interchangeably if this approach proved unsatisfactory.

The process is quite simple and follows the pseudo-code from Listing 26.2 closely. First, we compute the closest response value for the node and data set. If this is perfect, we return. Then, the attribute with the most information gain is identified, and a decision is created. This is used to split the data set into subsets. The same `Build()` procedure is applied recursively to the children, as discussed in Chapter 26.

Prediction

The algorithm to simulate the tree is very efficient and extremely compact. Essentially, the current node is set to the root. The node's decision is called and returns the index of the child. The recursion continues with the child chosen. Otherwise, if there is no child, the response value of the current node is returned.

Application

Given a modular DT with well-defined interfaces and a satisfactory implementation, it can be applied to weapon selection. Most of the remaining work lies in building a scaffolding to support it, providing the right inputs and outputs.

The exploitation of the DT is relatively straightforward, comparable to replacing the voting system with another component. Listing 27.2 shows how the senses are used to interpret the features, which are used by the classification process to predict the fitness.

Listing 27.2   A Function for Selecting the Weapon Called on Regular Intervals When It's Necessary to Change

```
function select_weapon()
    # use senses to determine health, enemy distance...
    env = interpret_features()
    # find best weapon among the ones available
    max = 0
    for each (weapon, ammo) in inventory
        # compute the fitness based on concatenated features
```

```
        fitness = dt.predict(env + weapon + ammo)
        # only remember if it's better
        if fitness > max then
              fitness = max
              best = weapon
        end if
    end for
    # weapon can be selected
    return best
end function
```

The induction of the DT and computing the sample for learning are slightly more complex. It involves three main phases:

➤ Interpreting the features of the environment from the senses

➤ Monitoring episodes of the fight when weapons are being used

➤ Computing the desired fitness for each episode

The implementation is built upon the same techniques used to monitor the effectiveness of rockets. The following sections explain these stages in greater detail.

Interpreting Environment Features

The features of the environment are collected using the senses from the interfaces discussed in Chapter 24, "Formalizing Weapon Choice," and other specifications (for instance, vision, inventory, and physics). The results are a set of predictor variables, with the representation shown in Table 27.1.

Table 27.1 Variables Used by the DT to Estimate the Fitness of a Particular Weapon

Variable	Range
Distance	Near, medium, far
Health	Low, high
Ammo	Low, medium, high
Traveling	Forward, backward
Constriction	Low, medium, high
Fitness	[0...100]

These variables are the most important features to incorporate into the model, although we could easily add and remove some as necessary to find the ideal balance. These predictor variables are used by the weapon selection, but the response variable is needed for learning. The response is evaluated by monitoring the fight.

Monitoring Fight Episodes

The AI gathers four different types of information from the game, all relevant to the applicability of weapons. Like the animat learning target selection, an event-driven mechanism is used to identify hits (pain signals) and potentially misses (explosion only):

➤ **Self-damage** is identified by any pain broadcast by the body, usually shortly after a projectile is launched.

➤ **Hit probability** measures the number of enemy hits, compared to the number of bullets fired (ammo query).

➤ **Maximal damage** keeps track of the most pain the enemy has suffered while a particular weapon was used.

➤ **Potential damage per second** computes the average damage over the total time the weapon was used.

Identifying the cause of damage can be the most difficult task, but can be solved by checking the location of the pain event, compared with the aiming direction. Alternatively, this information could be provided by the data structures used to store the messages.

Computing the Fitness

The principle at the base of the voting system is that the fitness of a weapon depends on the situation. This also means the criteria used to evaluate the weapons changes depending on the conditions.

It's somewhat difficult to go into this subject without considering high-level tactics (covered in Part VII), so we'll make a few assumptions. Looking at weapon selection alone, we want to take into account the following oversimplified criteria:

➤ **Low personal health** requires precautions to minimize self-damage.

➤ **Low enemy health** should incite the player to increase the hit probability.

➤ When the **enemy is facing away,** the animat should attempt to maximize the potential damage. Otherwise, a good policy is to try to maximize potential damage per second.

Because the overall fitness will represent these different criteria in different situations, we need to make sure that they're vaguely on the same scale. To do this, we'll rescale the values so that they fall into the range [0...100] as closely as possible, as summarized in Listing 27.3.

Listing 27.3   This Function Learns the Desired Fitness of Weapons Based on the Features of the Environment

```
function learn_weapon(weapon,episode)
    # gather the information from the senses
    env = interpret_features()
    # compute the fitness in terms of the monitored information
    if episode.self_health < 25 then
        fitness = -episode.self_damage
    else if episode.enemy_health < 40 then
        fitness = episode.accuracy
    else if episode.enemy_position.y > 0 then
    # enemy is facing away
        fitness = episode.max_potential
    else
    fitness = episode.enemy_damage_per_second
    # incrementally induce the fitness from concatenated features
    dt.increment(env + weapon, fitness)
end function
```

Practical Demo

An animat demonstrates the ideas described here. It can be found under the name of *Selector* on the web site at `http://AiGameDev.com/`. There's a step-by-step guide to get the animat up and running. *Selector* uses a DT to evaluate the benefit of each of the weapons based on the current situation. This is interpreted, with a few restrictions, to choose the best weapon.

Biologically Plausible Errors

By analyzing the data with statistics, it's possible to see how the problem is shaping up. Using a histogram of the potential damage per second, the main feature (distance of the enemy) offers visible trends. For example, the super shotgun is extremely efficient up close, but tails off as the enemy gets farther away. This is understandably caused by the spread of the fire.

On the other hand, some trends are quite surprising. The railgun performs well at a distance, as expected. But up close, the performance is higher than expected. Together with this, traveling backward imposes no additional difficulties on the aiming, so weapons are just as efficient—regardless of the direction of travel. Quite literally, the animats are like the mobile turret of a tank, and just as efficient.

The constant aiming errors were sufficient in the previous part to produce realistic aiming, but we need a more plausible error model for higher-level behaviors, such as weapon selection, to be more humanlike. The weapon selection is already very realistic, but believability could be taken a step further by increasing the variability of the accuracy.

To achieve this, we'll improve the aiming error model to take into account movement and relative direction of travel. The more the animat moves, the less accurately it will turn; also, moving forward is more accurate than running backward.

Evaluation

When playing against the animat, the selection of weapons does not particularly stand out. The choices seem reasonable, although very dependent on the context. Indeed, in many cases, the animat has only a few weapons available; unconventional weapon choices are mainly caused by limited alternatives.

In addition, the fact that combat is over within a few seconds implies there is little time for errors and bugs to become obvious! To really test the weapon selection, we need to artificially prolong the fights (for instance, by making the animats invulnerable), just to check the consistency of the decisions for a longer period. Making the animats immortal also allows them to accumulate all the weapons.

From a technical point of view, we can prevent redundant computation by discarding weapons with low ammo before they are evaluated. The DT is surprisingly efficient, but every little thing helps!

A conceptual problem with this solution is that it required a lot of supervision. We needed to compute the fitness of weapons manually, or use an expert to provide examples, so that we could train the DT. Once learned, the DT has its advantages (for instance, it is general and efficient), but a more implicit approach would have been easier; we want the system to be able to learn the best weapon that improves overall performance, and not have to worry about the criteria for weapon selection.

Summary

This chapter applied DTs to learn weapon selection. We actually had the luxury of being able to apply DTs to this problem in many different ways:

➤ Classification trees can learn the most appropriate weapon in each situation.

➤ Regression trees can estimate the fitness of weapons as a whole.

➤ Regression trees can estimate the different properties of weapons in practice.

➤ Regression trees can predict the weight of the votes for each feature depending on the situation.

We opted for the second option: estimating the overall fitness of the weapon, because it provides more challenges and reduces the need for external code. Then we drafted the interfaces for a modular DT, both runtime and initialization:

➤ The data used for initialization is left high level, only describing the variables types and ranges used during the prediction.

➤ The runtime interfaces are very similar to those used for the perceptron, with functionality for simulation and both varieties of training. The main difference is that any types of input variables are accepted.

The implementation itself is quite challenging to handle when multiple attributes types are possible:

➤ Three data types are required: attributes, decisions, and nodes. Each class depends on the one before.

➤ The implementation for incremental learning is done by storing the samples and updating the tree only if necessary.

In the application phase, we identified some key tasks:

➤ Gathering the information from the fight episode takes the most time for the implementation.

➤ When analyzing the data gathered, some trends arise as expected. However, the errors in the aiming need to be made even more dependent on the context (for instance, subject to movement, direction of travel) for the weapon decisions to be humanlike.

➤ Because the DT is supervised, the result must be computed to train the DT. This involves using a very simple function to compute the weapon's desired fitness.

The system performs well enough, and imposing timing restrictions (as with the voting system) also helps reduce idiosyncrasies. The advantage of the DTs is that the performance of the weapon in the game is learned, subject to individual skill and preferences—rather than objective statistics. On the down side, there is a lot of work needed to set up the DT, notably gathering the data and computing an example that the algorithm can learn.

Part V moves away from supervised techniques. Techniques such as genetic algorithms have the advantage of being directed by a very high-level fitness function, rather than individual examples. Before the next part, however, there's a lesson in the next chapter about understanding AI solutions in general, which provides guidance for the design of all AI systems.

Chapter 28

Understanding the Solution

KEY TOPICS

- Complexity of the Solution
- The Search Space
- Different Approaches to Finding a Solution

The importance of understanding the problem was discussed in Chapter 21, "Knowledge of the Problem." The lesson for Part IV provides insights into the solution itself. The role of the solution is to provide a direct mapping between the inputs and the outputs. The solution has many different aspects, so it's important to present the big picture before moving on. The solution consists of four different parts:

➤ **Representation** is the formalism used to store the solution, the structure of the expert knowledge about the problem.

➤ **Training** provides a way to find the right variation of the representation that manages to solve the problem.

➤ An **instance** is the result of the training, a particular set of internal values expressing the input/output mapping.

➤ **Simulation** is the algorithm that uses an instance to compute the correct response given a particular input pattern.

As always, it's easier to understand using an example or two. The concepts are depicted in Table 28.1. It's important to understand that AI techniques presented in this book provide design patterns for each of these four aspects of the solution. That said, we can generally consider the concepts separately during the design and development. (For instance, some training algorithms are interchangeable.)

Table 28.1 Different Aspects of Solutions to Problems

	Perceptron	**Decision Tree**
Representation	Connection weights between neurons	Decision nodes and branches
Training	Back propagation	Recursive partitioning
Instance	Values of weights	Decision criteria for each node
Simulation	Forward propagation of input pattern	Guided traversal of the tree

This chapter looks at the general concepts behind each of these four characteristics of solutions. This will help explain the general role of design when developing intelligent systems, and allow us to apply AI to novel problems. Sadly, it's not possible to discuss the process of simulation in general terms, because the algorithms depend on specific representations.

The remaining sections of this chapter cover the following topics:

➤ A description of AI solutions based on *information theory*. Specifically, we can express redundancy by compressing the mapping from inputs to outputs—exploiting patterns in the data. This is the idea behind the *minimum length description* principle, which helps determine the necessary complexity of the solution. This section also reveals the importance of representation of the solution.

➤ An explanation of the solution's representation in more detail, explaining search spaces as the number of possible instances of the solution. In a similar fashion to Chapter 21, the size and dimensionality of the search space is analyzed. A few examples reveal important properties of the search space (such as roughness and smoothness).

➤ An overview of the different design paradigms used to craft an AI system. These range from human solutions to expert tailored algorithms, including random and exhaustive search methods.

At the end of this chapter, we'll better understand the intricacies of AI solutions and have an enhanced comprehension of the approaches used.

Complexity of the Solution

The solution to a problem can be considered as raw data describing the mapping from the input domain to the output codomain. This raw data enables us to solve the problem by using it as a lookup to find the correct response. This approach is not particularly elegant or convenient, but it reveals the true nature of the solution.

Before we even start discussing more sophisticated ways to express a solution, we can use *information theory* to understand how complex the solution needs to be. In Chapter 21, we already managed to get a feel for the complexity of the *problem* by analyzing it from an external point of view. This section considers it from the inside.

Information Theory and AI

Beyond the raw data that expresses the solution, we're interested in the *information* stored within. Information is the essence of the data, the parts that cannot be predicted. Removing the redundant data reveals the fundamental aspect of the solution itself—which we're interested in.

In this context, the term "information" has its meaning from information theory. Information theory is a branch of statistics and probability theory dealing with the study of data, ways to manipulate it (for instance, cryptography and compression) and communicate it (for instance, data transmissions and communication systems) [Wikipedia03a].

This information can be obtained by *compressing* the raw data in various ways (that is, expressing it in a more compact form). Again, we use the term "compression" in its generic meaning—not limited to encoding bitstreams in small chunks. Such compressing takes into account *any* kind of pattern in the data, and not just statistical relationships: Symmetry involving arbitrary input or output configurations, and different levels of covariance between variables (as introduced in Chapter 21).

Taking a look at the solution from the point of view of information theory enables us to understand the complexity of the input/output mapping itself. For example, a solution that maps all the inputs onto one single output configuration can be highly compressed, potentially stored as one output element only (for instance, the move forward behavior). This reveals that the AI technique does not need to be complex at all. In a similar fashion, if the solution is extremely flexible (that is, many legal configurations), it's not important which output is chosen. This extra flexibility can also be highly compressed into a concise solution. (For instance, obstacle avoidance does not require any specific action in open space.)

On the other hand, if the mapping from input to output is seemingly unpredictable, and without any flexibility in the solution, the compression ratio will be one. In this case, the AI technique needs to store a lot of complex information to solve the problem, almost reaching the theoretical size of the problem space. This level of complexity is quite rare in practice; even a difficult task such as playing a deathmatch game has many patterns (which we extracted by design). That said, larger problems are more expensive to compress, because patterns are tough to find.

In a nutshell, raw data can describe the solution. The more patterns there are in this data, the better the compression of the input/output mapping. The better the compression, the less information is needed to describe the solution, which in turn simplifies the role of the AI technique.

Minimal Complexity

Not only does information theory enable us to estimate the complexity of a problem, it also provides us with a metric for identifying the best representation. The most compressed form of a data set is known as the *minimum description length* (*MDL*). There has been a lot of research on the subject over the past decades, combining the experience from many fields of science.

> *"The fundamental idea behind the MDL principle is that any regularity in a given set of data can be used to compress the data—that is, to describe it using fewer symbols than needed to describe the data literally." [Grünwald98]*

Essentially, the *description length* is measured by the number of bits needed to encode the patterns in the data, together with the bits required to express the divergences from these patterns. Generally, the patterns are encoded within the solution, and the exceptions to these patterns can be measured as the necessary adjustment to the output.

Ideally, we would like to find the best possible solution. It turns out *Occam's razor*, a principle for keeping everything as simple as possible, is an extremely useful bias in AI. Finding the MDL enables us to identify the simplest solution; the one that requires least information to express the entire data set as a collection of bits.

The MDL is a principle for trading off insignificant information in the data for the sake of finding better patterns in the data—and hence a better solution. Using the MDL, we can first identify the most suitable representation, as well as find its best instance.

Theory and Practice

It's important to understand the concepts of information, complexity in the data, and trading off generic-ness with precision. Entire algorithms have been developed around these principles, notably decision trees (covered in Chapter 26, "Classification and Regression Trees").

That said, when it comes to design issues and choices about representation, these insights are mainly useful as wisdom for the AI developer. Understanding the nature of the solution, different ways to express the mapping from input to output, and how to compare two different approaches enables us to design better systems. In the case of weapon selection, for example, it's possible to determine whether neural networks are more appropriate at predicting the weapon fitness than decision trees. By counting the amount of memory used by the representation and the number of bits to express the error of each sample, the developer can compare the lengths of the two descriptions and pick the minimal (neural network or decision tree).

Although such formal methods help, knowing which representation to use can be a matter of experience. This book has already covered AI techniques such as neural networks, rule-based systems, and decision trees, mentioning which types of solutions they provide best. Each provides minimal descriptions for certain problems. A summary of the elusive problem of choosing an AI technique is provided in Part VIII, after each technique has been explained. Until then, this lesson about the theoretical complexity of a mapping is a great guideline for understanding the difficultly of finding a solution.

The Search Space

Assume we've chosen a representation, hopefully one enabling us to express the patterns in the solution. Beyond its suitability to map inputs to outputs, other properties of the representation affect the solution. Among these, the concept of search space and its smoothness are crucial issues for the AI (affecting its efficiency and reliability).

One thing to keep in mind throughout this section is that the solution's internal representation may be entirely different from the problem's representation. In fact, it's often the case, because the interfaces to the components are often designed in a relatively generic fashion.

Internal Representation

The representation can be understood as a paradigm used to express the solution, as a blueprint for the internal variables—and not the solution itself. The solution is a particular instance of all the possible representations, consisting in a set of specific values for each of the internal variables.

The total number of configurations made up by these internal values is known as the search space; it's the set of all possible solutions—good or bad. Just like the domain of the problem, the domain of the solution is influenced by two things:

➤ **Dimensions**—The number of variables in the solution

➤ **Size**—The number of possible values that each variable can take

The domain of the representation affects the simulation (computing the answer) as well as training (finding a valid instance). Increases in the size of the search space tend to make both these tasks much tougher.

Examples

Let's take a few examples. For a perceptron, internal knowledge of the problem is stored in the weighted connections. Because the topology of perceptrons is generally frozen, the search space consists of the weights only. If there are 8 weights and 1 bias, the search space has a dimensionality of 9. The size of each dimension is theoretically the number of permutations of the 32 bits of a floating-point number (that is, 2^{32} = 4,294,967,296). In the case of the perceptron, however, the values of the weights are limited to a small range around 0, and fine precision is rarely required. So in practice, the size of each dimension is in the thousands rather than billions.

As for decision trees, let's consider the worst case: a complete tree. A tree with four Boolean attributes has three levels of branching, with the bottom nodes being leaves. The internal variables of the solution represent the decision used in each node. In the root, there are four possible attributes to choose from; in the next level, there are three choices, but two nodes; on the final level of branching, there are four nodes but only two possible attributes to choose from. The leaves have no decisions. So, the search space of a worst-case binary decision tree with n attributes would have a dimensionality of $2^0 * 2^1 * 2^2 * \ldots * 2^{n-2}$. Starting from the root, the size of these dimensions would be n, n − 1, n − 2, ... 2. Theoretically, that gives us a search space size of 576 for a full tree with 4 attributes—or worst case 6,480 if we allow the tree to be partial (1 extra option per decision).

Search Space Properties

Beyond just issues of size, the internal representation chosen is important for many reasons. Not only must the representation allow the problem to be modeled in a suitable fashion, it also must allow the AI technique to find the solution.

The smoothness of the search space is a consequence of the representation. How do small adjustments to the internal values affect the mapping from inputs to outputs? In some cases, a small adjustment leads to a small change in the mapping; this is a smooth part of the search space. On the other hand, small changes may also lead to large jumps in the mapping; this is a very jagged part of the search space (see Figure 28.1).

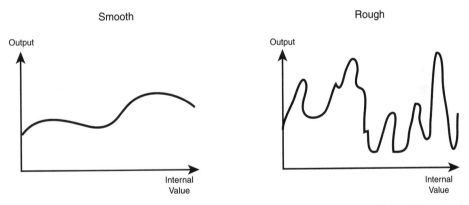

Figure 28.1　On the left, a smooth mapping that allows an easy adjustment of the internal values. On the right, a rough mapping that is hard to control and learn.

Significant changes in the mapping are particularly undesirable for two main reasons. If the search space is very rough, the control of human experts seems erratic when they make adjustments to the solution. This does not make their job of adjusting the solution very easy; whereas a with smooth search space, all the chances are on the experts' side. The same applies to AI techniques; in many cases, algorithms are used to find solutions to the problem. The mapping can be very unstable when the search space is jagged, which doesn't help the AI at all. Conversely, a smooth search space means that the adjustments in the solution are easy to control and understand by the AI.

In practice, it's relatively easy to check how smooth the search space is. Starting with random configurations of the solution, the internal values are adjusted and the corresponding changes on the output are measured. The jump in the mapping very much depends on the interdependency between the internal variables. For example, adjusting a single weight in a multilayer perceptron can have a knock-on effect for all succeeding neurons, completely changing the entire mapping. On the other hand, changing a single rule of a rule-based system will only change a few isolated output conditions.

The system designer has direct control over the properties of the search space. Chapter 21 discussed decisions at the problem level that affect the search space (for instance, selecting the right inputs and outputs). From the solutions point of view, engineers have control over the parameters of the representation (for instance, number of hidden neurons' maximum decision tree branching). The most appropriate technique can also be chosen without any prejudice. All these factors are in our control, and almost guarantee that a working solution can be developed with a smooth search space.

Different Approaches to Finding a Solution

Given the representation, we need to find the right instance of the internal values to provide a valid solution. The existence of a brute-force solution (revealed by information theory from the first section of this chapter) and the smoothness of the search space (analysis of the representation in the second section) provide little benefit if we can't solve the problem!

It's the job of the developer to pick the AI technique so that the internal variables of the solution are set correctly. Assuming it's possible for this type of representation to express the solution, there are different approaches to find the right values for each of these internal variables.

Expert Solution

Some AI techniques rely on the engineer to create the internal knowledge of the solution. This is the case for rule-based systems, where the developer crafts the rules (for instance, for wall following). An expert could also create a decision tree manually in the same fashion for weapon selection.

In this approach, the AI developer uses all his experience and wisdom to find the best possible instance. The developer is also responsible for updating the solution if it doesn't work immediately (common in the experimentation phase).

Expert Guidance

Taking a broader view of this approach, the developer can get involved on several levels to help find the solution. Instead of finding the solution directly (level 0 contribution), the expert can devise algorithms to find the right configuration (level 1). This is the case of multilayer perceptrons, where the gradient descent technique allows the adjustment of the weight to a near-optimal configuration.

With even less involvement, the expert can develop technology that helps general algorithms find the right solution (level 2). This is the case with decision trees; the statistical heuristic used to determine the best attribute helps the generic recursive partitioning algorithm find a solution.

The higher the involvement of the expert (level n), the less work needs to be done to have an effect on finding the solution. The understanding of the algorithms becomes more and more abstract, however, so it can be difficult to understand the consequences of high-level policies. In games, low-level involvement allows explicit control but can be time-consuming. Higher-level involvement results in less work but can suffer from the indirect nature control.

Exhaustive

A less sophisticated—but fully automated—approach relies on brute force to find the solution. All the configurations are tested until one of them matches the criteria laid out by the design. Each of the values is searched methodically, often in the form of nested "for" loops. All the instances are therefore searched exhaustively (hence the term "search space").

The major advantage of this approach is thoroughness. If there is a solution using the representation, it will be found! The cost of this guarantee is computation power—lots of it. This can be suitable for preprocessing in game AI, but nothing else.

Random

A random approach to finding a solution essentially chooses the instance stochastically. It is evaluated by a third-party component, and the process is repeated until the solution is acceptable.

The advantage of this approach is that there is no particular bias toward any type of solution. This means that we'll get a representative distribution of the possible instances of the solution before a satisfactory one is found. This approach is very unpredictable by nature, however, and no guarantees on a time scale to find a solution can be made.

Hybrid Approaches

Most AI techniques use a blend of these approaches. All the previous paradigms have tremendous advantages; often, they can be combined successfully. In many cases, particular solutions are better suited to different kinds of approaches, so we have the freedom of choosing the best technique for the job. In many cases, the choice is made among the techniques presented in this book, which provides a diversity of approaches.

Summary

This chapter described the various aspects of solutions in general, starting with an *information theory* study:

➤ The solution is a mapping from inputs to outputs, within which there are many types of patterns.

➤ Compressing this data leaves us with essential information that indicates the complexity of the mapping.

➤ There is a trade-off between finding patterns to approximate data and missing out on information with oversimplifications.

➤ We can measure the quality of a representation or instance using the MDL principle, which provides a trade-off between precision and generalization.

➤ Although algorithms use these principles, understanding these concepts helps AI developers find better solutions.

Then, the concepts behind the representation were analyzed in more depth:

➤ The solution's representation is often different from the representation of the problem.

➤ The representation indirectly determines the size of the search space.

➤ It's relatively easy to compute the total number of configurations by multiplying the size of internal variables together.

➤ The representation chosen has an effect on the smoothness of the search space.

➤ We can control the properties of the search space by tweaking parameters of the representation, or even selecting the right representation.

The simulation of the solution (that is, computing the result) depends on the representation. By contrast, there are some common concepts behind the training mechanisms:

➤ Human experts can intervene at various levels to provide guidance to find the solution.

➤ Other native approaches include exhaustive search and random scanning of the search space.

➤ Combinations of these different approaches are very common, if not essential, for any solution to work effectively.

The concepts in this chapter tend to come in handy while applying AI techniques to new problems. Although the ideas may seem somewhat abstract, they provide pertinent insights that guide the design of solutions. The only way to get comfortable with this process is to practice, practice, practice!

Practical Demo

Guinea is an animat that has modular capabilities for movement and shooting. These are used to collect all the solution data, ready for analysis. By examining the mappings for each of the capabilities, the best AI technique can be chosen. *Guinea* provides the necessary facilities to apply ideas from information theory, and can be found online at `http://AiGameDev.com/`.

Part IV

Conclusion

This part has proven extremely entertaining; two very successful prototypes for weapon selection have been developed, almost at opposing ends of the spectrum of techniques available (static design versus online learning)—yet surprisingly similar in many respects. The behaviors created certainly contribute toward the intelligence of the animats and provide additional realism. The AI is certainly much closer to providing a worthy deathmatch opponent!

Retrospective Overview

With the experience of Part IV behind us, a critical analysis is in order.

Techniques

Voting systems have many advantages in game development:

➤ **Powerful**—They can successfully handle many problems.

➤ **Flexible**—The system is based on customized voters.

➤ **Extendible**—New voters and candidates can be added easily.

Sadly, voting systems can require a lot of effort to tweak during the experimentation phase, notably to get the votes balanced right and the suitable weights.

Decision trees, too, are an incredibly useful AI technique. When used in the right context, they have many benefits. They are extremely simple conceptually; all we need is a tree. Decision trees are designed to be fast, and are capable of processing huge quantities of data in real time. They are also very good general-pattern recognizers, capable of dealing with continuous and categorical variables.

On the downside, decision trees can be somewhat painful to train, like other supervised learning techniques. Indeed, it's still necessary to find the data for the decision tree to learn! This requires preprocessing, or a separate phase for gathering information.

Behaviors

As for the weapon-selection behaviors, these generally prove quite satisfactory. In many cases, the choice of weapons is limited, and there are many acceptable options. This means that the AI has plenty of tolerance as to what is classified as a realistic weapon choice. As long as there's no fast switching, the behaviors are mostly acceptable.

Both the voting system and the decision tree rely on assumptions at a certain level. The voting system depends on statistics about the weapons, so that it can deduce the best weapon—in theory. The decision tree learns the properties of the weapons, but relies on assumptions used to compute the training data. We used a simplified voting system to do this, and the behaviors are satisfactory. However, the weapon selection is not optimal. There is no sense of survival or desire to score points, so the animat has no idea of the purpose of better weapon selection.

Outlook

In this part, we managed to disregard high-level tactics as much as possible. This was possible by using expert wisdom and supervised learning. In many cases, however, the weapon-selection behavior integrates with the tactics. Often, criteria used in choosing weapons depend on the tactical behavior and the current state. We'll cover high-level tactics in Part VII, and we'll discuss how to integrate the existing decision tree design then.

Parts III and IV focused on offensive behaviors, including shooting and weapon selection. Such capabilities often go hand in hand with defensive behaviors, such as dodging fire or picking up armor. The next part covers these capabilities and neutral behaviors, such as climbing ladders or using platforms. This will make our animats better-rounded individuals—and therefore more realistic to other players.

Part V

Using Items and Objects

The animats created so far are sensitive to particular aspects of the world (for instance, obstacles), but insensitive to most objects. They have broad senses but selective perception, because previous parts of this book focus on important behaviors and neglect little details.

This part remedies this problem, rounding out the animat's skills. Notably, they are taught how to interact with various objects in the world (for instance, picking up items, pressing buttons, and following on) and shown how to *not* use objects (for instance, putting a pin back in grenades and trying to catch rockets).

Motivation

The main goal of this part is to deal with all the little details that make a good deathmatch nonplayer character (NPC). This involves actively collecting items such as armor, weapons, and ammunition. We also want our AI not to look stupid when encountering a ladder, platform, or door. The animats should not avoid doors like obstacles, lacking the perception and capability to deal with such contraptions. Essentially, the AI must make the most of all the items in the world.

There's also another aspect to this part: defensive behaviors. Dodging behaviors or evasive maneuvers can be seen as ways to use objects in the world—specifically avoiding projectiles. These instincts of survival also balance out the offensive behaviors developed previously.

The animats also learn to rocket jump, using the same technology as dodging fire. In fact, technically speaking, the following chapters provide a way to deal with many heterogeneous behaviors using similar AI technology.

As far as learning is concerned, an intuitive representation bridges the gap between hand-designed behaviors and learned ones by encoding action sequences in a way that's convenient for the computer and the designer, with advantages for both parties involved.

Outline

As more of the AI becomes complete, less time needs to be spent defining interfaces, so the time is used to brush up on some technology. Three chapters cover theory, two focus on practice, one chapter has a lesson, and one chapter discusses preparations:

Chapter 29, "Analysis and Specification." The first chapter of this part merges the three predevelopment phases together as preparation: analysis of the environment's involvement, understanding the behaviors from a human player's perspective, and specification of extensions to existing interfaces.

Chapter 30, "Fuzzy Logic." In this chapter, we focus on the theory behind a popular AI paradigm known as fuzzy logic. We show how fuzzy logic is better suited to represent linguistic concepts as defined by humans. To use fuzzy logic in practice, we need a fuzzy expert system—similar to standard rule-based systems.

Chapter 31, "Enhancing Movement Behaviors with a Fuzzy System." In this chapter, fuzzy logic is applied to enhance movement behaviors. Notably, fuzzy rules control the animats up ladders, onto platforms, and through doors. The fuzzy approach enables us to create very smooth-looking behaviors.

Chapter 32, "Genetic Algorithms." Now it's time for another chapter on theory—specifically, genetic algorithms. In essence, evolutionary principles are applied to optimize behaviors by letting only the fittest solutions survive.

Chapter 33, "Learning Classifier Systems." Combining genetic algorithms and representations based on rules, this chapter introduces learning classifier systems. This technique can be used to adapt behaviors to problems by trial and error in the environment. The best set of rules can be learned this way.

Chapter 34, "Adaptive Defensive Strategies with Genetic Algorithms." By using a genetic algorithm and similar concepts to classifier systems, the animats learn action sequences. Specifically, they adapt defensive strategies by dodging fire or using preventive maneuvers. Rocket jumping also is learned in this chapter with an evolutionary AI technique.

Chapter 35, "Designing Learning AI." The last chapter of this part is a lesson on learning AI. We discuss the different ways of simulating it, and the various approaches that can be taken. This chapter also presents tips and tricks to design a learning AI that avoids common pitfalls.

Assumptions

By this stage, an impressive amount of work has been done. Most of the code will obviously be reused, along with the tools, framework, and game engine:

➤ The AI relies on **previous behaviors** for teaching the animats. The animats need to have basic movement, and their enemies must be able to shoot.

➤ The world needs to have **support for contraptions** such as doors and platforms that behave automatically, as handled by the game logic. We expect the characters to have necessary low-level animations.

➤ There are **items in the world** such as weapons, armor, and ammunition that the animat can perceive. The interaction with these items is also handled by the game engine, and the animations are dealt with transparently.

These are similar assumptions made throughout the previous parts and should be familiar by now. Be sure to visit the web site at `http://AiGameDev.com/` for the corresponding code and setup instructions.

Chapter 29

Analysis and Specification

KEY TOPICS

- Objects in the World
- Behavior Enhancements
- Specification

A t this stage of the book, the reactive animats are competent enough to perform various tasks such as wandering around and engaging basic combat. To make them more intelligent, we must increase their capabilities by allowing them to perform short sequences of actions (such as using doors or platforms and dodging incoming fire). Although these short plans are still short-term reactive behaviors, they can make the animats appear surprisingly realistic.

The next few pages prepare the development of these behaviors by analyzing the platform, understanding the problem, and specifying the world interfaces. This process is relatively familiar now, with the previous parts covering it in depth, so progression through these phases is much quicker here.

This chapter covers the following topics:

➤ The objects in the game environment, both items that can be picked up and contraptions that affect the movement. How they affect the player and how they are dealt with by the engine.

➤ The way human players manage to develop behaviors to use items and contraptions. A case study of each individual behavior for later use during the application phase.

➤ A specification that extends many of the existing interfaces described throughout this book.

At the end of this chapter, we'll have a code skeleton ready for an implementation of these behaviors.

Objects in the World

The game environment is scattered with many different objects, most of which have a purpose. The design of first-person shooters includes items such as health packs, armor, and silencers to enhance the experience. Contraptions such as ladders, platforms, and doors also diversify the gameplay.

Items

Some items in the game have a direct effect on the player's state. When picked up, health packs and stimpacks increase the player's health immediately. The same applies to the various forms of armor; the combat armor, the jacket and vest, as well as the shards contribute positively to the player's armor count. Although *Quake 2* has some subtleties with different armor types (for instance, conversions between green, yellow, and red), the general pattern is very similar to most first-person shooters; the player automatically benefits from health and armor and does not need to pay attention to it.

On the other hand, some items are not always used directly—such as quad damage (four times weapon strength), health regeneration, invincibility, and the silencer. In single-player modes, these items are stored in the inventory, and only activated when the player uses them. During multiplayer games, such as deathmatch or capture the flag, these items are activated automatically in *Quake 2*. This speeds up the game, requires strategy to maximize the benefits of object collection, and increases the importance of item placement.

Contraptions

Because the worlds in first-person shooters are quite realistic, players often encounter challenges such as doors, ladders, and elevators. In many cases, these contraptions have particular structural design goals, such as slowing down escape from a key area or preventing easy access to important weapons.

Specific sequences of actions are often required to activate these contraptions, as defined by the game logic. For example, pressing a switch calls the platform, a key unlocks a door, and the player needs to touch the ladder face on before climbing it. These actions are prerequisites for any player in the world to use these objects.

A Test Bed

Because health and armor are essential parts of deathmatch games, most levels are designed with many items scattered around. We'll have no trouble finding the levels with such items, or testing the AI's capabilities at collecting these items.

On the other hand, contraptions such as doors, teleporters, ladders, platforms, or even jump pads are relatively rare. When they are present, these elements are usually centerpieces to the architecture of a level. Developing the artificial intelligence (AI) requires a variety of different levels as a test bed, because a unique level with all the required features will be hard to find. Developing the AI for ladders and platforms proves somewhat challenging regardless. Indeed, contraptions are quite rare, so there won't be too many opportunities for the animat to test its behaviors.

Using customized simplified levels is a common practice applicable in this case, but precautions are necessary to guarantee that the AI is capable of generalizing to real game levels. To increase the likelihood of encountering training situations, the animat can be taught in phases by alternating complementary behaviors—for example, going up a ladder and down again. This will provide ample opportunities to develop the necessary skills in the animats, although this approach depends on a separate training period. (Running back and forth can't be done during the game.)

Behavior Enhancements

Players in the game can take advantage of these items and contraptions with specific behaviors. This section investigates such behaviors, starting with an examination of the human approach. The criteria for evaluating AI at this task are discussed, and a case study of the behaviors required finishes the section.

Human Approach

The use of items is the most important ability for humans, then dealing with contraptions, and, finally, behaviors involving objects indirectly.

Picking Up Items

Collecting objects in first-person shooters is mostly a matter of moving toward them and walking over them. The items are automatically used by the player, either added to the inventory or processed directly.

We've already discussed movement as a preventive measure for avoiding obstacles, and even movement with loose goals such as exploration or wandering. The process of picking up items is more focused; it requires moving in a very specific direction.

Humans do this almost subconsciously, combined with the other movement behaviors (such as preventing collision). Picking up objects can be considered a short-term goal-directed behavior that only leads to small detours. Rarely does seeking a target affect the primitive movement abilities, such as avoiding ledges and preventing collision; humans are very good at combining these sometimes contradictory requests.

Using Contraptions

Handling contraptions in the environment (for instance, ladders or platforms) is more of a challenge; the movement required is not a special case of wandering behaviors. Additional skills such as pressing switches (voluntary contact), waiting for an event, or moving vertically on ladders are more sophisticated behaviors.

On top of this, players also need to combine abilities together to get through contraptions. Sequences of actions are needed to move through open doors or catch an elevator. Each action is triggered by events or conditions that arise from the previous action. For this reason, these short "plans" can be considered as reactive because they are driven by direct observations.

These sequences of actions are therefore very simple. After the decision has been made to use the contraption, it's just a matter of acting reactively according to a set pattern—with little or no variation. Apart from the actions required to activate the contraptions, few other actions are taken.

Behavior Enhancers

This part of book covers not only the direct use of objects, but also behaviors that involve objects in a less-obvious manner—for example, animats that rocket jump or even dodge incoming projectiles. Just like the use of contraptions, behavior enhancers can be considered as a sequence of reactive actions. The difference, however, is that the behaviors are triggered at arbitrary moments rather than in specific locations.

Naturally, players determine the most appropriate moment to dodge weapons or rocket jump—instead of doing it all the time. The question of dodging projectiles is relatively straightforward, because it's only possible when a weapon has been fired. On the other hand, determining when to rocket jump is instead dependent on the height of the obstacle in front, and the desire of the player to lose health to get over that.

Criteria

Just like for other reactive behaviors, certain properties are expected to maintain the illusion of realism. Luckily, the AI relies on existing movement capabilities developed in Part II, so much of the work is already done—guaranteeing smooth, humanlike motion.

In this part, we must pay attention not to abuse the "enhanced" behaviors to prevent them from standing out too much. Even if they are realistic, it's good practice to try and keep their use to a minimum. A good way to achieve this is to abide by the following criteria:

➤ **Effectiveness**—By making the behavior as efficient as possible (for instance, no wasteful moves or pauses), the result will be close to what was intended by the design of the door or platform. The optimal behavior is easy for the AI to learn, but also comes close to human behavior.

➤ **Consistency**—The actions need to be justifiable. The last thing we need is an AI that performs one action, but does not follow up on it—for instance, opening a door but not going through it. The entire sequence of actions needs to be consistent.

These are the basic criteria we'll use to evaluate our animat's behaviors from a high-level perspective. We need a case study to explain the lower-level details.

Case Study

Because there's little common ground among the behaviors, they need to be analyzed separately:

➤ When opening a **door**, the player walks toward the switch and it gets pressed automatically on contact. The player stands back while the door opens, and walks through as soon as it opens wide enough.

➤ Getting onto a **platform** first involves pressing a switch, and then waiting for the platform to reach its destination. When it's in place, the player gets on and the platform will generally move up automatically.

➤ To get on **ladders**, the player must move forward until contact is made. The player must face in the direction of the ladder at all times in order not to fall off. Climbing is achieved by looking upward and moving forward.

➤ **Jump pads** just need to be walked on, at which point the player gets projected into the air. By moving when in the air, the player can control the fall.

➤ **Dodging** incoming missiles is a matter of moving away from the line of fire, as well as moving away from the estimated point of impact.

➤ **Rocket jumping** is a matter of looking down, jumping using the standard command, and then releasing a rocket into the ground.

Such capabilities will enhance our animats to a level that matches the reactive behaviors of humans.

Specification

Before implementing these behaviors, it's necessary to define world interfaces. At this point, more than halfway through this book, we are relying on many interfaces to improve our animat's behaviors. This section mostly extends existing interfaces, so the usual *sketching*, *rationalizing*, and *formalizing* phases are dealt with quickly.

Motion

Our existing world interface for movement currently supports turning and moving. There's a lot of flexibility in this specification; the AI can stop, walk, and run by providing movement vectors of different magnitude. It's also possible to look in any direction.

However, the AI has little control over the body's stance. The animat cannot crawl, for instance, or leap in any direction. Two additional modifier functions can be added, allowing the AI to achieve things such as rocket jumping or dodging fire:

```
void Jump();
void Duck();
```

The Jump command corresponds to the same action that human players can perform. Combined with a Move command, this produces a directed leap. The Duck command makes the animat crouch, and combined with a move command allows the animat to crawl.

Inventory

The previous part proposes a query for determining which weapons are available. To handle inventory items in general, the same interface is extended:

```
void ItemsAvailable(vector<Entity>& items, const Entity::Type&
unifier = 0);
```

The weapon interface is used quite often, so keeping this query separate makes it more convenient to use, and less code is required to interpret the result. To actually activate an item in the game, we can use the identifier symbol stored by an entity and call another function:

```
bool UseItem( Symbol& item );
```

Items such as the silencer, quad damage, or even keys can be used by the animats this way, if they are not activated automatically.

Vision

No functional extensions are needed for the vision interface; only additional data is passed through it. For example, doors and platforms also can be handled as entities, so a similar call to `VisibleEntities()` would suffice. The platform must guarantee to provide this information; ladders, for example, are not entities in the *Quake 2* engine, so the framework needs to deal with them.

Entities such as doors carry some additional information indicating whether they are open, closed, or locked. We can understand this as an inheritance of entities in the game. (That is, a door is a kind of object.) The simplest C-like way to handle this is to provide a custom data pointer with each entity, which the AI would have to interpret depending on its type. Alternatively, each entity could be inherited from the base class, passed through the interface by typecasting. Either approach is similar in means, although the C++ inheritance approach is safer.

The message-passing mechanism also needs to handle doors and platforms. For example, events must signal that a door is open or that a platform has stopped after reaching its destination. Callback functions also can be used to alert the animat of these events.

```
void OnDoorOpen( const Event& event );
```

The content of this message would provide the information required to determine the location of the door.

Physical State

Finally, we want to extend the physical interface to return information about the state of the animat. This includes queries such as holding on to a ladder, standing on a platform, or even the type of medium (for instance, air or water).

We can handle this with a collection of simple queries. This proves much easier than having one generic query with parameters and complex output types:

```
bool isPlatform();
bool isLadder();
bool isWater();
bool isAir();
```

These queries could easily be wrapped into one function taking an enumeration as a parameter if necessary.

Summary

This chapter started by analyzing the platform for the AI, notably explaining the objects and contraptions in the environment and how they are handled by the engine. We've identified the following information:

➤ **Assumptions**—Items are picked up automatically. Some are activated instanta-neously, whereas others are placed in the inventory. The contraptions operate mostly autonomously, occasionally requiring the player to press buttons.

➤ **Restrictions**—Certain items have limited applicability. (For instance, a silencer works when firing, and quad damage relies on damage.) Contraptions require particular sequences of actions to be used correctly.

➤ **Guidelines**—Environments with many items around are necessary to simplify the development of the AI. Many different game levels are needed for all the contrap-tions to be attempted by the AI.

The second section of this chapter tried to understand the problem, investigating the behavior of human players. This enabled us to define a problem definition on two levels:

➤ **Criteria**—High-level properties specific to this problem were identified (effective-ness and consistency) and used when evaluating the AI behaviors.

➤ **Problem definition**—A description of the expected outcome of each task was pro-vided as a step-by-step walkthrough. This serves as a reference in the upcoming application phase.

The final section of this chapter established a specification, or rather, extended existing interfaces. This provided us with additional inputs and outputs, allowing the AI to interface with the platform.

Before putting these interfaces to use, another AI technique is investigated. Fuzzy expert systems can be seen as an extension to rule-base systems, capable of expressing behaviors to use doors and platforms, or even climb up ladders.

Practical Demo

An animat, known as *Greedy*, demonstrates the concept behind collecting objects. *Greedy* attempts to collect every object in sight, moving on when the item is not picked up or remains inaccessible. The AI is built upon the steering behaviors used in Chapter 10, "Steering Behaviors for Obstacle Avoidance." See `http://AiGameDev.com/` for the code and binary.

Chapter 30

Fuzzy Logic

KEY TOPICS

- Set Logic Extended
- Fuzzy Representation and Conversions
- Fuzzy Logic
- Fuzzy Control and Decision Making
- Discussion

Classical logic can only model crisp values: The enemy is either dead or not. Probabilities express the likelihood of a crisp variable having a specific value: This door has an 80-percent chance of being open. Fuzziness is conceptually different because it models degrees of truth: The enemy is mostly dead, and this door is nearly shut. At times, crisp AI suffers from clear-cut decisions and very robotic control. The fuzzy approach resolves the issue by providing shades of gray between black and white, allowing animats to attack with moderation (decision making) or turn left slightly (smooth control).

This form of knowledge representation is very intuitive, and comes surprisingly close to modeling human thoughts. Using a model closer to linguistic definitions can simplify the design of systems, enabling humans (not only experts) to add knowledge to the system.

Although the concept of fuzziness is easy to include in most architectures (with fuzzy senses or actions), it's only thanks to fuzzy expert systems that the true power of fuzzy logic is harnessed.

This chapter covers the following topics:

➤ Fuzzy set theory as a logical foundation for the technique

➤ The concept of representation with fuzziness, and conversions to/from crisp representations

➤ Fuzzy logic as a way to manipulate fuzzy variables with operators and expressions

➤ How fuzzy principles are integrated into expert systems, capable of decision making and control

The theory from this chapter can be applied to a wide variety of problems in game development, providing levels of realism that other crisp techniques struggle to reach. Fuzzy techniques in the next chapter help the animats climb ladders and use platforms.

Set Logic Extended

Fuzzy approaches are primarily based on fuzzy set theory. As such, its foundations lie in formal definitions, which are explained in this section using parallels with classical logic. Indeed, fuzziness can be seen as an extension to Boolean set theory, used daily in programming.

Principles

In classical logic, all sets are *crisp*. True and false are crisply defined (for instance, 1 and 0). A value either belongs to a set, or it doesn't. Numbers are crisp, too, meaning each concept is perfectly known and expressed as such (for instance, health = 68, armor = 41).

As the saying goes, some things in life aren't just black and white. With crisp values, there's no way to express a value close to a set but not quite inside it. We can't have something that's *mostly true*, or *not entirely false*. With classical set logic, it's not possible to create a set that is not precisely defined, or a number that's relatively close to a value. We want to express part membership.

Fuzzy Sets

Fuzzy set theory can get around these limitations. Essentially, each set is defined by a membership function—with smooth variations rather than crisp borders. For each value in the *universe of discourse X*, the membership function defines a real number in the range [0,1]. This is the degree of membership; a value of 1 indicates the item is fully in the set, whereas 0 means the item is not in the set. Intermediate values indicate part membership:

$$\mu_A : \quad X \rightarrow [0,1]$$
$$x \, \alpha \ \mu_A(x), \ \rightarrow x \in X$$

A *membership function*, as shown in Figure 30.1, is generally denoted with the Greek letter mu (μ). The preceding equation explains that membership function μ_A—for a given set A—maps the universe X onto the interval [0,1]. Implicitly, this transforms every item x onto its degree of membership to set A, written $\mu_A(x)$. For the sake of simplicity, however, we often use the notation $\mu_A(x) = A(x)$.

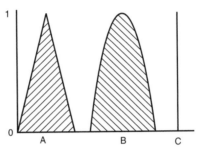

Figure 30.1   Example of different fuzzy membership functions: triangle (A), curve (B) and crisp singleton (C).

Strictly speaking, a fuzzy set is a collection of ordered pairs with items from the universe and their corresponding degree of membership $(x, \mu_A(x))$. A pair can be referred to as a *fuzzy singleton* [Jantzen98]. The following expression describes A as a set of such singletons:

$$A = \{(x, \mu_A(x))\} \ | \rightarrow x \in X$$

In practice, it's often easier just to represent set A with vector a, rather than a collection of singletons. The vector contains the grades of membership for elements in the universe. For this to be possible, we need to know the correspondence between membership values in the vector and items from the universe. The correspondence can be achieved by using the same order for declarations. Let's say A is the set of *hostile* objects, defined for all objects in X:

$$X = \{door, gun, fred, bot_1\}$$
$$a = \begin{bmatrix} 0 & 0 & 0.3 & 0.8 \end{bmatrix}$$

So, explicitly, the vector definition would correspond to the following definition of A:

$$A = \{(door,0),\ (gun,0),\ (fred,0.3),\ (bot_1,0.8)\}$$

This definition associates each object with its degree of hostility. So let's move on to manipulating these vectors. It's possible to combine such fuzzy sets, using similar definitions for classical logic.

Set Theory

We need *fuzzy set theory* to provide a basic definition for manipulating fuzzy sets. Two sets are equal if and only if ($\Leftrightarrow$) the two membership functions are the same for all ($\forall x$) values of x:

$$A = B \Leftrightarrow \forall x\colon A(x) = B(x)$$

Relationships between sets can also be expressed, such as containment (strict subset, denoted $\subset$). This can be combined with the definition of equality for *subset or equal*. A set is a subset of another if and only if the membership value is lower for all *x*:

$$A \subset B \Leftrightarrow \forall x\colon A(x) < B(x)$$

Operations on fuzzy sets such as AND (set intersection, denoted $\cap$) and OR (set union, denoted $\cup$) are defined as follows:

$$C = A \cap B \Leftrightarrow \forall x\colon C(x) = \min(A(x),\ B(x))$$
$$C = A \cup B \Leftrightarrow \forall x\colon C(x) = \max(A(x),\ B(x))$$

If we want to define a membership function that includes two sets, we use the maximum of the two functions (OR). If we need to find the common parts, we use the minimum (AND). This makes more sense graphically, as depicted in Figure 30.2.

The complement $\overline{A}$ of a set A is defined as follows (logical NOT):

$$\overline{A}(x) = 1 - A(x)$$

A set is empty if and only if the membership value is always 0:

$$A = \emptyset \Leftrightarrow \forall x: A(x) = 0$$

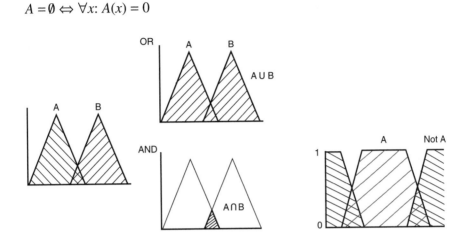

Figure 30.2   Operations on fuzzy sets. OR is the maximum of the two values; AND is the minimum of two values.

Fuzzy Modifiers

In the expression "very dangerous," the adjective "dangerous" would be a fuzzy set; players can belong to it with a degree of membership. The adverb "very" is a *linguistic modifier* that alters the meaning of such terms. Therefore, a *fuzzy modifier* can be seen as an operation on a set:

dangerous = [0   0.1   0.4   0.8   1]
very dangerous = [0   0.01   0.16   0.64   1]

From this example, we can see that an item that is not dangerous (0) is not very dangerous (0). At the other end, an element with membership of 1 to dangerous will also be very dangerous. For items in between, their membership is diminished, as shown in Figure 30.3.

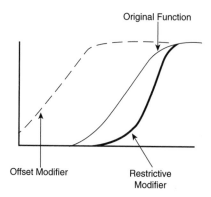

Original Function

Offset Modifier

Restrictive
Modifier

Figure 30.3   Example of modified sets based on a primary fuzzy set. One is a restrictive modifier (very), and the other is an offset modifier.

More formally, a modifier m can be seen as a function over the domain of all fuzzy sets $F(X)$. It converts any set a into another modified set $m(a)$:

$$m: \quad F(X) \rightarrow F(X)$$
$$a \; \alpha \; m(a) \quad |\rightarrow a \in F(X)$$

In practice, how do we determine how "very dangerous" an object is based on its danger? It's a direct mapping that can be applied to individual items and the entire set:

$$\text{very } a = a^2$$
$$\text{extremely } a = a^3$$

Both these examples are known as *restrictive* modifiers, because the modified fuzzy set is a subset of the original: $A \subseteq m(A)$, so all the modified membership values are lower. Conversely, there are also *expansive* modifiers verifying $m(A) \subseteq A$, where the membership values are higher or equal—as in the following example:

$$\text{more or less } a = \sqrt{a}$$
$$\text{slightly } a = \sqrt[3]{a}$$

It's important to remember that membership values are within the range $[0..1]$, so values of x above 1 will make a^x smaller, and values of x below 1 will make a^x bigger. With $x = +\infty$, the modifier would be called "exactly"; and for $x = 0$, the closest linguistic term seems to be "always" (as $a^0 = 1$).

There are also offsetting modifiers that "shift" a fuzzy set by a constant amount: $A(x) = m(A(x + k))$. Such modifiers are sometimes closer to the intuitive meaning of adverbs, as used in human communication.

Fuzzy Representation and Conversions

Using fuzzy set theory, it's possible to define fuzzy values that are stored in single fuzzy variables. These fuzzy variables can be combined to create a more intuitive concept known as *linguistic variables*.

To initialize these fuzzy values from crisp numbers, the membership function is used. Converting from crisp to fuzzy is known as fuzzification, and the opposite is known as defuzzification.

Fuzzy Variables and Values

A fuzzy variable can be considered as a term, associated with a single float representing a fuzzy truth value. There is nothing complex about this intrinsically; it's just a symbol/number pair. For example, the variables shown in Table 30.1 might represent an enemy in a deathmatch.

Table 30.1   Collection of Fuzzy Variables, Each Assigned a Particular Value to Represent an Enemy

Term	Value
Healthy	0.9
Dangerous	0.3
Moving	0.0

These variables are conceptually independent from each other. To give each concept a more intuitive definition, fuzzy variables can be combined.

Linguistic Variables

Linguistic variables are a more sophisticated representation, and prove more human-like. They harness the power of fuzzy logic to model real concepts without being limited to one fuzzy variable, or tied to the precision of crisp variables.

A linguistic variable is a high-level concept, such as health (see Table 30.2). However, instead of being associated with only one fuzzy variable, it corresponds to a collection of them—each a symbol/real number pair. Each symbol is known as a *term*; the group of fuzzy terms is known as the *term set*.

Table 30.2   A Linguistic Variable Representing the Concept of Allegiance

Term set	{enemy,neutral,friendly}
Values	[0.0, 0.4, 0.9]

These fuzzy variables are used in conjunction with each other to express the linguistic variable. Taken alone, they do not have the same meaning.

The linguistic variable is defined over *base variables*. The base variables correspond to the set of values over which the terms are defined. Base variables can correspond to continuous crisp values and fuzzy terms (see Figure 30.4).

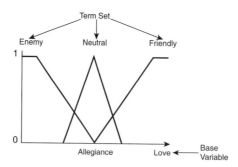

Figure 30.4   The linguistic variable allegiance defined as a collection of membership functions defined over a single base variable (love).

The terms appear as fuzzy sets. Some terms have modifiers attached to them, others remain without modifiers; these are know as *primary terms*.

Fuzzification

Fuzzification is the process of creating a fuzzy variable from a crisp value. This is done by using fuzzy sets. The membership function defines the value of a fuzzy variable, as shown in Figure 30.5. The universe of discourse is in fact the range of the crisp value. Evaluating the membership function in terms of this crisp value results in the degree of membership.

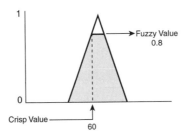

Figure 30.5   Using the membership function to determine a fuzzy value in terms of a crisp value in the universe of discourse.

Naturally, the speed of the fuzzification depends entirely upon the efficiency of the membership function. For simple functions, it's faster to evaluate it dynamically with a native implementation. Using more complex membership functions may warrant the use of lookup tables to speed up the process.

Defuzzification

The process of defuzzification aims to do the exact opposite of fuzzification: convert a fuzzy value to a crisp value. This is relatively straightforward for atomic fuzzy values, but can get trickier for linguistic variables. The problem is to find a single crisp value for a concept expressed as a set of fuzzy values.

This process fundamentally involves the loss of information; only in the simplest case can the conversion process be lossless (although not all techniques exhibit this property). Each method will therefore have its own set of assumptions and flaws. It's also the case that different approaches to defuzzification are appropriate for certain types of problems (see Figure 30.6). There is no unique equation, because even humans defuzzify linguistic concepts in problem-dependent ways.

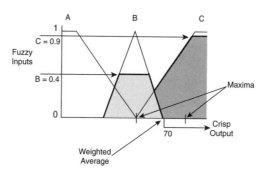

Figure 30.6 The fuzzy sets are used to determine the crisp value in terms of the fuzzy values.

There are two major approaches to defuzzification:

➤ **Maximum** approaches use the highest points in the membership function. The *first of maxima* approach essentially picks the crisp value corresponding to the highest point of all the membership functions. *Average of maxima* instead uses the average of all the crisp values. Sometimes, this average is weighted by the degree of membership.

➤ **Centroid** requires computing the area covered by the membership function. The crisp value can correspond to the center of gravity of the entire fuzzy set, or to the average of the center of each area. Such approaches are computationally intense, because they either rely on heavy analysis or mathematical knowledge of the integral of the membership function (to find the area).

When simple atomic sets are used as the fuzzy sets, the maximum approach works just fine. It's simple to implement, and faster by an order of magnitude. Indeed, we don't even need to compute the maxima, because we often know it (used to define the membership function). Centroid methods can be seen as more mathematically correct, but this seems out of place compared to the informal nature of fuzzy reasoning.

Fuzzy Logic

We've seen that fuzzy sets can be used to convert crisp values to fuzzy values, and vice versa, but we don't need sets to manipulate fuzzy values together. So how do we perform operations on fuzzy values? Cue fuzzy logic.

Operators

The concepts of fuzzy logic are similar to those used in fuzzy set theory—but much simpler. Once again, min/max are used as operators to replace the logical operands AND/OR. The basic operators in fuzzy predicate logic are defined in Table 30.3.

Table 30.3   Fuzzy Operators with Their Corresponding Notation from Boolean Logic, and the Equations Used to Compute the Resulting Fuzzy Value

Operator	Notation	Equation
NOT	$\neg$	1-x
AND	$\wedge$	MIN(x,y)
OR	$\vee$	MAX(x,y)
IMPLIES	$\Rightarrow$	MAX(1-x,y) MAX(0,x+y-1)

Fuzzy implication has been defined in different ways, because each alternative has analogies with its Boolean counterpart. All these operators can naturally be combined with each other to produce compound expressions.

Linguistic Expressions

In fuzzy logic, compound expressions correspond to intuitive statements in natural languages (such as English). This is one of the reasons why it's relatively easy for experts to translate their knowledge into fuzzy form, as shown in Table 30.4.

Linguistic expressions can be seen as a set of fuzzy values combined with fuzzy operators. Linguistic modifiers can also be used to change the meaning of fuzzy values (for instance, extremely, slightly), as discussed for fuzzy set theory.

Table 30.4   Some English Statements and Their Corresponding Fuzzy Expressions Using Fuzzy Values, Operators, and Modifiers

Statement	Expression
Dead or alive	$d \vee a$
Extremely nasty and more or less dead	$n^3 \wedge \sqrt{d}$
Shot and bleeding badly implies dying	$s \wedge b^2 \Rightarrow d$

Converting plain English to fuzzy linguistic expressions can present its challenges. It's obvious that most adjectives correspond to fuzzy values. However, assigning a meaning to the adverbs can be tricky; how do we define bleeding badly in terms of bleeding? In this case, badly is clearly a modifier. Finding an equation to match the meaning of a modifier is not as intuitive as writing English, so this often requires a knowledge engineer.

Objections to Fuzzy Logic

The set theory behind fuzzy logic is still somewhat controversial—especially within the classical logic community. It may seem obvious why we need fuzzy values with degrees of membership, but couldn't this be modeled using "standard" mathematical concepts?

For this reason, fuzzy researches have put a lot of effort into justifying the difference between fuzziness and probability. They are indeed similar, but there are conceptual differences. Fuzziness is in fact *deterministic uncertainty*. A fuzzy value measures the degree to which a statement is true. Probability expresses the likelihood of it being either true or false.

Another major problem with fuzzy theory is the apparent inconsistency. For example, given a smooth membership function for skilled gamers, the fuzzy set of gamers that are skilled and not skilled is not empty! There are formal explanations for this; it's because of assumptions from Boolean logic that do not apply to fuzzy logic. The nature of the fuzzy operators is to blame, but choosing anything else but MIN/MAX raises other consistency problems.

Regardless, it seems somewhat ironical for a theory that prides itself on intuitiveness (and similarities with human reasoning) to be logically inconsistent on such simple examples. Despite these flaws, however, fuzzy logic does appear to model human knowledge and reasoning better.

Luckily for fuzzy researchers, fuzzy logic has proven itself extremely successful as a control mechanism (somewhat unexpectedly). Practical applications span numerous domains, from pattern recognition to data mining, including regression and control systems, or even function approximation.

However, some systems use some important simplifications of the "fuzzy" theory (for instance, using Boolean outputs directly). This implies that the entire reasoning just collapses to standard logic. This happens regularly in game AI engines; fuzziness is used as a concept, but the fuzzy logic is simplified to crisp levels for efficiency [Alexander02].

Fuzzy Control and Decision Making

This section discusses how fuzzy logic can be applied to control systems or decision-making architectures. It's simple to understand why the applications are so successful when the technique is so close to rule-based systems (the single most successful AI technique, as discussed in Chapter 11, "Rule-Based Systems").

Isn't fuzzy control an oxymoron? Can it work at all? Of course. Humans do not require precise numerical information, yet they are capable of highly adaptive control. It seems obvious to try to program controllers to accept imprecise and noisy input. Then, the system may be able to deal with complex situations in a smarter fashion, and may be easier to implement. Decision making benefits from the same advantage: human-like reasoning on concepts with degrees of truth.

Working Memory

In fuzzy systems, there is also a working memory. Naturally, the symbols are not crisp values but fuzzy ones. Apart from the obvious fuzziness, there is little distinction between a working memory in a fuzzy system and a standard rule-base system. In fact, in most implementations, the same generic container could be used to store the fuzzy variables.

Knowledge Base

Just like rule-based systems, fuzzy systems rely on a knowledge base, containing a set of rules. Instead of being defined in terms of crisp symbols, fuzzy variables are used instead (see Table 30.5). Unconfident, vulnerable, attack, and retreat are fuzzy variables. Enemy and accuracy are linguistic variables, with healthy/damaged/dying and high/medium/low as fuzzy terms.

Table 30.5 Fuzzy Rules Defined Within the Knowledge Base

Index	Rule
1	IF NOT *unconfident* THEN *attack.*
2	IF very *unconfident* OR somewhat *vulnerable* THEN *retreat.*
3	IF *ammo* IS *low* AND extremely damaged THEN more or less *unconfident.*
4	IF *enemy* IS *healthy* THEN NOT *unconfident.*
5	IF *enemy* IS *dying* and *accuracy* IS very *high* THEN *attack.*

As in rule-based systems, the rules are composed of an antecedent clause (IF), and the consequent clause (THEN). However, there are two major extensions to rules in a fuzzy system:

➤ **Linguistic variables** can be used as elements in the rules. If allegiance is a linguistic variable, the rules could refer to a particular fuzzy term. This is done by using the keyword IS: IF allegiance IS friendly THEN happy. The construct (M is X) simplifies to a single fuzzy variable; it can be seen as an accessor to the X variable in M.

➤ **Fuzzy modifiers** can be applied to each of the variables to add nuance to their meaning. Modifiers are generally applied to the antecedent clause, but in some cases can be used on the consequent clause.

Despite these additions, the acquisition of knowledge is slightly simpler with fuzzy systems. Indeed, fuzzy rules are much closer to human knowledge, which can reduce the number of total rules required. The linguistic expressions and modifiers are also very intuitive to work with, so almost anyone can add rules to the system.

The major problem is creating the membership functions for each of the fuzzy variables. The membership functions have a tremendous effect on the output of the system, so it's important to get it right. Different approaches can be used to create membership functions:

➤ The **knowledge engineer** can consult with the experts in the usual way and extract enough information to understand the nature of the membership function.

➤ A **survey** can also be set up. Different people can be questioned about their understanding of different concepts, and statistics can be used to create a membership function that reflects the average opinion.

➤ In both cases, it's often necessary to perform **incremental tuning**. If the results are not as expected, the developer can attempt to trace the reasoning and correct the faulty membership functions.

After the knowledge base has been created, and all the rules and membership functions have been crafted, they can be manipulated by the interpreter.

Fuzzy Interpreter

The interpreter is responsible for manipulating the variables in the working memory using the rules. There are two key differences compared with crisp rule-based systems: the matching and the evaluation of rules. So almost everything changes!

Matching

In crisp systems, it's obvious which rules match the current working memory. All symbols are either true or false, so it's easy to identify the antecedent clauses that are applicable.

In fuzzy logic, true and false are just special cases. Most of the time, fuzzy values will have partial membership to sets. This is not a problem in itself; the fuzzy rules are meant to have fuzzy inputs.

The problem is that we cannot discard most of the rules. Even fuzzy values with small degrees of truth will need to be plugged into the relevant rules. In practice, most fuzzy values become nonzero after a short amount of execution. So almost every rule has to be checked!

The best way to deal with this is prevention. We can make sure there aren't that many rules in the system! There have been some suggestions to deal with the combinatorial explosion of rules by reorganizing the rules, but these have turned out mathematically inaccurate and only applicable in a few cases.

So it seems the only way to deal with many fuzzy rules is to approximate the computation, to discard rules as in crisp rule-based systems. To do this, the interpreter can just ignore fuzzy values below a certain threshold (considering them false). For example, all the fuzzy values below 0.5 can be ignored, and values above 0.5 can be rescaled to fit the [0,1] range. This can be seen as trimming all the membership functions, but dealing with this in the interpreter instead will be more flexible and no slower. The higher the threshold, the closer the system is to a crisp rule-based system.

This seems a good way to trade off precision with speed. Sadly, the results will not be the same at different thresholds, so precautions need to be taken when developing the system.

Inference

Inference is a process applied to each rule. Essentially, the purpose is to determine the degree of truth of the THEN part of the rule, based on the IF part. This can be achieved using fuzzy logic; the appropriate fuzzy operators can be used to reduce any linguistic expression into a single fuzzy value.

The resulting fuzzy value can be considered as the output of this rule. However, the output is also associated with a fuzzy set—as all other fuzzy variables. This set will only be used for defuzzification. There are two different ways to compute the fuzzy output set (see Figure 30.7):

➤ **MIN** inferencing essentially trims the top off the output membership function to produce the output set.

➤ **PRODUCT** inferencing instead scales the membership function by the output value.

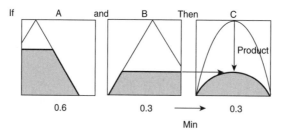

Figure 30.7   Example of fuzzy inference using the product method to scale the output set. The actual fuzzy values are denoted underneath the membership functions.

In the implementation, there's usually no need to manipulate any fuzzy sets. The two different operations—MIN and PRODUCT—can be understood as an interpretation the output value and set. As such, we can take this interpretation into account during the defuzzification; this is lazy evaluation.

Composition

Many rules may have the same fuzzy variable in the body of the rule. The composition stage must take into account each consequent clause that affects a single variable, and combine them together (see Figure 30.8). Again, there are two common ways to do this:

➤ **MAX** composition uses the maximum value of each of the rule outputs. Therefore, the final fuzzy value can be considered as a conjunction (AND) over each of the results for the inference stage.

➤ **SUM** composition takes the total of all the membership values. This can be a problem because the final fuzzy value may be greater than one. As such, summation is often followed by a defuzzification that can handle this problem. The alternative is to average the membership values.

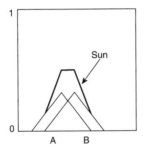

Figure 30.8   Example of fuzzy composition over two sets using summation.

Again, the composition can be interpreted as having two outputs: the actual fuzzy value, and a corresponding fuzzy set. The set itself is only used when defuzzifying, but the fuzzy value is reinserted into the working memory.

Algorithm

The simulation of the fuzzy system requires two copies of the working memory to be consistent. One stores the current results, and the other remembers the previous state (until the update is finished). This is necessary because updating the same working memory leads to somewhat unpredictable results, which depend on the order of processing.

All the rules are processed as shown in Listing 30.1. The system could discard some rules where the antecedent clause is exactly 0. Doing this efficiently requires a treelike structure, as discussed for the rule-based systems. For fuzzy systems, this trick will not pay off because the values are rarely 0.

Listing 30.1   Main Simulation Loop of the Fuzzy System

```
current is the working memory with the latest fuzzy variables
previous is the last state of the working memory

for each value in the working memory
previous[value] = current[value]
current[value] = 0
end for
for each rule
     result = evaluate( rule.expression, previous )
     current[rule.body] = MAX( current[rule.body], result )
end for
```

Discussion

Fuzzy systems are surprisingly robust, managing to cope with noisy and incomplete data. However, the fuzzy output is still extremely smooth and can deal with tight control problems. Little feedback is needed to perform well.

Fuzzy expert systems can mimic human reasoning surprisingly closely, which makes it ideal for decision making. The rule-base systems apply the rules of thumb in a similar fashion to experts, and the fuzzy representation is close to human knowledge representation.

Like rule-based systems, fuzzy systems are easy to extend incrementally. Each rule is modular, and different rules can be tweaked independently from others.

It's even easier to write the rules for the system. The close links with natural language means that anyone can add rules. The linguistic expressions pose no problems to the underlying fuzzy logic.

With fuzzy systems, there is no need for mathematical models of the problem. We use simple rules of thumb created by experts to guide the system, which can cope with complex nonlinear problems.

An intrinsic requirement of fuzzy systems is that most of the rules need to be evaluated at each cycle. This is because even values that are close to false cannot be disregarded—as with standard rule-based systems. This can be quite computationally expensive, although the time required is proportional to the number of rules.

In addition, it can be difficult to create membership functions for fuzzy systems. This is a very informal process that can easily require many iterations.

Combinatorial explosion is a commonly cited problem with fuzzy systems. Indeed, if we want to enumerate rules for all possible inputs combinations, the number of required rules will grow exponentially with the number of fuzzy variables. Frankly, there are few cases when this is necessary! Not only is this time-consuming (making it unfeasible for experts to enter the rules into the database), but also extremely naive. In most problems, there is no need for all possible rules to be present; the solution doesn't need such complexity. Borrowing the ideas from rule-based systems, knowledge in fuzzy systems can be represented implicitly instead. So the only rules required are the ones that solve the problem (which should at least match the number of fuzzy variables).

Summary

Fuzzy techniques are based on foundations in fuzzy set theory, as well as fuzzy logic:

➤ A fuzzy set is modeled as a membership function with smooth variations within unit range.

➤ A fuzzy variable is a symbol associated with a degree of membership to a function.

➤ Linguistic variables are collections of fuzzy variables defined over a base variable.

➤ Logical operations such as conjunction (AND) and disjunction (OR) are performed with MIN and MAX operators.

➤ Fuzzy modifiers are functions applied to change the meaning of sets and values.

Because the fuzzy representation and the processing of fuzzy values differ from standard crisp values, it's often necessary to convert between the two:

➤ Fuzzification is the process of converting a crisp value to a fuzzy value using a membership function.

➤ Defuzzification is a matter of interpreting fuzzy values and their corresponding membership function to determine the most accurate crisp estimate.

To harness the full power of fuzzy logic, fuzzy expert systems are used in a similar fashion to rule-based systems. However, key differences exist:

➤ All the rules are matched, but the fuzzy value of the body differs depending on the fuzzy value of the condition.

➤ To determine the value of a fuzzy variable, the bodies of rules are combined by composition.

➤ Two working memory arrays are needed to maintain consistency, one with the current fuzzy values and one that's being computed.

Fuzzy systems are particularly suited to providing smooth control and making decisions with partial truths. In the next chapter, fuzzy logic is applied to control the behaviors of animats, notably climbing ladders and opening doors.

Practical Demo

An animat known as *Dominator* uses a fuzzy expert system to drive all aspects of the AI. Fuzzy rules are used as a control technique for movement and shooting, whereas the weapon selection uses fuzziness in the decision making. Of all the animats using pure AI techniques as brains, *Dominator* performs among the best. The source and data files can be found online at `http://AiGameDev.com/`.

Chapter 31

Enhancing Movement Behaviors with a Fuzzy System

It's clear that animats with simple obstacle avoidance will struggle in complex environments. To remedy this problem, fuzzy logic is used to craft behaviors necessary for dealing with contraptions—such as ladders, doors, and platforms. These capabilities are created by design, and are not acquired through learning. Other short sequences of actions would be equally as easy to create. Despite the focus on the three major contraptions, any other behavior discussed in the previous chapters could be implemented using an identical methodology.

Having a fallback is the main motivation for tackling the toughest behaviors first—particularly if the learning solution fails or takes too much time to develop for little benefit. This is good practice in a professional setting.

This chapter covers the following topics:

➤ The fuzzy variables involved both externally (interface to the problem) and internally (used by the solution), with an explanation of their membership functions when necessary

➤ Specific fuzzy rules for each of the behaviors, involving combinations of pressing buttons and moving forward

> ➤ The variables for climbing a ladder, using a door, and taking a platform

> ➤ The design of a simple fuzzy logic module to execute the rules, revealing the similarities between rule-based systems and fuzzy interpreters

> ➤ Minor flaws that cause idiosyncrasies in some rare cases, and possible improvements

At the end of this chapter, the artificial intelligence (AI) is enhanced to deal with a complex environment—still using reactive behaviors.

Fuzzy Variables and Membership Functions

The enhanced movement behaviors are defined in terms of concepts in the world, which must be modeled using either fuzzy variables or linguistic variables (that is, a combination of terms). Conceptually, these variables are used by a fuzzy expert system, either inputs to the system or outputs linked to actions. There's no need for internal variables in the actual fuzzy interpreter because the behaviors are truly reactive.

Actions

First, the fuzzy system needs to control the movement. A linguistic variable called move is defined with three different terms: forwards, stop, and backwards. The base variable is defined as the movement velocity. Forwards is defined as half a triangular membership function, corresponding to 0 degree of membership (DoM) when the velocity is null, and a DoM of 1 when the velocity is full. Backwards is defined as the exact opposite, defined as 1 DoM when the full velocity is in reverse. To define the third term, we use a fuzzy equation of the primary terms:

```
stop = not (forwards or backwards)
```

This relationship is relatively intuitive. However, want to sharpen the meaning of stop, because the slope is a bit too gentle. So, we use the fuzzy modifier extremely to obtain a steeper curve, much closer to the informal meaning of stop.

The second form of control needed on the movement is turning the body to influence the direction of travel. To achieve this with a fuzzy interpreter, we'll use another linguistic variable called `turn`. The base variable for `turn` is defined as the relative yaw turning angle in degrees. There are five fuzzy terms defined over this base variable to form the linguistic variable, each of which indicates objects that must be turned toward: `button`, `door`, `ladder`, `platform`, and `exit`. These are dynamic membership functions, because the relative position of these objects changes over time. The triangle membership function is used; the point of the triangle matches the angular position of the object, and the base always goes through the origin. (That is, zero membership means no turn.)

A final variable, called `look`, controls pitch separately. This is a simpler linguistic variable, defined statically. There are two fuzzy terms: `up` and `ahead`. The term `up` corresponds to a pitch of 90, with the base of the triangle going through the origin. The term `ahead` corresponds to a pitch of 0, with the base of the triangle at ±90.

Senses

The senses are other linguistic variables. The `door` is defined over the height of the opening (base variable); the door is defined as "open" if the player can crawl through, which tails off to a DoM of 0 as the door touches the floor. We can also define the fuzzy term "fully open" as a combination of the primary term `open` and the offset modifier `fully`. When the player can walk through, the DoM is 1, and 0 when the player can crawl through.

Then, we define a `button_pressed` term, which is really more of a Boolean singleton than a fuzzy variable. There is no continuous base variable to use (except maybe time), and more to the point, there's little benefit in using one.

The linguistic variable `platform` is defined as two terms: `ready` and `arrived`. Readiness is measured as the distance off the floor, and how easy it is to climb on. The DoM is 1 when the platform is at the starting point, fully on the floor; the DoM triangle then reaches 0 when the player needs to double-jump to get onto the platform. The state `arrived` is measured as the distance to the final location; full DoM corresponds to a distance of 0; when 0, DoM requires a double-jump to get off.

Another simple term, called aboard, indicates whether the animat is on the platform. It's defined with a membership of 0 when the animat is not on the platform. This peaks at the center of the platform to a degree of membership of 1. The base variables are the x and y coordinates on the floor, rather than the distance to the center of the platform. This makes the membership function seem like a pyramid on the platform.

Finally, the linguistic variable for the ladder is defined as two terms: held and top. The term held is defined over time, taking its full 1 DoM value after 1 second of touching, and back to 0 after it has released for a second. The term top is defined over height as a base variable. When the player can just walk off, it has 1 DoM; the DoM triangle reaches 0 one step away from the top.

Fuzzy Rules

Given the variables just defined, we're ready to create the behaviors as a set of rules. To achieve this, we'll use the case studies from Chapter 29, "Analysis and Specification."

Using Doors

The set of rules required to move through a door is that we need to press the button first, and then move through the door when it's ready. The rules, displayed in Table 31.1, reflect the simplicity of the task, involving only four fuzzy terms.

Table 31.1   The Fuzzy Rules That Control the Animat While It Opens and Moves Through an Arbitrary Door

Condition	Action
If not button_pressed	Turn to button, move forward
If button_pressed	Turn to door
If button_pressed and door not fully open	Move stop
If door fully open	Move forward, turn to door

It's important to note that this set of fuzzy rules relies on being interrupted once the door is crossed. The higher-level AI identifies this is the case, and stops calling this fuzzy behavior. The problem is that the animat will continue to try to get through the door again (backwards) once the door has been used. Preventing this problem would require another few symbols and additional rules, thereby complicating the system. It's is certainly feasible—and even desirable—to only let these rules handle the door scenario, and nothing else.

In brief, the behavior does need to specify to stop turning toward the button; in rule 1, the membership value of the action will drop toward 0 when the button is pressed. The same applies for the movement.

Using Ladders

Ladders are equally simple to deal with by using fuzzy rules. The hardest work has been done by the time the rules are written. To climb a ladder, the animat must first move toward it and grab hold of it (handled automatically). Then, it must look up and press forward until the top of the ladder is reached, at which point the animat can look ahead to dismount. Table 31.2 lists the fuzzy rules that express this.

Table 31.2   Set of Fuzzy Rules That Guide an Animat Toward a Ladder, Up the Rungs, and Dismount at the Top

Condition	Action
True	Move forward
If ladder is not held	Turn to ladder
If ladder is held	Look up
If ladder is top	Look ahead, turn to exit

Once again, we'll assume that these fuzzy rules are no longer called by the higher-level AI after the animat has dismounted from the ladder. These fuzzy rules are only expected to be applied to their intended domain.

Using Platforms

The use of platforms involves more actions in the sequence than the previous two behaviors. Consequently, the rulebase is slightly more complex, but the principles remain the same. The animat presses the button and gets onto the platform (see Table 31.3).

Table 31.3   A Longer Sequence of Rules Needed for the Animat to Climb onto Platforms, Wait, and Disembark

Condition	Action
If not button_pressed	Turn to button, move forward
If button_pressed and platform not ready	Move stop
If button_pressed and not aboard	Turn to platform
If platform is ready	Move forward
If aboard	Turn to exit
If aboard and platform has not arrived	Move stop
If aboard and platform has arrived	Move forward

Again, we assume the behavior is disengaged after the platform has been dismounted. By making the rules as specific as possible, we can also avoid having to specify behaviors such as "stop looking toward the platform."

Module Design

Before we start the application, the interfaces to the fuzzy module must be defined. The implementation is a straightforward application of the theory in Chapter 30, "Fuzzy Logic," but interfaces are necessary to interact with it. Because fuzzy expert systems are surprisingly close to rule-based systems, the design is mostly borrowed from Part II.

Initialization

First, we'll consider how the fuzzy module can initialize itself from disk, loading the different components separately.

Working Memory

The *working memory* contains the fuzzy terms used by the interpreter. These terms may be individual variables or part of linguistic variables. There is no difference between these two types of fuzzy terms, except the way they are referred to later by the rules.

Some fuzzy terms need to be associated with a membership function. This is necessary for fuzzy variables that need fuzzifying by the system (inputs), or those that need defuzzifying automatically (outputs). We'll define the membership function for a symmetric triangle, which is often sufficient (see Listing 31.1).

> **NOTE**
>
> The term `open` is defined as a membership function over the base variable of `door`. The other two terms will be set manually by the user.

Listing 31.1   A Set of Two Linguistic Variables Containing a Total of Three Fuzzy Terms

```
<memory>
     <Variable name="platform">
          <Term name="ready" />
          <Term name="arrived" />
     </Variable>
     <Variable name="door">
          <Term name="open">
               <triangle center="0" base="45" />
          </Term>
     </Variable>
</memory>
```

For the trickier membership functions or ones that change dynamically, the client is encouraged to do the conversions manually instead. This implies that the membership functions can be omitted.

Rulebase

The *rulebase* must express the relationships between the fuzzy variables. This is done by a set of rules, each with conditions and actions. In the example from Listing 31.2, the rule is defined by a single fuzzy term and a linguistic one. An arbitrary number of statements are allowed within both the head and body of the rule.

The conditions are understood implicitly as a conjunction (AND) of all the statements. Just like for the rule-based system, there are no particular limitations with this paradigm, because disjunctions (OR) can be split into multiple rules.

Listing 31.2   A Rulebase for a Fuzzy System Containing a Unique Rule

```
<rulebase>
<Rule>
     <conditions>
          <Term name="aboard" />
          <Variable name="platform" value="arrived" />
     </conditions>
     <body>
          <Variable name="move" term="forward" value="1" />
          <Variable name="turn" term="exit" value="1" />
     </body>
</Rule>
</rulebase>
```

Modifiers are handled by nesting the fuzzy terms within a modifier tag such as very, extremely, somewhat, and so on. Currently, these need to be defined within the fuzzy system.

Interface

After the mechanisms for initialization, the discussion can focus on the runtime functionality. This *native* interface handles callbacks automatically for convenience and efficiency. The other type of interface allows dynamic queries, covered shortly after.

Synchronization

To prevent having to feed data into the fuzzy system, a native interface is defined. Using C++ callbacks allows the fuzzy system to gather the information by itself. This proves more convenient and simplifies the code tremendously:

```
void SetSensor( const SensorFunc& s, const string& symbol );
void SetEffector( const EffectorFunc& e, const string& symbol );
```

Two functions are used: one to gather the content of a fuzzy term (sensor), and the other to pass the value of the fuzzy term back to the client (effector). The callback functions must be defined according to an existing prototype, specified by the fuzzy system.

Because these two functions are only convenient for accessing single fuzzy terms, there are actually another two ways to declare sensors and effectors. These take two string parameters rather than one; the first specifies the linguistic variable, the second refers to the nested fuzzy term.

Dynamic Access

For those situations that do not need regular callbacks, two simple accessor functions provide the extra flexibility needed:

```
void Set( const string& symbol, const float value );
float Get( const string& symbol ) const;
```

These can query the content of any single fuzzy term. Once again, two more of these functions deal with linguistic variables, using two strings as parameters.

Further Information

The implementation of the fuzzy expert system is a direct application of the theory in Chapter 30, branched from the rule-based system module. Although there are certainly programming and software design challenges, these are discussed in the documentation on the web site at `http://AiGameDev.com/` and as comments within the code itself.

Evaluation

The fuzzy control is very smooth. Only when the switch is pressed is the movement a bit jerky, but we would expect that because there's often a wall in the way. In some cases, the reaction times may seem a bit slow. For example, the animat can be a bit slow in looking up when climbing the first step of the ladder, or anticipating the arrival of the platform. We can fix this by adjusting the membership functions, generally using a translation modifier (for instance, so that DoM reaches 1 only half a second after the ladder is touched).

Practical Demo

The animat with these fuzzy abilities is known as *Jacky*. *Jacky* can climb ladders, open doors, and call elevators. Otherwise, the default behavior is reactive wandering. The source and fuzzy rules can be found on the web site at `http://AiGameDev.com/`.

The movement itself in relatively effective, because the animat does not seem to waste any particular time. In fact, after pressing the switch, the animat tends to head directly to the door/platform, using the shortest path. Indeed, the movement is very close to the wall, and animats take no step back at all. Telling the animat to step backward after the switch has been pressed would be possible, although this makes some other assumptions about the layout of the terrain.

This leads into the essence of the problem: The fuzzy interpreter is given direct control of the movement. This works fine in most cases, but some cases stand out because of the assumptions made by the rules. For example, animats struggle to go around obstacles between the button and the platform; they tend to bump into the wall and slide off it, or fall into holes when the opportunity arises.

Ideally, the output of the fuzzy system should be used as a higher-level suggestion to the movement behaviors already developed. For example, the heading would be taken as the heading for the seek behavior, but not overriding obstacle avoidance.

As for the fuzzy rules themselves, they are not particularly well-suited to modeling sequences of actions such as these. In a sequence, conditions can trigger transitions to the next action in the sequence. The interpreter needs to implicitly keep track of the position in the sequence. This doesn't show too much in the rules, except that we have to keep the rules as specific as possible. (For instance, avoid looking at the platform's button when aboard the platform.) A better approach to such low-level control would involve a fuzzy finite state machine; it does the same thing, but is conceptually easier to design. Fuzzy rules are instead well-suited to decision making rather than control (that is, finding answers to well-identified static problems, such as selecting the best weapon). Naturally, both approaches can be combined beautifully!

Summary

This chapter applied fuzzy logic to create robust and realistic reactive behavior sequences, capable of dealing with tricky contraptions. The development started with two important steps that need to be undertaken whenever fuzzy logic is applied to a problem:

➤ A declaration of each fuzzy variable is provided, necessary to solve the problems.

➤ The membership functions are described for the fuzzy variables that need to be fuzzified and defuzzified.

Given these variables, we had to define the fuzzy rules and ways for them to achieve their task simply:

➤ The fuzzy rules kept track of the position in the sequence using sensory input only.

➤ The knowledge is represented as implicitly as possible to reduce the number of rules.

➤ Each rule is made as specific as possible to prevent nasty side effects of rules executing out of order.

Then, we needed to create a simple fuzzy logic interpreter, mostly inspired by the rule-based system from Part II:

➤ There is a data interface to load persistent information from files on disk.

➤ Native interface are necessary for handling C++ callbacks.

➤ Dynamic accessors, such as `Set()` and `Get()`, provide all the additional flexibility needed.

The evaluation reveals that movement is pleasingly smooth and effective—to an untrained eye. Some of the assumptions made by the rule can cause a few problems, so we need to integrate the fuzzy logic output with lower-level navigation behaviors for the best results.

The major problem with the fuzzy approach is that it requires the designer to specify the behaviors. The next chapter covers genetic algorithms that provide ways to find near-optimal behaviors given high-level criteria.

Chapter 32

Genetic Algorithms

Evolutionary algorithms are a collection of solutions based on the theory of evolution. As such, genetic algorithms are a popular process that can optimize parameters in multi-dimensional space. Genetic algorithms use a simulation of the problem to determine the fittest solutions among the population. Improvements of the results over time are encouraged by only letting the fittest individuals survive and contribute to the gene pool.

For example, *Quake 3* uses a genetic algorithm to adjust the weapon strategies [Waveren01]. Different parameters, such as the ideal distance for using the weapons, are optimized based on the performance. This evolutionary approach allows the behaviors to be adjusted to the game design in postproduction.

This chapter covers the following topics:

➤ Biological evolution and natural selection as the inspiration for an artificial model

➤ The importance of representation in genetic algorithms (the concepts of genotypes and phenotypes)

➤ An outline of the algorithm used in artificial evolution

➤ The details of specific genetic operators and evolutionary policies at each stage of the evolution

Biological Evolution in a Nutshell

Evolution is a phenomenon that happens to species on a large time scale, driven during reproduction by the underlying genetics of each organism.

Theory of Evolution

Darwin—among others—observed that every creature is unique. Each organism has its own set of attributes that are transmitted to offspring. These lead to unique children, but with common features to the parents. Humans have managed to harness these changes by *selective breeding* (for instance, by mating pets that have desirable attributes).

Evolution is the result of nature's effect on this process, causing entire species that change slowly. According to Darwin, evolution is a consequence of the *universal struggle for life*. There are three major forms of pressure on each individual:

➤ **Environment**—Each creature is constantly working to survive in the environment by finding resources such as food and water.

➤ **Competition**—Creatures within the same species also compete with each other, because they are each trying to do similar tasks (for instance, find a partner to mate).

➤ **Rivalry**—Different species can affect the life of others, either by direct confrontation (for instance, hunting), or indirectly by fighting for the same environment resources.

Darwin suggested that such constraints affect the behavior of each and every creature, as well as its chances of survival. Creatures unsuccessful in different aspects of life (for instance, hunting or mating) have fewer chances of having offspring. On the other hand, slightly more effective creatures are more likely to transmit their attributes to the next generation. This is the "preservation of favorable individual differences."

This is made possible by the fact that breeding happens relatively quickly; therefore, there are more creatures born that can survive. The constraints of the environment imply that the fittest survive. This is known as *natural selection*.

Natural selection happens on a short time scale—a daily or even hourly basis. However, evolution is a very slow progress, requiring generations for favorable attributes to spread throughout the species.

Biological Reproduction

What makes evolution possible is the underlying biology of reproduction, allowing creatures to transmit beneficial attributes to their offspring. This happens on a cellular basis with the genetic code contained within chromosomes. Let's take humans as an example.

Each cell has 23 pairs of chromosomes. The chromosomes can be seen as the structure carrying the genetic code. Reproductive cells (sperm and ova) have just 23 single chromosomes. One normal cell divides into two reproductive cells during a phase called *meiosis*. Before the cell splits, the chromosomes pairs cross over: Their genetic code is mixed up a bit. Each reproductive cell has genes from both members of a chromosome pair.

During fertilization of the ova by the sperm, these chromosomes recombine together to reform the 23 pairs. The resulting cell is the first cell of the offspring, and contains half the genetic code from the father and half from the mother.

The entire process is extremely complex, because many different molecules are involved. In some cases, *mutation* can happen. Mutation is an error in copying the genetic code, either at the gene level or at the chromosome level. This can turn out beneficial in some cases, but often causes irrevocable problems in the reproduction.

Inspiration

Evolution can be seen as an optimization process. The attributes of the creatures are optimized over time with respect to the environmental constraints. John Holland introduces these ideas in his book *Adaptation in Natural and Artificial Systems* [Holland75]. Computer scientists have managed to simulate evolution and apply these ideas to optimize problems such as genetic algorithms.

The genetic code at the roots of most life forms on earth makes evolution possible, by allowing successful attributes to be transferred to the next generation. For genetic algorithms, representation is also the most crucial issue.

Genetics and Representation

Genetic algorithms are essentially an optimization strategy. However, unlike most domain-specific optimization techniques (that is, gradient descent), they do not rely on any particular representation. This doesn't mean that representation isn't important for genetic algorithms—quite the contrary. It just implies there's a lot of freedom in the choice of knowledge representation. A large proportion of chapter discusses knowledge representation, and this is another direct application.

Because biology is the inspiration for the field of genetic algorithms, much terminology is borrowed, too. This makes it convenient to explain, but once again, this intuitiveness can lead to unfounded assumptions. These are pointed out when appropriate.

Genome and Genotype

The basis of evolution is genetic code, composed of a sequence of genes. This sequence is known as a *genome*. Each species has a different kind of genome, with various lengths and different genes. There is one important thing to note about the genome: It describes the overall structure of the genetic code (its meaning and not the actual value).

Genomics is the study of the meaning of these genes for particular species. The genomes found within a species are almost identical. Each gene will occur at the same position—or *locus*—in the genome, as shown in Figure 32.1.

In each individual creature, these genes can carry specific values known as *alleles*. An allele is one of the possible forms a gene can take. The sequence of alleles is called the *genotype*. The genotype is a sequence of information, and not just the structure. (That's the genome.) The field of genetics aims to study the role of alleles (forms of genes) in biological inheritance.

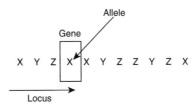

Figure 32.1 Conceptual representation of a genotype, displayed as a sequence of letters representing the genes.

As programmers, we can understand the link between genome and genotype as a class/instance relationship. The genotype is a particular instantiation of the genome, with each gene assigned values as alleles.

The human genetic blueprint is a genome, and each of us comes from one genotype. In our case, the genotype is a set of *chromosomes* contained within each cell. Chromosomes can be found in most living creatures, which explains why some people use the word "chromosome" in the context evolutionary algorithms. Because this is only one particular option (found by nature) for representing a genotype, its use is often incorrect in this context—strictly speaking. However, most people will understand this terminology as well. We'll use the term "genotype" for the sake of semantic accuracy, historical reference, and convenience. (It's a shorter and unambiguous word.)

Generally, the genome is a highly implicit way to store information. For humans, it contains all the information needed for our cells to develop themselves into a fully grown body. We're still somewhat amazed how the genetic code can allow a collection of cells to grow into a "working" human being. These concepts are borrowed by genetic algorithms.

This genotype's information is typically compact and needs to be somehow "interpreted." To do this, human cells use the genetic code to decide how to behave, which indirectly drives the growth of the body. However, this is very difficult to achieve with simulation— and still produce useful solutions to problems.

Genetic algorithms use much more explicit formalisms to represent the genotype, because this proves easier to work with in practice. However, the principles remain; the genotypes contain the essential information about a solution, usually in the most compact form possible. The idea is that we can build a solution to solve a problem from the genotype.

Phenome and Phenotype

Phenetics is the study of physical properties and morphology of creatures, regardless of their genetic background. This field of science isn't too popular, but attempts to provide understanding of the concept of phenome. The *phenome* is the general structure of a creature's body: cells, nerves, veins, brain, organs, skin, and so on. This can be seen as a set of physical attributes.

Unlike this example, phenomes can be very complex and very detailed—especially for humans. There are different levels at which the phenome can be modeled, each with increasing complexity (cells, organs, limbs) as shown in Table 32.1. In fact, the human phenome is not fully understood by the fields of biology/anatomy/medicine!

Table 32.1   Simplified Description of a Phenome as an Incomplete Set of Attributes, and the Values of a Particular Phenotype

Phenome	Phenotype
Hair color	Blond
Tone of skin	Dark
Number of legs	2
Height	2m 10

The *phenotype* is a particular instance of a phenome, namely a unique creature like each of us. Each of the physical attributes will be associated with a particular value.

Once again, these are very high-level properties. The phenotype itself is basically every cell in our body. Unlike the genotype, the phenotype changes quite rapidly over time. (Cells die, organs get injured, the body grows and ages.)

The phenotype is the product of the genotype and the constraints of the environment. For genetic algorithms, this is an explicit representation of the solution. In fact, it's the representation that will be applied to solve the problem—directly or using a third-party algorithm. As such, the structure of the phenotype is often designed to be convenient to manipulate, so solving the problem is made easy.

Conversions

There's a similar relationship between genome/genotype and phenome/phenotype. In each pair, the second is an instance of the first. But what link exists between the genotype and the phenotype?

As discussed, in humans the genotype specifies the way each cell grows, indirectly creating the phenotype. As such, attributes of the phenotype itself aren't determined by a single gene, but rather the observable effect of all the genes on the organism.

The genotype has a strong influence on the outcome of the phenotype, but not an exclusive influence. Because the genes provide a very implicit form of controlling growth, the environment itself has a strong part to play in the equation. This too leads to observable characteristics in the organism (for instance, physical conditioning or accidents).

In artificial intelligence (AI), things are nowhere near as complex. There is usually a direct mapping between genotypes and phenotypes. The AI engineer needs to devise a function to handle this conversion. The representation of the genotype must be converted to a suitable phenotype (see Figure 32.2). In most cases, this happens by decoding the same representation into a different data structure.

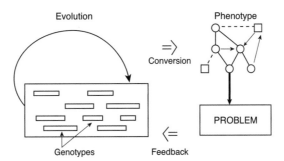

Figure 32.2   The conversion from a genotype to a phenotype, showing the relationship to the evolutionary algorithm and the problem itself.

Because there is little distinction between genotype and phenotype in most simulations, why not disregard the genotypes and evolve the phenotypes directly? This would prevent the software from having to convert information from one format to another.

Using the representation of the solution for evolution is becoming common practice. This is sometimes referred to as an *evolutionary data structure*, although it's really about phenotype-specific operators. It's often much easier to adapt the genetic operators to work with different data structures than it is to encode and decode phenotypes. This is discussed in the next two sections.

> **NOTE**
>
> The simplicity of the conversion between genotypes and phenotypes is one of the reasons why genetic algorithms just do not have the power of biological evolution; the representation is nowhere near as sophisticated. Nature has taken billions of years to evolve a robust representation itself, and a sophisticated way to transform it into living organisms. In AI, representations are chosen in a few hours by engineers, and even implicit encodings in AI are designed by hand.

Genetic Algorithms

Biological evolution relies on autonomous creatures living and reproducing within an environment. Most problems will not want such sophisticated creatures, or even the complexity of an environment that can drive evolution. Therefore, there is a need to understand the evolutionary process and replicate the important operations that drive evolution.

Evolutionary algorithms model the process step by step, so it can be performed artificially within a computer (see Figure 32.3). Instead of relying on living artificial creatures, genetic algorithms can "apply" evolution to static data structures (for instance, strategies or behaviors). These may be solutions to any problem that requires a solution using the power of evolution.

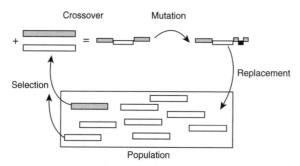

Figure 32.3   Bird's eye view of an evolutionary algorithm, including the main cycle that creates new offspring from existing parents.

Here's the generic outline of such an evolutionary process:

➤ **Initialization**—A population of individuals is created.

➤ **Selection**—Parents are picked from the population.

➤ **Crossover**—Their genetic code is combined together to form the child.

➤ **Mutation**—A few genes of the offspring are changed arbitrarily.

➤ **Replacement**—The offspring is potentially reinserted into the population.

This is the template for artificially simulating life as we know it. Naturally, the techniques used at each stage will influence the outcome. The remaining part of this section presents the purpose of each stage and their major requirements. The next section introduces a wide variety of policies from which to choose.

The Population

The population is essentially a set of individuals. In the software, the population is essentially the container that stores each of the genotypes. Like living populations, the ones in genetic algorithms change over time, too. Newly born offspring become part of the population, whereas others die out.

The computer model has the luxury of being able to preserve individuals for any number of generations. This is a problem as much as an advantage, because we have to manually discard individuals when appropriate.

Conceptually speaking, the population can be *steady-state* or *generational*. A steady-state population will change incrementally very slowly, on a per-individual basis. This means a new genotype is inserted into the current population, and the process starts again. For generational algorithms, a new population is created each generation, and new offspring from the previous individuals are added to the next generation until there are enough to continue. Figure 32.4 shows different types of populations.

There are also different forms of storage, not as a data structure, but conceptually speaking. On one hand, the population can be seen as a group of individuals with no particular organization. Alternatively, it can have spatial coherence. The individuals can be organized in 1D or 2D space, in a line, or on a grid.

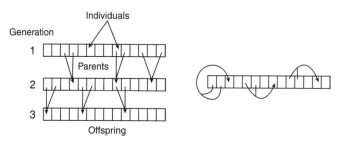

Figure 32.4 Different types of populations. On the left, three generational populations, and one steady-state population on the right.

This models some important properties of real environments in the simulation, and different stages in the algorithm can benefit in some way. The major advantage is that the propagation of genes can be constrained spatially.

Initialization

Ideally, the initial population must be a representative sample of the search space (that is, all the possible solutions). This gives the genetic algorithm a vague idea of the fitness in each area. To do this, initializing each individual completely randomly is a good policy.

Given a good random number generator (such as the Mersenne Twister [Matumoto02]), and a procedure that can create a wide variety of random genotypes, the coverage of the initial search space will be very broad. The more the individuals are in the initial population, the better the coverage (see Figure 32.5).

During initialization, it is also possible to reuse existing genotypes (a.k.a. *seeding* the evolution). For example, the population can include good solutions that have been created with other mathematically based algorithms, or solutions modeled or inspired by human experts, or genotypes from previous evolutions. This has the advantage of immediately revealing areas of high fitness in the search space, for the genetic algorithm to explore and improve them.

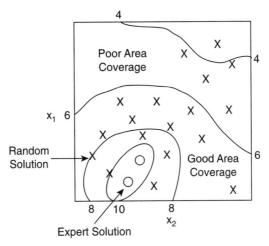

Figure 32.5   The initial population in a 2D search space. There is good coverage of most areas, as well as some expert solutions.

Evaluation

Before getting to the genetic algorithm itself, you need to understand the concept of fitness and evaluation. This is crucial; it allows biasing the process in favor of the fittest individuals, allowing the quality of the solutions to improve.

Each individual in the population can be seen a solution to a problem. The purpose of the evaluation is to determine how good the solution is. This measure represents the *fitness* of the individual.

The process of evaluating an individual is known as the *fitness function.* This function takes a phenotype, and returns its fitness as a floating-point number. The implementation of the function itself will simulate the problem with the proposed solution. Then, depending on how well the phenotype does, it is assigned a score. The scale for the scoring is quite flexible, as long as it ranks the individuals relatively to each other. The rest of the genetic algorithm can be developed to take care even of disparate fitness values.

This fitness function is fundamental to genetic algorithms—and multidimensional optimization strategies in general. It drives the optimization process by rating the benefits of individuals:

➤ Simplicity is the major **benefit** of this approach. There's no need for mathematical models in genetic algorithms; we just use simulation to check the value of a solution. This is as simple as setting up the problem itself.

➤ As for **pitfalls**, the fitness function is really the most important aspect of the entire genetic algorithm. Despite it seeming simple, it can become the bottleneck for the entire optimization.

The fitness function is naturally problem dependent; if we want to evolve game characters that creep slowly, our fitness function will differ from the one evaluating animats at running. Even within each problem, there are many different ways to implement the fitness function.

In fact, it's safe to say that creating fitness functions is the primary problem with genetic algorithms. With a perfect system and a poor evaluation, nothing worthwhile will arise from the evolution. On the other hand, it's possible to get good results with a minimal genetic algorithm and a well-considered fitness function.

Further Information

The process of designing a fitness function can prove tricky for many problems. When it comes to behaviors, however, it's close to a black art! This topic is very important for computer game AI, and is discussed at length in Chapter 35, "Designing Learning AI."

Selection

The selection process aims to pick out individuals from the population, in order for them to spawn offspring. Two different methodologies affect the selection process (although these are sometimes used together):

➤ **Sexual** breeding requires two parents; they are combined to form the offspring.

➤ **Asexual** reproduction implies that only one parent forms the offspring.

The selection process has a very influential role on the fitness of the offspring. Darwin observed that the genes of successful individuals are more likely to spread throughout the gene pool. By favoring better individuals during selection, the average fitness of the population tends to increase over the generations. This is known as *elitism*, selecting fit individuals in preference.

Elitism can be applied to other stages of the genetic algorithm, but is especially important when selecting parents. When fit individuals are chosen for breeding, the offspring is likely to be fit, too—although there is absolutely no guarantee. Unfit parents could also spawn miracle offspring. However, using elitism, the average fitness of the population will generally rise to find better solutions.

There is a trade-off between exploration of the search space (that is, allowing any individual to breed) and the elitist approach. With lower elitism, more parts of the search space are explored. Higher elitism implies areas around the fitter individuals are under focus instead. Evolution is slower with little elitism but guarantees a better coverage of the search space. On the other hand, evolution with strong elitism tends to converge quicker to a result (although not necessarily the optimal one).

Crossover

In this phase, the genetic code of both parents is combined together to form an offspring. This is only possible if sexual reproduction is used; using crossover on one parent has no effect whatsoever (because the genes to be "mixed" are identical).

This idea is modeled on the creation of the reproductive cells. Before becoming the sperm and ova, the pairs of chromosomes are split right down the middle and reassembled together in alternate pairs. This way, about half the genes of each parent are found in the reproductive cells.

For living creatures, this process is done entirely by chemical reaction. In artificial evolution, we need to perform crossover manually. This is generally done by copying some genes from the father and others from the mother. Using random factors in this selection ensures that parents will not always have the same offspring—as in real life.

It's good practice for the crossover to preserve a good balance of genes between both parents, for example 60 percent / 40 percent. (Just swap the genes to create the complement offspring, as discussed in the following section.) Other unbalanced distributions aren't as common, because we want to borrow good traits from both parents. A genetic sequence of sufficient length is needed to transmit these attributes intact. (Of course, there are no guarantees this is always true, but it works in nature.)

Distributions such as 95 percent / 5 percent negate the benefits of sexual crossover, becoming closer to asexual reproduction. This is generally modeled using a high mutation rate instead.

Mutation

In living organisms, mutation happens regularly during cell division, but this is especially likely when reproductive cells are created. The chemical reactions that happen during the division process are error prone; chromosomes and genes can be changed permanently. In some cases, the cells die or the fertilization fails. In other cases, the changes persist in the offspring, although mutation leads to "abnormal" individuals with arbitrary fitness.

The mutation can happen on two levels, in the chromosome (genome level) or in the DNA (genotype level). Changes in the genome are generally much more threatening to the process, and happen quite rarely.

In genetic algorithms, mutation is generally applied to the genotype of the offspring after it has been created—to fake the errors that happen during fertilization. Typically, only alleles are mutated by changing their value with a small probability (for instance, 0.001). The structure of the genetic code (genome) is often left intact.

The importance of mutation is underlined by evolution strategies that use only mutation and no crossover. It has many beneficial properties, notably maintaining diversity in the genetic code. That said, mutation is not as important as geneticists originally thought it was for the evolution of intelligence—but mutation is more important than they believe it is now (no doubt somewhere in the middle of the spectrum).

In a simulation, the way mutation can be performed really depends on the representation of the genome itself. Generally, only the genes will be mutable, so only a simple traversal is required to mutate some genes randomly. If the genome is open to mutation (that is, the rest of the genetic algorithm can deal with arbitrary genomes), it may be beneficial to mutate that too.

Replacement

Each of the previous steps contributes to creating one (or more) offspring. The purpose of the replacement scheme is to determine whether to insert these individuals into the population. If not, they should be discarded. Otherwise, the replacement policy should decide how to reinsert the individual into the population. If the population has no particular organization, it's not important *how*, but *whether* replacement occurs.

The genotype of offspring is fully known at this stage so it can be evaluated if necessary. Indeed, most replacement schemes rely on the fitness value to determine whether to replace the individual in the population.

The replacement function affects the evolution of the population directly. Because we want to control the quality of the solutions, we need to favor fit individuals. The principle of elitism affects the design of a replacement scheme, too. Indeed, it's possible to prevent offspring's with low fitness from entering the population at all. Likewise, existing individuals with low fitness can be replaced in the population.

The replacement function must take into account that evolution may be either steady state or generational. In the steady-state case, each individual is processed one by one and reinserted into the same population. In the second case, there is a different population containing the next generation, and individuals are inserted into that instead.

A genetic algorithm has the luxury of being able to preserve individuals for any length of time. Using a generational approach, the genetic code of an individual will only survive in the offspring. However, using a steady-state approach, it's possible for fit individuals to remain throughout the evolution. The replacement policy is indirectly responsible for this, too, because old individuals or the parents can be replaced by new genotypes.

Genetic Operators and Evolutionary Policies

Genetic operators are tools used at each stage of the genetic algorithm. These model the biochemical process that happens at the genetic level. Evolutionary policies are principles enforced during other parts of the genetic algorithm to influence the outcome of the evolution. This section describes a variety of genetic operators that are commonly used, as well as evolutionary policies.

Initialization

When spawning random individuals, it's important to make sure they are as diverse as possible. This means our phenotype-generation mechanism should ideally be capable of creating all legal solutions. The initial population can thereby be representative of the search space. Other genetic operators have this requirement of completeness, too.

Making sure that we can randomly generate any solution is not a particularly difficult task, especially with common genotypes. With more exotic solutions, we'll require some understanding of the data structure used.

Arrays and Lists

Typically, *arrays* contain a sequence of genes of one data type only (for instance, used to express sequences of actions). Floating-point numbers and single bits are common choices. When initializing such structures, their length must be selected as well as the value of each gene.

Lists are traditionally not restricted to one single data type. They can contain floats, integers, Booleans, and so on. This can certainly be modeled with an array (using one of many programming tricks), but the distinction is historical. Similarly, the length of the list is chosen as well as the values of each gene, but also their type.

Each individual may be somehow constrained. This means the problem requires specific properties from the genotype. For example, an array may need to be a certain length, or the data types in the list may be restricted. In this case, the initialization mechanism should take the constraints into account. This will save valuable time in both the evaluation and the genetic algorithm itself, and improve the quality of the solutions. Figure 32.6 shows a randomly initialized array and list.

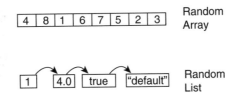

Figure 32.6   Example of an array and a list that have been randomly initialized.

Trees and Graphs

Data structures with higher levels of connectivity prove harder to initialize randomly. A good general-purpose method generates the nodes first, and then connects them together randomly.

For a tree, each node would have one outgoing connection, except the root, which has none. When selecting a neighbor to connect the current node to, the algorithm must not pick one of the descendants (already connected to it). This will ensure that no loops are produced. This will also ensure that the tree is a *spanning tree* containing all the nodes. To get a binary tree, only parents with fewer than two incoming connections must be chosen.

For graphs, things prove slightly easier. There is no need to prevent cycles because they are allowed—and necessary—in graphs. However, the problem of a single graph spanning all the nodes remains. Sometimes, two subgraphs may be created. If this proves problematic, this case must be identified by a traversal of the data structure. If the graph does not span all the nodes, another random connection can be established. Repeat these steps until the final graph has been built.

Crossover

The genetic operator for crossover is responsible for combining two genotypes. In doing so, a healthy blend of genes from both the father and the mother need to be present in the offspring. This can be problematic, because we want to preserve the good combinations of genes and discard the inappropriate ones. However, it's tough to determine which gene combinations are "fit," so the crossover function needs to be flexible enough to extract these combinations.

Once again, the representation of the genotype is crucial for developing a crossover function. Linear data structures will be able to benefit from biologically inspired crossover techniques, whereas custom designed operators will be needed for data structures with high connectivity.

Regardless of the type of genotype, it's important for the crossover to maintain a consistent data structure; if a specific syntax need to be respected, the operator should not invalidate it. Once again, this will reduce the redundant computation done in the genetic algorithm.

Arrays and Lists

For such linear data structures, a wide range of crossover operations is possible (see Figure 32.7):

➤ **Unary crossover** (single point) defines one split point in the parent genotypes. Both are split at this point, and the four parts are permuted and reassembled.

➤ **Binary crossover** (two point) instead uses two points to split the parents. This defines a middle segment of the genotype, which is inserted in place of the other parent's segment of genetic code.

➤ **Uniform crossover** does not rely on split points. Instead, each gene is randomly copied from either parent. This corresponds to a single split point, but not respecting the order of the genes.

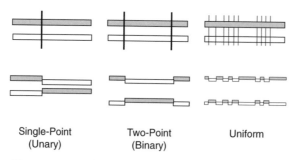

| Single-Point (Unary) | Two-Point (Binary) | Uniform |

Figure 32.7 Applying different kinds of crossover to two genotypes.

The benefit of each of these operators depends on the meaning of the underlying genome. A fairly safe choice, however, is uniform crossover because it consistently provides a good blend of the genes.

Trees and Graphs

For trees, it's fairly trivial to isolate subtrees and swap the nodes in the genetic code. Doing this once can be sufficient for small trees, but the operation may need to be repeated for larger data structures (see Figure 32.8).

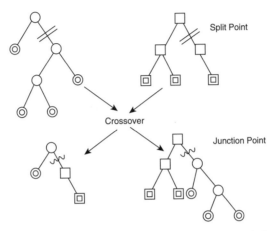

Figure 32.8 The crossover operator on trees swaps sub-branches.

If the trees have well-defined syntax, it's important that the operators check this consistency. (It's often the case here, more so than on lists or arrays.) For each problem, it's important to perform crossover with these constraints in mind.

As for graphs, the issue becomes trickier. Some effort is required to find a good splitting line. First, the set of nodes is divided into two. All the edges that lie within a set (internal) are left intact. The external edges are disconnected and reconnected to random nodes in the other parent genotype (see Figure 32.9).

Because keeping all the external edges may lead to dense connections within the graph ($O(n^2)$ edges), only half the external edges can be kept. These can be either inbound or outbound edges in directed graphs, or just the mother's or father's edges for undirected graphs.

Mutation

This operator is responsible for mutating the genotype to simulate the errors during fertilization. Such operators generally modify the value of single genes, changing the allele. However, some operations can happen on the genome level, too.

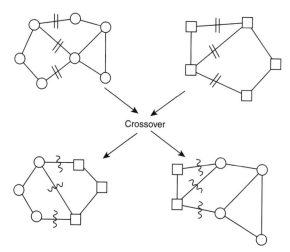

Figure 32.9   On graphs, crossover splits the data structure into two and rejoins the parts in alternate pairs.

Mutation is responsible for introducing new genetic code into the gene pool, so it's important that this operator be capable of generating any genetic variations. Ideally, the mutation operator should be capable of transforming any genotype into any other—given a sequence of arbitrary transformations. This ensures that the genetic algorithm is capable of exploring the entire search space.

Mutation on single genes is the most common, and applies to almost all data structures. For bits, the mutation can just flip the value. For integers and real numbers, these can be initialized randomly within a range. Another popular approach is to add a small random value to the numbers, as determined by a Gaussian distribution (provided by most random-number generators).

Arrays and Lists

The most common form of mutation happens at the gene level, which is convenient for linear data structures. The mutation operator only needs to know how to generate all the possible alleles for one gene. With a low probability—usually 0.001—the value of a gene should be mutated. Alleles can also be swapped if appropriate.

Given an even lower probability, the length of the data can be changed. The size of arrays can be increased or decreased by a small amount, and list can be similarly mutated. Such operations are done globally, actively changing the size of containers before proceeding. However, a more implicit approach is possible; genes can be inserted or removed from the sequence with an even lower probability. These changes implicitly mutate the length of the genetic code (see Figure 32.10).

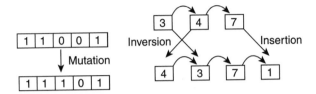

Figure 32.10   Mutation is applied to the value of an array, and twice to elements in a list.

This actually can affect the genome itself, which can correspond to meaningless genotypes. Again, if this is the case, the mutation operator should be capable of identifying and preventing this problem. Such structural changes are sometimes not necessary, because the genome is usually well defined and fixed in structure.

Trees and Graphs

For more elaborate data structures, mutation is just as easy on the gene level. Indeed, it's just as easy to mutate an allele if it's a node in a tree, or a graph. These can be swapped also.

In trees, there are also many possible structural mutations. The order or the number of the children can be mutated. Some operators can even swap entire subtrees.

In graphs, structural mutations are trickier. A similar trick can be used as in crossover; the nodes can be split into two groups and reassembled randomly. New nodes can be inserted individually, but it can be beneficial to grow entire cycles at a time. Indeed, in graphs the main difficulty of the evolutionary process is to evolve meaningful cycles.

Selection

The purpose of the selection policy is to decide which parents to pick for breeding, and those that should not reproduce. By using a policy based on the fitness values, elitism can be enforced.

Although each of the genetic operators (that is, crossover, mutate) can be designed to have a beneficial effect on the performance, it's rarely successful and often comes down to educated guessing. On the other hand, the selection policy has a direct influence on the quality of the population—and measurably so.

Fitness Scaling

Before selection occurs, preprocessing of the evaluation results can take place. This may be necessary for multiple reasons [Kreinovich92]:

➤ The values need to be positive to be interpreted as probabilities.

➤ The search may be wrongly misled by "super individuals" because of the lack of selective pressure.

➤ There is no evaluation score per se, because only ranking is possible.

There are some common functions to do this [Goldberg89]:

➤ **Linear scaling** uses the function $f(x)=ax+b$, where the parameters are generally chosen each generation.

➤ **Exponential scaling** is based on simulated annealing, where $f(x)=e^{-\beta x}$ renormalizes each of the scores given β.

➤ **Ranking** associates a fitness for each individual based on their rank, so the result no longer proportional. For example, 1st: 10, 2nd: 9, 3rd: 8, and so on.

This can help iron out the problems with irregular fitness functions to maintain selective pressure on the top individuals. Given the scaled fitness value, different policies can be used in the selection:

➤ **Roulette wheel** assigns a slice of the circle proportionally to the fitness. The wheel is spun randomly, and the winning individual gets to mate!

➤ **Tournament** selection picks the best from a random group of individuals. One variation involves generating a random number of the magnitude of the fitness, and then picking the highest.

➤ A **ranking** policy essentially only allows the top n individuals to mate. This can be done in order.

➤ **Random walk** traverses the population stochastically, and picks the best individual encountered. This works well for populations with spatial coherence (for instance, 2D).

➤ **Remainder** stochastic sampling allows individuals to mate a number of times , if their fitness is over the average. The remainder of the quotient can be used as a probability to mate again.

Often, fitness corresponds to probabilities for reproduction. These policies provide a way to use the probabilities to create new populations (or parts thereof).

Replacement

This policy varies a lot depending on the nature of the evolution. Generational approaches will not replace any individuals, but rather avoid including them in the next population! On the other hand, replacement is an intrinsic part of steady-state approaches, because room needs to be made for the newest individuals. This section discusses the general techniques used to discard or replace individuals, regardless of the type of population.

It's possible to simulate the generational approach incrementally—potentially using a temporary population—so the steady-state approach can be seen as more generic. When designing the software for this, it may be beneficial to opt for this flexibility.

Two main criteria can be used to replace individuals: fitness and age. However, replacing individuals can be completed by other specific tricks. Common policies include the following:

➤ If the individual is in the top n%, find another individual at the lower end of the fitness ladder and replace.

➤ Replace the parents with the offspring (optionally, if the child is less fit).

➤ Replace the oldest individual in the population with the newest offspring. (This is a hybrid steady-state/generational approach.)

➤ Individuals found nearby in the population (in 2D grid) can be replaced by local offspring.

These different criteria can combine to estimate the likelihood of an individual being replaced. This value can be interpreted in a similar way to the selection policy (for instance, tournament to determine who dies, and a random walk to find the least fit).

Advanced Issues

When the policies, operators, and other parameters of the genetic algorithm combine together, unexpected phenomena can arise when solving problems.

Premature Convergence

Really successful individuals tend to see their genes spread throughout the population. If a particular allele is much better than all the others, it will start taking over. Eventually, there may be only one allele left for that gene. This is known as *genetic drift*.

Isn't keeping the fittest alleles of all genes desirable? If the solution is optimal, such convergence is desirable. However, like other forms of optimization, convergence can happen too soon; the solution may not actually be the best. In this case, genetic drift is a problem because diversity in the gene pool is lost. Once particular alleles have taken over, it is difficult to get evolution back on track.

Genetic drift is especially problematic for small populations. In this case, it will take few generations for the genetic code of successful individuals to take over. With larger populations, the risk of premature convergence is reduced.

An easy solution to genetic drift involves using a much higher mutation rate, especially toward the end when convergence is detected. This will change the values of genes with a higher probability, and attempt to reintroduce some new allele. This is an appealing alternative to premature convergence, but the high levels of randomness don't help the genetic algorithm.

A better way lies in preventing genetic drift rather than curing it. The trick is to impose constraints on the population, allowing them to breed with only a subset of the population:

➤ **Multiple populations** can be introduced, which can be relatively small. They exchange individuals among each other to allow the spreading of genes, while still preventing premature convergence.

➤ Single populations with **spatial structure** are a popular alternative. Here, individuals live on a 2D grid, and are only allowed to breed with others nearby. Offspring are reinserted locally, too. The spreading of genetic code is constrained by space, which introduces *fitness islands*: places where the genetic code is similar.

These techniques have proven very powerful in preventing premature convergence. Multiple populations are likely to use more memory, but this is an improvement over the huge populations required to cure genetic drift. Using spatial organization in populations is an easy alternative.

Slow Convergence

It can also be difficult to get the algorithm to converge at all. This is an issue when the fitness function gives few hints about the solution. (That is, all fitness values are similar.) Noise in the fitness can also make it difficult to converge to a result.

In this case, redesigning the fitness function would be strongly recommended (see Chapter 35). As an alternative, however, we can turn up the elitism to really encourage fitter individuals to spread their genes. This runs the risk of premature convergence, but it's a trade-off that often has to be made!

An adaptive elitist policy can improve the situation slightly. Starting off with high elitism will encourage the results to improve at the start. Then, decreasing elitism as the fitness increases often manages to prevent premature convergence. Together with this, increasingly random mutation can be used to explore the search space better.

Parameters, Parameters

Genetic algorithms suffer from having lots of parameters. These are mutation rate, crossover type and parameters, population size, and fitness scaling policy—just to name a few. There are good values to start experimenting with, but often the ideal values will depend on the problem itself.

There are alternatives to manual experimentation, but these generally cost computation time:

> ➤ It's possible to use a **hierarchy of genetic algorithms**. One *meta-genetic algorithm* sits on top of the ordinary genetic algorithm and optimizes the parameters mentioned, which is particularly slow.

> ➤ There is also a so-called **parameterless genetic algorithm**. It actually does have parameters, but they are chosen so that no human input is needed. This uses a combination of suitable parameter choices for the crossover rates and mutation rates, but then uses brute force by simulating many different population sizes [Harik99].

In practice, the default parameters work well. Although it wouldn't take long to implement either of these strategies, it seems like overkill for the kind of problems that are likely to be encountered. It's far more constructive to spend time on the design instead.

Domain Knowledge

Genetic algorithms can be relatively naive; they do not exploit knowledge of the problem to help solve it quicker. It's possible for the AI engineer to give hints to the genetic algorithm by designing specific policies and genetic operators.

For example, during the initialization there can be a bias for certain genotypes. If an expert can tell which ones are likely to do well, the algorithm can generate more similar solutions randomly.

As for the genetic operators, custom crossover and mutation routines can be designed. These will take into account the good places to split the genetic code, use gene-dependant mutation rates, or even prevent fruitless manipulation of genes before they happen.

Finally, the representation itself can help the genetic algorithm. It may be possible to choose a representation that minimizes the size of the search space, or even its complexity. Interdependent genes can be placed close to each other so that they will be kept together when transmitted to the offspring.

Discussion

Genetic algorithms are a very flexible form of optimization, and can be applied is a generic fashion to most problems. There is a little amount of work required to choose a representation and write the conversion routines, but this is acceptable in most cases.

Genetic algorithms tend to do well at avoiding local minima, and given time can often find a near-optimal solution. This is due to their global nature; the search is not restricted to certain areas of the search space.

In many cases, it's possible to extend evolutionary algorithms by designing custom genetic operators. This allows the AI engineer to inject his knowledge about the domain to improve the quality or speed of the convergence.

On the other hand, although genetic algorithms can be assisted by custom operators, they cannot take advantage of properties of the problem to solve them more efficiently (for instance, mathematical insights).

Genetic algorithms perform well on a global scale, but are not very efficient at local optimization (that is, making small changes in the solution to improve it). They can do this thanks to mutation, but this generally happens slowly over time. Greedy hill-climbing techniques work better in such cases.

Randomness is the essence of genetic algorithms. Therefore, they can be hard to predict. One moment they may find the right solution in a few generations; in others, however, it may take entire dynasties! It's not a good idea to rely on randomness if a solution is required quickly.

Genetic algorithms require entire populations of solutions to work. Even with simple genotypes, this becomes costly very quickly, in both memory and computation. For complex problems, it's often unfeasible to run the optimization at fast enough rates for it to be interactive.

Summary

The primary concepts behind genetic algorithms are biological evolution and representation:

➤ Genetic algorithms are based on natural selection, in which only the fittest individuals survive.

➤ Solutions are encoded as sequences of genes, known as genotypes. Arbitrary data structures such trees or graphs can also be evolved.

➤ An evaluation function is used to estimate the fitness of each solution. The fitness value can be postprocessed to maintain evolutionary pressure.

The genetic algorithm itself consists of multiple stages:

➤ During initialization, a population of random individuals is created. Seeding enables the engineer to guide the evolution.

➤ The selection process picks two parents from the population, generally with an elitist policy.

➤ Crossover is used to combine the genetic code of two parents, and mutation randomly changes select genes.

➤ The replacement policy decides whether the resulting offspring should be reinserted into the population.

Watch out for a few details in practice, such as premature convergence and slow convergence. These issues can be resolved by tuning the parameters appropriately. Despite not being particularly efficient, genetic algorithms are an extremely robust and flexible optimization strategy.

Chapter 34, "Adaptive Defensive Strategies with Genetic Algorithms," applies genetic algorithms to learning simple behaviors such as rocket jumping and dodging rockets. The next chapter discusses a popular use of genetic algorithms, which are combined with a rule-like representation.

Practical Demo

There's a simple animat that uses a genetic algorithm to learn its behaviors. *Evolvee* uses existing representations—such as neural networks—which are evolved according to a high-level metric. The realism of *Evolvee* is relatively poor, although simple tasks (such as attacking an enemy) do not pose a problem.

Chapter 33

Learning Classifier Systems

Learning classifier systems (LCSs) are best understood as a combination of three popular AI techniques: genetic algorithms, rule-based systems, and reinforcement learning. LCSs are capable of learning to predict the best action based on the current situation (a classification problem).

Rule-based systems require significant involvement from a human designer—the knowledge acquisition bottleneck. Instead, a system could use the creativity of genetic algorithms and the guidance of reinforcement learning to find the right behavior autonomously—as most animals do. By using information gathered from the environment and a high-level measure of performance as feedback, it's theoretically possible for a system to find the most appropriate set of rules. In practice, the adaptation can be difficult to apply at runtime in a realistic fashion, but LCSs have their advantages compared to other approaches (for instance, they're automated).

This chapter covers the following topics:

➤ The underlying representation of an LCS as the set of rules known individually as *classifiers*, consisting of the head (matching the sensory input) and the body (corresponding to the effectory outputs)

➤ The additional information stored by the rules, notably the prediction of their benefit and an estimate their error

➤ An introduction to classifier systems, including their internal functioning from an architectural point of view and each of the components

➤ The different aspects of LCSs, their different practical problems, and their applicability from a game developer's perspective

As well as introducing the theory behind classifier systems, this chapter shows one way genetic algorithms can be applied in practice.

Representation of Classifiers

The basic element of classifier systems can be compared to a rule with both a head and a body, known individually as a *classifier*.

Head and Body

Typically, the condition of the classifiers is modeled as a ternary string (that is, each symbol can have three values). The ternary representation includes the standard binary values of 0 and 1, as well as a "don't care" symbol denoted #—allowing the system to generalize. The length of this ternary condition string is the same as the length of the binary input string (usually perceptions of the animat). By using the "don't care" symbol #, it's possible to match the inputs with the conditions of classifiers. A match occurs when corresponding bits are equal or one of the symbols is #.

As for the classifiers' actions, they are generally encoded as *binary* strings, corresponding to the effectors of the animat. Classifiers have specific actions, so no abstraction is needed on the outputs (that is, without # symbols).

Other Attributes

Each classifier also stores a *prediction*, which corresponds to the expected *return* if that action is taken. Return can be defined as the accumulation of the reward over time (for instance, armor units successfully collected in the game). Essentially, return measures how good this particular classifier is in the long term.

Together with prediction, we also store its estimated *accuracy*. It's important to measure the accuracy of a prediction to emphasize the consistency of a classifier. If the classifier has low accuracy, it's just no good at predictions (regardless of the return). In this case, how can we trust it as a policy? On the other hand, rules with high accuracy demonstrate understanding of the world, and therefore are more likely to succeed when applied.

Before Wilson's XCS system [Wilson94] (a groundbreaking classifier system), the *fitness* of a classifier was based on its prediction of the return. Essentially, the system rewards how well a classifier *thinks* it does. This is often inconvenient because very general classifiers tend to have high return predictions, but are particularly inaccurate. All encompassing rules are therefore encouraged, implying the classifier system does not find the best representation, but rather a blur of generic concepts. Instead, using the accuracy as the fitness allows the best set of classifiers to be found. This is, in fact, a key insight into modern LCSs.

To compute the return and the prediction error, a counter is used for each rule. When the counter is 0, the values are not initialized. As the counter increases, so does the accuracy of the values. (More learning examples are available.)

Overview of the Classifier System

The classifier system is an aggregation of many components, reminiscent of three other AI techniques (genetic algorithms, rule-based systems, and reinforcement learning). Learning happens online by default, but the simulation can be used as a preprocess for games.

Architecture

The process follows the flow of data through the system, as depicted in Figure 33.1. The process starts by checking the sensory input and computing the matching classifiers. The matching classifiers are potentially evolved by the genetic algorithm. Then, the match set is processed to extract predictions for each of the actions. Given the predictions, it's possible to select the most appropriate action. The match set is then filtered to leave only the rules suggesting the selected action. The action is executed by the effectors.

Then, at the next step of the simulation, the reinforcement component adjusts the classifiers in the action set, given the reward and the predicted return.

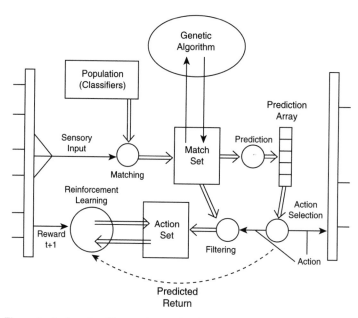

Figure 33.1 Flow chart of a classifier system, with functional components represented as circles, and data structures as rectangles.

This outline gives us preliminary ideas of how the system works overall. The following sections cover the components separately.

Matching Classifiers with the Input

The *matching* phase essentially analyzes the sensory input of the LCS (binary), comparing it with the conditions of the individual classifiers (ternary). Taking into account "don't care" symbols, all the applicable classifiers are stored in a *match set*, ready for further processing (see Table 33.1).

Table 33.1   A Population of Classifiers, Revealing the Condition, Action, Prediction, and Error

Condition	Action	Prediction	Error
01101	11	48	0.1
0#011	00	10	0.09
10110	01	25	0.14
#011#	01	17	0.05
1##1#	10	31	0.23

The classifiers below the double line are the ones that match the input of 10110.

Creation of New Classifiers

Evolution aims to create new classifiers from the match set. This is performed in two cases: when there are insufficient matching rules (covering), and when there's a low probability (discovery). This phase is actually performed by a genetic algorithm. Genetic operators used are the random initialization, mutation, and crossover.

Covering

Covering guarantees that there are always enough matching classifiers by generating new ones randomly if necessary. This introduces diversity into the population of classifiers, thus reducing the likelihood of premature convergence (in the population), or getting stuck in local traps (in the environment). The prediction and the error are left uninitialized with the counter at 0, as the reinforcement phase provides the first estimate.

Discovery

One noticeable property of classifier systems is that they are not directly driven by the genetic algorithm. Instead, the genetic algorithm is considered the creative component that finds new behaviors, only applied with a low probability.

The probability of selecting a classifier from the match set is proportional to its fitness (an elitist policy). Generally, two parents are chosen, two new classifiers are created, and they are inserted directly into the population. Again, the counter is set to 0 with the other values initialized in the reinforcement phase.

There are separate probabilities for each genetic operator; there's a probability of μ (Greek mu) that mutation will occur on a bit, and χ (Greek chi) probability that one-point crossover is applied (see Chapter 32, "Genetic Algorithms").

Removal of Classifiers

Because classifiers are added to the population at random intervals, it's necessary to remove the least fit to keep the population size under control. Deletion of classifiers also applies evolutionary pressure onto the population and increases the fitness of the system.

There is a fixed upper limit on the size of the population. When there are too many classifiers, the worst are deleted stochastically. Generally, each classifier keeps an estimate of the size of the match sets it was involved in. The probability of a classifier being deleted is proportional to this estimated size and the classifier's fitness. In essence, frequently used classifiers are more likely to be removed when unfit.

Using match-set size as a criterion for killing classifiers has the effect of balancing out the match sets. In genetic algorithms, such a technique is known as *niching*. A *niched* genetic algorithm essentially splits up the search space into different parts, and considers them as mostly separate. Genetic operators, including the deletion operators, are based on these niches. When done correctly, this has a consequence of balancing out the niches.

Therefore, niching enforces diversity in the population of classifiers in an LCS. Individual classifiers apply to a certain part of input space. Ideally, we want to force the system to cover all the possible inputs (either explicitly or by generalization) so that it always suggests an action. Niching is necessary for the classifier system to acquire broad knowledge of the problem, and not just knowledge of the local areas of the search space where the fitness is high.

Prediction

In the match set, the conditions of the classifiers are similar because they match the same inputs. The prediction phase separates the classifiers further by sorting them by identical actions. Each classifier has a different prediction of the return, so the prediction phase tries to estimate the total return for each action, taking into account potentially different predictions (see Table 33.2).

Table 33.2   A Match Set Has Been Grouped by Action to Extract a Final Prediction of the Return

Condition	Action	Prediction	Fitness
10110	01	48	47
#011#	01	31	13
1##1#	01	7	81
##1#0	10	27	92
10##0	10	13	58

Generally for each action, the estimated return is a weighted average of the predictions of the classifiers. Wilson advocates using the fitness to perform the weighted average, so that the prediction of most accurate classifiers is given priority [Wilson94].

Action Selection

Given the return predictions for each of the actions, it's possible to select the one that's most appropriate. Naturally, the action with the highest return is the most promising choice. However, it can also be beneficial to use randomized choices of actions to provide the system with more experience about the world. These two approaches are known as action selection *policies*:

➤ A **deterministic** policy selects the action with the highest prediction of return (greedy).

➤ The **roulette wheel** policy chooses the action with a probability proportional to the fitness.

Generally, a combination of the two policies is used to provide a trade-off between *exploiting* the best results, and *exploring* random actions.

Reinforcement

The reinforcement component is responsible for updating the values of the rules in the action set, only after the reward is received from the environment. Generally, the AI has to wait until the next step $t+1$ of the simulation to get the reward (that is, $r(t+1)$). Therefore, the implementation must keep the action set until then.

Values that need to be updated include the prediction, the error of the prediction (accuracy), and the fitness. The principle used for updating these values is based on Widrow and Hoff's *delta rule*—as described in Chapter 17, "Perceptrons." The idea is to adjust the values toward a desired target, with a small step of β.

We define the desired prediction P as the maximal value from the prediction array, multiplied by a discount factor $\gamma \in [0..1]$ (Greek gamma), summed with the reward feedback $r(t+1)$. This is used to update the error estimate, denoted by the Greek epsilon ε_j:

$$\varepsilon_j \leftarrow \varepsilon_j + \beta(|P - p_j| - \varepsilon_j)$$

In the case of the prediction of the return p_j, we adjust that toward the desired value P using the delta rule, after the error has been updated:

$$p_j \leftarrow p_j + \beta(P - p_j)$$

The accuracy is defined as a function of the error, which increases the accuracy toward one as the error diminishes. The function $\exp(-\varepsilon_j)$ models this, and can be adjusted by scaling the error by alpha α. This is a simplification of the original function defined by Wilson [Wilson94], but works fine in practice.

The fitness is defined as the *relative* accuracy of the classifier. The relative accuracy is computed as the difference of the accuracy and the average accuracy of the population. The fitness is estimated using an average for the first n updates and then using the delta rule (with $\eta=1/\beta$).

Discussion

LCSs are particularly good at estimating the benefit of actions, which implies they are also able to take advantage of the best actions. Because the classifiers are rewarded for their accuracy, the knowledge of the world modeled by LCS is generally representative of its true nature.

The basic representation of classifiers is relatively easy to understand, being almost as expressive as rule-based systems. Sadly, the binary and ternary values aren't especially friendly to read. Although they may be very efficient, binary sensors are somewhat clumsy to deal with; given heterogeneous data from the interfaces (for instance, floats, integers, arrays), we need a lot of "serialization" to convert them to binary values.

As for game development, LCSs can be applied in many situations. LCSs are primarily intended to provide adaptation in online simulations—although offline problems are safer choices. Control problems are the most popular application, although this technology is applicable to optimize a set of rules used for problem solving instead.

Adapting the representation to other categorical data types is relatively straightforward. It's just a matter of using symbols rather than the binary values, but retaining the "don't care" symbol. By providing a hierarchy of symbols (for instance, Marvin is-a player), the LCS can learn precise generalizations. On the other hand, continuous values are not a trivial extension of the same principle, because generalization would prove less straightforward.

This means LCSs, and slightly adapted versions, can theoretically be applied to almost any game AI task, ranging from obstacle avoidance to learning to assess weapons, including all reinforcement learning problems we'll discuss in Part VII. All we really need is a form of reward signal or a fitness value, and the creativity of genetic algorithms will find an appropriate set of rules. In practice, however, other techniques may be more appropriate.

Summary

This chapter covered classifier systems, which can be seen as hybrid combination of different fields. The representation itself is a combination of rule-based system and genetic encodings in binary:

➤ Each classifier has a condition that can use "don't care" symbols to generalize on the sensory input.

➤ The actions match directly with the effectors, without abstraction.

➤ The classifiers all store statistics about their recent application: predicted return, error (used to compute the accuracy), fitness, average size of the match set, and so forth.

The internal organization of classifier systems is surprisingly close to that of rule-based systems, notably including matching and conflict resolution phases. However, some key improvements allow the system to learn:

➤ An evolutionary component is applied to the match set. If the set is empty, a random classifier is created. Otherwise, with a low probability, two classifiers are mutated and crossed over and reinserted into the population. The most redundant and least accurate classifiers are occasionally removed.

➤ To update the values of the classifiers (for instance, prediction and error), a reinforcement component uses the reward signal from the environment, together with existing estimates of the classifier's benefit.

Over time, this tends to find a good set of classifiers. Such technology can be applied directly to control problems where a solution needs to be learned online. However, the ideas can also be modified to various degrees to handle different representations (any categorical variables) and problems (evolutionary approach with fitness rather than reward).

Practical Demo

Cascador uses a classifier system to learn to play deathmatch games according to a high-level performance indicator. *Cascador* benefits from hints provided by the designer as feedback. Still, the classifier system performs worse than a heterogeneous AI architecture, but manages to achieve (mostly) satisfactory behaviors autonomously.

Chapter 34

Adaptive Defensive Strategies with Genetic Algorithms

KEY TOPICS

- Representation of Action Sequences
- Genetic Operators
- Evolutionary Outline
- Genetic Algorithm Module Design
- Computing the Fitness
- Application
- Evaluation

Because two entire parts of this book focus on offensive strategies (for instance, shooting and weapon selection), it seems appropriate to balance out the animats' skills with defensive strategies—such as dodging fire or jumping unpredictably.

The preceding two chapters discussed new technology that allows the creatures to adapt to their environment, based on Darwinian concepts. So, instead of manually crafting fuzzy rules as defensive strategies (as we learned in Chapter 31, "Enhancing Movement Behaviors with a Fuzzy System"), the creatures learn how to defend themselves successfully within the game. We'll achieve this by placing them in a competitive environment and use evolutionary techniques to select the fittest behaviors (specifically, using genetic algorithms). We'll focus on dodging fire and rocket jumping in the following sections, but jumping unpredictably to prevent being shot will be left as an exercise—extending directly from the principles behind dodging.

This chapter covers the following topics:

➤ A custom representation for sequences of actions, notably focusing on the parameters for each action and timing issues.

➤ Some genetic operators that can be used to manipulate these sequences of actions. These mutate and crossover operations will be capable of manipulating the behaviors as if they were genetic code.

➤ An outline of our evolutionary algorithm, with a description how to create better sequences over time.

➤ A general-purpose genetic algorithm module. This will interface with any other components that can be evolved. At least we'll have the option of using this robust solution, despite the simplicity of our problem.

➤ A discussion of the fitness function from a behavioral perspective and the different fitness components that prevent loopholes (leading to undesirable behaviors).

➤ An overview of the different implementation issues, as well as testing issues.

➤ An analysis of the behavior of the animat briefly and theoretical limitations of the solution.

At the end of this chapter, the animats are no longer defenseless in the face of oncoming rockets.

Representation of Action Sequences

Once again, the concept of representation is the primary issue to resolve. In this case, we're interested in representing sequences of actions that produce reactive behaviors.

Actions and Parameters

There is clearly a subset of all possible actions that will allow animats to achieve the two behaviors described (see Table 34.1). Limiting the representation to only the actions needed will not only make the development easier, but also speed up the learning. It would be trivial to extend this at a later date if necessary; the genetic algorithm would cope just as well, if a bit slower.

Table 34.1   Limited Set of Actions Used in Each of the Sequences and Their Corresponding Parameters

Action	Parameter
Look	`direction`
Move	`weights`
Fire	—
Jump	—

The `direction` parameter is a symbol taking values (`up`, `down`, `ahead`). The `weights` are used to blend possible moving directions together.

Some actions are given parameters, which means we don't have to use large numbers of parameterless actions. This also separates the concepts of *what* to do, and *how* to do it in the representation (which helps the evolution). There are two parameters to explain:

➤ `Direction` is a parameter used by the `look` action. This is only needed in rocket jumping, and the animat only really needs to look down. For flexibility (and to not make the problem too simple), we'll include the three directions as possible values for this parameter: `up`, `ahead`, and `down`.

➤ `Weights` are used by the `move` action. Instead of letting the action specify every possible movement, we provide it with a set of default directions—chosen as expert features. There are three of them; move away from (1) the projectile, (2) the closest collision point, and (3) the estimated impact location (see Figure 34.1). The genetic algorithm can decide upon arbitrary weights (both positive and negative) to move almost anywhere.

Now it's just a matter of combining parameters and actions into sequences of actions.

Sequences

Simple arrays are commonly used to represent sequences. However, by using actions as the elements in the array, our sequences have no sense of timing; the actions will be ordered, but no hints about delays are provided.

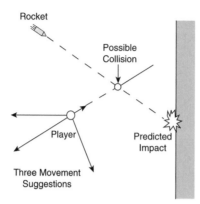

Figure 34.1   Top-down representation of the three different direction vectors provided to the genetic algorithm. A weighted combination of the three allows almost any point in space to be chosen.

For this reason, the AI needs to associate each action with a time. There are two ways to do this, using either of the following:

➤ A time offset relative to the previous action

➤ Absolute timing, based on the start of the sequence

To make this decision, it's necessary to consider how small changes in the representation affect the sequence. Using relative times, changing the timing of one action will have a knock-on effect on the absolute times of all the other actions thereafter. On the other hand, with absolute times, changes to any particular value will be completely independent from the rest of the action times. Because the absolute approach minimizes the interdependencies between variables of the search space, it provides the most flexibility to the genetic algorithm.

As a consequence of global action times, the order of the actions in the array is not important; it's just a form of storage. The first action in the sequence could easily be the last element of the array. There are two different ways to interpret this:

➤ It's beneficial for the genetic algorithm to have a loose representation because it will be able to group actions that work well together.

➤ The fact that the order of the array is not important implies there are many symmetric solutions; this is the cost of the loose representation. The size of the search space could be reduced by ordering the array of actions by time.

Both of these factors will affect genetic algorithm. Because the problem does not seem too complex, however, we'll settle for the loose representation. The arrays can be ordered after the evolution is over, for efficiency reasons (to avoid scanning the entire array to check the timings of actions).

Genetic Operators

Given a representation for a sequence, we need to define basic genetic operators. These are necessary for evolution to be possible, however simple the process.

Random Generation

Let's start by considering the random generation of actions, divided into three separate concepts: the type of action, its parameters, and the time offset:

➤ The time offset will always be a floating-point value, so it can be initialized randomly within the maximum length of a sequence.

➤ As for the action type, it can be trivially encoded as a symbol. This can be initialized randomly to one of all the possible actions.

➤ The parameters depend on the action, so we'll make sure to initialize the values at the same time, depending on the random action selected. All values are selected randomly among their maximal range.

The random generation of sequences must also decide on sequence length (that is, number of actions); this is done randomly, too, but within the limits of a maximal sequence length. Each of the actions can then be generated randomly to occupy each slot in the array. Finally, we have the option of re-offsetting all the times so that the first action starts at 0. This postprocess saves a lot of time in the sequence, although it removes some options for the evolution (for instance, waiting before triggering an action).

Crossover

The simplest possible operator handles crossover: one-point crossover. The idea is to find a random split point on both the parents and swap the subarrays to create two offspring. The advantage of using this approach is that the sequence of genes is left mostly intact, so actions that combine well together have a high chance of still being together after the crossover. This concept is discussed in depth in Chapter 32, "Genetic Algorithms," and this operator presents no particular programming challenge either.

Mutation

The random mutation happens in two ways. First, with a particularly low probability, the length of a sequence can be modified. If the array needs additional elements, they are added randomly; otherwise they are removed.

Mutation also happens to individual actions, with a small probability (different to the one previously discussed). The gene storing the time is mutated by adding a floating-point value generated by a Gaussian distribution (like the parameters). The action is mutated by selecting a different action randomly. If there is a change in action, the parameters are automatically changed to match.

Evolutionary Outline

The population is kept of constant size, which reduces unnecessary memory allocation and de-allocation. The population is initialized randomly, with all the fitness values left unassigned.

An evolutionary step happens on request; if there is an individual in the population with an unassigned fitness, it is chosen and passed to the evolved component. Otherwise, two parents are chosen with a probability proportional to their fitness. These are crossed over and mutated to form two offspring, which are reinserted into the population.

When individuals need to be removed from the population, they are selected probabilistically according to the inverse fitness and the similarity with other sequences. As for classifier systems, the idea is to enforce diversity in the population by removing the worst behavior when two are similar.

Genetic Algorithm Module Design

The preceding two sections mentioned that most of the work is done in custom genetic operators. The evolutionary procedure itself is relatively simple, too. This predicament is quite common, so the need for a genetic algorithm code is often as a set of helper functions. Common idioms and patterns for evolutionary algorithms are easily created as standalone functions.

Having the genetic algorithm as a separate module is very debatable in this case, and in fact, we may not use it at all. However, creating a robust genetic algorithm module will give us the luxury of the choice. The component will come in handy in other situations where more robust solutions are required. Ideally, we want a module that brings together the common evolutionary patterns and genetic operators, one that also allows configurability and customizability.

Role of the Genetic Algorithm

It's important to realize that the genetic algorithm is nothing more than an optimization strategy in most cases. This implies that the functionality of the evolved object does not change in any way; only a different quality of service is provided.

Many genetic algorithm libraries focus on the evolutionary loop and provide various hooks for evaluating custom objects defined by the user. This approach is appropriate when there is one simple component being optimized as a precomputation. For complex systems with multiple components, or animats that evolve throughout their lifetime, however, the genetic algorithm needs to take a supporting role—leaving the center stage to the components providing the functionality.

Interfaces

The external interface (exported) of the genetic algorithm consists of a unique entry point, used to report the fitness of the candidate currently being evaluated. This could easily be handled by message passing if this proves more convenient:

```
void ReportFitness( const float f );
```

The internal interface (imported) lies between the genetic algorithm and the component being evolved (for instance, rule-based system). This interface is called *evolvable*, exported by all components that can be optimized by an evolutionary algorithm.

The main principle to implement a truly flexible genetic algorithm module is to let the evolved component perform all the genetic operations. This avoids the major overhead (in coding and execution time) of converting each of the phenotypes to genotypes and back. This is sometimes known as *evolutionary data structures*, although I prefer the term *phenotype-specific operators*. The main idea is that it is unnecessary—and inconvenient—to convert between representations. The genetic operators often need to be customized anyway. When standard data structures and genetic operators are used, common helper functions can be reused.

The phenotype-specific operators are exposed by the evolvable interface. There are also functions available to initialize the population and control the evaluation:

```
void Crossover( const Individual& a, const Individual& b,
Individual& c );
void Mutate( const Individual& a, const Individual& b, Individual&
c );
void Randomize( Individual& a );
void Allocate( vector<Individual*>& population );
void Deallocate( vector<Individual*>& population );
void Evaluate( const Individual& a );
```

The genetic algorithm is thereby completely independent from the implementation details of the client component. The `Individual` is an empty base class defined with a pure virtual copy operator (so that the genetic algorithms can perform assignments without knowing the details of the data structure).

To use the genetic algorithms module to evolve our sequences of actions, we need to implement each of these functions. Most of this functionality will need to be implemented anyway, so it's mainly a matter of preference whether it's modular or not.

Computing the Fitness

A minimal amount of code is required outside of the modules. Mainly, the artificial intelligence (AI) must compute the fitness of the behavior at regular intervals and pass the information to the genetic algorithm. Because we're interested in two different behaviors, there are two fitness functions to think about.

Rocket Jumping

Ideally, we don't want to test for rocket jumping directly, instead letting the evolution discover rockets as the best approach to jumping very high. (Double-jumps or jump pads could be other solutions.) Therefore, we want to assign reward for upward movement only. To prevent the animat from getting high fitness for running up stairs, upward movement is only considered when the animat is not touching the floor.

We also want to reward very high jumps more than many smaller jumps. To achieve this, the reward can be the square of the distance traveled upward. Genetic algorithms are particularly notorious for finding loopholes in fitness functions, but all these criteria seem to cover all our bases.

Dodging Fire

To rate skills at dodging incoming fire, we'll measure the distance of the player to the point of explosion. If the rocket hits the animat full on, the distance—and therefore the fitness—will be near 0. On the other hand, if the animat successfully scampers far away from the collision point, it'll get a high fitness. Because all rockets explode quickly enough, no limit is imposed upon the fitness. (Clamping the distance would remove useful information for the evolution.)

To prevent the animat from getting high fitness for standing still (but far away), the AI monitors the *difference* in distance. This is like measuring the average velocity away from the point of impact. This will only be measured at the start and end of the sequence (called when a rocket is fired).

Although these hints to the genetic algorithm indicate that distance is important, the AI also needs to measure a crucial factor: damage. Any damage taken will be subtracted from the animat's fitness (decreasing the estimate of the capability to dodge fire).

In the unlikely event that these two fitness components fail to guide the evolution to desirable avoidance behaviors, a more continuous reward feedback can be used (instead of the fitness computed at the end of the sequence). Any movement away from the closest point of contact is rewarded, measured with time as the fourth dimension. So we're finding the closest 3D point given 4D trajectories in time and 3D space. Any movement away from that point results in positive fitness.

Application

The genetic algorithm provides an endless stream of candidate sequences, which need to be evaluated by the animat as behaviors. Execution of the sequences is just a matter of starting the timer. The rest of the AI can proceed normally, but when the next time step is beyond the time offset of an action, it must be executed.

Instead of scanning the sequence for actions that need to be executed, the sequence can be sorted for efficiency—copying the old sequence if the genetic algorithm requires it intact. For additional efficiency, we can request a callback specifically at the time of execution of the next action. This approach requires separating the sequence execution from the rest of the AI, but proves to be a much more elegant design.

To prevent any problems, we can force the first action to happen at the start of the sequence. This is done by offsetting all the actions to 0, if the genetic algorithm doesn't do that during the evolution. We must guarantee that sequences are always finished or terminated, no matter what happens to the animat. (Even death must cause the AI to abort the sequence.)

Testing the animats is much easier than using the contraptions. Indeed, rocket jumping and dodging fire can be performed at any location in the terrain. There's no need for any particular game environment; all we need to do is give the bots rocket launchers, and let them fire away.

As usual, it's possible for the animats to learn the behaviors respecting the rules of embodiment. However, making each of them invulnerable (but still aware of normal damage) during the learning can save them a lot of time. As for combining the fitness values and learning phases, this should get the animat to rocket jump away from the impact points (assuming the rocket jumps have lower damage than incoming projectiles).

Finally, it's best to separate the learning for both rocket jumping and dodging fire. (The behaviors are conditionally independent anyway.) The are two ways to achieve this separation: Use distinct learning phases with one unique fitness function, or manually split the fitness according to the behavior and learn the behaviors at the same time. Both achieve the same thing, but in different ways, obviously.

Practical Demo

The animat demonstrating these principles is called *Kanga*, and lives on the web site `http://AiGameDev.com/` with all its friends. The code is extremely well documented, and there's a walkthrough to get the AI up and running within the game. *Kanga* actually learns its jumping and dodging behaviors during the game.

Evaluation

The animats are certainly very quick to learn how to jump! Multiple jumps seem to cause no problems either. It takes a bit longer in evolution terms to discover the rocket jump, but there is evolutionary pressure toward that behavior—thanks to the squared height fitness function. The problem is not too difficult, so keeping the population small helps.

The dodging behavior is learned relatively quickly, thanks to the simplicity of the representation. Generally, any balanced combination of weights for the vectors works well, engendering movement away from the estimated point of impact, from closest collision point, and from the projectile itself.

In some cases, this approach is suboptimal; on average, however, it performs well. The genetic algorithm would need more information about the relative positions to perform better (instead of blindly optimizing weights).

The fitness function providing rewards on a per-jump or per-dodge basis actually works very well; we don't need to provide a more regular form of reward. The fact that fitness is continuous is of great help to the genetic algorithm, because it guides the evolution better than Boolean success indicators.

This scheme reveals how it's possible to evolve behaviors, using simple genetic operators and a customized representation. The representation is better suited to modeling sequences than learning classifier systems and fuzzy rules; the learning benefits from this explicitness.

However, the representation is incompatible with these other schemes based on rules. In addition, the linear flow of the sequence and its insensitivity to environmental stimuli would be problematic, particularly when applying this representation to the behaviors from Chapter 31.

For this reason, it may be advantageous to merge the two representations, including the best of sequences (nonlinear ones) and rules together. In fact, the next part covers this in the introduction to the discussion about finite state machines, which represent sequences with transition rules. Then, we cover hierarchical finite state machines, which enable us to integrate classical rules and other finite state machines within each other.

Summary

This chapter started by creating a custom representation for the desired behaviors:

➤ The representation of the sequences is designed to be linear. Sequences are purely reactive, mostly insensitive to sensory input after they have started.

➤ Genetic operators were defined—both for initialization and discovery—and were capable of generating all the possible sequences within acceptable length and time.

After that, we moved on to ways to optimize the behaviors using genetic algorithms:

➤ The evolutionary process is extremely simple, selecting the fittest and discarding the weakest.

➤ The module is designed to be plugged straight into any other component that can be evolved. This is done by defining an evolvable interface that provides phenotype-specific evolutionary operations.

Back into the practical world of in-game behaviors, we talked about dodging fire and rocket jumps:

➤ Two fitness functions were defined, and we made sure they had few loopholes for the genetic algorithm to find. We also attempted to make the values as continuous as possible, to guide the evolutionary process.

➤ The application phase discussed implementation details (for instance, sorting the array, using callbacks, and guaranteeing the sequence finishes), and pointed out the simplicity of the testing phase.

The resulting behaviors are relatively close to what human players would do, despite not being perfect. The dodging behavior is useful in practice when triggered at the right moment, but rocket jumping is used just to show off! We need a higher-level AI to decide when to use it.

The technology used in this chapter manages to express sequences of actions very well, but fails to provide some other functionality we take for granted in expert systems. Part VI will actually look into a way of expressing arbitrary sequences with rules—resulting in finite state machines. These are more powerful, but would be less tailored to this particular problem at hand.

Chapter 35

Designing Learning AI

KEY TOPICS

- Purpose of Learning
- Approach to Learning
- Varieties of Learning Components
- Methodologies for Learning Behaviors

Learning systems are extremely appealing for computer game developers, because they can speed up development and increase the levels of intelligence in nonplayer characters (NPCs). However, the task of creating a learning system is complex; beyond just knowing about artificial intelligence (AI) technology, it's a matter of system design to create functioning behaviors and capabilities.

Right at the beginning of the book, Chapter 2, "The Design of Intelligence," provided a very quick introductory overview of learning. Having covered much more ground on the subject, we can look into the learning in more depth. Using examples, we'll investigate learning AI from different viewpoints (for instance, behaviors, technology, and components). We'll discuss advantages and disadvantages, giving guidelines for future implementations.

This chapter covers the following topics:

➤ An overview of learning from a high-level point of view, trying to understand what this technology can achieve

➤ The different approaches to learning, both in terms of the game development (online and offline) and the technical point of view (incremental and batch)

➤ A description of AI components, showing how they deal with the data to learn facts or behaviors (that is, using examples or feedback)

➤ The creation of behaviors using learning, and different methodologies that can be used to get animats to behave correctly

This in-depth review will provide the information necessary to make design decisions about what learning AI to use. This high-level approach is undoubtedly the best way to get the learning to work (that is, a preventive measure for any potential problems). Chapter 48, "Dealing with Adaptive Behaviors," discusses practical tips and tricks for getting any adaptive AI to "work"—however inappropriate the design!

Purpose of Learning

As with any new technology, users can be overwhelmed by its potential and forget to take a critical perspective. The main reason for failure in projects based on learning AI is *overuse*. AI technology has made great progress over the past few years, but it's still at a stage where it's best kept focused on domain-specific problems.

Therefore, we'll try to approach learning from an engineer's point of view, analyzing what benefits it provides, and at what cost. By trading off both aspects of the technology, design decisions become more obvious.

Why Learn?

There are two main reasons for learning, both of which attempt to find intelligent solutions to problems. The main difference is the goal of the learning; is the desired result static or dynamic? We choose the terms *optimization* and *adaptation* to refer to these different cases.

Optimization

Optimization attempts to find the solution to a known puzzle, which does not change over time. We rely on knowledge of all the variables involved in the problem, as well as the criteria to evaluate the solution. In fact, the entire task can be considered as static.

An example of this is obstacle avoidance; the goals are clearly identifiable, and we can develop competent behaviors that do not need to change to deal with new situations.

Adaptation

In the case of *adaptation*, the problem actually changes over the course of time because of hidden factors affecting the behavior in unforeseeable ways. The goal may be clear, but not how to achieve it. This is the case when an animat enters a fully unknown environment.

Alternatively, adaptation is necessary when the actual goal of the learning changes—regardless of the problem being well identified. If an animat's feelings about certain players change for the worse, for example, the behavior will shift from helping them to making their life difficult.

Successful adaptation therefore involves using the facilities available in new ways, so that unforeseen factors—both changing problems and changing goals—are taken into account.

Similarities and Differences

The static and dynamic nature of the problem is the major difference between optimization and adaptation. It's important to realize that dynamic-ness arises from variables not being *modeled*. In many cases, information about the full problem is freely available from the game; indeed, the world is at least very predictable, if not fully deterministic (for instance, physics and logic). The designer voluntarily discards much information about the environment, for efficiency and simplicity reasons. In a few rare cases, dynamic problems arise from truly *unknown* parameters (for instance, emergent phenomena).

So fundamentally, both problems are really the same thing. Static problems are better identified, because most of the variables have been identified, since the problem is small or the designer has spent time on it. Dynamic problems are poorly described by the variables chosen, because the scope of the problem is too large or the designer wasn't able to identify all the parameters.

As far as the AI is concerned, the closer to a static problem the better the final result. For example, we may not want an animat that struggles to adapt to all situations, but rather one that handles a great majority of them by using a good AI optimized statically. Defining a satisfactory static problem is about knowing the variables involved and choosing all (or most) of the relevant ones. Chapter 21, "Knowledge of the Problem," discussed this in depth.

Learn What?

Different forms of learning can be applied to various tasks.

Facts and Knowledge

By observing the world, it's possible to understand it using facts or statistical predictions. "If I jump, I'll fall back down" is an example of a fact. "This platform spends most of its time in its original position" is an example of a statistical prediction. Given enough experience, this knowledge can become surprisingly accurate.

It's also possible to extract general principles from a collection of distinct facts. (For instance, "All objects that are in the air will fall to the floor.") This is a more implicit way of representing knowledge, known as a generalization. It can be quicker to learn, but less accurate.

Behaviors and Procedures

An alternative to learning facts is learning behaviors. Synthetic creatures can learn how to control their movement, to use weapons, and to move through doors. These behaviors can be simple actions as well as complex sequences guided by stimuli from the environment. It's also important for the animats to learn how to apply the behaviors in general situations.

Overlaps in Representation

In some cases, it's relatively intuitive what classes as a *behavior*, and what classes as a *fact*. However, there can still be some confusion, because it often depends what words are chosen! For example, shooting (behavior) is partly about knowing where to aim (fact). So conceptually, it's possible to learn behaviors as facts. Conversely, animats implicitly know facts about the world when they perform behaviors.

When it comes down to the representation, things are equally ambiguous between these declarative and procedural forms. For example, a decision tree stores facts but it can be used for behaviors, too. Neural networks can be used for control, but also learn information about the problem.

The implementation of the technique is the best hope of distinguishing *knowledge* from *behaviors*. Knowledge learned online (ontogenetic) will be queried by a component that's fixed (phylogenetic). On the other hand, learned behaviors will be handled by a component that changes itself dynamically. Naturally, if we look deep enough it all comes down to "information," regardless of the technology used.

In practice, game developers will almost always learn facts directly, which enables them to debug and optimize the AI component responsible for using this knowledge. It's also much easier when animats can be understood as a form of data with a developer-friendly representation.

Approach to Learning

With the purpose of learning clear, this section looks at different ways to achieve it.

Two Game Phases

Learning can take place during the development (offline), or after the game has started (online).

Offline

When learning is used during the development, it can be considered as a preprocess—on the same terms as compacting graphical data structures or compressing sound files. Offline learning generally assumes that the problem is static, and that an optimal solution can be found automatically. The developer can assist and manage the learning by using tools and methodologies.

This approach is used by cunning and efficient developers who have the experience to let the AI do their work for them—quicker than they would do it themselves. It's possible because there is a well-identified goal and the system remains the same in the game.

Online

Online learning happens after the game has shipped, whenever the player launches the simulation. In many cases, this form of adaptation is used as part of the design to provide a more immersive world and believable creatures.

This approach requires much more thought, because the developer must foresee many possible situations and outcomes. In many cases, the AI engineers are responsible for guaranteeing that their *design* is safe, because no amount of beta testing will take into account all the situations. We'll discuss the issues that arise in more detail during Chapter 48.

Misidentification

Although online learning can be a justifiable design feature, sometimes developers believe they need online learning, but in fact, it's because they are incapable of defining a good solution offline (for instance, too big or too complex). This is a perfectly valid justification for online learning, as long as the AI engineer is aware of the alternative! When trying to find a solution, both online *and* offline solutions should be equally considered.

For example, most simple NPCs (for instance, cannon fodder) do not need to learn online; they can be trained offline. Their behavior is simple to identify: The problem is mostly static. It's also very good practice to use offline learning even when online adaptation is required. This allows near-optimal default behaviors to be present, allowing the AI to look reasonable from the start.

Two Fundamental Techniques

Technically speaking, there are two ways of learning information: batch and incremental.

Batch

Batch learning uses a large data set to extract relevant facts. The idea is to rely on vast quantities of information to extract general trends. This is the principle behind *data mining*, for which decision trees and neural networks are commonly used. Decision trees are batch learners because they process all samples to build the tree recursively.

Batch algorithms are generally very efficient, and can be easily optimized because they operate on large data sets in one pass. They also provide great quality solutions, because they consider such a wide variety of examples. For this reason, batch algorithms should always be preferred, or attempted first as a proof of concept.

Incremental

The *incremental method* takes samples one by one, and tweaks the internal representation by a small amount every time. Eventually, a good solution arises from the learning.

Incremental learning uses much less memory than batch algorithms, because in incremental learning, data is immediately discarded after it has been learned. However, the quality of the results can suffer from this, because it's much tougher to learn incrementally without "forgetting."

Interoperability

Generally, it's the case that incremental algorithms are used online, and batch algorithms offline. However, both these design decisions are not connected; either form of algorithm could easily be used in both contexts.

It's certainly feasible for an incremental algorithm to learn from a full data set (for instance, perceptron back propagation to learn target selection), and to get a batch algorithm to update the decision tree (for instance, learning weapon selection). Both these combinations are somewhat inefficient computationally, especially the second. However, they have their uses on a case-by-case basis, when needing low memory usage or better quality behaviors respectively. Naturally, there are a few precautions to take in each of these cases, but—once again—we'll discuss these in Chapter 48.

Varieties of Learning Components

Both batch and incremental techniques are methods for processing (sensory) data. This section discusses particular ways to extract the essential information and find the right solution.

Supervised

Supervised learning uses examples of mappings from inputs X to outputs Y, where Y is the desired output. This can be expressed formally as the relation $X \to Y$. This approach is extremely explicit; it's clear what the answer should be given an input. This captures the essence of reactive techniques.

An example of supervised learning would be to build a decision tree based on a collection of examples gathered from expert play. For supervised learning to work well, it's best to gather lots of data. This is important for learning generally; it gives the AI system the opportunity to find the best solution.

Supervised learning is very efficient, because it can be handled directly by reactive components. It's literally about adjusting a direct mapping, which is arguably the fastest form of learning. The quality of the results is also very good, because most AI techniques have been fine-tuned over the past decades of research.

Reinforcement

Reinforcement learning problems are less explicit. They require the animat to try an action X in a certain situation Y, and for the animat to receive a reward according to the outcome. This is formally modeled as a relation $X \times Y \rightarrow \mathbb{R}$. As usual, $\mathbb{R}$ is the set of real numbers, to which the reward value belongs.

Taking another example from reactive movement, the animat would be given a positive reward signal for moving forward, and a negative one for bumping into obstacles.

This problem is difficult for two reasons. First, it's difficult to find the best behavior without a lot of experimentation. Second, complex problems have complex reward signals that often must be interpreted and distributed into subcomponents (that is, *modular* rewards rather than *holistic*).

As far as using this approach in practice is concerned, it's important to realize the amount of time it takes to get to the right result. This approach requires many exploratory actions that may be particularly unrealistic. So either:

➤ The search space should be minimized.

➤ An offline approach should be preferred.

These design tricks maximize the benefits of the reinforcement approach.

Evolutionary

The *evolutionary approach* is based on a fitness function. This is conceptually similar to reinforcement problems, because a scalar value is used to provide evaluative feedback of the behavior quality. However, the difference in the evolutionary approach is that the fitness is generally computed on a per-trial basis, not for every action. Conceptually, this means n pairs of inputs and outputs correspond to the fitness; formally speaking, it's the relationship $(X \times Y)^n \rightarrow \mathbb{R}$.

For example, we could evolve the entire shooting behaviors using a set of trials on moving targets, and use genetic algorithms to mate the best shooters together.

Evolutionary approaches are extremely impractical in anything but offline learning, because lengthy trials are required to set up the animats. These phases are particularly unrealistic to watch, albeit entertaining! That said, the results produced are generally extremely efficient.

Unsupervised

Finally, there are specific *unsupervised techniques*—such as self-organizing feature maps—that are not covered directly in this book. The principle is to feed lots of data to the component, and let it automatically organize an internal representation that extracts patterns in the data. After this has been done, the internal representation can be analyzed for pattern details. Naturally, independent AI techniques are needed to interpret these patterns, so purely unsupervised techniques are not useful alone.

However, it's possible, for example, to combine reinforcement learning technique with an internal evaluation mechanism (for instance, a reward script). As a compound component, these approaches can be considered unsupervised (and are covered in Part VII).

Synopsis

As a general rule, supervised learning is the way to go. It's a safe bet because of the predictable results, and is undoubtedly the most efficient form of learning. This makes it ideally suited to game development.

Other techniques provide less control over the final behavior. Although there are many ways to get them to work in practice (as depicted in this book's examples and exercises), this generally incurs an overhead in both development and computation. Also, even though reinforcement and evolutionary components can achieve better behaviors, their learning phase is quite unrealistic (for instance, experimenting with actions or behaviors that are inappropriate).

In brief, supervised components are the best way for game developers to keep control. Components based on feedback may be tempting from a design point of view, but we should be aware that they require longer development times.

Methodologies for Learning Behaviors

In contrast to the technical nature of the previous sections, the next few paragraphs take a practical perspective on learning. We discuss the different ways that designers interact with the AI to get it to learn.

Training

Training involves providing examples from which the AI can learn. In most cases, experts analyze the problem and design a solution. After the knowledge is expressed with a convenient representation, it's possible for the animats to learn those examples, as well as provide suitable interpretations of the cases where no examples are provided.

Imitation

Imitation is similar to training in that data samples are required for the animat to learn. The difference is that examples are gathered from observing any other player in the game. In this case, there is no longer any need for experts; random players can be used as a reference for the learning.

Trial and Error

Trial and error is another way for animats to acquire the desired behavior. The idea is to provide no guidance about what to do, and instead rate the quality of actions (at every step) or behaviors (in larger intervals). Thus, the designer is involved in a much higher-level fashion, usually designing the way the feedback is given to the animat. Learning is achieved by attempting to maximize the reward received—regardless of the granularity.

Shaping

Shaping is a way for designers to provide their knowledge of the task to help the animat find the solution [Perkins96]. Generally, medium-level insights are provided by breaking the problem up so that it's easier to solve. In practice, the developer sets up a series of trials, incrementally revealing different aspects of the problem. Generally, these trials are spaced out so that the fundamental concepts are presented first and the more difficult ones later.

Similar principles to shaping can be combined with the three previous approaches. When training, the important cases can be learned first. With imitation, the teacher can make a point of demonstrating simple issues first. Finally, learning based on trial and error can focus on essential concepts first.

Critical Review

In games, training is used the most often because it provides the most predictable results. It's advisable to use this as a default approach. Imitation is becoming increasingly common for small problems, but usually takes more time and effort to set up. Trial and error is extremely powerful, but presents the most technical challenges. A form of shaping is present throughout AI development generally, notably in the iterative nature of the design process (with significant involvement from the engineer).

Summary

Many of the concepts presented in this chapter overlap to a great degree. For very good reasons, particular combinations of design decisions are more common than others. However, it's important to realize that these design decisions are orthogonal (that is, mostly independent from each other). Table 35.1 summarizes the reliability of the different approaches.

Table 35.1   Decisions That Need to Be Made When Designing a Learning AI, Ranked by Their Likelihood of Success

	Reliable	**Higher Risk**
Type	Optimization	Adaptation
Representation	Knowledge	Behaviors
Phase	Offline	Online
Technique	Batch	Incremental
Component	Supervised	Feedback
Methodology	Training	Trial and error

The more reliable design decisions made, the more control the developer has over the NPC. In addition, the animats are likely to perform better and the AI to run more efficiently. There are challenges even with these safer options, but the higher-risk technologies complicate matters by an order of magnitude. Chapter 48 discusses this issue further.

Practical Demo

A skeleton animat, known as *Loony,* sets up to illustrate the ideas in this chapter. The animat provides three forms of feedback: supervised, reward, and fitness. Callback functions are called when this information is available, which can be interpreted as the AI engineer sees fit.

Part V

Conclusion

The last few chapters covered a nice blend of technology, discussing a wide variety of little behaviors that make a tremendous difference when it comes to believability and realism.

Retrospective Overview

Let's recap the important observations made throughout this part.

Techniques

Fuzzy logic represents facts in an extremely intuitive way using degrees of membership. Fuzzy expert systems are particularly suited to deductive reasoning, determining new facts from a set of statements in a surprisingly humanlike fashion. Fuzzy rules can also be used to provide smooth control, but this requires a few precautions to handle correctly; indeed, long sequences can be confusing to describe with consistent rules.

On the downside, fuzzy expert systems require all the rules to be processed at each step, which can be relatively costly. Combinatorial explosions can often be avoided in practice by representing the knowledge in an implicit fashion, regrouping and simplifying rules as appropriate.

As for *genetic algorithms*, they are an extremely powerful optimization paradigm that can be applied to almost any problem. They are powerful at finding near globally optimal solutions.

Genetic algorithms rely on a good representation of the solution they are optimizing. So the evolutionary technique is only a small part of the development. Very often, custom encoding/decoding methods need to be created. Alternatively, phenotype-specific genetic operators are required.

On the downside, genetic algorithms suffer from one of their essential concepts: the fitness function. They can be very easy to set up with simple criteria (for instance, efficient), but prove challenging to adjust for more complex behaviors (for instance, realistic). This is because of the implicit, high-level form of control and the particularly slow optimization that makes incremental tweaking a nightmare. It's particularly difficult to prevent unintended loopholes, although it can be entertaining to watch.

These shortcomings apply to all techniques based on fitness values, and not particularly to genetic algorithms. The solution is to lower the level of control back down to supervised learning as much as possible, expressing the fitness in terms of specific situations and actions.

Learning classifier systems is a great example of how to apply genetic algorithms within simple architectures. As a matter of fact, learning classifier systems is an extremely efficient technique for adaptation, and even optimization. The representation of individual classifiers has the advantage of being quite expressive, so they are easy to understand at a glance. That said, modifying the binary representation to include arbitrary symbols is more useful in practice.

Behaviors

We developed a variety of behaviors together, either using handcrafted rules or learned sequences. In many cases, these approaches could be swapped—for example, learning the more complex behaviors such as using doors. Only a decent environment is necessary, making it easy for the animat to learn (that is, shaping the behaviors using customized game levels). Conversely, it would be fairly easy to develop arbitrary behaviors using fuzzy logic.

Most of the behaviors based on fuzzy logic are very satisfactory, providing smooth control and effective movement. Some behaviors don't rely on existing lower-level behaviors, and fail because of invalid assumptions (for instance, walls between the button and the door). To keep up the effectiveness and realism of the behaviors, they must reuse the existing capabilities.

As for dodging, the behavior is surprisingly successful despite the simple model of weighted suggestion vectors. This is a good example of providing expert-designed features to assist the learning algorithm. That said, there are some issues of suboptimal policies in some cases, but generally, they are equally as effective as humans.

As for rocket jumping, it seems like a circus act. The behavior has no purpose until analysis of the terrain reveals that a rocket jump is necessary. This is performed by a higher-level AI, and is practically never suggested. In fact, this is a tremendous example of a behavior that would benefit from broadcasting of *affordance* signals; items that require a rocket jump would broadcast that fact to the animats capable of doing so, saving them the computationally expensive effort of analyzing the situation.

Outlook

All the techniques from this can be reused for previous problems or upcoming ones, and everyone is encouraged to see some suggested exercises on the web site at http://AiGameDev.com/.

This chapter provides a good set of techniques and methodologies to solve simple problems by using a custom representation. It also reveals how to use learning to create sequences of actions that are very easily edited manually.

However, as far as manually crafting behaviors is concerned, no technique comes close to the simplicity of finite-state machines. They provide a practically perfect representation for arbitrary sequences of actions, taking away this flaw from (fuzzy) rule-based systems. In the next part, we'll discuss ways to combine state machines with other techniques using heterogeneous hierarchies of components.

Our animats are also much more flexible now; in fact, they have an almost complete set of reactive behaviors. In the next part, we'll be making them a bit more realistic, giving them the kind of instincts that animals have. To do this, we'll attempt to model different aspects of emotions, which will lead to more believable behaviors.

Part VI

Emotions

Over the course of this book, the animats have become relatively intelligent. They are capable of primitive motor control, handling objects, and making some decisions. However, the behaviors are not particularly believable, mainly because the AI focuses on intellectual capabilities.

This part covers emotions, used as a tool to improve the believability of the animats. In the spirit of adding errors to the actions (for instance, noise in the aiming), emotions provide a biologically plausible way to modify the sensors and effectors to affect behaviors. Emotions also provide a high-level bias for decision making.

Motivation

The emotions improve the simulation of the animat's body, modeling essential human characteristics (such as adrenaline). Not only is this likely to improve the realism of low-level actions, it's also likely to improve higher-level behaviors that arise from the simulation.

As well as affecting existing behaviors, the emotional system provides guidance for intelligent decision-making components. The emotions can be understood as desires and motivations, which are often subjective to each player.

The technology developed in this part also demonstrates systems composed of multiple subarchitectures. In this case, the emotional architecture and the intelligence architecture are mostly independent, with emotions providing influences only during interaction with the body.

Finally, this part covers an AI technique better suited to modeling simple states—and therefore, sequences of actions. Finite-state techniques are often easier to design and provide a greater form of control.

Outline

Chapter 36, "Emotive Creatures." This chapter provides an overview of emotions, studying the different approaches in AI and psychological research. We identify the need for emotions in games as a way to interact with human players.

Chapter 37, "Sensations, Emotions, and Feelings." This chapter defines sensations, emotions, and feelings and provides examples of such common in games. This chapter presents an interface used for communicating emotions with the game engine and discusses ways to portray them.

Chapter 38, "Finite-State Machines." This chapter covers finite-state machines from a theoretical and practical perspective. They are a control technique particularly suited to keeping track of states—and therefore sequences.

Chapter 39, "Under the Influence." In this chapter, we use finite-state techniques to model emotions and sensations. This subarchitecture affects the intelligent behaviors by degrading the senses and actions, according to mood.

Chapter 40, "Nondeterministic State Machines." Probabilistic, nondeterministic, and fuzzy models are presented as extensions to finite-state machines in this chapter, each resolving practical issues with the original technique.

Chapter 41, "Hierarchical State Machines." Hierarchical approaches are discussed, and examples of how they are applicable within games are shown—notably how they considerably simplify the design of finite-state machines.

Chapter 42, "An Emotional System." In this chapter, each of the extensions to finite-state techniques is applied to create a hierarchical system that models emotions, feelings, and sensations. The animats also include simple memories and manifestations of their emotions as behaviors.

Chapter 43, "Emergent Complexity." The last chapter of this part discusses the concept of emergence. Different aspects of the behaviors and functionality can be considered emergent. After defining emergence and covering why emergence is desirable, this chapter provides hints to harness the power of emergent phenomena by design.

Assumptions

Emotions rely on other aspects of the AI to provide purposeful behaviors and need the game engine to portray them:

➤ **Existing behaviors** are required, although they can include various levels of complexity. The architecture providing intelligence is assumed to be self-standing.

➤ **Parameters** influence the interfaces between the body and the brain, modeling degradation from perfect senses and actions.

➤ Emotions can be **portrayed** by the game engine using a variety of technologies, not limited to gesture animation, fixed expressions, and text messages.

The following chapter covers the origins of emotions and their different aspects. Understanding provides the foundation for this analysis and specification, which prepares us to develop an artificial system to model emotion.

Chapter 36

Emotive Creatures

Many people have love/hate relationships with their emotions. Sometimes, moods are very enjoyable, and in other cases they seem utterly useless. What purpose do emotions have in biological creatures, and why do synthetic creatures need them?

The next few pages provide a preliminary survey of emotions in biological and synthetic creatures and examine their role in computer games.

This chapter covers the following topics:

➤ The background of human emotions in evolutionary terms

➤ Biologically inspired emotional systems and their approach

➤ The relationship between emotions and intelligence

➤ Emotions as improving believability in human interaction (including a few examples)

➤ The role of emotions in computer games

This chapter lays the foundation for the next chapter, which contains examples and a practical AI developer's perspective on artificial emotions.

Emotions Within Human Evolution

As a product of evolution, emotions have a particular purpose: They have helped humans become the most successful species on earth. Emotions bypass the need for deliberative thought by providing biases toward the behaviors with better chances of survival—short-circuiting time-wasting rationalization. Other kinds of mammals also exhibit emotional capabilities with very similar reactions to humans.

Psychoevolutionary scientist Robert Plutchik shares such theories [Plutchik80]. According to Plutchik, there are eight primary emotions—associated in complementary pairs: anticipation and surprise, joy and sorrow, acceptance and disgust, fear and anger. His theory states that it's not possible for humans to experience two complementary emotions at the same time; they balance out to provide diversity in the behaviors.

In psychoevolutionary terms, each emotion serves its purpose by triggering a reactive behavior that's appropriate for survival. For example:

➤ Fear stimulates the body to release hormones, awaiting flight (or fight) for survival.

➤ Surprise awakens the senses and forces the brain to pay more attention to perceptions.

➤ Disgust leads humans to reject the object in question.

➤ Anger causes humans to destroy obstacles that prevent them from achieving their goal.

➤ Sadness encourages humans to seek comfort.

According to Plutchik, these primary emotions can be observed in varied intensities (for instance, rage, anger, annoyance, terror, fear, apprehension). Primary emotions also combine together into complex moods; acceptance and joy can be understood as love, fear and acceptance lead to submission, sadness and surprise form disappointment, and so forth.

Psychoevolutionary theory succeeds at explaining the reasons for emotions and provides a basic understanding of their roles as evolutionary tricks to improve survival rates. However, Plutchik's approach fails to take into account the cognitive process associated with emotions.

Biological Models for Emotion

To gain a better understanding of emotional reactions in mammals, it's necessary to model their cognitive abilities at least in part. Indeed, animals must perceive and interpret their surroundings before they can feel emotions.

Researchers in various fields related to AI attempt to reproduce different aspects of biological creatures to simulate adaptive behaviors. Generally, systems are based on two different components: cognitive and emotional. This is often done in the spirit of *nouvelle AI*, but with additional biological insights:

➤ The *emotional* component is often hard-coded (phylogenetic). With this approach, the designer can impose biologically accurate emotions (for instance, fear, pain, and pleasure) and test their role in the learning. Complementary emotions can be considered as extreme values of a single variable, used to drive the learning toward positive emotions.

➤ The *adaptive* component provides the ability to learn behaviors dynamically during the simulation (ontogenetic). Techniques such as neural networks and reinforcement learning allow the creature to adapt to its emotional status and behave in a better fashion (as explained in Part VII).

The primary objective of such biologically inspired approaches is to build understanding in mammals. However, it's possible to investigate the benefits of emotions as a tool for creating intelligent creatures—with less focus on biological accuracy.

From Emotions to Artificial Intelligence

To most AI developers, such research in biologically plausible emotion systems sounds extremely promising. In many cases, however, the main goal is to improve upon classical AI instead. Traditional approaches with strong representation and rigorous search mechanisms can benefit tremendously from instinctive reactions and subjective preferences; in fact, that's the premise of this book (learning and reactive behaviors). In many ways, artificial emotions—and the reactive AI techniques used to produce them—represent an ideal complement to classical AI.

On the other hand, the whole concept of artificial emotions is easily blown out of proportion (just as reactive AI is not a silver bullet). Emotions also have their pitfalls; they are not easily controlled, very inflexible, and are hard to understand.

Emotions are a small part of evolution's approach to creating intelligent species. Engineering generally produces very different solutions than evolution; it's very likely engineers will create intelligence with little or no resemblance to biological emotions—although some concepts may be similar (for instance, reactive actions or heuristics). So although emotions are not what make us intelligent, they define us as humans. Therein reside our interests from a game developer's perspective: emotions are a key factor in realism and believability.

Human/Machine Interaction

Emotions are certainly a defining characteristic of all mammals, and particularly humans. Emotions play a crucial role in the interaction between people. Because humans have grown accustomed to interaction using emotions, computer interfaces could emphasize this to improve their intuitiveness. The most useful and practically justifiable application of "emotional systems" therefore lies in improving the interaction between humans and machines by making the AI more lifelike.

Humans communicate emotions in a wide variety of ways. Researchers are attempting to convey artificial emotions in the following forms:

➤ **Expressions**—Static facial expressions carry a tremendous amount of information about emotions (for instance, smile or frown). In fact, another perspective for studying emotions uses facial expressions to distinguish primary emotions [Ekman79].

➤ **Gestures**—Body language and gestures are also strong indications of emotions. For example, slouching is a sign of depression, and nodding shows acceptance [Perlin96].

➤ **Behaviors**—Over longer periods of time, behaviors are stronger manifestations of emotional state [Bécheiraz98]. For example, ignoring someone is a sign of rejection, taking care of people shows affection.

➤ **Language**—The choice of words is an extremely strong indication of mood during a conversation (for instance, familiar or formal). Rhythm in sentences also conveys emotion; shorter sentences are more authoritative and sound angrier (as reflected by the artificial language Lojban [Lojban03]).

➤ **Voice**—The tone of the voice the sentence is pronounced with also reflects mood. Loud voices indicate anger, faster speech often implies anxiety, and so forth.

As indicated by the preceding list, the portrayal of emotions in synthetic creatures requires more than just AI. The fields of modeling, animation, linguistics, and speech synthesis are key aspects of the development.

Emotion in Games

As far as behaviors are concerned, the animat's intelligence is the initial bottleneck. Failing to accomplishing a task can almost be considered as a bug in the game AI (for instance, running into a wall). The reactive behaviors discussed throughout this book can provide such functionality—without the need for solutions inspired by emotions.

On the other hand, when an animat is fully functional, the problem is increasing the levels of realism. Emotions can help tremendously with this by enhancing the quality of the behaviors with a biologically plausible approach. There's particular interest in the following features that emotions will bring to game design:

➤ **Attachment**—Individual characters that can display moods are more believable, and human players become emotionally attached to them. Such bonds can be strong enough to change the course of the game.

➤ **Storylines**—By providing nonplayer characters with emotions, their interaction with humans is greatly improved. The essence of story lines happens between players, so emotions can greatly enhance the entertainment.

➤ **Immersiveness**—With emotions, all nonplayer character behaviors would seem more realistic and generally increase the immersiveness of the game environment.

Each of these features increases entertainment value. Our responsibility is to achieve this by focusing on the different aspects of emotions (for instance, gestures, behaviors, or language) and using an AI system to drive them in a suitable fashion. To find out more about creating emotions in games, see *Creating Emotion in Games: The Craft and Art of Emotioneering™* by David Freeman (New Riders, 2003).

Summary

This chapter covered the background behind emotions from many different perspectives, and the information provided here will help us develop emotional systems in the rest of this part:

➤ In evolutionary terms, emotions increase the likelihood of survival by providing instinctive reactions and high-level biases for behaviors.

➤ Biologically inspired emotional systems generally combine an adaptive component with a fixed emotion component.

➤ Emotions are a small part of human intelligence, although they serve their purpose like other abilities.

➤ The main purpose of artificial emotions is to improve the interaction with humans.

➤ Games can benefit from emotions because the emotions improve believability and realism.

With the purpose of artificial emotions now obvious, we can take a game developer's approach to the problem in the next chapter.

Practical Demo

Sensitiv is a combination of previous capabilities and behaviors, each triggering simple emotional reactions. *Sensitiv* is not affected by these emotions, but keeps track of them by logging them to the debugging console. These primitive sensations are explained further and taken into account in the next chapter.

Chapter 37

Sensations, Emotions, and Feelings

Emotions arise from complex interactions between the body and the brain. Emotions begin in the body, influenced by stimuli from the environment (such as an explosion). The brain generally responds to these low-level perceptions, which translate into persistent characteristics of the creature (as fear). These emotions can potentially become visible externally via behaviors (running away).

This chapter defines the different concepts involved when creating artificial emotions in animats. The lower-level concepts are presented first as we move toward higher-level emotions.

This chapter covers the following topics:

➤ A definition of sensations as the brain's reaction to perceptions, which drive emotions

➤ A description of emotions as a persistent characteristic, with the concepts of moods and feelings derived from emotions

➤ An interface used by the AI to communicate emotions to the game engine

➤ (New) ways to portray the emotions in practice within the game world

At the end of this chapter, an understanding of the different aspects of emotions permits the implementation of an emotional system. Extending the animats is possible thanks to new interfaces dedicated to emotions.

Sensations

All emotions in embodied creatures are initiated by sensations.

> A *sensation* is an immediate reaction to a creature's current status.

By definition, sensations are experienced practically instantaneously, based on changes in the current situation. Two factors may cause sensations: the current perceptions (that is, stimuli from the environment), or cognitive activity (that is, thinking). Table 37.1 lists common sensations.

Table 37.1   Common Sensations That Can Be Observed in Living Creatures

Surprise	Anticipation
Disgust	Attraction
Confusion	Discovery
Pain	Pleasure

Perceptual Sensations

Typically, a sensation is triggered by *perceptions*. The body detects stimuli from the environment, and the information causes an immediate reaction in the brain. For example, a nonplayer character (NPC) may experience a sensation of surprise when a player appears suddenly.

Embodied creatures are defined by their interaction with the world, so the perceptual type of sensations will be the most common (see Table 37.2). The reactive techniques studied throughout this book are appropriate for creating such reactive emotions.

Table 37.2 External Stimuli from the Environment That Cause Sensations

Health and armor lost	Blood splat
Sparks/explosion	Object disappears
Arriving lift	Door opening
Enemy presence	Desirable object

Cognitive Sensations

Sensations may also be triggered by reactions to the mental state (for instance, knowledge of the world or other emotions). Here, basic processing of information in the brain causes the sensation. For instance, surprise can be caused by an object not being present, when the animat thought it should be there.

Sensations based on cognition and perception have common traits: Both are triggered when a pattern is matched in the brain. With perceptions, this pattern is matched instantly based on sensory information. On the other hand, some cognition is necessary before a pattern develops in the brain (by thinking), which eventually engenders a sensation instantly when a pattern is matched.

Emotions

Sensations can be considered low level because they are instantaneous patterns. Higher-level trends arise from cognitive activity, too. These are called *emotions*.

An *emotion* is a lasting characteristic of a person's state.

Emotions change relatively slowly over time (compared to sensations, which are instantaneous). For example, fear and anger are lasting emotions, so are joy and sorrow. The changes in emotions are generally triggered by the animat's sensations. An emotion could also correspond directly to a single sensation (for instance, surprise).

Each *primary* emotion may have variable intensity (for instance, fear, as shown in Table 37.3). We term each of the different values *secondary* emotions (for instance, terror and apprehension). Primary emotions may also be defined such that two of them may not be present at the same time; we call these *complementary* emotions.

Table 37.3   Examples of Primary Emotions Found in Humans

Pride	Shame
Fear	Anger
Joy	Sorrow
Amusement	Weariness

Moods

A *mood* is the complete set of emotions that constitutes someone's mental state at a particular time.

A mood will generally be represented as a set of primary emotions, each with many possible states: the secondary emotions. For example, a good mood might be a blend of acceptance (primary), satisfaction (secondary to joy), and awe (secondary to surprise). Such combinations of primary emotions produce *complex* emotions (for instance, love and optimism).

Feelings

A *feeling* is a persistent association of an emotion with a class of object.

Feelings are a more powerful concept; unlike emotions, they can be expressed about the past or future, and unlike sensations they do not rely directly on current state. Instead, feelings can be associated with arbitrary objects, in the past or future.

Feelings are also very broad in that they can be applied to any concept (for instance, attributes or categories of objects). Examples of feelings are disgust with varieties of food, hate for different types of car, or a phobia of moving obstacles (see Table 37.4).

Table 37.4 Some Feelings That Can Be Found in People

Pity	Cruelty
Love	Hatred

Interfaces for Communicating Emotions

When developing a complete animat capable of emotional response, there is often non-AI technology involved in portraying emotions—as discussed in Chapter 36, "Emotive Creatures." To abstract the AI from the animation (for example), an interface is needed between the two components. This section covers the design of such an interface.

Design Principles

The next few chapters assume that the platform has support for expressing emotions, and the AI is only responsible for driving them. This assumption is similar to all the other parts, with the engine always taking care of the lower-level details within the 3D world. (This is a challenge beyond the scope of this book.)

Because the platform provides the functionality to express the emotions, the AI must interact with it to express these emotions. The interface should have the following characteristics:

➤ **Backward compatible**—All the existing interfaces should work without emotions.

➤ **Extensible**—It should be simple to express arbitrary emotions with the interface, without having to change its specification.

➤ **Portable**—Some game platforms may not support every emotion expressed with the interface, but the system should work nonetheless.

An interface with these properties will enable both AI engineers (creating emotions) and the game engine developers (portraying emotions) to program the functionality independently from each other. Naturally, they'll eventually need to agree on the particular emotions, but the framework will remain the same.

Rationale

One option is to include the emotions with each effector. When an animat executes an action, the game engine will be provided with the details of how to execute it. This approach provides the flexibility of per-action emotion control. However, because moods are consistent over time, such fine control is generally not necessary. Including emotional status in each interface would probably prove somewhat cumbersome, difficult to extend, and backward incompatible.

A better approach is to separate the emotions from the effectors and sensors. This distinction allows the current mood to be set independently from the rest of the AI—and this approach reduces the overhead because the emotions can be changed. After the emotions have been communicated via a separate interface, the AI would assume the game engine does its best to portray them in every subsequent action.

With this approach, the game platform can just ignore select emotions—effectively providing backward-compatible support. This also makes the interface portable, because it can be integrated to any game engine regardless of the technology present to portray the emotions. Extending the system will be a matter of providing extra functionality via a single interface, which may not even require extending the system.

Specification

Each component of the AI that can be affected by emotions depends on the `emotion` interface. This interface provides information about the current emotional state that can be taken into account by the implementation.

The most obvious way to query emotions is via a function call. This returns the value of an emotion, with 0 indicating no emotion and 1 corresponding to full emotion (similarly to fuzzy logic definition):

```
float GetValue( const string& emotion );
```

This approach has a relatively low overhead, but is particularly suitable when components are not updated regularly, or do not need up-to-date emotion values. This *polling* approach could be replaced by *event handling*, whereby the implementation is passed messages when the emotions change. This second approach is more efficient, but requires memory to store copies of the emotion values passed by events.

Portraying Emotions in Games

Having covered the definition of emotions and how to communicate them to the game engine, it's possible to discuss the ways emotions can be portrayed in practice.

Existing Senses and Actions

Taking a practical perspective, portraying emotions is about using whichever means can be perceived by the other players. In the case of first-person games, many existing actions can display emotions (for instance, movement, turning, or jumping). Senses also contribute indirectly to conveying emotional state.

Actions

Fundamental skills such as movement are ideal for conveying emotions because they are so obvious to external observers. For example, walking slowly may be a sign of depression; running especially fast can indicate fear. Turning toward an object reveals attraction, whereas turning away shows disgust. Jumps may also indicate happiness.

The other actions used in previous parts play a lesser role in portraying emotions. For example, weapon selection and firing and picking up and using objects leave little room for emotions in terms of animation. However, the higher-level principles involved in the decisions portray emotions (for instance, selecting a weak weapon to ridicule an enemy).

The lack of action can also be interpreted as a manifestation of emotion (for instance, melancholy). Higher-level decisions such as fleeing and fighting reveal emotions, too.

Senses

Although there needs to be a behavioral response for emotions to be perceptible, any part of the animat affecting the response plays a role in the production of emotions. Senses are surprisingly important for this reason, because they provide perceptions to the brain—affecting the flow of information from the source.

Emotions primarily affect vision, because the senses may be less alert in some situations (for instance, no anticipation). In these cases, creatures do not perceive nearby entities as well—if at all. Conversely, when creatures are surprised or afraid, their senses will be attentive to the smallest movement. Other senses such as touch are generally less susceptible to emotional status.

New Interfaces

This part reuses existing technology—focusing on the emotional system from the AI point of view. However, two additional means are used by human players to convey emotions in games: gestures and chat messages. Both are supported by our first-person game engine (*Quake 2*), so it's just a matter of defining interfaces to them.

Each of the gestures supported (such as wave, salute, point, or taunt) are defined in an enumeration. Using these values as the parameter of a function causes the animat's body to perform that gesture:

```
void Gesture( const GestureType g );
```

Chat communication is supported by one function, taking the text string as a parameter. The second parameter is used to specify who to broadcast to (that is, the team or everybody):

```
void Say( const string& text, const GroupType g = Everybody );
```

Wrapper functions could make the interface simpler if necessary (for example, `Wave()` or `SayTeam("text")`).

Example Manifestations of Emotions

The following list of scenarios illustrates the kind of emotion-driven behaviors that our animats should be capable of portraying:

➤ Jump, wave, or dance of joy.

➤ Loose turning precision when frightened, but allow quicker turns. Run faster with fear, simulating adrenaline rushes.

➤ Stop thinking and freeze when affected by panic (for instance, if many enemy players present).

➤ Diminish accuracy of all actions when boredom sets in (for instance, sleepiness, complacency). Also fail to perceive distant enemies when standing still.

➤ Turn away in disgust (for instance, blood splat), or focus on attractive other player.

➤ Reduce perception delay when surprised (for instance, player appears), but increase it when anticipating an action (for instance, door opens).

➤ Insult the enemies when they get killed, or perform a taunting gesture.

➤ Run away scared when the enemy is more powerful.

➤ Select the enemy to target from personal vengeance, based on past fight history.

The aim of the next chapter is to understand new technology to handle these situations elegantly, and the chapter after that applies the new technology to the creation of such emotions.

Summary

This chapter looked at the different levels at which emotions affect the animat:

➤ Sensations are reactions to patterns that trigger changes in the emotions, generally based on perceptions.

➤ Emotions are persistent characteristics of a creature's state.

➤ Feelings are emotions associated with arbitrary objects.

➤ The latter sections defined an interface for communicating the emotions from the AI to the engine, so that they can be portrayed within the game by animation technology.

A dedicated interface for emotions has many advantages thanks to the separation of the emotions with the behaviors.

Existing actions as well as the new gesture and text interfaces remain independent of emotions, and the AI can assume the engine does its best to display the emotions.

Finite state machines are discussed in the next chapter, which focuses on the theory. Chapter 39, "Under the Influence," applies finite state machines to model the emotional state, and discusses the role of the sensations in influencing the emotions.

Practical Demo

Actor is an animat with a large database of actions and mannerisms that reveal emotions. *Actor* is content using these gestures arbitrarily, and does not attempt to use them meaningfully within the context. Each mannerism is implemented with a previous AI technique—as appropriate.

Chapter 38

Finite-State Machines

KEY TOPICS

- Formal Definitions
- Representation and Simulation
- Control Logic
- Optimization
- Discussion

F*inite-state machines* are a model of computation with a limited amount of memory known as a *state*. Each machine has only a finite number of possible states (for instance, wander or patrol). A transition function determines how the state changes over time, according to the inputs to the finite-state machine. There are two different categories of state machines.

➤ **Finite-state automata (FSA)** do not generate any output until a *terminal* state is reached. They can be used to recognize patterns (for instance, interpret enemy actions) or classifying sequences (for instance, determining a strategy).

➤ **Finite-state machines** provide an output every time an input symbol is consumed. They can be used to model the state of thought of nonplayer characters (NPCs), such as their current task and how they need to react to the situation (that is, sequential control).

The game AI designer who crafts behaviors manually generally creates finite-state systems. Because they are so intuitive and simple to implement, they are the most widely used form of AI used in games. Not only are they widely applicable, they are also very efficient.

This chapter covers the following topics:

- ➤ The theory behind finite-state automata

- ➤ The differences in representation between Mealy and Moore machines, and variations of finite-state techniques

- ➤ The array- and graph-based representations

- ➤ Finite-state systems as a control technique that can be used to drive the behaviors of NPCs

- ➤ The problems with procedural implementations of finite-state techniques

- ➤ The benefits and pitfalls of the finite-state machine as a technique for game AI development

The theory in this chapter is not only used to provide behavioral control for an example animat, but also to model the emotions in the preceding chapter.

Formal Definitions

Although the concepts at the base of each category of finite-state system are similar, there are different definitions for finite-state automata, Mealy, and Moore machines.

Finite-State Automatons

Finite-state automata (FSA) are a computational model, often used as *recognizers* or *acceptors* (see Figure 38.1). Intuitively, the entire input sequence allows the automaton to output the corresponding class or a Boolean (if the pattern was recognized or accepted, respectively). For example, an FSA could be used to recognize the actions look down, fire rocket, and jump as a rocket jump. FSA could also categorize enemies or friends based on their behavior. (For instance, fire twice is accepted as an enemy.)

Essentially, an FSA consists of a set of states connected together by transitions. Because it is provided with a data stream, the active state changes if a transition matches the input character. After all the characters have been consumed, the current active state can determine whether a pattern was recognizable.

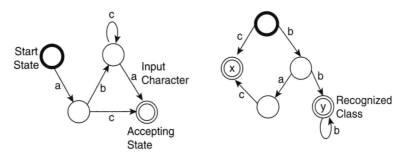

Figure 38.1 Graphical representation of a finite-state automaton used for accepting and recognizing input patterns. On the left, the sequence *abccca* is accepted. On the right, the sequence *bbbb* is recognized as category Y.

More formally, a finite-state automaton can be considered a quadruple:

$$FSA = \{\Sigma, Q, \delta, F\}$$

Q is the set of states, and δ is the transition function defined over an input alphabet Σ. There is one particular state: the start state q_0, where the computation begins. There's a special subset of states $F \supseteq Q$ known as terminal (or accepting) states. Each of these concepts is now explained in greater depth.

Input Alphabet

The finite-state automaton is fed a stream of data. Each element in this data stream can be understood as a specific character, taken from a finite alphabet Σ (see Table 38.1).

Table 38.1 Some Examples of Input Sequences and the Corresponding Input Alphabet

Sequence	Alphabet
0010001000110	$\Sigma_1 = \{0,1\}$
Abbabcbabbacc	$\Sigma_2 = \{a,b,c,d\}$
Flash shout explosion smoke	Σ_2 set of in-game events

In the first case, the alphabet Σ_1 has two characters corresponding to on and off bits. The second string has characters from the alphabet Σ_2 consisting of the first four letters, although *d* is not present in the string. Although it's easier to discuss these ideas with letters, each of them can be substituted to game events, such as jump, fire projectile, drop weapon, and so on.

The role of the finite-state automaton is to process the characters from this input stream one by one. This allows computations to be performed. For example, the patterns in the data can be identified and classified as necessary.

States

A state can be understood as a node from a graph. Because same states have a particular meaning for the problem, they are assigned names as well as identifiers (which are more intuitive to work with).

In FSA, some states have a special meaning. One state, denoted q_0, is active in the initial configuration of the finite-state automaton (for instance, assume neutral player). It is generally denoted by a bold circle in graphical representations. There are also some accepting states, called F, which usually contain a class type (for instance, decide friend or foe). These are double circles.

Table 38.2 All the States in a Finite-State Machine, Along with Their Different Properties (Class, Terminal, and State)

State	Terminal	Class
1*	No	
2	Yes	X
3	No	
4	Yes	Y

Start state is denoted with an asterisk.

If the pattern causes the finite-state automaton to finish with one of these states active, the pattern is recognized as the corresponding class.

Transition Function

The transition function determines the next active state q_{t+1} based on the current state q_t, and the input character σ_t. (The subscript t denotes the index in the sequence.) Mathematically, it can be modeled as a function mapping the set of states and the input alphabet onto the set of states:

$$\delta: \quad Q \times \Sigma \to Q$$
$$(q_t, \sigma_t) \, \alpha \ \ q_{t+1} \ \ \longmapsto (q_t, \sigma_t) \in Q \times \Sigma$$

The transition function essentially changes the internal state of the finite-state automaton based on the input patterns. Graphically, transitions can be modeled as directed connections between two nodes in a graph (see Figure 38.2 and Table 38.3).

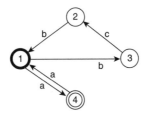

Figure 38.2   The example finite-state automata in graphical form.

Table 38.3   Transition Table Containing the Start and End of Each Transition and the Input Character Required, Corresponding to the FSA in Figure 38.2

Start State	Character	End State
1	a	4
1	b	3
2	b	1
3	c	2
4	a	1

Each transition is triggered by a particular character in the input stream. The transition is said to consume the character; this is indicated in the graph by writing the character near the transition. Strictly speaking, all connections (including recurrent ones) need to be expressed by the transition function. However, often it's easier to assume the state stays the same if there are no applicable outbound links.

Mealy Machines

Finite-state *machines*—unlike the *automata* just discussed—produce an output while the input stream is processed. *Mealy machines* (named after their inventor) output symbols based on each transition. Mealy machines can be understood as a superset of FSA that dispose of more flexibility. They are better suited to sequential control problems (for instance, to provide a response action for each comment of the enemy).

Accordingly, there is a different definition for what a Mealy finite-state machine is—a quintuple this time:

$$FSM = \{\Sigma, Q, Z, \delta, \lambda\}$$

Just like for finite-state *automata*, Σ represents the set of characters in the input alphabet, Q is the set of states, and δ is the transition function. Now for the new ones: Z is another set representing the output alphabet, and λ is a function to determine the output based on the transitions. We'll look into these new concepts a bit further.

Output Alphabet

At each step t of the simulation, a Mealy finite-state machine can output a symbol. Each symbol belongs to the output alphabet, which can be animat actions, as shown in Table 38.4.

Table 38.4   A Collection of Output Sequences and the Corresponding Output Alphabet

Sequence	Set
000101010111	$\Sigma_1 = \{0, 1\}$
eggheheif	$\Sigma_2 = \{e, f, g, h, i\}$
jump shoot crouch	Σ_3 set of animat actions

There is absolutely no correlation between input and output alphabets. They can be different sizes and contain different symbols.

The role of the state machine is to produce a sequence of output symbols based on the input pattern. The output at every step t of the simulation may not always be necessary, but it's almost just as easy for the finite-state machine to compute it regardless!

Output Function

In practice, the output is computed by another function. This is done in a fashion similar to the state transition, using a function mapping the current state and the input symbol onto the output value:

$$\lambda: \quad Q \times \Sigma \to Z$$
$$(q_t, \sigma_t) \, \alpha \; z_t \; \mapsto (q_t, \sigma_t) \in Q \times \Sigma$$

Because the transition and output functions are defined over the same set, they can be represented in the same way. Graphically, this means it's possible to attach an output symbol to each link in the directed graph (see Figure 38.3).

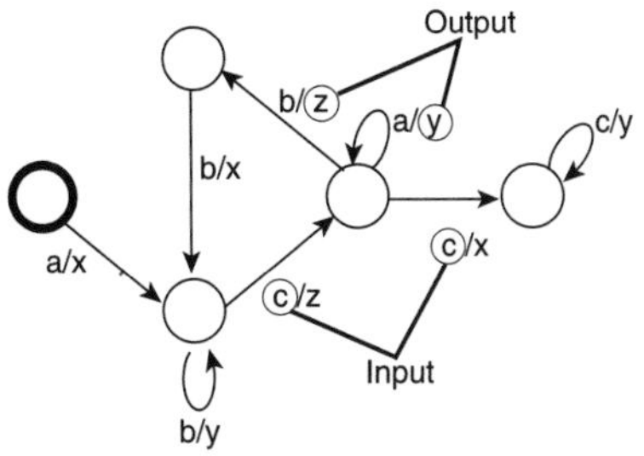

Figure 38.3 Finite-state machines produce output on each transition. The output is noted alongside the input character consumed, in the input/output order.

To output a symbol every step while a state remains active, it is necessary to have a recurrent connection. Although this proves the most flexible approach, this is not always the most elegant way to proceed.

Moore Machines

Moore machines provide a simpler alternative to finite-state machines. Instead of outputting symbols for each transition, the states determine output. The formal definition of a Moore machine is the same as a Mealy machine, although the output function λ is simpler but less powerful. These are used more often because they are easier to design for game AI.

In this case, the transition function can be expressed in much simpler terms, mapping the current state onto the output:

$$\lambda: \quad Q \rightarrow Z$$
$$q_t \; \alpha \; z_t \quad | {\rightarrow} q_t \in Q$$

This has repercussions on the graphical representation, too. Instead of writing the output near the transitions, they can be displayed within each state, as shown in Figure 38.4.

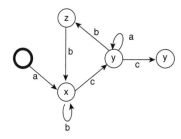

Figure 38.4   Moore machines have an output value associated with each state rather than the transition.

As a nice consequence of this, we no longer need to explicitly model recurrent connections; the output will remain the same while no external transition is taken.

Representation and Simulation

Data structures and algorithms can be derived from the theory to assist the programmer.

Transition Array

One popular way to encode the transitions is to store them inside a 2D array (see Table 38.5). The two dimensions are state and input, and each cell stores the next state. All transitions are therefore explicitly encoded. There needs to be a specific symbol to indicate an empty cell, which allows the finite-state machine to be sparse (that is, not fully connected).

Using only a transition array, a finite-state *automaton* can be modeled. To represent a finite-state machine, an additional output table is required. This stores the output in terms of the current state and input.

Table 38.5   Transitions Stored as a 2D Array, with Each Cell Pointing to the Next State (Some cells do not have following states.)

State\Input	a	b	c
1	4	3	-
2	-	1	-
3	-	-	2
4	1	-	-

Such an approach does prove quite fast—given a reasonable size table—because it's a plain lookup. The major benefit lies in simplicity, and minimal knowledge of programming is required to implement a 2D array. Very little effort is required to test and debug it, too.

On the downside, this representation is not compact. In an average case, a lot of redundant information is stored; indeed, most finite-state machines are sparsely connected (that is, many empty cells). An array that can store all the transitions is wasteful, and scales very poorly.

Directed Graph

A *directed graph* proves a more compact representation of a finite-state machine. This corresponds exactly with the graphical representation, so encoding it as a directed graph is little trouble. Typically, the states are stored as an array (at least conceptually). Each state is then responsible for keeping track of outward transitions. This can be done with a nested list or another array, as shown in Table 38.6.

The active state can be determined with a single lookup. The bottleneck of this approach lies in finding the applicable transition. A traversal of the array at each state is necessary, checking whether the current input symbol matches at each step.

Table 38.6 Representation of a Directed Graph Using an Array of States Containing Lists of Transitions

State	Transitions
1	a: 4, b: 3
2	b: 1
3	c: 2
4	a: 1

Even a naive traversal of this array may prove faster than a lookup in a large array, because of the cache consistency. Indeed, all the transitions can often be stored within the same cache line. To squeeze every possible cycle out of the search, each of the transitions could be sorted according to the input symbol consumed. This would allow a binary search, and reduce the complexity of the traversal to $O(log\ n)$ rather than $O(n)$. Finally, a hash table could make this a near constant lookup at the cost of additional memory.

These tricks are often unnecessary because of the simplicity of the finite-state machine used and because the overhead is negligible compared to other aspects of the AI. If an early prototype reveals that large finite-state machines are required, however, such optimizations should be considered.

Grammar

Finite-state machines recognize a distinct set of patterns. All these patterns fall into the category of *regular languages*, which have limited complexity. Finite-state machines are not a model of computation as advanced as the Turing machine (which can emulate any form of computation).

Intuitively, regular languages correspond to regular expressions commonly used for text processing (mainly in the Perl programming language). Such regular expressions are a compact way of representing a regular grammar, which can thereby be compiled into a finite-state machine:

```
 (baab)*
((.*)ab+){1,2}
```

Grammars can be used to store the essential structure of finite-state automata, but are not appropriate for finite-state machines with outputs. This representation should be considered mainly for recognizing and accepting text. Those not familiar with regular expressions may prefer the graphical approach to design!

Some constructs are easier to model as finite-state machines, but operations such as counting can be difficult to express in a simple fashion. The {1,2} shown actually specifies that the previous pattern should be present either once or twice; this requires duplicating the sub-FSA capable of accepting that pattern, and connecting it twice. This gets worse for larger numbers, so alternative approaches (that is, counters, using an additional variable to count) are generally used in combination to create simpler, hybrid finite-state machines.

Control Logic

Until now, we've discussed finite-state machines as computational models capable of creating an output string in terms of an input string. These outputs can also indicate whether the input was recognized or accepted. When embedded within a real system, these outputs can also be used as a control mechanism. Although the theory behind finite-state machines is very robust, the extent of the practical applications reveals the finite-state machine to be an undeniably useful tool.

All the finite-state machines discussed can be directly applied to control already. This section discusses specific tricks that are often used, and points out potential problems that can arise. Solutions to these problems are explained.

Procedural Approach

Although the symbol processing model captures the essence of control logic, this is a very formal way of proceeding. A more practical approach is often taken instead: the procedural approach. In this case, each transition is a hard-coded function, which can be queried to determine whether the transition should be taken.

The states themselves are also native procedures performing tasks when the respective state is active. This approach proves often easier in the short term; building one state machine will involve minimal overhead and allow all the code to be explicit. There is also no need for a mechanism to pass symbols around; everything can be programmed as sensors (transitions) and actuators (states).

Potential Problems with Procedural Finite-State Machines

Aside from the practical problems (that is, code complexity), there are also theoretical issues to deal with. The finite-state machine that is implemented may not behave as expected—diverging from the design.

Sequential Chaos and Ambiguity

In theory, finite-state machines are passed a sequence of input characters that are used for the transitions. These inputs are implicitly ordered because they belong to a sequence; that's the way the problem is defined. In procedural code, there is no dedicated queue where all the symbols are placed; the transition functions are checked by the simulation. The order in which the transition functions are processed has a great impact on the result of the simulation; the transitions checked first have an implicit priority over all the other transitions.

Consider, for instance, an animat is in a *wander* state. If the presence of an enemy is checked first, the *hunt* mode will be engaged. On the other hand, if nearby armor is identified first, the *gather* state may become active. These variations potentially result in unintuitive bugs.

Theoretically speaking, the finite-state machine basically interprets the order of the symbols based on the implementation, which results in an unforeseen bias in the design. (Some transitions are preferred.) This poses problems because there's no formal way to model such ambiguity. So the procedural implementation may behave differently than the design itself. This can be understood as a type of nondeterminism (discussed further in Chapter 40, "Nondeterministic State Machines").

Loss of Data

If the code is purely procedural, each transition is checked on-the-fly. There's no intrinsic way to remember sequences of events that happen. Given two transition conditions that are true at the same time, only the first transition is processed; the second is ignored. In general, this approach intrinsically discards all the information about transitions conditions that occur after the first has been taken.

For example, the animat is in *combat* mode. Simultaneously, the health drops very low and an armor object appears nearby. The armor is checked first, so the *gather* state becomes active. The low health transition to the *flee* state is ignored and forgotten, and the animat gets shot as a result.

This problem is a consequence of dealing with ambiguity using plain procedural code. In many such cases, ignoring transitions can lead to incomplete or inconsistent behaviors. Once again, this results in buggy behaviors that are not obvious from the finite-state machine design.

Flow Control

In the code, transitions may be processed within the states' procedures. Indeed, it's often easier to check for transitions during the update—which can also prevent redundant processing. The problem is deciding where the control goes next. Is the transition followed immediately? Does the simulation continue processing the procedural state code instead? In this second case, how do we deal with multiple transitions that happen at different times during the state update?

Remedies for Procedural Control

The first step for solving these problems is to identify them. Precautions can then be taken when they are encountered. However, a better approach defines methodologies preventing the problems from arising at all.

When to Redesign?

Most of the problem can be understood as having to deal with large state procedures (for instance, wander behavior) that can be interrupted by multiple transitions (for instance, to flee or gather).

A programmer's solution would find a programming language trick that can be used to simplify the issue. For example, the state procedure could check the transitions itself, and return a code indicating the necessary transition. If multiple nested procedures are required to simulate this state, the return codes need to be cascaded.

However, the AI engineer would realize that a lot of redundant work is being done, and that each of the code paths can in fact be handled by the finite-state machine. Enforcing this requires respecting a single constraint; *state procedures are atomic and cannot be interrupted.* The entire finite-state machine can be designed around this principle, instead of using programmatic hacks as temporary solutions.

Code Structure

Given these principles of atomicity, the code can be reorganized. It's good practice to keep transitions and state procedures separate. Then, a convention can be established to decide when to process the transitions. Usually, they are all checked after the state update has been done.

The great advantage of grouping all the transitions at once is that they can be easily identified in the code. Problems of ambiguity can be resolved very simply; the transitions can be given a priority. The transition with the highest priority can be checked first, and the rest discarded. These priorities can be built in to the design and translated directly into code.

There are still two problems remaining that code organization doesn't solve. First, there is a small efficiency price to pay for this, because the transitions may do some redundant processing (which could be made common in the state procedures). Second, there is no way to deal with multiple transitions and storing events for later.

Message Passing

A small data structure solves both these problems by temporarily storing requests for transitions. This can be as a simple message-passing mechanism, but used to simulate the sequence of input characters. This is not as efficient as the purely procedural finite-state machine, but still beats all the other AI techniques in the book in terms of raw performance.

The state update procedure can queue transition messages so the transitions do not need to process redundant information. These messages can also persist, such that important events are not forgotten, and will eventually be taken into account. (For instance, the need to *flee* is important and should affect the state.)

Naturally, not all the messages generated by the state update procedure need to be stored until processed. These can be called *temporary* messages. These need to be collected separately from the message queue, and discarded if they are not needed.

Merging this queuing system with the transition priorities, we get a priority queue that is capable of dealing with all the problems discussed. In this case, only the temporary message with the highest priority needs to be kept, and is discarded if its priority is lower than the priority of the message at the front of the queue.

> **NOTE**
> The priority queue is not adding extra power to the finite-state machine. The simulation uses a data structure to transform procedural information into a more formal input sequence, mainly to maintain coherence—ensuring that the behaviors in the game correspond intuitively to the design.

Optimization

Let's assume a designer isn't too familiar with the tools provided and has generated an overly complex finite-state machine. If the finite-state machine is substantial in size, or if the number of NPCs using it is large, the computational overhead may be hard to neglect. Instead of having the AI developer check through each of them for optimality, why not create a tool to do so?

Finite-state machines have the advantage of being a well-understood, simple computational model. Unlike more elaborate models such as Turing machines, there are known algorithms to optimize finite-state machines. In fact, creating canonical finite-state machines (that is, the simplest possible graph) is a proven technique to compare finite-state machines to one another.

One algorithm to perform such optimizations compares all the states together and merges them where possible (see Figure 38.5). The state comparison is best done in pairs. Two states can be merged if all outgoing transitions point toward the same state. The two states are merged by using one set of the duplicate outbound transitions, but all the incoming transitions. It's a good idea to rename the merged state to something indicative of the previous two states.

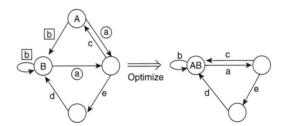

Figure 38.5   Optimization of the finite-state machine by folding states with identical outgoing transitions together.

A naive implementation of such an optimization process would be of complexity $O(n^2)$. This proves more than satisfactory for modern computers; given the small size of finite-state machines, we're talking milliseconds and not seconds of optimization time, which is also an offline preprocess. By doubly linking the transitions to the start and end state, this can be optimized almost $O(kn)$, where k is the degree of connectivity. In this optimized version, the algorithm checks the inbound links of each state. Each of the states connected is compared to each other state for similarity. The intuition is for two states to be identical; they need to be connected to the same state, so tracing inbound links reduces the total number of nodes that need to be compared to each other.

Regardless of the technique used, finite-state optimization has mostly benefits. If we can simulate the same behavior with fewer states, it makes sense to do so. However, smaller finite-state machines are often less intuitive. If the designer added extra states, it's usually because they are easier to understand that way. As such, it is beneficial to keep the human-designed finite-state machine, and only compile them down to an optimized finite-state machine during the release build.

Discussion

With regards to finite-state machines in game AI development, there are some observations to point out.

Advantages

Finite-state machines are so incredibly simple. They're easy to implement, visualize, design, debug, and work with in pretty much any other stage of the development pipeline.

Their theory is extremely well understood. We have formal definitions of finite-state machines, which can be optimized and manipulated by various algorithms. It's also clear that finite-state machines can deal with regular languages only.

Finite-state machines have been proven to work well with computer games, and are in fact one of the most popular AI techniques. This is because of the fact that they can be used for control, and almost anyone can create them.

Disadvantages

The pitfalls of finite-state machines seem insignificant compared to avalanche of benefits, although there are quite a few:

➤ Designing finite-state machines can get very complex when building large machines.

➤ They are computationally limited to certain problems.

➤ Finite-state machines are not suited to many simple tasks, such as counting.

➤ The design of finite-state machines is frozen at runtime.

➤ There can be problems dealing with procedural control.

➤ The output of finite-state machines is very predictable, and not necessarily suited to creating behaviors.

The disadvantages of finite-state machines can be easily taken into account during the design (and selection of the right solution), so these issues have not affected finite-state machines as the most popular game AI technique.

Summary

There are two different subtypes of finite state techniques:

➤ **Finite-state automata**, used to *recognize* or *accept* sequences of input symbols by producing one output.

➤ **Finite-state machines**, capable of *transducing* an input stream into the corresponding outputs. Mealy and Moore machines are particular variations on the representation.

The essence of finite-state models is the transition function. There are different ways to represent and simulate it in practice:

➤ An array can be used as a lookup to find the next state based on the current state and the input.

➤ A directed graph allows the next state to be looked up as a link from the current state using the input symbol.

The graph-based implementation scales better with the number of states, and tends to perform more efficiently. Simple declarative models of the theory can be used as decision-making components, but procedural approaches are more convenient for control problems:

➤ Each transition is represented as a function that returns true if the state should change.

➤ Each state has an update procedure that is used to perform the corresponding actions.

Occasionally, there are problems with the procedural approach, notably loss of information and ambiguity in the transitions—which can result in unforeseen bugs in the behaviors. These can be resolved with a simple priority queue of messages if necessary.

Finite-state machines are one of the most suitable AI techniques for game AI development. That said, they have some conceptual problems that cannot be resolved by clever implementation. Chapters 40 and 41 discuss nondeterministic machines, probabilistic finite-state machines, fuzzy-state machines, and hierarchical-state machines. These remedy most of the other problems associated with finite-state machines.

The next chapter applies finite-state machines to modeling emotions, and provides a few examples of how to use finite-state machines in practice.

Practical Demo

Fizzer is an animat that uses finite-state machines as an implementation of its deathmatch behaviors. Although the design is not particularly complex, *Fizzer* shows how behaviors can be crafted explicitly by a designer. Scaling up the capabilities of this animat is particularly challenging because of the rapid increase in complexity.

Chapter 39

Under the Influence

This chapter shows how combinations of finite-state machines can be used to create emotions. Two additional levels are added to the AI architecture. A low level generates sensations based on the perceptions, and an emotive layer keeps track of the primary emotions. The behavioral response of the animats is affected only by degradation of the senses and actions. Essentially, the emotions determine how effective the body parts are.

This emotional model influences the behaviors of the animats, providing more diversity and increasing their believability.

This chapter covers the following topics:

➤ A description of important stimuli from the environment and their corresponding sensations, as well as primary emotions and how to portray them.

➤ A data-driven finite-state module supporting finite-state machines and finite-state automata. Both functional interfaces and message passing are considered.

➤ Modeling of the emotions using the finite-state AI techniques and integrating the system within the previous architecture (that is, the behaviors developed so far).

➤ The effect of emotions on the creatures, and the system's limitations.

The prototype developed throughout this chapter reveals the benefits of emotions. This provides an elegant paradigm that is extended with better technology in Chapter 42, "An Emotional System."

Designing Artificial Emotions

The design phase must decide which emotions are experienced by the animat, which sensations trigger changes in emotions, and how they are portrayed in the behavior. This prototype will be extended later in Chapter 42 with additional primary emotions, secondary emotions, and moods.

Primary Emotions

Because this chapter builds the first emotional prototype, it seems appropriate to include the most important emotions only. As such, the animats have only four of the primary emotions defined by Robert Plutchik in his psychoevolutionary theory [Plutchik80]:

➤ Fear and anger

➤ Surprise and anticipation

As complementary emotions, only two of four may be observable at any point in time. Each of the emotions is defined as a binary value: either fully active or inactive.

Sensations and Stimuli

The sensations are patterns that cause changes in the emotions. These patterns can be present in the current state, but also over periods of time. In this prototype, the sensations are based directly on the stimuli from the environment. Sensations are identified as sequential combinations of stimuli (see Table 39.1).

Table 39.1   Stimuli from the Environment Triggering Sensations

Player appears	Object respawns
Unexpected sound	Item picked up
Low health	Small/large damage
Explosion	Death
Switch pressed	Door/platform ready
Blood splat	Body part

These sensations are considered as Boolean triggers that cause the emotions to change. Specifically, a sensation of fear will toggle the corresponding emotion fear *on* and anger *off*.

Behavioral Response

The emotions need to be portrayed by the behaviors for them to have any purpose. Selecting the most obvious manifestations of emotions improves the realism, and keeping their number to a minimum keeps the system simple. In this chapter, we'll use the following parameters—applied via the interfaces to the body:

➤ **Action precision and power**—Depending on its mood, an animat will run quicker or slower and have varied control over each step. It will also turn with different speed, sometimes with additional precision when aiming.

➤ **Sensing delay and accuracy**—The entities present in the nearby world may take a short amount of time to be perceived by the animat, modeling human reaction times. Animats also have trouble estimating the distance of objects in some cases.

These are restrictive modifications, because they decrease the capabilities of the animats. In the best case, the animat will not be affected by its emotions. Chapter 42 extends upon these ideas by influencing the decision making with moods, too.

Finite-State Module Development

In the preceding chapter, three finite-state techniques were presented: transducers (finite-state machines), recognizers, and acceptors (finite-state automata). Both modules have different interfaces, but there are common concepts in the passing of information within the architecture.

Data Exchange

Like other AI modules, finite-state machines take inputs and produce outputs. The data can be passed as parameters to functions (used synchronously to pass control), or messages between the components of the architecture (used asynchronously to interrupt control). In the case of finite-state machines, it's often convenient to support both of these paradigms. The functions provide efficient support for batch processing, whereas the events allow incremental updates driven by events.

Depending on the approach taken, a different representation may be the most efficient. For example, the functional approach needs to identify transitions based on the current state, whereas the event-driven approach needs to identify the state based on the transition symbol.

A Finite-State Automaton

finite-state automata can recognize and classify sequences. The input of finite-state automata is therefore an array of characters, or any other type of symbol that can trigger transitions between states. The output can be any form of data, although usually a categorical variable (for classification) or a Boolean (for recognition):

```
bool Accept( const vector<Symbol>& sequence );
Symbol Recognize( const vector<Symbol>& sequence );
```

Using these functions, the automaton will be reset before the simulation starts. Using message passing, the inputs will be processed incrementally. An output message will be sent when a terminal state is reached. The automaton is reset automatically in this case, but this is also possible using the Reset() function in the interface if necessary.

A Finite-State Machine

Finite-state machines, on the other hand, provide an output for every input symbol. The interface to the finite-state machine could alternatively provide a step-by-step approach, or take a sequence of symbols and return another:

```
Symbol Tick( const Symbol in );
void Simulate( const vector<Symbol>& in, vector<Symbol>& out );
```

These functions provide synchronous behavior. On the other hand, the asynchronous approach works incrementally, generating messages immediately as others are received. Again, an explicit `Reset()` call may be used to initialize the machine.

Specification

The file format used to store the layout of the finite-state machines is XML, as shown in Listing 39.1. The file is an arbitrary number of states, each with outgoing transitions. The transitions have a target state and matching inputs. Both states and transitions can optionally have outputs.

Listing 39.1   An Example of a Single State of a Finite-State Machine Described Using XML

```
<state name="surprise">
      <transition input="door_open" target="anticipation" />
      <transition input="explosion" target="fear" />
      <output
            precision="0.4"
            delay="0.1"
      />
</state>
```

The definition for a finite-state machine that processes symbols is relatively straightforward. When the finite-state machine relies on procedural code and the declarative approach, the specification needs additional syntax. This will be introduced in Chapter 42.

> **Further Information**
>
> The Library Reference on the web site at `http://fear.sf.net/` contains more information about the specification and implementation of finite-state machines in FEAR.

Implementation

The finite-state automata and machines need to store their internal graph, as well as the active state. The current state itself can be represented as an index into the array of states, or even a reference to a C++ instance. The transition table is stored as an array of states, each mapping the input symbol onto the destination state. Each state also stores the data that has been defined by the user.

The generic containers from the Standard Template Library provide a convenient way to load the layout from a file and allocate arbitrary arrays at runtime—without having to worry about memory issues.

After the interfaces have been defined, the data structures have been declared, and the layout of the finite-state machine has been loaded, the simulation is surprisingly easy to implement, as shown in Listing 39.2. The declarative approach used in this chapter simplifies the module significantly.

Listing 39.2   A Single Update of a Moore Finite-State Machine

```
function Tick( Symbol in )
     # look up the next state in the array of lists
     state = transition[state][in]
     # locate the data stored for this state
     return data[state]
end function
```

Creating Emotions as Finite States

Another component is included in the overall AI architecture to handle emotions. Internally, it is composed of two nested finite-state components, handling sensations and emotions.

Finite-State Machine for Emotions

The finite-state machine used to model the four emotions contains four states. However, each emotion is associated with two states, such that each state corresponds to two emotions. When pairs of complementary emotions are considered as dimensions, the finite-state machine can be understood as a 2D grid—as shown in Figure 39.1. This enforces the restriction that two complementary emotions may not be active at the same time.

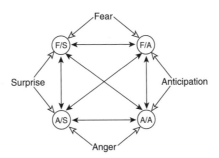

Figure 39.1   The four different mood states, each with two emotions.

The finite-state machine is fully connected, so there are transitions from each state to every other. The conditions for the transitions are left generic, and are defined by the sensations. The design of this finite-state machine is therefore frozen. All the flexibility comes from the sensations finite-state machine, which defines active emotions; transitions in this finite-state machine match the desired mood.

Each state contains specific values for each of the parameters used to control the behaviors. These are defined in Table 39.2, but can be adjusted by the designers. The parameters are defined for the turn and move actions, and the visual senses are defined as follows:

> ➤ **Accuracy** indicates the randomness of an action; a value of 1.0 means the requested action is executed, a value of 0.0 means that a randomized action is picked based on the request.

> ➤ **Power** is used to scale the value of actions. A 0 power means the animat is completely frozen, whereas 1 power implies the actions have their maximal value (turning and moving).

➤ **Delay** represents the number of seconds after which an event is passed to the animat. A 0 delay means the animat perceives the object as it appears, whereas there may be almost a second delay in other cases.

➤ **Precision** defines how the senses interpret the position of objects in space. A value of 1 indicates the position is exact, whereas 0 means that a large random value is added to distance and angle.

Table 39.2 Parameter Values That Affect the Behaviors Based on the Current Mood (Precision and power affect the actions, whereas delay and accuracy affect the senses.)

	Surprise	Anticipation
Fear	Precision 0.7	Precision 0.9
	Power 0.2	Power 0.4
	Delay 0.0	Delay 1.0
	Accuracy 0.9	Accuracy 0.2
Anger	Precision 0.0	Precision 0.1
	Power 1.0	Power 0.9
	Delay 0.3	Delay 0.8
	Accuracy 0.8	Accuracy 0.3

Finite-State Automaton and Sensations

A finite-state automaton is used to process the perceptions into concise sensations that can be interpreted by the finite-state machine used for emotions. An example finite-state automaton is shown in Figure 39.2. Because these sensations are crafted by the designer (and the emotions are frozen), they implicitly affect the personality of the animats. Some creatures may be likely to react better in combat, whereas others become complacent when nothing happens. These personalities can be controlled indirectly by adjusting the sensations.

The system could be modeled with only one finite-state automaton with five states (one start state and four states corresponding to the recognized sensations). Arbitrary intermediate nodes can be used to simplify the model as necessary. Although this approach is the simplest possible, it does not provide much diversity in the behaviors. Instead, using one finite-state automaton for each of the moods provides the flexibility to customize each of the transitions, while still keeping the complexity of the system low.

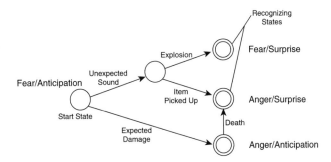

Figure 39.2   Finite-state automaton to recognize the sensations based on the stimuli.

Integration

The two finite-state components are built separately, but need to work closely together to produce the final system. The stimuli from the environment are passed as events to the finite-state automaton. The sensations are passed asynchronously as messages to the finite-state machine modeling the emotions, as shown in Figure 39.3. With this approach, the emotional state is always up-to-date, driven reactively in a very efficient fashion.

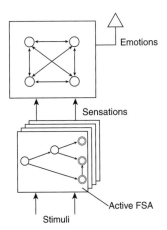

Figure 39.3   Integration of the sensations and the emotions using message passing.

Similarly to biological creatures, the emotions are experienced subconsciously. In this system, the moods are essentially an underlying layer for the AI already developed. The previously developed AI architecture is therefore required as another layer to provide the intelligence.

These two layers need to interact for the mood to affect the behavior, as shown in Figure 39.4. The mood is queried by sensor and effector components that manifest the emotions (that is, vision queries or movement actions). Depending on the component, the emotions are queried on-the-fly when necessary or they are passed by messages and cached.

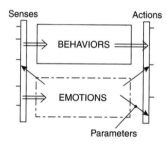

Figure 39.4 High-level view of the architecture with the emotions and the reactive behaviors working independently. The emotions affect the senses and actions with parameters.

Evaluation

The animat's moods are implicit and are not easy to identify at first glance. Nonetheless, the emotions certainly have an effect on the gaming experience over time. The changes in the animat's behaviors can be understood with observation and insights into the underlying model—although printing out the emotional state in the debugger also helps.

Despite the AI behaviors being identical, this emotional model provides more diversity in the behaviors. In terms of the shooting behaviors, the emotions have a similar effect to the context-dependent aiming errors—but applied throughout the AI in a biologically plausible fashion. This leads to unexpected situations arising, which makes the game more interesting. In no cases were the behaviors unacceptable in terms of realism, although the skills of the animats occasionally seemed rather poor (because of the negative effect of the emotions degrading the senses and actions).

That said, the emotional model is incredibly simple to adjust. The values of the manifestations are stored in a configuration files and modifiable with a text editor, which allows easier experimentation. The precision or delay attributes can be changed by the game logic, or even by the players themselves, to adjust the skill dynamically.

Technically speaking, the system showcases the benefits of a modular approach to AI. The existing modules providing the intelligent behaviors remained completely unchanged, and the emotions are inserted as an additional layer in the architecture. The emotional layer is completely independent from the reactive behaviors. This design pattern provides the base of a better model, which is explained in Chapter 42.

This system suffers technically because of the limitations of finite-state machines. The transitions are Boolean; the mood changes states completely or it stays the same. As a consequence, the emotions are essentially black and white, with no shades of gray possible—although this is not immediately obvious in the behaviors. The emotions are also very predictable, and remain the same throughout the game.

There are minor issues with emotions changing too quickly. Because mood changes can be triggered by sensations, a quick succession of stimuli could cause rapid changes in mood. Luckily, the way the animats emotions are portrayed (degradation of the senses) does not cause unrealistic behaviors. In general, a low frequency of updates to the emotions can be used to prevent such oscillations (for instance, manually driven rather than by events).

From a design point of view, the improvement in realism is already noticeable, but choosing only four emotions limited the full potential of the technology. It would be particularly challenging to implement more emotions with the finite-state machine, because the number of transitions necessary would grow exponentially.

Practical Demo

The animat demonstrating the ideas in this chapter is called *Moody* and can be found on the web site along with the other examples at `http://AiGameDev.com/`. Based on the AI of the previous parts, the architecture includes two kinds of finite-state components to implement the emotions. These emotions are portrayed by degrading the senses and effectors.

Summary

The design for this prototype was based on a simple model of sensations and emotions:

➤ Four primary emotions were chosen to represent the mood.

➤ The sensations are Boolean triggers that change the mood based on stimuli.

➤ The emotions are portrayed by degrading of the senses and actions.

Two finite-state components are developed to implement the design:

➤ A finite-state machine models changes in emotions and keeps track of the mood.

➤ A finite-state automaton determines the sensations as Boolean conditions from the stimuli.

➤ Both components communicate by passing messages between each other, to affect the inputs and outputs.

Evaluation of the system reveals the benefits of simple emotions for improving believability, but also technical problems:

➤ A limited number of emotions are chosen; modeling complex moods becomes increasingly difficult with finite-state machines.

➤ The system is fully predictable and does not change over time.

➤ Sensations and emotions are defined as Boolean values.

The next two chapters investigate extensions to finite-state machines that can solve these problems. Fuzzy-state machines can have partial degrees for emotions, probabilistic models make the sensations less predictable, and hierarchical systems simplify the modeling of complex moods.

Chapter 40

Nondeterministic State Machines

There are various types of extensions to finite-state machines. These range from nondeterministic models (with ambiguous transitions) to probabilistic models (each transition has a probability), including fuzzy models (where every state is a fuzzy variable).

There are few changes to be made to finite-state machines to support these variations. The representation is still graphlike, and the data structures remain very similar.

Each extension to finite-state machines has its own advantage. Nondeterministic models greatly simplify the modeling of large finite-state machines and the combining of smaller ones together. Probabilistic models can be used to analyze the likelihood of obtaining different sequences, or even to generate stochastic output sequences. Fuzzy models combine the advantages of fuzzy logic with finite-state machines; partial degrees of truth on the inputs and state values are supported, and smooth outputs can be generated.

In games, this can simplify the development of nonplayer character (NPC) behaviors, as well as improve the final results by making the outputs less predictable and with smoother transitions.

In the nondeterministic case, it's best to convert the machines to deterministic ones before simulation. For probabilistic models, the simulation of the finite-state machines is updated to take into account the changes in representation. Each transition is just chosen stochastically.

For the fuzzy system, the finite-state machines can be trivially converted to a set of rules and fuzzy variables. Therefore, the same fuzzy engine can be used to simulate the fuzzy state machine.

Overview

This chapter documents all the different variations of finite-state machines that prove useful in computer games. This includes fuzzy, nondeterministic, and stochastic state machines. Further *extensions* to finite-state machines—such as hierarchies—are left until the next chapter.

Before starting the explanations, it seems appropriate to make clear distinctions between the different approaches, but also try to point out similarities (see Table 40.1). This can be somewhat confusing, because the mathematical background spans over multiple domains; terminology, and even interpretation, varies from one subject to another.

Table 40.1   The Different Variations of Finite-State Computational Models and Their Relationship to Each Other

	Acceptor	Transducer
Deterministic	Finite-state automaton	Finite-state machine
Nondeterministic	Nondeterministic FSA	Nondeterministic finite-state machines
Probabilistic	Hidden Markov chain	Markov model
Fuzzy	Fuzzy FSA	Fuzzy FSM

For each of the paradigms, there are *acceptors* (that determine whether an input sequence is valid), *recognizers* (classifying an input sequence), and *transducers* (outputting values matching the inputs):

➤ **Deterministic** models are fully predictable and present no ambiguity when computing the results.

➤ **Nondeterministic** models are less explicitly defined; they allow ambiguous cases, but no hints are provided as to which is correct. The option that generates the right result should be chosen; the trick is to decide how to achieve this.

➤ **Probabilistic** models have probabilities associated with each of the transitions. These can be used for analysis or interpreted stochastically.

➤ **Fuzzy** models have each state represented as a fuzzy variable. The transitions can be interpreted as fuzzy rules applied over the states. Each of the fuzzy states has a degree of membership that changes throughout the simulation.

This brief overview is intended to remove any possible misinterpretation of the techniques. Everything will become clear with the following technical coverage.

Fuzzy State Machines

A *fuzzy state machine* is an extension to standard finite-state machines. Instead of processing crisp symbols, both the inputs and outputs are fuzzy values. This has the advantage of smooth control and reasoning with degrees of truth, which often proves more humanlike.

Internally, each state is defined as fuzzy variables, too. Like other fuzzy systems, this leads to a combinatorial explosion of applicable rules determined by the number of states and input/output symbols.

Contrary to common beliefs, a fuzzy state machine is intrinsically deterministic—just like a fuzzy rule-based system. Common terminology among game developers associates fuzzy state machines as probabilistic ones. This is not only misleading, but also ambiguous and inconsistent, so we'll stick to the standard definition.

Definitions

As with their nonfuzzy counterparts, fuzzy automatons are used as acceptors, and fuzzy machines used as transducers.

Fuzzy Finite-State Automaton

A fuzzy finite-state automaton (FFSA) can be seen as an acceptor that outputs degree of membership. It is defined as a quadruple:

$$FFSA = \{\Sigma, Q, F, \delta\}$$

Here, Σ is an alphabet of fuzzy input values, Q is a collection of fuzzy variables representing the states, $F \subseteq Q$ is a subset of accepting states, and δ is a fuzzy transition map that defines the next state R_{t+1} of the fuzzy automaton in terms of the current state R_t. The state of the automaton corresponds to the set of all fuzzy values Q:

$$\delta: \quad F \times \Sigma \to F$$
$$(R_t, \sigma_t) \,\alpha\; R_{t+1} \;|\!\to \sigma_t \in \Sigma, R \in F$$

$F(Q)$ is the set of all possible states of the fuzzy automaton, so δ is defined as a mapping this set onto itself, given a fuzzy input symbol.

Fuzzy Finite-State Machine

Like its nonfuzzy counterpart, a fuzzy finite-state machine (FFSM) is a version of the fuzzy automaton that can output symbols as it consumes input symbols. The outputs, obviously fuzzy symbols too, can be defined in terms of the transitions or the states (corresponding to Mealy and Moore machines). It is defined as a quintuple:

$$FFSM = \{\Sigma, Q, Z, \delta, \lambda\}$$

Z is the output alphabet, namely a set of fuzzy symbols. λ corresponds to the fuzzy output map, defined in terms of the inputs and current state.

$$\lambda: \quad F(Q) \times \Sigma \to F(Z)$$
$$(R_t, \sigma_t) \,\alpha\; Z_t \quad |\!\to \sigma_t \in \Sigma, Z_t \in F(Z)$$

In this case, the output isn't only one symbol, but a set of fuzzy symbols defined with a smooth membership function.

Representation

The graphical representation of a fuzzy state machine shown in Figure 40.1 is still graph based. The active state cannot be denoted as a unique bold node, because many states may have nonzero degrees of membership. To visualize this aspect of the finite-state machine, the size or shade of gray of each state can indicate the degree of membership. This is especially useful when debugging the machine or trying to explain the outcome of a situation.

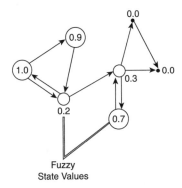

Figure 40.1   A fuzzy finite-state machine with the degree of membership of each state indicated by the size of the node in the graph.

The finite-state machine itself may be unfolded into a set of fuzzy rules defined over the states and the input/output alphabet. Because none of these rules can be discarded when simulating the state machine accurately, there is little hope for significant optimizations in the representation. In the end, the rulebase contains fuzzy rules with the following format:

```
IF <state1> AND <transition> THEN <state2>
```

If the FFSM is not unfolded into a set of rules, the transitions themselves must be stored differently compared to a finite-state machine's graph. Crisp finite-state machines associate the transitions with the active state, so the simulation can check each transition when it becomes active. With a fuzzy model, state activity is not passed forward as a crisp Boolean. Instead, each state inherits the combined activity of the predecessor states (weighted by the fuzzy transition symbol). This implies that it's easier to compute the fuzzy value of a state based on its predecessors, instead of trying to propagate activity to the successors. The implementation stores the predecessor states for each state, which allows the fuzzy rules to be applied to each state to determine their next value in one pass.

Look at the example behavior in Listing 40.1. A crisp finite-state machine would store transitions from the three states (`wandering`, `attacking`, and `gathering`) to the `fleeing` state. On the other hand, the fuzzy finite-state machine needs to store backward links from the `fleeing` state, so its fuzzy value can be computed in terms of the antecedents states (an OR relationship between the three rules).

Listing 40.1 A Small Subset of Rules That Represent Part of a Fuzzy Finite-State Machine Graph

```
IF <wandering> AND <attacked> THEN <fleeing>
IF <attacking> AND <near_death> THEN <fleeing>
IF <gathering> AND <surprised> THEN <fleeing>
```

Simulation

Because the representation can be converted to a set of fuzzy rules, the simulation too will be little different from a fuzzy rule-based system.

There are two aspects of the simulation: computing the next fuzzy state using δ, and computing the output with ω. Computing the next state is done as a set of IF-THEN implications. Let's take an example, defining a state's degree membership as a disjunction over the neighboring state/transition pairs:

$$q_0 = (q_1 \wedge \sigma_4) \vee (q_2 \wedge \sigma_3)$$

The fuzzy OR $\vee$ is defined as the maximum of the two operands; the fuzzy AND $\wedge$ is expressed as a minimum. Using MIN/MAX inference leaves us with the pseudo-code in Listing 40.2 to determine the degree of membership of a state.

Listing 40.2 Determining the Fuzzy Value of a State s, and the Degree of Membership of the Output

```
s = 0
for each predecessor state q and input i
      output = MIN( q, i )
      s = MAX( s, output )
end for
```

The output itself is defined as a rule mapping the input symbol σ_4 and previous state q_1 onto the output $z_{1/0}$. This is the conjunction:

$$z_{1/0} = q_1 \wedge \sigma_4$$

No operations on sets are needed to simulate the FFSM. However, these may be required if the output variables need to be defuzzified.

Discussion

Fuzzy state machines have the advantages of both fuzzy expert systems and finite-state machines. They are straightforward to create, especially using graphical tools. They operate with fuzzy terms and linguistic variables, which prove more intuitive for humans. FFSA can recognize partial degrees of membership in input strings, whereas FFSMs have the capability to generate smooth output—ideal for control.

The major problem with fuzzy state machines is the combinatorial explosion, which follows from fuzzy expert systems. It's difficult—if not impossible—to reduce this problem without simplifying the problem. The sparse nature of the state machine is a small advantage here, because the numbers of rules does not reach its upper bounds. FFSMs also have problems dealing with complexity, as the design process becomes tougher with large machines. Although given the use of fuzzy concepts, this proves generally simpler than with crisp states.

Nondeterministic State Machines

All previous models (both fuzzy and crisp) are fully deterministic; for each state/input combination, it's clear what the next state should be. Nondeterminism enables us to define machines where more than one next state is defined for each situation. The model does not even specify which should be chosen; there doesn't necessarily need to be only one next state—all the specified options could be correct.

There is nothing uncertain about nondeterminism; there are no probabilities associated with transitions. Nondeterminism just reflects a lack of information about the next transition, essentially a gap in the formal definition. How we decide to deal with that is

not a consequence of nondeterminism itself. Nondeterminism is just a less-explicit way
of representing a state machine. In fact, most nondeterministic state machines are used
in a deterministic fashion.

There can be two types of nondeterminism. One is nondeterminism in the *transitions*
(present in automatons), the other is in the *outputs* (visible in transducers). The fact
that no deterministic transition or outputs are specified is generally interpreted as,
"Use an option that gives the correct answer." We'll discuss how to implement this in
the next sections.

Definitions

Acceptors, recognizers, and transducers can be created with nondeterministic models.

Nondeterministic Finite-State Automaton

Formally, a nondeterministic finite-state automaton (NFSA) is defined in a similar way
to a deterministic finite-state automaton. It's a quadruple:

$$NFSA = \{\Sigma, Q, \delta, F\}$$

Again, Q is the set of states including the start state q_0, $F \subseteq Q$ is the subset of accepting
states, and Σ in the input alphabet. Only δ is defined differently; it's a transition *relation*,
which means there can be multiple transitions suggested. Formally speaking, it's not a
one-to-one mapping from the current state and input symbol onto the next state.

A transition *function* is in fact a special case of a transition *relation* with at most one
next state possible. To this extent, an FSA is a special case of an NFSA. So conceptually, the inputs and outputs are the same in both cases. In fact, we'll also show how a
nondeterministic automaton can be converted to a deterministic one!

Nondeterministic Finite-State Machines

Both types of deterministic finite-state machines—Moore and Mealy—are also available
in nondeterministic flavors. In both cases, the Moore machine is a simplified version of
the Mealy machine, so the same differences about the output function apply; one is

based on states, the other on transitions (see Chapter 38, "Finite-State Machines"). We'll study them both together this time.

The formal definition of a nondeterministic finite-state machine appears to be the same as the deterministic one:

$$NFSM = \{\Sigma, Q, Z, \delta, \lambda\}$$

Most terms are the same as for NFSA. Z is the output alphabet. However, again both δ and λ are in fact *relations*, and no longer *functions*. Let's look at the consequences of nondeterminism in both these relations:

➤ First, the transition relation δ implies that multiple next states can be suggested for any state/input pair (q, σ). In fact, no input is actually needed to trigger a transition (known as epsilon transitions ε). This form of nondeterminism is the most common in both theory and practice.

➤ Second, for the output relation λ, the symbol produced may vary based on the current state/input. This form of nondeterminism is not as common. In fact, λ can often be interpreted as a deterministic function based on δ. In this case, there is only one possible output per nondeterministic transition.

These changes in the definition also impose a few restrictions on the representation.

Representation

The data structures for finite-state machines were optimized to store only one transition per state/input pair. Nondeterminism does not guarantee this.

Problems with Arrays

Nondeterminism means that the standard array-based representation of the finite-state machines is no longer feasible. Indeed, many state/input cells in the array would require holding more than one value, as shown in Table 40.2. This would be necessary to represent all the transition and output options.

Table 40.2 An Array Attempting to Store the Transitions for a Nondeterministic Finite-State Machine (Some cells have more than one value.)

Input/State	1	2	3	4
a	2 & 4	-	-	-
b	-	3 & 4	-	-
ε	- -		2	3

A somewhat inefficient solution to this would include a list of transitions for each cell. This overhead may be reduced by only having lists in the necessary cells, but a small flag would be needed to indicate whether the cell contains a list or a single value.

At this point, the array representation has lost its major advantage: simplicity. The efficiency of the lookup will also be reduced, so it would seem better to consider the graph-based approach.

Directed Graphs

The graph-based representation, as shown in Table 40.3, remains mostly unchanged by nondeterminism. The additional transitions needed to model the additional options can be added using the same representation. Only one additional type of transition is needed, the ε transition to model the case where no input symbol is needed to trigger a transition.

Table 40.3 Using a Single Dimensional Array Storing Linked Lists to Represent the Same Nondeterministic Finite-State Machine

State	Transitions
1	a: 2, a: 4
2	b: 3, b: 4
3	$\varepsilon : 2$
4	$\varepsilon : 3$

This confirms the advantages of the graph-based representation. It will be needed to perform nondeterministic simulation of the state machine, or just to store it temporarily while it is converted to a deterministic model.

Algorithms

As mentioned, there are two ways to deal with nondeterminism. First, we can just simulate the machine in a way that is compatible with its nondeterministic definition (see Figure 40.2), putting up with the inconveniences and overheads (a recursive traversal that consumes memory exponentially). Second, we can decide to convert it to a deterministic finite-state machine, so we don't have the trouble of dealing with nondeterminism.

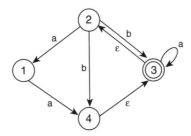

Figure 40.2   A nondeterministic finite-state machine with epsilon transitions and ambiguous ones.

Nondeterministic Simulation

With standard finite-state machines, only one possible transition is applicable. This implies that the active state will change, but there will always be only one. With nondeterministic simulations, there may be more than one transition, which implies more than one active state.

Let's consider the algorithm with finite state automata first. It's simpler because no output is generated, and it's most common anyway. Start with a set of active states (usually just one), and read in the next symbol. If a transition from any of the current states matches, the corresponding next state is added to the next set of active states. This parallel simulation avoids backtracking (rewinding the input if we reach a dead end). Empty ε transitions should be expanded immediately. This process continues reading in symbols and determining the next active states. If one of the states is an accepting state, the simulation ends.

For finite-state machines with deterministic outputs (but nondeterministic transitions), the algorithm needs to keep track of the output sequence for each of the active states. When a correct output sequence is detected, the simulation can stop.

In the case of nondeterministic outputs, things are even more complex. A set of the possible outputs needs to be maintained for each of the active states. This is quite cumbersome, and has little practical benefit, so it seems easier to use deterministic outputs.

Conversion to Deterministic

The procedure for creating a deterministic automaton from a nondeterministic one is known as the *subset construction* algorithm. Essentially, each state in the FSA is associated with a set of states in the NFSA. This is because of the fact that ε transitions and ambiguous transitions may cause the same input string to reach different states in the NFSA (as in the simulation where multiple states can be active). So, during the construction, the corresponding subset of states in the NFSA is stored in each FSA state.

The algorithm starts with the ε closure of the start states from the NFSA. This is the set of all states that can be reached from the start states by transition. Then, all the input symbols that can trigger a transition from this subset of states are considered. For each unique input symbol, one state in the FSA is created corresponding to the set of states in the NFSA that would be accessible with that input symbol. This set of states is stored along with the state of the FSA, so it can be expanded later. This process repeats until all the states of the FSA have been considered (see Listing 40.3).

Listing 40.3   Converting a Nondeterministic Finite-State Automaton to a Deterministic One Using a Subset of the Construction Algorithm

```
create the start state in the FSA
associate it with the subset of start states in the NFSA
while there is an unmarked state in the FSA
      scan the corresponding subset of NFSA states
      for each unique input that can trigger a transition
            find the corresponding subset of states in the NFSA
            create a new FSA state associated with this subset
            connect it the current state to this new one
      end for
      mark this state
end while
```

This same procedure can be applied to nondeterministic finite-state machines as long as the outputs are deterministic. If this is not the case, the final model cannot be made deterministic with this algorithm. It's best to resolve these problems manually or simulate the machine nondeterministically.

Discussion

Nondeterminism can simplify the process of creating FSA and finite-state machines. This is possible by using a less rigorous definition that allows multiple ambiguous transitions per input character, and ε transition when no input characters are needed. For example, merging two finite state machines together (for instance, to combine and extend behaviors) can be done with a simple ε transition between the appropriate states. An algorithm can then convert the most resulting finite-state machine to a deterministic one.

The simulation of nondeterministic machines can be slower, because the number of active states can potentially grow exponentially. Likewise, when converting nondeterministic finite-state automata into deterministic models, the number of total states can explode exponentially in the worst case—although that rarely happens in practice. Finally, nondeterministic output of finite-state machines is relatively awkward to handle, and generally ends up being exploited as a probabilistic finite-state machine.

The benefits of nondeterminism have not been identified by game developers, because they are never used in game AI. The major advantage lies in simplifying the modeling for the designer. Consider having to create an FSA to recognize enemies from teammates. It's often simpler to create two small FSA for each problem. An ε transition can join the two together trivially. The result can be converted to a standard deterministic model for efficiency. Nondeterminism provides the best compromise between design simplicity and runtime efficiency. Another example would be to design the "replenish inventory" and "avoid combat" behaviors separately and use nondeterminism to combine these together.

> **NOTE**
> Nondeterminism can be used to emulate many of the advantages of hierarchical finite-state machines by using a standard representation and simulation algorithm. The concepts of hierarchy can be modeled using ε transitions, and an algorithm can remove any form of nondeterminism—effectively flattening the hierarchy into a standard finite state machine. This can be an effective build-time procedure.

Probabilistic State Machines

So far, all the models have in fact been deterministic. Even the nondeterministic ones turned out just to be a more compact deterministic model. In games, a bit of variation is often needed; voluntarily random behaviors can have a positive effect on the realism.

By assigning probabilities to the transitions or outputs, we can use the finite-state machines to estimate the likelihood of an input sequence occurring, or—more commonly—to generate random sequences of outputs.

Definitions

In both the case of probabilistic finite-state automaton and machines, there is a strong correlation with other fields of mathematics—notably statistics. We'll present this angle too, because this discussion benefits from a comprehensive background.

Markov Chains

A probabilistic finite-state automaton (PFSA) can be seen as a *Markov chain*. A Markov chain is a sequence of random events—known formally as a stochastic process—with a particular property; the likelihood of an event occurring next depends entirely on the past sequence. A Markov chain of degree *one* expresses that only one past event is needed to determine the probability of the next event; this is a *state-determined* Markov chain. A Markov chain of high order is called a *history-determined* Markov chain, relying on more past events to model the probability of the next event.

We're interested in Markov chains of degree one, because they can be seen as finite-state automata with probabilities associated to each of the transitions (see Figure 40.3). Sticking with definitions similar to the previous finite-state automata, consider the following:

$$PFSA = \{\Sigma, Q, F, \delta\}$$

Once again, Σ is the input alphabet, Q is the set of states, and F is the subset of accepting states. δ is still the transition function, but associates state/input pairs with the next state and a probability:

$$\delta: \qquad Q \times \Sigma \to Q \times [0,1]$$
$$(q_t, \sigma_t) \,\alpha\; \big(q_{t+1}, p(q_{t+1})\big) \;\mapsto (q_t, \sigma_t) \in Q \times \Sigma, \, p(q_{t+1}) \in [0,1]$$

This is subject to a condition applying to every state q_t. The sum of the probabilities $p(q_{t+1})$ (of the outgoing transitions) for all the possible inputs σ_t should be equal to 1. If this is not the case, the probabilities can be renormalized (that is, divide by the sum):

$$\mapsto q_t : \sum_{\sigma_t} p(q_{t+1}) = 1$$

Most often, δ remains a *function*—extending the deterministic FSA model. However, it can become a *relation* if necessary, where multiple transitions from a state would be possible for one input. It wouldn't be any additional problem to handle these with the simulation or representation.

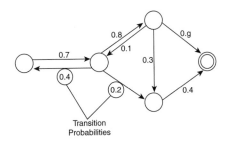

Figure 40.3   A probabilistic finite-state automaton and a simpler finite-state machine.

Hidden Markov Models

A probabilistic finite-state machine can be interpreted as a *hidden Markov model*. A hidden Markov model (HMM) is like a Markov chain in that it has probabilistic transitions. However, an HMM is a more complex model because the outputs are stochastic, too. Formally speaking, a probabilistic finite-state machine can be defined as follows:

$$PFSM = \{\Sigma, Q, Z, \delta, \lambda\}$$

Again, most of the terms are identical to Markov chains. As a reminder, Z is the output alphabet, and λ is the output relation. (It's a relation because there is more than one possible output per state/input pair.) Because the definition of δ was extended to handle probabilities, we need to do the same for λ:

$$\lambda: \quad Q \times \Sigma \rightarrow Z \times [0,1]$$
$$(q_t, \sigma_t) \, \alpha \, \left(z_t, p(z_t)\right) \, |\!\rightarrow\! (q_t, \sigma_t) \in Q \times \Sigma, p(z_t) \in [0,1]$$

Here also, the sum of the probabilities needs to be 1, for each of the possible pairs (q_t, σ_t). This ensures consistency in the probabilities (which can also be enforced by normalization):

$$\sum_{(q_t, \sigma_t)} p(z_t) = 1$$

Given this definition, we can use a variety of algorithms to extract information from it. It's also possible to create some sample outputs given the model.

Algorithms

There are two principal ways to traverse probabilistic finite-state models: one for evaluating probabilities, the other for generating pseudo-random symbols.

Evaluation

There is an algorithm to compute the probability of a given sequence occurring. The animats can use this technique to evaluate their chances of success, for example. Taking each of the input symbols, the probabilities for each transition can be multiplied together to determine the total probability of this sequence occurring.

Generation

It's also possible to perform a random traversal of the graph, taking each transition according to its probability. Randomized NPC behaviors with a common pattern can be generated this way. When the probabilities are respected, the sequences generated are a sample distribution of the Markov chain (that is, representative of all the possible sequences). So if we were to gather the statistics to compute the probabilities, we would get the same result.

Discussion

Probabilistic state machines are extremely simple to model and implement. However, they can provide very interesting patterns simply thanks to a stochastic traversal. This is ideal to influence characters to perform in one particular way, while allowing them to diverge occasionally. For the designer, this proves to be an extremely powerful control method.

One disadvantage is that random behaviors aren't very predictable! This can be awkward when debugging or trying to develop the finite-state machine. Probabilistic state machines are also subject to the same disadvantages of the standard models, notably limitations in capabilities and complexity of large models.

Summary

Various extensions to finite-state machines prove useful in game development:

> Fuzzy finite-state machines bring the benefits of fuzziness to finite-state models. These provide smooth control and reasoning with degrees of truth, which can increase realism in some cases. FFSM are best simulated using a fuzzy expert system, although they have the advantage of being easy to create with a graph-based representation.

> Nondeterministic finite-state machines are less strict as a mathematical model, which implies the design of finite-state machines in game AI is much simpler. Instead of leaving uncertain transitions, tools should be used to convert NFSM to their deterministic counterparts.

> Probabilistic models can be used to evaluate the likelihood of sequences occurring, or even to generate random sequences according to a random pattern. This is the simplest and most common extension to finite-state machines in computer games.

The next chapter covers an extremely powerful concept: hierarchies of finite-state machines. Although the theoretical complexity of finite-state machines is not increased by hierarchies, behaviors and capabilities are much easier to model this way. Chapter 42 uses extensions of this chapter and the next to create a better emotional system that makes the animats seem more lifelike.

Practical Demo

There's an animat that uses the concepts in this chapter to create behaviors and capabilities. It's known as *Masheen* and can be found on the web site at `http://AiGameDev.com/`. *Masheen* has some advantages over the plain finite-state machines, notably smoother behaviors and a simpler design.

Chapter 41

Hierarchical State Machines

Complex behaviors are difficult to create as regular finite-state machines. Tasks can generally be decomposed into increasingly detailed subtasks. (For instance, playing death-match relies on the capability to gather items, attack, and defend.) This approach is reminiscent of AI architectures in general—as discussed throughout this book. In the case of finite-state machines, individual finite-state machines are designed in the normal fashion, but these are accumulated in layers by nesting finite-state machines within each other. Thanks to abstraction and modularity, hierarchical finite-state machines (HFSMs) significantly reduce the complexity of the asset development pipeline. Hierarchies, however, do not increase the computational power of the system.

This chapter covers the following topics:

➤ The problems with finite-state machines that are resolved using hierarchies.

➤ The different types of hierarchies commonly used with finite-state machines, notably nested states and nested finite-state machines

➤ Semantics that formalize the interaction between levels in the hierarchy. The system is simulated according to these principles.

➤ The advantages and disadvantages of HFSM.

The technology presented in this chapter is used in the next chapter to improve the model of animat emotions.

Overview

Hierarchical state machines are born as solutions to the flaws with standard finite-state machines. The biggest issue is complexity of the representation. With classical finite-state machines, it is difficult to express the following examples:

➤ "During any attacking or wandering behavior, run away if the enemy boss appears."

➤ "When a flash grenade is thrown, enter dodge mode!"

➤ "The attack behavior consists of the tasks of finding, following, and shooting at the enemy."

➤ "The camping behavior is independent from weapon management."

The flat nature of finite-state machines does not allow these concepts to be expressed. The four following criteria can be identified from such examples [Harel87]:

➤ **Clustering**—The first example indicates the need to group together all states for attacking and wandering. The compound state itself is known as a *superstate*.

➤ **General transitions**—In the second case, there's a need to express a transition from any state, so that the behavior is overridden.

➤ **Refinement of states**—Some behaviors in the finite-state machine are defined as a combination of other simpler activities. The third case is an example of this.

➤ **Independence and orthogonality**—The fourth point illustrates that components of a system are not always directly connected.

The first three properties can be captured using a hierarchical model. The last property is about concurrency instead, and can be considered separate.

Hierarchies

Understanding HFSMs involves defining a hierarchy. A *hierarchy* is a set of objects assembled together on multiple levels, generally contained within each other. As objects are nested inside others, hierarchies can be represented as trees, with the root node of the tree being the top object of the hierarchy (see Figure 41.1).

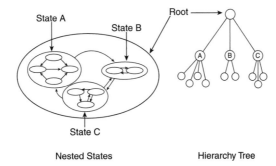

Figure 41.1   Example of nested nodes and the corresponding tree representing the hierarchy.

In the case of finite-state machines, hierarchies can be defined just as nested states or entire machines. This proves to be a good way of understanding the different benefits of hierarchical state machines (HSMs).

Nested States

The definition of an HSM primarily allows states to be defined within each other. States that englobe other states are known as *superstates*. This has no effect on the computational capabilities of finite-state machines, because all hierarchical models can be flattened out with each transition made explicit. In many cases, the hierarchy leads to simpler models.

The number of states in the HSM will generally not diminish compared to the flat finite-state machine. In fact, if the higher-level states are counted too (that is, superstates), the total number of states increases. This kind of hierarchy allows the abstraction of transitions (see Figure 41.2).

Transitions that are outbound from a group of states should be interpreted as connected to each of the nested states (known as *generalized* transitions). Conversely, inbound transitions are only redirected to specific states.

By grouping states together with the same outgoing transitions, it's possible to cut down on the number of transitions. This is the initial interpretation of a hierarchy, on the state level. Nested states will accept only a subset of the input/output alphabet.

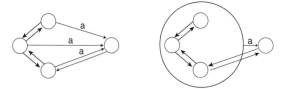

Figure 41.2   A superstate defined as the parent of three nested states, each having the same outbound transition.

In practice, the benefits of such nested states are not restricted to strict hierarchies; the states at the top of the hierarchy are not necessarily mutually exclusive. Instead, super-states are defined to englobe standard states. These are known as AND states, because the outbound transitions apply to all the nested states. It's possible to define superstates around arbitrary areas of the finite-state machines to reduce the number of transitions.

Hierarchy of State Machines

Instead of just simplifying the representation with superstates, the hierarchy can be considered as a functional decomposition. Specifically, each nested state is a compo-nent providing exclusive functionality. The outer finite-state machine can assemble these components in the most suitable fashion to provide functionality.

Abstraction

A hierarchy provides different levels of detail for each of the finite-state machines. By not displaying the lower levels of the tree, it's possible to mask out the details of the underlying implementation. Essentially, this abstracts out the complexity of the imple-mentation. This operation is known as *zooming out* (see Figure 41.3).

In many cases, it is beneficial to consider a state as a black box, disregarding the layout of the nested finite-state machine. During the design phase, this can increase produc-tivity. When a higher-level finite-state machine is created, certain functionality is assumed from a state and it is used transparently. In a similar fashion to programming, this requires a clear definition of the state's behavior and the facilities it provides.

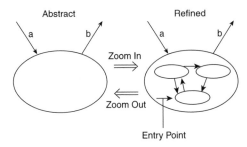

Figure 41.3   Zooming in and out. A nested finite-state machine is abstracted by hiding the lower levels of the hierarchy, which are then reinserted when required.

Refinement

After the higher-level finite-state machines have been created, it's necessary to *zoom in* to each of the states. The underlying implementation is thereby revealed, as the state itself is refined into a nested finite-state machine.

When the requirements of any state are too large to handle with simple procedures, refinement provides the methodology to expand the state transparently. A set of nested states can be created trivially, while still maintaining the same output behavior.

Modularity

Given the two previous properties of HSMs, it's trivial to extend the definition to deal with modular finite-state machines. Reminiscent of object-oriented programming, each finite-state machine can be treated as a modular component (see Figure 41.4). This implies it can be reused in any place and any in level of the hierarchy.

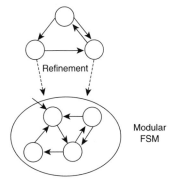

Figure 41.4   Two states reuse the same modular finite-state machine as a nested component.

During the design phase, modularity allows working finite-state machines to be stored in a common library, and imported into models when necessary. It's also convenient to spread the workload among multiple AI designers.

Heterogeneous Computational Models

Flexibility is one of the major advantages of these hierarchical models. Thanks to the high levels of abstraction and modularity, it's possible to use various different models of computation within each state. This is a tremendous advantage because finite-state machines are ill suited to certain tasks (for instance, counting).

Some models of computation related to finite-state machines have been integrated within finite-state machines (including synchronous data flow, discrete events, and reactive systems) [Girault99]. In games, however, other AI techniques such as rule-based systems or scripts are usually used within states to provide specific behaviors.

Interaction Semantics

To simulate the components in the hierarchy, a clear definition of the interaction between nested states is necessary. This enables us to understand what happens in these situations:

➤ In what order are the states processed?

➤ How are transitions handled on multiple levels?

With standard finite-state machines, there is little room for ambiguity. Therefore, a reliable approach to simulation would first convert the hierarchical state machine to a flat one. In this simpler case, stepping through the states is a well-defined process (especially if symbols are processed one by one).

Sadly, this discards some of the benefits of HSMs (such as abstraction and modularity). Also, a deterministically flattened hierarchy assumes that the process of simulating an HSM has been defined already. The following sections discuss different ways to simulate the HSM.

Master and Slave

Typically, the relationship between two nested finite-state machines is known as *master/slave*. The outer finite-state machine is the master, whereas the nested finite-state machine is the slave. This relationship implies that finite-state machines higher up the hierarchy are in control of the execution. Indeed, the master finite-state machine has the opportunity to override the slave.

In the simulation, the slave is simulated first and the master next, moving up the hierarchy (see Figure 41.5). This allows the master finite-state machine to override the output, and trigger a transition away from the nested state.

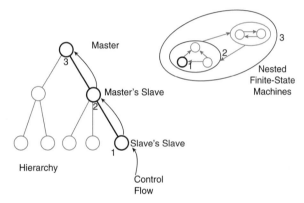

Figure 41.5   Flow of control in the hierarchy using the master/slave configuration. The slaves are processed first, allowing the master to override the output.

When using a mechanism for passing input/output symbols, conflicts are rare because all the messages are ordered and interpreted one by one. If there is ambiguity in the execution, the HSM is in fact nondeterministic and should be fixed by design (or using the automated procedure of Chapter 40, "Nondeterministic State Machines"). However, the procedural approach with hard-coded sensors can become troublesome—even as a deterministic model. Transitions at different levels of the hierarchy may be triggered "simultaneously."

There are guidelines for resolving this using the master/slave paradigm. If a possible conflict exists (ambiguity of what to do during the execution), all the transitions affecting the master would have priority. Because the slave went first, all changes to nested finite-state machines will be discarded if there is a transition inside the parent finite-state machine. (That is, this child finite-state machine will no longer be active.)

Stack Based

During the simulation, the active finite-state machine at each level can be stored on a stack. The most generic finite-state machine (at the root of the hierarchy) resides at the bottom of the stack, whereas the most detailed finite-state machine lives on the top. The process of zooming in to a state can be seen as a *push* operation, adding another finite-state machine to the stack. The process of zooming out is a *pop* operation, because the last finite-state machine is discarded off the stack, returning to the parent.

The finite-state machine in focus is the one currently on the top of the stack (see Figure 41.6). One common approach is to only simulate this finite-state machine until it decides to terminate. Termination can be measured by reaching a certain state, or just by issuing a *pop* command to remove itself from the stack.

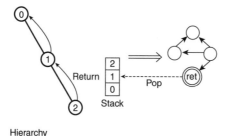

Figure 41.6   A stack of finite-state machines and the corresponding hierarchy. The finite-state machine in focus is responsible for *popping* itself.

This has the advantage that only one finite-state machine needs to be simulated at a time. There's no need to know how many other levels there are in the hierarchy, or even how big the stack is. Careful design can ensure that each state machine is capable of removing itself of the stack.

Levels of Detail

Each level in the hierarchy is an additional level of complexity; states are refined into substates, containing an expansion of the original task. As such, the different levels of the hierarchy add more detail to the behaviors.

Among the game AI community, there is a certain amount of interest in level-of-detail (LOD) solutions, providing varying quality of behaviors at different computational cost (see Figure 41.7). LOD schemes assume that it's possible to estimate the required detail for each nonplayer character (NPC). This is usually done by distance to the creature, or its visibility. Given this detail coefficient, the LOD technique should be capable of providing a trade-off between the quality of the behavior and the computational overhead.

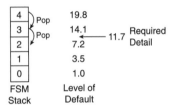

Figure 41.7   Controlling the level of detail by managing the stack of finite-state machines.

HSMs are relatively well suited to this purpose. At design time, the designer can manually assign detail coefficients for each state machine (for instance, based on their computational cost). During the simulation, it's possible to keep track of the total detail in the HSM (that is, the sum of all the detail values of the finite-state machines in the stack). Then, comparing the potential detail of a nested state enables us to decide when to refine a state. If there is enough detail, the refinement is skipped and a simpler approximate behavior is used.

The detail can also be controlled proactively, forcing changes in detail when necessary. If a character goes out of view, for example, the required detail can drop drastically. At this point, finite-state machines can be popped off the top of the stack until the detail level matches. Likewise, states can be pushed onto the stack if more detail is suddenly required. Sadly, both push/pop operations can lead to unwanted idiosyncrasies.

It turns out that the intrinsic problem lies with losing detail, and not the technique itself. So most of the problem is about design: Is a LOD solution feasible at all, and if so, how do we lose detail gracefully? LOD behaviors created with HSMs suffer from this problem, too. It's taken the graphics community a couple of decades to handle visual LOD smoothly; essentially, choosing the right representation can reduce the appearance of the "popping" effect, notably allowing continuous LOD techniques. This is a long way off in AI because no convenient uniform representation can handle all aspects of AI (unlike triangles in computer graphics).

One of the advantages of HSMs is that the state machine can handle the changes in detail itself, as shown in Figure 41.8. Each state can consist of two nested states: One corresponds to the rest of the hierarchy, whereas the other will be a unique state providing an approximation of the behavior. The changes in LOD can be seen as a transition between these two nested states using a threshold test as a condition. To handle the inconsistencies in changing detail, these transitions can be connected to temporary states responsible for ensuring the graceful degradation (or addition) of the information.

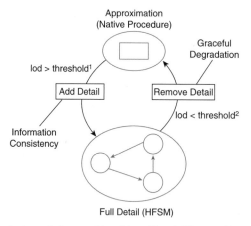

Figure 41.8   Zooming in to a state capable of handling LOD transitions itself. The two states correspond to full detail and approximation, while intermediate states take care of graceful degradation. This could be extended to handle multiple levels of detail.

Essentially, it's possible to achieve LOD smoothly with HSM under the following conditions:

> ➤ The designer can create a cheaper **approximation** of the behavior of nested finite-state machine.

> ➤ It's possible to create two procedures that will **handle transitions** between the two levels of detail in each finite-state machine.

> ➤ If any aspect of the AI or gameplay becomes inconsistent because of these changes, HSMs may not be the right approach.

Custom Semantics

HSMs are relatively simple to deal with as long as the simulation process is well defined. The previous pages describe the most popular interaction semantics. However, these approaches may not always be suitable. In such cases, spending time defining the interaction within the HSM is important to prevent nasty surprises.

One useful way to do this right is to abstract the internal processing of each state. This is the approach used by heterogeneous HSMs. Essentially, each state provides a function to step the execution, which must return within a finite time.

All the previous semantics can be reproduced, but this approach also allows custom processing algorithms to be inserted instead:

> ➤ The **master/slave** approach steps into the slave first, then simulate itself—overriding the transitions if necessary.

> ➤ The **stack-based** approach just steps into the slave until the focused finite-state machine is reached (top of the stack).

> ➤ A **level-of-detail** approach only steps into the nested finite-state machine if the detail is below the threshold.

So the processing is straightforward to abstract out. All we need is a base finite-state machine class, providing a step function. To create custom HSM semantics, we override the default step and manipulate the nested states as appropriate.

Discussion

Although standard HSMs have been used in some computer games, they are not widespread by any means. This may be because of terminology more than anything. The combination of finite-state machines with other nested techniques (for instance, rule-based systems or scripts) is popular, but these barely class as HSMs.

Advantages

HFSM really push finite-state machines to their best. Modularity does wonders to reduce the complexity of the design, which in turn simplifies the development process. Hierarchies make the creation of complex finite-state machines with graphical tools feasible. The ability to refine states into nested finite-state machines is a tremendous advantage when the behaviors are crafted incrementally.

The computational model itself is extremely flexible. It's possible to consider a state as an abstract component, letting it simulate its internal hierarchy as it deems necessary. Using this technique, it's relatively easy to customize the interaction semantics between nested states.

Disadvantages

HSMs, however, can get quite complex (on the same terms as software), although this paradigm seems one of the best suited to deal with such complexity. Debugging can be tricky for large models.

Although HSMs can be created manually with a text editor, advanced use relies heavily on graphical user interfaces—more so than finite-state machines. It's difficult to get the most out of a hierarchy without being able to display it and improve it with visual tools.

When it comes to the implementation itself, it's extremely important to define the interaction between states in the hierarchy. Still, unexpected events can occur—especially when native functions are used as transitions (that is, a procedural rather than declarative approach). Such problems are also common in standard finite-state machines, but the hierarchy really emphasizes these.

Summary

HFSMs improve upon standard state machines by adding the ability to cluster state, to express general transitions, to refine states that are to complex to handle with one procedure, and even to express independent components. In practice, this can be achieved using different concepts:

➤ Nested states allow states to be defined within others. Generalized transitions apply to these resulting superstates.

➤ Entire state machines can be nested within each other instead, with each finite-state machine forming a level in the hierarchy.

To implement the system, it's necessary to define the interaction semantics. This specifies how control is passed from one state to another:

➤ The master/slave approach processes the child components first, moving toward the root of the hierarchy. Higher-level state machines get priority.

➤ A stack-based simulation only processes the active finite-state machine, which lies on top of the stack. This changes only when the state machine removes itself from the stack.

➤ A level-of-detail approach uses a traversal of the hierarchy based on a threshold value, refining the behaviors when more detail is needed.

HFSMs are an incredibly powerful concept, ideally suited to game AI development. They extend finite-state machines—one of the most popular game AI techniques—and make them easier to design. Because pure finite-state machines are not appropriate for every problem, the concept of heterogeneous hierarchies (or AI architectures) can be used interchangeably.

The next chapter uses the concept of a hierarchy along with extensions to finite-state machines to create realistic emotions in animats.

Practical Demo

There's a simple animat, known as *Rarchy*, that uses nested finite-state machines to produce death-match behaviors. The top-level task is refined as subtasks, each corresponding to its own modular finite-state machine. The system is best understood as a tree representing the hierarchy, available online at http://AiGameDev.com/. *Rarchy* performs well and provides explicit control easily.

Chapter 42

An Emotional System

The emotion architecture described in Chapter 39, "Under the Influence," provides a proof of concept, but suffers from binary sensations and oversimplified emotions. The next few pages improve this previous architecture using extensions of finite-state machines—as described in the preceding two chapters.

The low-level technical problems are resolved using sensations based on fuzzy logic, and a wider variety of emotions and influences are included. The architecture itself is extended with mannerisms to portray short distinctive behaviors. Feelings are expressed about personal relationships, and the moods provide high-level guidance for the intelligent behaviors.

This chapter covers the following topics:

➤ The architecture from a high-level point of view, pointing out the additions and improvements to the previous prototype.

➤ The components of the architecture, revealing theoretical issues and practical details.

➤ The AI components used to handle these designs. Both extensions to the specification and customized functions are considered.

➤ An evaluation of the animat within a real game to reveal the improvements and analyze the technology.

At the end of this chapter, the animats not only have intelligent reactive behaviors, but realistic emotional responses to common situations.

Hierarchical Architecture Overview

Technically speaking, almost all the concepts are modeled with finite-state techniques—explained progressively in their own detailed section:

➤ Memories are gathered using statistics.

➤ Feelings are expressed as a nondeterministic automaton.

➤ Sensations are represented as fuzzy automata.

➤ Emotions are fuzzy-state machines.

➤ Mannerisms are selected by nested probabilistic automata.

➤ Moods are modeled with nested states.

The system is hierarchical in that many components depend on each other. There are also components included within others, as depicted in Figure 42.1.

Modeling Feelings

Because feelings are associated with categories of objects, the animats require a minimal memory to be capable of "feeling." In this section, we'll focus on feelings for other players as they vary from one character to another—unlike objects that have mostly constant benefits. Fascinating interpersonal behaviors could arise from this design.

Memory of Relationships

Players experience emotions while in close proximity with each other (such as anger or joy). These emotions could be remembered to express the feelings (for instance, as the average *anger* or *joy* value). However, a more compact approach only stores essential facts, and derives the feelings from them implicitly. This approach enables us to add feelings that are not necessarily emotions.

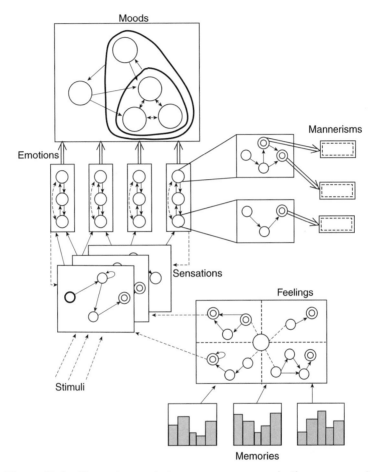

Figure 42.1 The system as heterogeneous communicating components.

Data is collected in a statistical fashion, although moving averages allow the trends to change over time (unlike a standard average where the results eventually converge). The following information is gathered over time:

➤ Damage taken and inflicted

➤ Number of shots fired and received

➤ Value and difference of the "kill counters"

This information is used to measure negative feelings (for instance, hatred). Positive feelings (for instance, attraction) are instead based on fixed properties such as gender. Such information is sufficient for deathmatch games, but could be trivially expanded to remember other little details.

Recognizing Feelings

The animats will be subject to four independent feelings: *pity*, *hatred*, *attraction*, and *disgust*. These are relatively easy to portray in the behaviors (especially in deathmatch games), and are sufficiently distinct from each other.

Each feeling is recognized by a finite-state automaton. The automaton uses the data collected about the players to decide what the animat's feelings are. For example, pity is triggered for large differences in the number of wins versus losses; hatred instead is felt for particularly accurate enemies (that is, high ratio of shots to damage).

Instead of keeping each finite-state automaton (FSA) separate, these are grouped into one large nondeterministic FSA (NFSA) for convenience. Nondeterminism allows the different automata to be merged together very simply, using (epsilon) ε transitions, as shown in Figure 42.2.

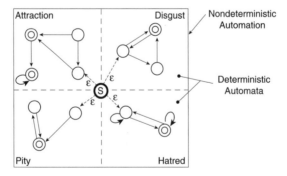

Figure 42.2   Four deterministic FSA connected into one NFSA to recognize feelings.

Additional feelings could be added very easily thanks to this mechanism. The FSA for the new feeling can be modeled separately, and grouped with the NFSA during the design. The subset construction algorithm described in Chapter 40, "Nondeterministic State Machines," can be used to factor out nondeterminism and create an FSA instead. Alternatively, the algorithm can simulate each NFSA separately to find all the feelings.

The feelings will mainly be used to generate new sensations. However, the feelings can be used by other behaviors as necessary—for example, selecting which enemy to combat.

Improved Sensations

The sensations in Chapter 39 were defined with a standard finite-state automaton. This caused problems by defining the sensations as Boolean values. This section extends the emotions with a fuzzy representation, and models sensations from sources other than the environment (for instance, from feelings and emotions).

Multiple Influences

Although perceptions are often the primary cause of changes in emotions, other aspects of the creature's state also cause mood alterations. The same concept of sensations can be applied to detect patterns in the emotions and feelings as well.

The source of the sensations can be fuzzy as well as crisp values. The stimuli and the feelings are in fact interpreted as Booleans. Emotions are also considered as fuzzy values in the next section. All these types are handled indiscriminately, resulting in fuzzy sensations that change smoothly over time. Note that at least some of the transition values need to be fuzzy; otherwise, the model becomes a particularly inefficient crisp FSA.

In essence, the following sources influence the sensations:

➤ The stimuli from the environment described in Table 37.2 (various game events— refer to Chapter 37, "Sensations, Emotions, and Feelings")

➤ The four feelings defined in the previous section

➤ The changes in the emotional state machine

Using sensations based on different aspects of the animat's brain increases the accuracy of the simulation, which may potentially improve emotional reactions.

Sensational Combinations

The sensations used in this model are defined in Table 37.1 of Chapter 37. They are surprise, anticipation, disgust, attraction, confusion, discovery, pain, and pleasure.

These sensations are modeled as fuzzy states of an automaton, very similar to the crisp counterpart in Figure 39.2 (refer to Chapter 39). Other intermediate states are also fuzzy variables.

The influences—whether from perceptions, emotions, or feelings—are considered as transitions in the fuzzy FSA (FFSA). These are handled indiscriminately by the automata, mostly passed by messages rather than queried.

Preventing Degenerate Automata

The crisp version of this automaton is fully event driven. The active state changes when matching stimuli are observed. When an accepting state is reached, the FSA is automatically reset. There are a few problems with this approach in the fuzzy model that stem from the simulation itself; all the states have degrees of membership, and need to be considered at all times. This implies that all the transitions need to be considered simultaneously, too. We need to take a few precautions with the FFSA version to ensure correct functioning (for instance, that the fuzzy values won't all become 0). It's possible to do the following:

➤ Force the initial state to have full degree of membership.

➤ Maintain the initial state to the opposite of the accepting states (a fuzzy equivalent to binary reset). Intuitively, high degree of membership values flow from the initial state to the accepting states.

Given these either of these solutions, the FFSA can be updated when a matching event is received. The asynchronous approach can be somewhat inconsistent (because the result depends on the messages received), so a synchronous approach seems a viable alternative. In this case, the transition strengths are determined over a small period of time (using messages), but the FFSA is simulated at regular intervals.

Accumulating Emotions

The prototype from Chapter 39 used a total of four complementary emotions. Because the emotions were interdependent, using more emotions would have caused the number of states in the model to grow exponentially. Instead, this section models each of the emotions separately, so adding emotions incurs a linear growth of states. We'll use the emotions listed in Table 37.3 (refer to Chapter 37); specifically, pride, shame, fear, anger, joy, sorrow, amusement, and weariness.

Complementary emotions are grouped together in a single fuzzy finite-state machine (FFSM), which acts as an accumulator, as depicted in Figure 42.3. finite-states are not typically suited as accumulators, but using fuzzy states resolves the issue. The FFSM is comparable to linguistic variables in fuzzy logic. For example, one finite-state machine will include three fuzzy states, two extremes, and the neutral emotion: amusement, weariness, and boredom.

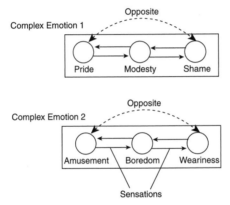

Figure 42.3 Two complex emotions made of three primary emotions. Sensations drive the state changes, and the complementary states are linked together by a "not" fuzzy relationship.

Each state in the FFSM is connected with transitions triggered by the fuzzy sensations. The transitions can be expressed as fuzzy rules; the target state value is the MIN of the source state value and the input condition.

As with the fuzzy FSA used to model sensations, FFSMs may degenerate, too. Using both synchronous and asynchronous approaches may lead to each of the fuzzy states becoming 0 if no precautions are taken. Similar to the tricks described for sensations, the fuzzy variables for complementary emotions are linked with fuzzy rules (both defined as the opposite of one other).

Revealing Emotions with Mannerisms

In the previous prototype, the senses and actions of the animats are degraded according to the emotional status. However, the emotions are often portrayed in a more explicit fashion, using quasi-subconscious behaviors (known as *mannerisms*). For example, a nonplayer character (NPC) may jump from surprise, insult the enemy with words and gestures, wave to a partner, or perform a celebratory dance.

In this system shown in Figure 42.4, the mannerisms are triggered by emotions. When an emotional state has a fuzzy value above a certain threshold, a nested FSA is called. This component is responsible for deciding which mannerism to execute—if any.

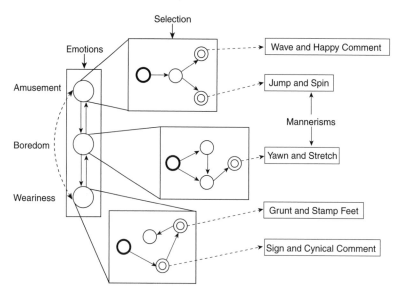

Figure 42.4   Primary emotions are potentially associated with a probabilistic FSA (PFSA) for selecting mannerisms.

The nested FSA is probabilistic. It provides diversity in the selection of mannerisms and enables the designer to control how often the behaviors execute (on average). The transitions are based on feelings (for instance, only insult an enemy who's hated) and recent events (for instance, wave if a teammate appears).

The mannerisms themselves can be implemented using almost any technique described so far. That said, the most applicable methods are rule-based systems, small scripts, or even native C++ code.

Mood Hierarchies

In the previous prototype, only combinations of primary emotions were represented. The architecture in this chapter makes the concepts of moods explicit, using separate finite-state machine component in the system.

The moods correspond to certain emotional patterns, such as cautious, complacent, entertained, depressed, or aggressive. Each mood corresponds to an atomic state in the finite-state machine. The transitions between these moods are determined by changes in the emotions. When the animat gets frightened, for example, it becomes cautious; animats show aggressiveness with anger and sorrow, entertainment arises from amusement and joy, and so forth.

When modeling the moods based on emotions, remember that many of the transitions—especially outbound ones—are similar to each other. This causes a spaghetti layout, which can be simplified with the concept of superstates; transitions from the super-states also apply to the nested states. This is demonstrated in Figure 42.5.

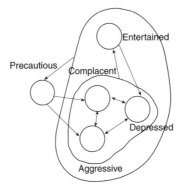

Figure 42.5   The five moods are defined as atomic states. The superstates around them reduce the number of transitions.

The moods are in fact used to store parameters for the senses and actions—as the emotions in Chapter 39. However, moods are also used to provide high-level biases for the reactive behaviors. For example, mood will influence the desires of the animat: Prevent damage when scared, inflict damage when angry, or minimize violence when happy. The moods provide preferences, but other AI techniques are needed to create behaviors that take these preferences into account. The next part of this book uses moods as guidance for a reinforcement-learning algorithm, creating behaviors that adapt near optimally to the desires. This chapter just prepares the emotional aspect of the system, ready for integration with high-level behaviors in Part VII.

Practical Demo

The animat illustrating this emotional system is known as *Remote*, with source code and guidelines for experimentation at `http://AiGameDev.com/`. The intelligent behaviors remain the same as in the previous example, but the subarchitecture for emotions is improved with a hierarchy. *Remote* demonstrates feelings based on memories, sensations about its own emotional state, as well as perceptions, and displays mannerisms as well as improved plausibility of the body simulation, not forgetting high-level mood biases.

Evaluation

The most significant addition to the model—mannerisms—makes an impressive difference to the realism of the animats. Most game engines randomly play different animation cycles to add variation to the default animations (for instance, looking around while standing still). The mannerisms provide similar breaks from the standard animations, although they are driven by higher-level patterns in the animat's state. Mannerisms also offer unique insights into the emotional state of NPCs, which are much easier to identify than the implicit parameters for senses and actions.

The fuzzy sensations and emotions also imply that the changes in the manifestations are much smoother (for instance, loss of precision aiming). This difference is hard to notice when playing the game, but a spectator observing the animats closely can recognize the changes in crisp emotions—whereas the changes in fuzzy emotion do not stand out. Overall, from a spectator's point of view, the emotions implicitly seem less mechanical and somewhat more believable.

From a technical point of view, the fuzzy-state machines can be difficult to handle. Whether updated every time an event is received or on a regular basis, there's always the risk of the fuzzy state values becoming 0. Precautions need to be taken to prevent degenerate FFSMs, and in-depth experimentation must check their validity and adjust the transitions.

Although each concept benefited from tailored models (for instance, FFSA for sensations, HFSM for the moods), the system generally suffers from heterogeneity. A simpler design reusing only one type of finite-state technique could recapture the essence of the design, with extra simplicity. That said, the different components were extremely useful as proof of concepts, and demonstrated increasingly complex hierarchical architectures.

Summary

This chapter modeled emotions using a hierarchical system of heterogeneous components:

➤ Memories of relationships are kept using moving averages for important facts.

➤ The separate FSA for feelings are grouped with nondeterminism, simplifying the model.

➤ Sensations are modeled as fuzzy automata, but are experienced as triggers from multiple sources.

➤ Emotions are similar to fuzzy linguistic variables, although changes are triggered by sensations.

➤ Mannerisms are called by nested probabilistic automata, which are activated when a threshold is crossed.

➤ Moods are modeled as hierarchical collections of states, used to reduce the number of transitions.

From a technological point of view, there are a few problems:

➤ The fuzzy state machines can be difficult to design, because particular combinations of events may cause degeneration.

➤ Customizing the system is a matter of exploiting the flexibility of the specification, and calling user-defined routines.

➤ The system as a whole is somewhat heterogeneous, and despite the advantages, a homogenous systems may prove to be a better trade-off between development and results.

As a whole, the emotional system improved the believability of the characters (mannerisms), and made the changes in emotions more realistic (fuzzy models).

The next chapter examines a concept that was exploited by the design of this emotional system: *emergent* behaviors. Simple interacting components generate complex patterns in the behaviors. Emergence is particularly important for game AI developers, because it can be so powerful and dangerous at the same time.

Chapter 43

Emergent Complexity

Emergence is a particularly popular topic in both the artificial intelligence (AI) and game-development communities. Emergent phenomena are particularly interesting yet somewhat mystical. AI researchers are keen to capture emergence properties to improve their intelligent systems, and designers are keen to increase the entertainment of their games.

As game AI developers, our interests lie in producing more efficient nonplayer characters (NPCs) with simpler techniques and producing more interesting behaviors. The combination of the emotional system with intelligent capabilities—generating fascinating scenarios—is a good example of an emergent system. We want to understand and reproduce such phenomena.

This chapter covers the following topics:

➤ The concept of emergence, its intricacies, and the different types of emergent patterns.

➤ The most popular example of emergence in games: behaviors at the individual and the collective level

➤ One particularly popular form of emergence that involves smart environments providing functionality to simple AI creatures

➤ The emergence of functionality as the general case, and various techniques from AI and modern software engineering to harness the power of chaos

First, a clarification of the concept of emergence is in order.

A Definition of Emergence

Emergence can be tricky to define, because capturing all the intuitive examples of emergence with a single plain-English definition is difficult. Here's a reasonable definition—even if overly generic:

> *Emergence* occurs when complex patterns arise from simple processes combined in a straightforward fashion.

A few examples help illustrate emergence in a more intuitive fashion. In each case, low-level rules cause patterns in the higher-level behavior:

➤ The movement patterns created by a flock of birds, a school of fish, or a group of cyclists. Locally, the individuals avoid each other while staying close, but the groups coordinate to flow smoothly around obstacles.

➤ The evolution of intelligence to increase changes of survival is a pattern that arises from the manipulation of genes.

➤ Neural networks produce high-level cognition from collections of simple neurons.

➤ Daily trading drives patterns in the economy.

➤ The flow of traffic based on the desire of individuals in their automobiles.

Although these examples provide insights into emergence, they also open up gray areas. The next section investigates these issues, and the following subsections present the types of emergence.

Clarification and Discussion

The primary notions behind emergence are common discussion topics in the AI community [Chalmers90].

Design Goals

Intuitively, many people associate emergence with patterns that arise unexpectedly—almost by magic. By this definition, if a designer tries to reach a particular result, it does not emerge. Patterns only emerge if they are indirect consequences of the design and its goals. Interestingly, this interpretation implies that only the first occurrence of the pattern is emergent. Voluntarily trying to re-create a pattern in the same way implies that it's no longer emergent.

For example, one might consider obstacle avoidance as an emergent approach to implementing navigation. (Simple steering behaviors combine together.) If the goal is navigation, however, some developers no longer consider steering behaviors as emergent.

Deductibility

A property of a system is only emergent if (a) it's not a property of the subsystems, and (b) it cannot be deduced from other properties. The problem is now about explaining *deduction*. In this context, emergent property is understood as a *nonobvious* combination of properties, instead of being completely *improvable*.

The emotional system from Chapter 42, "An Emotional System," obeys this rule; it's not possible to deduce how and when moods are manifested, but they can be understood by stepping into the emotional state.

Irreducibility

Emergent systems are often considered as irreducibly complex, which means that removing any component breaks higher-level patterns. When removing a component from an emergent system, major effects on the patterns should be observed. If there are only minor changes, the components are combined in a trivial fashion—and therefore are not emergent.

A navigation system that uses a combination of wall following and goal-directed obstacle avoidance to reach targets in space is irreducible. By removing either of the two sub-behaviors, the navigation policy can no longer reach arbitrary locations.

Complexity

It seems emergence requires a certain increase in complexity between the combined components and the final system. This jump in complexity implies that trying to understand the underlying rules from the final pattern is extremely difficult. As such, from an observer's point of view, it may be easier to understand the higher-level patterns rather than the lower-level ones (for instance, macroeconomics).

Types of Emergence

From a conceptual point of view, three distinct types of patterns are created by emergence:

➤ Phenomena that would take huge amounts of resources to reproduce otherwise

➤ Patterns that cannot be created otherwise

➤ Emergent results that have not been identified at design time

The first two types of emergence are beneficial in games; emergence allows some problems to be solved very efficiently, and provides unique solutions to complex problems. The third type of emergence results in creative new outcomes to situations, which can be both positive and negative in game development. Harnessing the power of emergence involves understanding how it happens in games. Emergence can be exploited in games in different ways, including emergent behaviors and functionality.

Emergent Behaviors

The most common type of emergence is visible in the behaviors at the individual level. Simple actions can emerge as follows:

➤ **Combinations** of separate actions form meaningful behaviors.

➤ **Sequences** of independent actions can emerge into complex patterns.

Arguably, much of the AI design is about emergence. Most of the components in the architecture are not aware of each other (transparency); they just provide an output. As this output is assembled, it emerges into purposeful behaviors.

Reaching a goal in space with reactive movement is an example of emergence by sequence (see Figure 43.1). The policy is to head toward the target while avoiding obstacles. If a turn of over 90 degrees away from the target is necessary, a wall-following behavior is engaged until the target is within a direct line again. This approach works for a majority of layouts—but not all.

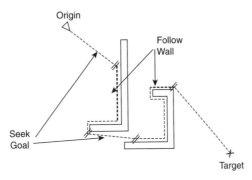

Figure 43.1   Emergence of goal-oriented movement using sequences of simple reactive behaviors.

An example of emergence by combination of actions is circle strafing. The two primitive actions are to look toward the enemy and to step sideways. Emergently, the pattern created is a circle around the enemy's location—ideal for combat behaviors.

Another example is the emotional system from the previous chapter; neither the emotions nor intelligent reactions could provide complex behaviors, but combined, they offer believable results.

Even high-level strategies emerge from straightforward tactics. For example, retreat when the enemy is dominating, locate items or weapons, and attack with the element of surprise. Even such reactive behaviors can match the levels of complexity of planned tactics in many cases.

As well as behaviors of individual creatures, emergence also applies collectively (a more popular definition of emergence). Groups of NPCs with simple behaviors can perform complex tasks together. Ants, for example, are particularly effective as a colony. In single-player games, combinations of different enemy types can be particularly tough to conquer as a group, despite being simple to defeat as individuals.

In large realistic worlds (for instance, simulations of small cities), the environment is so rich that each character has vast possibilities. Such designs leave room for emergence to create very interesting patterns—even with NPCs of fixed behavior. This can be somewhat problematic for designers, because the outcome can emerge to completely unforeseen patterns—which could become bugs!

Embodiment can help tremendously from this point of view. When the design of individual NPCs is biologically plausible, the higher-level patterns that emerge from the simulation are likely to be realistic—and therefore acceptable.

Smarter Environments, Simpler Behaviors

The previous example reveals the importance of the environment in creating emergent patterns. In fact, in some cases, the environment is the cause of the patterns, such as *Conway's Game of Life* [Conway70]. The environment is a grid, which defines the likelihood of cells surviving or dying in terms of their neighbors. Surprisingly complex patterns, both stable and chaotic, can arise from very simple rules.

AI engineers can exploit the importance of the environment to increase the functionality of their NPCs and simplify the design. An early trend in robotics was to enhance the test world, such as painting white lines on the floor or decorating walls with sensor-friendly materials. This allowed the robots to cope with simpler AI—hence smaller processors.

Nowadays, a popular trend in robotics research is pervasive computing, whereby rooms are filled with miniature interacting devices—sensors and actuators (for instance, detecting doors or shutters, controlling lights). These devices collaborate together and with local robots who emergently provide the expected functionality with simple signals.

As game AI designers, we have the luxury of manipulating virtual worlds in a much simpler fashion to assist the development of synthetic characters. There are two different aspects to consider: what information is available, and how to provide it.

Affordances

Not only can each object be used in a variety of ways, different players can also use the objects in various fashions. The objects are said to *afford* being used. For example, a door affords to be opened, a ladder affords to be climbed, and an item affords to be picked up.

A perceptual psychologist introduced the concept of *affordance* [Gibson77, Gibson79]. According to Gibson's theory, affordances are relationships between actors and objects.

These relationships exist naturally, regardless of whether they are desired, known, or even visible [Norman99].

Because affordances are *actionable* relationships, they only exist between actors that can perform an action on the object. For example, a door switch affords being pressed by humans only, but not by most mammals. So, affordances can be understood as being context dependent.

The Sims takes advantage of such ideas by placing smart furniture in the houses. Each avatar (that is, human-controlled game characters) can immediately tell what to do with each of the items in the world. More conveniently, the avatars know exactly what each item provides. Just like with the robots, this approach allows the AI to be much simpler because the environment provides additional hints about its functionality. The NPCs have simple reactions but rely on concise information, which together produce complex intelligent behaviors.

Associating affordances and functionality with items in the world benefits the development, because it prevents having to compute that information. But how should this information be provided to the AI?

Perceiving and Broadcasting

Affordances simplify the processing of the perceptions in the brain by modeling relationships between actors and objects. As we may expect, there are many possible implementations, each corresponding to different ways of organizing the data: perceiving or broadcasting.

In one case, the animats interpret their perceptions and associate them with the corresponding information. This approach is particularly suitable when players in the game have different capabilities and, therefore, different affordances.

Alternatively, the game engine can broadcast the affordances along with each of the objects. This approach is particularly appropriate when all the players have the same abilities, so the objects have the same affordances.

Once again, hybrid solutions are also very appealing. The animats can alert the game engine as to which affordances they are aware of, and the engine can broadcast them with the visible objects. This has the advantage of flexibility and convenience, providing an efficient solution while respecting principles of embodiment.

Emergence in Functionality

As a general case, it's possible for *functionality* to emerge from systems. Given a set of simple components connected together, the result is often more complex than a mere combination of its parts. With different interpretations of the definition, algorithms composed of multiple independent phases may be considered emergent.

We'll take the perspective that emergence cannot be foreseen, so it shouldn't be possible to devise an algorithm purely based on theory. However, we'll assume that emergence can be designed thanks to experimentation. This approach is more constructive because it means two things:

➤ Developers can harness emergence to solve problems.

➤ It's possible to adjust emergent phenomena.

In many ways, when complex reactive systems (or behaviors) are created, their functionality emerges by design. Game AI development can benefit from emergence in many ways, so any methodology that can help harness such chaos is welcome. In some systems, emergence is debatable, but the methodologies presented here apply equally to both scenarios.

Just as intelligence is an emergent phenomenon based on straightforward chemical mechanisms, many believe that complex software programs emerge from simple rules of the computer. Taking this software engineering approach provides practical insights into dealing with the development of AI—particularly how to craft simple reactive rules into complex behaviors.

Assembling simple components together to produce elaborate emergent functionality is a matter of engineering in different forms:

➤ **Architectural patterns** provide outlines for creating emergent systems with concepts that are likely to work. For example, both voting systems and the subsumption architecture are well suited to provide emergent patterns, but remain easy for the developer to adjust.

➤ **Design methodologies** provide methodologies to control resulting functionality. Agile development techniques match perfectly with AI creation, because it advocates evolutionary design to harness the chaos of the development process.

In practice, agile development is based on the following principles (although not exclusively limited to emergent patterns). Each principle is presented along with its benefits for AI:

➤ **Feature-driven** development focuses on important features desired by the customer. In game AI, the designers are the main customers; primary features are the forms of implicit control that need to be handled immediately. Secondary features are explicit behaviors required in particular situations.

➤ **Test-based** validation of the behaviors ensures that the system does not break as functionality is added. It also provides a measurement of progress. Each AI behavior can be tried by setting up a script with game logic and testing the result—as with evolutionary approaches. Minimal fitness is required for the test to pass.

➤ **Fast iterations** in the development build the functionality of the system incrementally. In AI, the engineer can focus on establishing the behaviors one by one, building up the system as an architecture (for instance, with a flat organization or a hierarchy of layers).

➤ **Extensive refactoring** is used to extract common functionality from each of the behaviors and place them into common components when necessary. By implementing the behaviors first, the interfaces to the components become obvious. The refactoring also keeps the code clean and maintainable, which makes it easier to debug and extend.

These procedures are considered part of *evolutionary design*. In this case, there's no planned design, but the functionality emerges incrementally. Evolution is thought to be the strongest way to create emergent patterns, and borrowing these methodologies can help us harness the power of emergence as game AI developers. The result is NPCs composed of simple components that interact with simple mechanisms to provide complex functionality.

Summary

This chapter investigated the concept of emergence and its presence and importance in computer games:

➤ Emergence is a phenomenon whereby combinations of simple rules cause intricate patterns.

➤ Intuitively, emergence is associated with patterns that are not expected, deductible, nor reducible, but with added complexity.

➤ Emergence can be the only way to create patterns, the most efficient way, or used as a means to find new patterns.

In games, behaviors are the most common manifestation of emergence:

➤ At the individual level, emergence can arise by independent combination or sequence of actions.

➤ Both behaviors and strategies can emerge in NPCs.

➤ The advantages in creating emergent behaviors lie primarily in efficiency, because reactive behaviors can be used.

➤ One particularly popular way to exploit emergence is to make the environments smarter.

➤ The objects in the world are associated with functionality and affordances.

➤ When the environment broadcasts this information, purposeful behaviors can arise from simple NPC reactions.

➤ The design of the AI is thereby greatly simplified.

Finally, it's possible to harness emergence generally by following certain designs and methodologies borrowed from agile development:

➤ Feature-driven development with extensive testing

➤ Rapid iterations with extensive refactoring

Creating complex NPCs using reactive behaviors is possible using emergence. The benefits are tremendous for game AI, and the methods described in this chapter will certainly help the engineer reach that goal.

Practical Demo

An animat known as *Penguin* illustrates the ideas in this chapter. *Penguin* has an extremely simple AI, but interesting patterns arise when it's placed in the world in large numbers. The animats notably gather to keep warm and run around in groups.

Part VI

Conclusion

Instead of using reactive techniques to model instinctive intelligence, this part shows how a plausible emotional model increases believability. The animats seem more life-like and interact in a way that's easier to identify with.

Retrospective Overview

The big picture is more obvious with this part finished, so a synopsis is in order.

Techniques

Finite-state machines are extremely popular in computer game AI, and justifiably so. Not only are they simple to design, they are also very efficient to simulate. As a control technique, finite-state machines are extremely versatile, although particularly well suited to modeling sequences of events.

Finite-state machines provide the capabilities of a transducer (converting inputs to outputs). However, automata are often disregarded; they provide the capability to accept and recognize regular sequences of characters in a very efficient fashion.

In cases where finite-state machines fail or lose simplicity, extensions are available to provide elegant solutions. Nondeterministic models allow numerous independent finite-state machines to be combined simply. Generally, tools are used to convert the model into a deterministic one. Probabilistic models add random variations to the results, which often leads to interesting behaviors. Both these extensions have little or no additional computational cost.

Fuzzy-state machines have the same benefits as fuzzy expert systems over crisp rule-based systems. Because each state is a fuzzy variable, fuzzy finite-state machines are often easier to handle using a fuzzy interpreter instead of extending the finite-state component. The benefits are visible, but the computational cost needs to be considered.

Hierarchical finite-state machines provide two advantages. They simplify the modeling of flat finite-state machines, but also allow nested components. The hierarchies can be built of heterogeneous components, as long as interaction semantics specify their relationships.

Behaviors

Although intelligence is an essential element for creating functional animats, *emotions* significantly enhance their believability. Therefore, they seem an essential component for computer games. Together, the emotions combine with the intelligent capabilities to create interesting emergent patterns.

Because the interaction with the world can be modeled near perfectly in virtual worlds, an approach that degrades the senses and actions is ideal—providing the widest range of effectiveness. Using a plausible emotional model as an underlying drive for the parameters leads to realistic reactions.

Using mannerisms to display the emotions makes a huge difference, contributing to the lifelike properties of animats. The mannerisms emphasize the mood of the creatures, causing the players to identify with them.

Generally, such emergent behaviors are an extremely powerful concept. Thanks to emergence, reactive techniques fail to reach the purposefulness of planned behaviors, appearing that way to the player. Evolutionary design and agile development practices increase the chances of reaching the desired "emergent" results.

Outlook

Because emotions make such an important improvement to the system, they are integrated with any new interface between the body and the brain—whether senses or actions. It's also important for different (cognitive) components in the brain to provide sensations, too (for instance, surprise when discovering objects).

Finite state machines are used ubiquitously in game AI, and there are plenty of reasons to use them in nouvelle game AI, too—notably as a phylogenetic (frozen) component to help manage the system. Therefore, finite-state machines can be applied as exercises to many other problems in this book.

Finite-state machines, however, are very static; they suffer from not being able to learn or adapt. Part VII of this book explores *reinforcement learning*, which can in fact be understood as a learning finite-state machines technique. The weights of the transitions are adjusted according to positive and negative feedback.

The moods created with the hierarchical finite-state machines are used to provide high-level guidance. In humans, emotions are often used to make high-level decisions about what to do, whereas intelligent abilities are used to bring these to life. The moods are put to use in the next part, as guidance for the learning algorithm in our animats.

Part VII

Action Selection

This is the final practical part, bringing together the best of all the previous chapters under the control of an adaptive AI. Many of the existing capabilities and behaviors were designed as standalone components, but can be reused in more complex architectures. The result is an animat capable of learning to play a game, one which most game producers would be proud to include in their engine.

Motivation

The overall aim of this part is to produce competent deathmatch behaviors based on each of the existing components. Fixed reactive behaviors are very satisfactory, but adaptive behaviors will keep the players on the edge of their seats.

Each of the capabilities developed so far have been relatively narrow, only capable of performing specific tasks. This part brings each of them together with a top-level component in the architecture. We'll show how (mostly) reactive components become very capable when combined.

As usual, the first prototype does not learn the behaviors, instead allowing the designer to specify the animat's strategies. The second prototype uses an adaptive learning technique. Both these models have advantages and pitfalls, and are compared with each other.

Outline

Chapter 44, "Strategic Decision Making." The first objective is to explain deathmatch strategies and analyze the roles of the environment and game engine. Then, we reintroduce decision making in the concept of high-level tactics.

Chapter 45, "Implementing Tactical Intelligence." Reusing capabilities from previous chapters develops a set of default tactical behaviors. A subsumption architecture is designed to integrate each of the behaviors in a coherent fashion. This provides a system that is easily controlled by the designers—and is therefore predictable.

Chapter 46, "Reinforcement Learning." The theory behind reinforcement learning is introduced in this chapter to remedy the limitations of the previous prototype and introduce adaptability at the same time. This chapter explains different algorithms applicable to game development in depth.

Chapter 47, "Learning Reactive Strategies." In this chapter, the reinforcement algorithms are applied to creating adaptive deathmatch behaviors. This is done in a modular fashion by decomposing the strategies into capabilities instead of reusing default tactics. This approach provides more flexibility and power for the learning.

Chapter 48, "Dealing with Adaptive Behaviors." Building on previous chapters that explain how to design learning AI, this last chapter in this part explains the most challenging problem: how to deal with adaptive AI that learns within the game. Tips and tricks are presented, as well as traps to avoid.

Assumptions

Although the technical requirements from the other parts still persist, the assumptions here are of a much higher level—closer to the nature of the game itself:

➤ The **purpose of the game** has been described using game logic and can be interpreted by the animats.

➤ Each animat has a **set of criteria**—expressed as moods—that determine what they want to achieve in the game.

➤ The animats can **compete against each other** in the game, for training and evaluation purposes.

➤ **Basic capabilities** are available and can be customized to produce different variations at will.

The first chapter in this part discusses these issues in greater depth during the analysis phase.

Chapter 44

Strategic Decision Making

KEY TOPICS

- Game Situation
- Personal Objectives
- Tactical Behaviors
- Animats and Decision Making
- A Training Zone

With specific capabilities in place, the focus can shift toward higher-level behaviors. This chapter combines the *analysis* and *understanding* phases of the AI development. A solid grasp of the decision-making process in the context of high-level strategies is necessary for manually reproducing human behaviors, as well as for developing a learning AI capable of adapting to deathmatch situations.

There's no need for specification of the world interfaces, because the higher levels of AI only depend on lower levels rather than senses and actuators.

The chapter covers the following topics:

➤ Factors in tactical decisions, some of which are used as features of the problem

➤ Objectives in the game, both global and personal ones

➤ Base components of tactical behaviors that are combined

➤ The decision-making process in the context of strategies

➤ A training zone that can be used for learning and evaluation

At the end of this chapter, the necessary elements are ready for a hard-coded solution to be developed (as well as a learning AI to deal with deathmatch games).

Game Situation

When making a strategic decision in a deathmatch game, players consider many aspects of the game world. The concepts behind both *factors* and *features* are introduced in greater depth in Chapter 22, "Fighting Conditions," which covers decision making for weapon selection.

Influential Factors

The most important factors in the decision are those depicting combat situations and the progression of the fight. Strategic decisions have an even broader scope than weapon selection, so additional factors of the game are considered.

Player State

Decisions are very subjective by nature. Aspects of the player's status play an important role in influencing the outcome. For example, both health and armor levels may affect tactical decisions, as do weapons and ammunition available. To a lesser extent, other items in the inventory may become factors of the decision.

Enemy Status

In deathmatch games, strategies revolve around the other player(s), too. Visible properties of the enemies, such as their position or orientation, contribute the decision because they affect the player's situation in the game. As well as the relationship between players and their situation in space, the observed weapons and estimated health can become decision factors.

Environment Layout

The terrain affects the movement of all players, as well as the projectiles. The layout of the world can serve as cover and secure an escape, but can also trap the players and make them vulnerable. The disposition of the items is space also affects the best tactic. As such, high-level decisions should take the role of the environment into account.

Features of the Decision

Although factors are aspects of the game that could potentially be taken into account, *features* are used as inputs to the problem. Features are relevant bits of information required to make the best decision. Different properties of the environment, situation, and progression of the combat are used as features in the decision.

A set of features can be considered as an array of floating-point values corresponding to the strength of the feature: $F = [f_1, f_2, K, f_n]$. This strength value is easily understood when constrained to the range [0..1]—interpreted as either a probability or plausibility (fuzzy degree of truth). The decision process can take into account either interpretation as long as all the values are consistent.

Personal Objectives

The global objectives of the game are established by design (for instance, destroy all aliens to prevent invasion, build and manage a city). These are neutral objectives that form the essence of the game. The game is often designed to assist the players in achieving these objectives—for example, using a mission briefing, tutorial, or inline help.

In many cases, however, the player has much freedom in the way the objectives are achieved (for instance, choosing paths and weapons in first-person shooters). In fact, some games enable the player to roam free of explicit objectives (for instance, in large-town simulations such as *Grand Theft Auto III*). There is always some freedom in deciding what to do and how to do it. This is the core of the gameplay experience.

For human players, the personal interpretation of the game's objectives is often instinctive, as if driven by feelings. Intelligent abilities allow the players to achieve their personal objectives, but responding to their emotions is usually the top priority.

In the previous part, high-level moods were modeled (for instance, aggressive and complacent). Desires and motivations can be derived from these moods. The examples in Table 44.1 serve as a basis for reinforcement-learning AI, developed later in this part.

Table 44.1   Example Moods and the Corresponding Objectives That Influence a
Player's Behavior

Mood	Personal Objective
Precautious	Look around and explore
	Proceed slowly
	Prevent self-damage
Complacent	Keep fight short
	Cause a lot of damage
	Move fast
Aggressive	No desire to collect armor or health
	Collect weapons and ammo
	Inflict most damage per second
Entertained	Use various items and objects
	Prolong the fights
	Curiosity, seek new sounds or entities
Depressed	Increase long-term kill probability
	Minimize actions
	Even stand still occasionally (camp)

The personal objectives can be considered in two ways, each with varying levels of abstraction. These desires can be expressed as follows:

➤ **Criteria** used by the AI to evaluate the fitness of tactical decisions manually

➤ **Fitness functions** containing the evaluation procedure for the behaviors—handled transparently from the AI itself

The criteria can be considered a particular way of implementing a fitness function. Again, this subject is discussed in more depth for weapon selection in Chapter 22.

In psychological terms, humans often use emotions as means for guiding and evaluating intelligent behavior. However, this process can be considered as a hierarchy instead; a higher-level component—sometimes known as a *reflective* process—could decide which criteria to comply with. The hierarchy is a way to interpret and refine goals in an intelligent manner. In classical AI, the layers usually correspond to planning algorithms, although reactive techniques would be equally appropriate. Emotions instead bypass this hierarchy by providing a suitable approximation, which proves more realistic rather than intelligent (and more efficient for game AI).

Tactical Behaviors

Fundamentally, strategies are composed of low-level actions, although it's more convenient to express them as tactical behaviors. Of course, behaviors are brought to life using individual actions, but abstracting out the actions simplifies the development of high-level tactics.

Tactical behaviors can be decomposed into independent actions—including movement:

➤ **Seek**—Move toward another player.

➤ **Flee**—Move away from a player.

➤ **Wander**—Move around randomly.

➤ **Stand**—Keep still.

Vision is one of the most important senses; players can look in different ways in different situations:

➤ **Look away**—Turn the view in another direction.

➤ **Focus**—Track a particular player.

➤ **Scan**—Look around the world.

➤ **Ahead**—View follows the movement.

When it comes to deathmatch games, the attack method is also important:

➤ **Violent fire**—Cause as much damage as possible.

➤ **Prevent self-damage**—Prevent losing health.

➤ **Increase probabilities**—Try to hit the player more often.

➤ **Decrease damage**—Enemy suffers little.

➤ **No fire**—Stop shooting.

Finally, gathering behaviors are considered useful in tactical terms:

➤ **Weapons**—Locate new arms.

➤ **Ammo**—Pick up rounds for the weapons.

➤ **Armor**—Find protection.

➤ **Health**—Locate medical treatment.

➤ **None**—Do not worry about gathering.

Specific tactical behaviors—such as hunting or escaping—can be expressed in terms of existing components providing functionality (for instance, movement or aiming). These can be created by customizing any AI techniques discussed throughout this book.

Animats and Decision Making

Conceptually, the tactical decision process is about mapping features of the game situation and criteria for the decision onto the desired behavior: $F \times C = B$; where $C = [c_1, c_2, K, c_m]$ is the set of criteria, and $B = [b_1, b_2, K, b_p]$ represent the possible behaviors.

Just as with the weapons, it's possible to assess the fitness of a behavior, given the features and criteria: $F \times C \times B \rightarrow R$. Indirectly, this allows the best behavior to be extracted, because we can compare the fitness of each behavior.

To determine these values in practice, various methods can be used. Deduction is used to combine fixed knowledge about strategies (for instance, ambushes are likely in a valley), whereas experience would learn from examples (for instance, this spot is vulnerable). These processes—along with hybrid combinations—are discussed further in Chapter 22.

Monitoring the performance of tactical behaviors is the major problem. Behaviors are executed over periods of time, so the criteria apply continuously. Therefore, the benefit of the behavior needs to be accumulated over time, converting incremental feedback into a fitness value for that period.

The animat's decisions also need to take into account the fact that behaviors will be executed over time, and their benefits may not be immediate.

A Training Zone

The ideal game environment used to test and evaluate high-level behaviors is a combination of all others. As usual, using multiple genuine worlds ensures that the behaviors developed will transfer straight into the real game. These environments should offer the following:

➤ Many weapons and items

➤ A variety of combat situations

➤ Different terrain layouts

By using accelerated simulation of the game, the AI will encounter sufficiently different situations, because of the unpredictable nature of most game designs.

Summary

The situations and the progression of the game are taken into account by the strategies:

➤ Factors of the decision include enemy status, player state, and terrain layout.

➤ Features are equations capturing these factors, used to model the problem. Features should represent concepts consistently within unit range.

Decisions need to be made according to various objectives:

➤ There are usually global objectives, but players have the freedom to interpret them according to their mood.

➤ Moods guide the intelligent behaviors by providing a fitness function, or criteria to evaluate performance.

The result of the decision is a tactical behavior, appropriate for the situation:

➤ Tactical behaviors can be considered as compositions of components.

➤ The existing functional components (for instance, movement or shooting) can be customized for each tactical behavior.

Another AI component is needed to bring all these concepts together:

➤ The actual decision-making process uses features and criteria to pick the correct behavior. This can be achieved with experience or deduction, or arbitrary combinations thereof.

The next chapter focuses on using this knowledge to create an AI with deathmatch strategies determined by design. The following chapters elaborate on this prototype by adding learning capabilities.

Practical Demo

The animat called *Ratty* uses the moods system as guidance for strategies. *Ratty* does not take these into account, but just tells other players what it's trying to do. The debugging log also reveals what criteria it's trying to satisfy. The binary is available on the web site at `http://AiGameDev.com/` with the source code.

Chapter 45

Implementing Tactical Intelligence

KEY TOPICS

- Crafting Tactical Behaviors

- Behaviors and the Subsumption Architecture

- Applying Subsumption to Tactics

- Evaluation

To reveal practical issues when creating deathmatch behaviors, a prototype must be designed manually. As usual, this provides a reference animat that potentially justifies the use of learning behaviors (if better AI leads to visible improvements). The design in this chapter does not aim to satisfy the emotions of the animat, but rather to conform to strategic patterns established by the engineer.

This chapter covers the following topics:

➤ Basic tactical behaviors that can be combined to form deathmatch strategies

➤ A description of the *subsumption* architecture in more detail, including a model based on finite-state machines, which simplifies to a layered approach conceptually

➤ An application of the subsumption architecture to provide deathmatch strategies with a behavior-based solution

➤ An evaluation of the solution in terms of performance and the design of the system

At the end of this chapter, the animats will be fully competent in the art of deathmatch combat.

Crafting Tactical Behaviors

Tactical behaviors are high-level components composed of primitive actions. Defining commonly used behaviors not only assists human engineers in developing strategies, but also simplifies the task of learning AI.

Reusing and Customizing Capabilities

Because most behaviors exhibit common functionality, each will depend on the components developed throughout this book (for instance, moving, shooting, or selecting weapons). This is shown in Figure 45.1. Although the behaviors depend on common functionality, the parameters passed to these components are customized as necessary.

Some of the behaviors do not depend on existing capabilities because they are trivial to handle without modularity (for instance, looking around). In the other cases, customization can happen in multiple ways:

> ➤ **Runtime parameters**—The interface is used to pass the custom information.

> ➤ **Initialization data**—Information is stored in XML and loaded from disk.

> ➤ **Wrapper component**—A simple component is used to simplify and customize the capability.

The tactical behaviors themselves can be created freely with any technique. Most behaviors discussed in this book are well suited to managing the functionality of nested components in a hierarchy. For example, finite-state machines consider nested states as dependent functions; rule-based systems depend on functionality to provide the body of production rules; scripts or native programming languages can be used.

Despite each of the child components being customizable, we'll assume that each of the behaviors can be called without any parameters (an `Explore()` function, in this case). Nevertheless, the behaviors can—and often will—be context dependent; the parameters will be gathered implicitly by the behaviors (for instance, query of the environment).

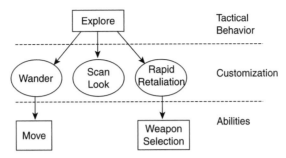

Figure 45.1 Hierarchy of dependencies with AI modules that are customized to provide specific functionality. The explore behavior relies on wandering movement, looking around, and selecting a weapon for rapid retaliation.

Sample Behaviors

Using the behaviors of human players as examples will assist the development of the AI. Neutral behaviors are analyzed first:

➤ **Explore**—Attempt to cover as much terrain as possible using sight, assisted by movement.

➤ **Investigate**—Move toward a point of interest in space and check the area.

➤ **Gather**—Collect armor and items that provide health as needed.

➤ **Wander**—Randomly patrol around a particular area.

In deathmatch games, offensive behaviors are needed to score points:

➤ **Attack**—Fire projectiles at the enemy.

➤ **Hunt**—Pursue enemies while assaulting them with weapons.

Naturally, there are defensive counterparts to these behaviors:

➤ **Dodge**—Move out of the line of fire.

➤ **Evade**—Avoid incoming projectiles and flee from the enemy.

➤ **Retreat**—Move to safety away from a danger zone.

It should be possible to combine these behaviors to produce satisfactory deathmatch strategies.

Behaviors and the Subsumption Architecture

The subsumption architecture provides a way for designers to organize independent behaviors that combine to produce the desired result [Brooks91]. This approach has the advantage that it's very simple to implement and remains fully predictable.

The subsumption architecture is known as an *arbitration* mechanism. The technique is used to select—or *arbitrate*—between multiple agents (for instance, behaviors or components) that compete over control for the same outputs.

Augmented Finite-State Machines

The subsumption architecture is based on a detailed process that involves creating intricate control networks. These are known as augmented finite-state machines (AFSMs), which are essentially finite-state machines with built-in timers that allow the state to change after a short delay [Wray94].

The inputs to the AFSMs are sensory values, and the outputs correspond to the effectors. When the inputs exceed a certain threshold, the AFSM is activated and an output is produced.

This approach makes it easy to manipulate the flow of information. Two techniques are used: *suppression* overrides inputs, and *inhibition* restricts the output. Multiple AFSMs can collaborate together using these mechanisms. This makes subsumption architectures well suited to controlling robots and animats.

Layered Approach

Despite being seemingly complex under the hood, conceptually the architecture is interpreted as a layered approach. Each layer corresponds to a behavior associated particular output. The behaviors are layered vertically; the ones at the top have the highest priority and have the luxury of subsuming layers with lower priority—as shown in Figure 45.2.

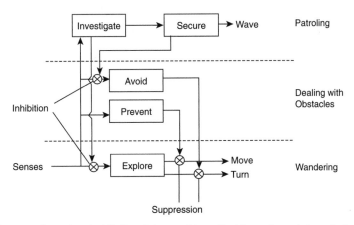

Figure 45.2   Layers of augmented finite-state machines that have been integrated with each other.

The layered approach also allows for simpler integration of existing components. Each layer can be considered as a black box whose output can be overridden by other layers. The passing of control between the layers can be understood as a Boolean condition.

Implementation and Optimizations

The implementation of an AFSM is very similar to a standard state machine, except there are timers built in that can trigger state changes. By using message-passing mechanisms as the transitions, inhibition and suppression are supported by overriding messages.

Because the behaviors are considered as components with a hidden implementation, however, we'll take a layered approach that does not depend on AFSMs. Instead, each level of the hierarchy can override the output of layers with lower priorities. This is implemented by a traversal of the layers, starting with the highest priority and traversing downward. When the component is active (that is, the condition is true), the output inhibits all other layers and the iteration stops. The output of the highest priority behavior is used as the action.

As far as optimizations go, the original model suggests that each layer is run asynchronously. With the layered approach, the traversal identifies the active behavior, and only that will be simulated. Also, during the traversal, common Boolean tests can be cached to prevent recomputation, and each of the lower layers can assume the higher-priority tests are false.

Applying Subsumption to Tactics

The process used to build a subsumption architecture is one commonly used in nouvelle AI, namely incremental development with testing. In fact, Brooks introduced this approach to robot design—similar to evolutionary design in the software engineering community.

That said, the subsumption architecture itself is not particularly simple to develop with incremental development, because it requires planned design. Without foresight, the entire architecture may need to be rebuilt if the wrong bottom layer is used. Because the flow of control is very linear, this imposes restrictions on the possible configurations.

A good complementary design strategy is needed to increase the likelihood of success initially, and to get around the limitations of the arbitration mechanism. The essence of the task is to sort the behaviors from generically applicable ones to the most specific. Understanding the general behaviors as applicable by default and the specific behaviors as exceptions helps interpret the role of the arbitration; when an exception to the default behavior is necessary, the subsumption architecture detects this situation and overrides the default.

In practice, we design the defensive behaviors as highest priority, and then the offensive behaviors, and finally the neutral ones. These are organized as in Table 45.1, with the highest priority behaviors on top.

Table 45.1   Layers of Behaviors That Are Activated with a Condition, Overriding All Other Behaviors with a Lower Priority

Priority	Behavior	Condition
7	Retreat	Low chances of winning
6	Evade	Incoming projectile
5	Hunt	High chances of success
4	Attack	Enemy present
3	Gather	Low health
2	Investigate	Possible enemy
1	Explore	*Always*

Evaluation

Once designed, the animat performs relatively well. In fact, the great advantage of systems based on subsumption—and other highly explicit AI techniques—is that they are very predictable; they execute the behaviors as expected.

The concept is so simple that little debugging is required; the conditions used to inhibit the outputs require testing for validity. The planned design actually works better than anticipated, mainly because of the fact that we're dealing with layers rather than AFSMs.

The subsumption architecture is relatively powerful, enabling the designers to achieve models that would be difficult with finite-state automata (for which many transitions are needed). However, despite being a hierarchy, subsumption has a linear flow of control. Together with this, the inhibition is done by Boolean conditions, so behaviors are triggered crisply. This is sufficiently realistic, but leaves room for improvement using smoother transitions.

As designed, the system does not separate the different components of tactical behaviors. It may be more appropriate to have different high-level controls for movement, aiming, and gathering, for example. This is not a problem with subsumption itself, but rather the way it was applied to this problem.

Practical Demo

The animat demonstrating these principles is called *Inhiboy*. It has a subsumption architecture with seven behaviors that inhibit ones with lower priorities. The result is a static deathmatch strategy that favors cowardly behaviors over brave attacks. The code and demos, as well as a guide for evaluating the behaviors, can be found on the web site at `http://AiGameDev.com/`.

Summary

The basic behaviors are the most important part of the system, and are designed manually:

➤ Tactical behaviors depend on existing capabilities, customized using wrappers while programming, by passing data at initialization or via runtime interfaces.

➤ Default behaviors combine different forms of movement with various ways of shooting and collecting items.

This chapter also covered Brooks's subsumption architecture in more detail to prepare for the implementation:

➤ The subsumption architecture is an arbitration mechanism, using a behavior-based approach.

➤ Fundamentally, behaviors are defined as augmented finite-state machines that pass messages and have timers for state changes.

➤ Behaviors are combined in layers, using suppression and inhibition points that interrupt and override messages.

➤ From a conceptual point of view, the vertical layers are prioritized with the most important behaviors on top.

Applying the behaviors is a matter of combining the components together with subsumption:

➤ Planned design can be used to organize the behaviors in order of importance.

➤ The condition under which the behaviors activate must be determined by the designer.

➤ The implementation scans each layer in order from the highest priority down until one is found.

The system performs very well, and predictably so. However, there are minor problems with Boolean activation. The control is somewhat limited by the default tactical behaviors, which combine basic elements. Finally, the fact that the system cannot learn is also a limitation. These problems will be remedied by redesigning the prototype using reinforcement learning discussed in Chapter 47, "Learning Reactive Strategies." But first, we'll cover the theory in the next chapter.

Chapter 46

Reinforcement Learning

The essence of playing games is to take the best action given the current situation. A *policy* expresses what should be done in each situation. Although the environment is usually nondeterministic by nature, most AI algorithms assume that underlying trends can be learned. *Reinforcement learning* (RL) is a collection of problems whereby the policy must be adjusted by trial and error, according to feedback from the environment.

Numerous problems can be modeled using reinforcement signals from the environment—for example, learning to aim, move, or even play deathmatch. Adaptation allows the animats to act in a more intelligent fashion without needing scripts or other designer assistance.

General optimization strategies (such as genetic algorithms) can be used to solve reinforcement problems, but they do not take advantage of the essence of the problem. Instead, specialized RL algorithms use the reward signal itself to learn the best policy in a more efficient fashion.

This chapter covers the following topics:

➤ The theory behind reinforcement models, and concepts such as states and policies, rewards and returns

➤ The common insights used by most reinforcement algorithms, notably the concept of state values that estimate the benefit of a situation

➤ The three major algorithms used for reinforcement learning, specifically dynamic programming, Monte Carlo, and temporal difference approaches

➤ The advantages and disadvantages of reinforcement learning used in game development

In practice, RL can be used in games to learn the best tactics based on trial and error. Intuitively, this can be understood as a learning finite-state machine, as covered in the next chapter.

Defining Reinforcement Theory

For reinforcement learning to be necessary, the problem needs to be modeled in a particular way, although only the concept of reward differs from supervised learning techniques.

In-Game Situation

Let's assume the animat is on the top floor of a level, and has the opportunity to throw a grenade down to the lower levels. There are three different gaps to drop the grenade, each leading to an explosion in a different room. Other players frequently traverse the three rooms. The traffic in the rooms varies from one second to another, but the statistics show there is a regular trend over time. So, at each point in time a constant probability is that one player will be present.

Sadly, as visibility is occluded, there is no way to check how many people are in each room at any moment. In addition, the animat has no experience or inside knowledge about the terrain, so it doesn't know about player traffic and the probabilities of rooms being occupied. The only way to check is to actually throw a grenade and listen for cries of pain!

If the animat has only one grenade, a random throw is the best thing it can do; at any time, it's arbitrary whether the room is occupied. If multiple grenades are available, however, the animat can learn to perform better over a period of time—specifically, attempt to cause as much third-party damage as possible. Therefore, the problem is to determine the best place to throw the grenade (that is, find the room with the highest traffic) to maximize long-term damage.

Reinforcement Model

This particular game scenario is one of many examples of a reinforcement problem. There is only one situation and a set of actions available to the animat. After an action has been executed, the environment immediately returns feedback about the result in the form of a scalar number.

The general architecture of RL can be adapted to other problems, as shown in Figure 46.1. Specifically, any situation in which a reward is given for particular actions is classified as an RL problem. This includes an animat learning actions according to a designer's wishes.

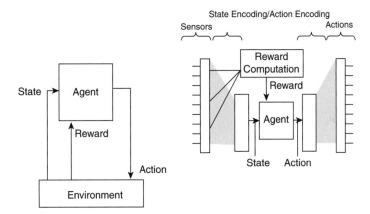

Figure 46.1   On the left, a typical model of the interaction between the agent and the environment. On the right, an embodied agent that uses a reward function created by the engineer.

States and Actions

In the grenade-throwing example, there is only one situation: "The animat is on the top floor with a grenade." Often, there are many more situations in a world. Each of these is known as a *state*. For each state, a set of actions is available to the agent. In the example, the actions were described as follows:

1. Throw grenade into the first gap.
2. Lob the grenade through the second hole.
3. Drop the grenade down the third shaft.

Naturally, in theory, there can be an arbitrary number of actions in each state. In game situations, however, we can expect there to be a reasonable number of actions in each state.

Reward Signal

After each action has been executed, the environment returns feedback immediately. This feedback takes the form of a scalar number, which can be understood as an evaluation of the action—hence the term *evaluative feedback*. The reward at time t is denoted r_t (both real numbers). Intuitively, a beneficial action has positive feedback, whereas a poor action has negative feedback. The range of the feedback value is in fact not important for the learning algorithms, as long as it can express the various levels of performance.

In our grenade example, the feedback could depend on the number of other players injured. If no players are hit, the feedback is 0 (not negative in this case). The feedback from the environment is also known as *reward signal*. The allusion to a signal implies that it can be monitored over time, as shown in Figure 46.2. Such graphs are found relatively often in RL, because with a quick glance they reveal the performance of an agent.

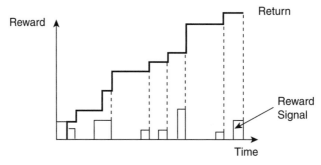

Figure 46.2 Graph of the reward values obtained over time. The return (accumulated reward) is superimposed.

In some cases, the reward associated with an action may not be immediate. This is called *delayed reward*—obviously! As long sequences of actions can lead to a goal, delayed reward is an important concept for most RL algorithms. The algorithms need to associate delayed reward with actions that lead to an immediate reward.

Behavior Policy

The purpose of learning is to find a good policy. A policy expresses what action should be taken in each state (such as where to throw the grenades). Because it's defined for every state, the policy is essentially a representation of the agent's behavior.

A policy is denoted π (Greek pi). A *stochastic policy* provides the probability of select-ing an action in a given state. Formally, it's a function mapping each state/action pair onto a probability p in the range [0,1]. Noting that $S = \{s_0, s_1 \mathrm{K}\, s_n\}$ is the set of all states, and $A = \{a_0, a_1 \mathrm{K}\, a_m\}$ is the set of actions, we have the following:

$$\pi: \quad S \times A(s) \to [0,1]$$
$$(s,a)\, \alpha \quad p \quad |\to (s,a) \in S \times A(s), p \in [0,1]$$

This definition expresses the policy π mapping the states and actions onto a unit range, for all ($|\to(s,a)$) valid states and actions. In many cases, not all actions will be applicable in every state. In this case, the policy is subject to a constraint that each action suggested is valid for the current state. The set of valid actions for state s is written $A(s)$ in the preceding equation.

Stochastic polices can be very useful as behaviors, but especially during learning. (For instance, it keeps track of the probabilities explicitly.) In some cases, however, a *deter-ministic policy* is more useful, notably when only the best action is needed for each state (and not the entire probability distribution).

$$\pi: \quad S \to A(s)$$
$$s\,a \quad \alpha \quad |\to s \in S, a \in A(s)$$

Generally, more than one policy is suitable for an animat within a game. However, one policy is defined as the target for learning. This is the optimal policy, written as π^*. The asterisk used as a superscript indicates optimality in RL theory.

Defining Optimality

Because a wide variety of problems can be modeled using RL, different kinds of results may be required, too. The final performance of the policy and learning speed are both desirable criteria in computer games. Let's look into the most common metrics for judging RL algorithms [Kaelbling96].

Optimal Return

To measure the performance of an agent over time, it's necessary to introduce the concept of *return*. The return is generally an accumulation of the reward signal over time. The agent's responsibility is to maximize the *expected return* at time t, denoted R_t. There are three principal ways to define the return, each leading to different behaviors.

➤ **Finite horizon** expresses the return as the sum of rewards within a certain time frame (in this case, bounded to the next h steps):

$$R_t = r_{t+1} + r_{t+2} + \mathrm{K} + r_{t+h} = \sum_{i=1}^{h} r_{t+i}$$

➤ **Infinite horizon** is not limited to a finite range (∞ denotes infinity). To limit the computation, a *discounted reward* is used instead; the further into the future, the less the reward affects the return. At each step, the reward is scaled by a power of γ (Greek gamma):

$$R_t = r_{t+1} + r_{t+2}\gamma + r_{t+3}\gamma^2 + r_{t+4}\gamma^3 + \mathrm{K} = \sum_{i=1}^{\infty} r_{t+i}\gamma^{i-1}$$

➤ **Average reward** models express the return in terms of the average of the reward over time. This can be understood as a special case of the infinite horizon model, except that $\gamma=1$ and the total is averaged:

$$R_t = \lim_{h \to \infty}\left(\frac{1}{h}\sum_{i=1}^{h} r_{t+i}\right)$$

The major disadvantage with average rewards is that no sense of time is included. A potential reward far in the future is just as important as the next one. The discounted reward is preferred instead.

Learning and Performance

Convergence is defined as reaching the optimal policy after a certain number of iterations (just as with optimization algorithms covered in Chapter 17, "Perceptrons"). Different properties of the convergence are used to measure the performance of learning algorithms:

➤ **Speed of convergence** is a popular measure of the algorithm's capability to learn quickly. Fast convergence means the optimal policy is reached very quickly, whereas slow convergence means the policy takes many iterations to improve. Most algorithms convergence asymptotically: very fast at first, and then infinitely slow as they get toward the optimal policy.

➤ **Convergence quality** is also an important measure of performance. However, it's not as common because most algorithms actually have proofs of convergence! So given enough time, these algorithms would perform in the same way.

It's often practical to visualize the convergence. We can do this by plotting the reward as a function of time in a graph. Generally, nonplayer characters (NPCs) in games need to learn both fast and accurately.

Markov Decision Processes

Most reinforcement learning problems class as Markov decision processes. In a Markov decision process, two additional concepts are defined; the probability of an action succeeding, and the expected reward. Assuming action a is taken from state s, the probability s' being the next state is written as $P_{ss'}^a$. Then, the expected reward is defined as $R_{ss'}^a$, although it doesn't matter what s' is, because the reward is independent of the next state (so it's really just R_s^a).

Both P and R are considered as the *world model*, because they define the environment and its typical reaction. There are two categories of RL problems: those where the world model is known, and those where it is not.

> **NOTE**
> There is a common background between finite-state machines and RL theory. In Chapter 40, "Nondeterministic State Machines," we studied probabilistic finite-state automata, with probabilities associated to each transition; these are classed as Markov chains. Probabilistic finite-state machines define probabilities for each output, and are considered as hidden Markov models. In RL problems, we have reward signals rather than outputs; they fall into the category of Markov decision processes.

Fundamental Elements

Each of the RL algorithms defined in the following sections relies on common insights to provide solutions.

Value Functions

All the techniques presented in this chapter—and most in RL—are based on the concept of *value functions*. Essentially, a value function is an estimate of the benefit of a situation. In practice, there are value functions defined for *states*, and for *actions* given a specific state, as shown in Figure 46.3. This allows RL algorithms to any reward signals to learn the policy, whether delayed or not [Sutton97].

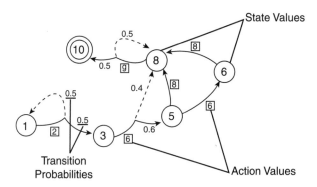

Figure 46.3   State values and action values drawn within the world model. Some transitions are probabilistic, denoted by dotted lines. The double circle represents a state where a reward of 10 is collected.

State Values

State values are an indication of how good it is to be in a certain state. (For instance, this bridge has a low value; it must be unsafe.) These values are generally defined as the expected return if the policy is followed from this state onward. The value of state s for policy π is written $V^{\pi}(s)$. Formally, it's defined as follows:

$$V^{\pi}(s) = E_{\pi} \{R_t | s_t = s\}$$

Remember that R_t is the expected return, usually defined as a discounted reward. E_{π} is the estimate of this return value starting given s as a start state at time t.

Action Values

Likewise, *action values* indicate the benefit of taking an action in a current state. (For instance, using an axe on a tank has low benefit.) These correspond to the expected return by following the policy π after taking action a from state s. The action value is also known as a Q value, and written $Q^\pi (s,a)$. Formally speaking:

$$Q^\pi (s) = E_\pi\{R_t \mid s_t = s, a_t = a\}$$

Because there are many actions per state, the action values require more storage than state values. Using Q values estimates the benefit of actions separately, whereas everything is considered together with state values.

Recursive Definition

One of the problems with the previous equations is that there's no obvious way of computing the estimated return E_π. This is the task of the various learning algorithms. However, the definition of state/action values can be reformulated to expose a recursive definition. This recursive property is exploited by most of the RL algorithms to compute the policies.

The intuition is that neighboring states also contain state/action values, so we can define a relationship between a state value and its neighbor's estimated return.

Using the transition probabilities and the expected reward, we can express the estimated return of a state. Assuming a discounted reward with coefficient γ, the following holds (see Listing 46.1):

$$V^\pi (s) = \sum_a \pi(s,a) \sum_{s'} P_{ss'}^a \left[R_{ss'}^a + \gamma V^\pi (s') \right]$$

Intuitively, the state value is the average of the discounted neighboring state values, including the reward collected by taking the action. The pseudo-code snippet in Listing 46.1 explains the equation in more practical terms.

Listing 46.1 Direct Application of the Preceding Equation, Which Can Be Used to Compute State Values

$P^a_{ss'}$ is the probability of action a leading to state s'
R^a_s is the expected reward for taking action a
γ is the discount factor for the reward (for instance, 0.9)
v is an array containing the state values

```
function state_value( s )
      s = 0
      for all actions a in state s
            action-return = 0
            for all possible states s' resulting from a
                  action-return += (R_s^a + γ * V(s')) * P_ss'^a
            end for
            s += action-return
      end for
      return s
end function
```

There could be an RL algorithm based on this equation. However, there are a few small details to be resolved—notably how to keep track of the various estimates.

Optimal Value Functions

The purpose of the learning is to find the optimal policy π^*, which acquires the most return over time. We've discussed this already, but now we can associate optimal value functions with it [Sutton97]. A policy π is better than another π' if and only if ($\Leftrightarrow$) the corresponding state values are above or equal, for each state $s \in S$:

$$\pi \geq \pi' \Leftrightarrow \forall s \in S : V^{\pi}(s) \geq V^{\pi'}(s)$$

We can also express the optimal state value as the maximal value, for all states:

$$V^{\pi}(s) = \max_{\pi} V^{\pi}(s) \quad \forall s \in S$$

Similar equations can define the optimal state/action value for each state/action pair, denoted $Q^*(s,a)$. These values are targets for all of the learning algorithms described.

Types of Reinforcement Problems

Reinforcement problems form a broad category. The can generally be classified into subproblems (for instance, episodic and incremental). In many cases, we can convert our problem to either of these options, depending on the preferences of the algorithm:

➤ **Episodic** learning problems are composed of multiple training instances. These correspond to training runs, which last a finite amount of time. Each episode corresponds to a short sequence of states and actions, as well as a reward signal.

➤ **Incremental** problems form one continuous set of states. There is no pause in the problem, and there is no end, either!

In game development, it's generally appropriate to use incremental learning within the game (online), and episodic problems during the development (offline).

Exploration Versus Exploitation

Reinforcement problems present a perfect example of a fundamental problem to learning AI. When do we assume we've learned enough, and start using what we've learned? Two different strategies are in opposition, as shown in Figure 46.4:

➤ **Exploration** attempts to cover all the possible states by trying every action. This gathers essential experience for learning algorithms.

➤ **Exploitation** instead uses the best-known action at each stage, trying to collect the most reward. This strategy confines itself to the domain of actions known to be valuable.

Often, these two strategies are combined into policies that are used during the learning. For example, ε-greedy (pronounced "epsilon greedy") policies use the best-known action, but make a random choice with a probability of ε. This is a special case an ε-soft policy, where the probability of each action $\pi(a,s)$ is at least ε divided by the number of actions in this state $|A(s)|$:

$$\pi(a,s) \geq \frac{\varepsilon}{|A(s)|}$$

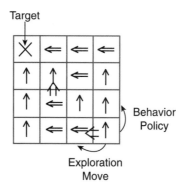

Figure 46.4   The behavior policy in a 2D grid, where the actions lead to the top left. Double arrows denote exploration moves that diverge from the learned behavior.

The concept of exploration and exploitation enables us to identify two types of learning algorithms: those that depend on the policy chosen to learn the optimal policy, and those that don't. These are known as on- and off-policy algorithms respectively:

➤ **On-policy** methods use the same policy for exploration and exploitation. Most on-policies guarantee that no actions are ignored (a.k.a. ε-soft policies). The algorithms for evaluating this policy typically depend on this precondition to produce the right results.

➤ **Off-policy** algorithms instead separate the exploration and exploitation. Both phases are generally done separately, each with its own policy. The policy for exploration is called the *evaluation policy*, and the one for exploitation is the *behavior policy*.

In brief, the policies chosen are influent factors for the quality of the learning as well as the final behavior.

Learning Tools

The algorithms presented in the next section make use of similar techniques, as well as the common definitions already provided.

Bootstrapping

Bootstrapping is the process of updating an estimate based on another estimate. This can prove useful during learning because it can improve the quality of the estimates over time. In RL, bootstrapping can be used to optimize the state values. Intuitively, it's possible to estimate how good a state is based on how good we think the next state is.

In contrast, nonbootstrapping techniques learn each state/value separately, without using estimates of neighbor states. Both approaches have been shown to have their own set of advantages, and there are numerous algorithms based on either (for instance, temporal-difference learning).

Backup

Backup is the process of using future return to estimate the expected return of the current state. So the return is percolated backward from any point s_{t+h} in the future toward state s_t we want to evaluate. The backup process can be seen as a treelike structure, spanning out from the current state [Sutton97]. This tree has different properties, as shown in Figure 46.5:

➤ The **depth** of backups can vary. There are backups of depth one that use state values from the next state. Backups can also have full depth, going all the way to the end of the problem!

➤ The **breadth** of backups is also an important parameter. Some backups only percolate the return from one state; these are *sample backups*. Other approaches perform *full backups*, the return from all the states are used.

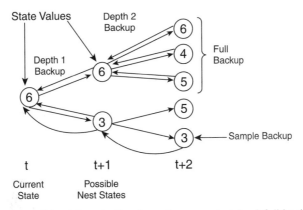

Figure 46.5   A tree of possible states starting from the current state. A full backup uses the state values of all the children, and a sample backup only checks one child branch.

The backing-up process usually works from one state value to another. However, this can also apply to action values, too.

Reinforcement Learning Algorithms

There are three major types of algorithms based on mathematical models, statistics, or incremental learning.

Dynamic Programming Techniques

Essentially, there are many brute-force approaches—based on dynamic programming (DP)—for computing policies and state values. Despite being exhaustive, they prove surprisingly efficient. DP works in two phases; the first estimates the state values of the states based on the policy (policy evaluation), and the other improves the policy using the state values (policy improvement) [Sutton97]:

➤ **Policy evaluation** essentially uses iteration to solve a large system of equations. These equations express each of the state values in terms of each other—using the recursive definition. The algorithm itself goes through all the states, and computes equation from Listing 46.1 exactly as described.

➤ **Policy improvement** uses the state values to investigate better suggestions. Intuitively, checking for actions that lead to improved return does this. If the estimated action value is higher, this action improves the policy, so we use this action instead.

Taking a popular example with a 2D maze, the policy evaluation computes the distance of each square from the exit, and the policy improvement tries to change individual steps to reach the exit quicker.

One thing to note is that DP solutions rely on knowledge of transition probabilities $P_{ss'}^{a}$ and expected rewards $R_{ss'}^{a}$ (from state s to s' given action a). Let's look at two ways to combine these separate phases into algorithms for computing ideal policies.

Policy Iteration

This method works by alternating phases of policy evaluation and policy improvement. This is an iterative process—as the name suggests—which continues until a convergence criterion is met.

The initialization is done by assigning suitable estimates to states (for instance, 0) and randomly picking any policy. Then, phase 1 evaluates the policy by computing the most up-to-date state value (see Listing 46.2).

Listing 46.2 Knowing the World Model, Policy Iteration Can Be Used to Compute the Value of Each State (The loop terminates when the updates are small enough. The state value estimation function from Listing 46.1 is used.)

```
repeat
      max = 0
      for each state s
            old = V(s)
            # compute the new estimate for this state
            V(s) = state_value( s )
            # check if it was improved
            max = MAX(max, ABS(old-V(s)))
      end for
until max < threshold
```

Then, to improve the policy, we check all the actions to see whether there is a better one. Both algorithms in Listing 46.2 and 46.3 are within the same larger loop, interleaving computation until the policy is stable.

Listing 46.3 Policy Improvement Is Used to Scan Each State, Checking Whether There Is a Better Action to Be Taken

```
π is a deterministic policy suggesting one action per state
Q is the value for each state/action pair

stable = true
for each state s
      previous = (s)
      best = -∞
      # determine if any other action is better than the current
      for each action a
            value = Q(s,a)
            # if this action offers an improvement, store it
            if value > best then
                  best = value
```

```
            π(s) = a
        end if
    end for
    # determine if this iteration was stable
    if previous != π(s) then stable = false
end for
if stable then halt
```

The policy iteration terminates when no changes are made to the policy. Note that throughout the iterations, only one array is used; V is necessary for storing state value estimates. In some implementations, the next iteration is stored in a separate array. This requires more memory and takes longer to converge, so one array is often sufficient.

Value Iteration

Value iteration is a simpler algorithm because it does not interleave phases. Both are handled together by evaluating and improving state value estimates at the same time. The policy is only computed after the value iteration has finished.

The pseudo-code in Listing 46.4 assumes that all the estimates of the state values in V are worse than the optimal value. (That is, $V(s) \leq V^*(s)$.) This relatively easy to ensure, and simplifies the code somewhat. If this is not possible, we need to compare the action values among each other, and assign the best to the state value (instead of comparing the action values to the current state value). After the iteration has finished, a policy evaluation can generate the corresponding policy (which should be close to optimal).

Listing 46.4   Value Iteration Algorithms Improve and Estimate the State Values at the Same Time

```
repeat
max = 0
# process all the states to improve the policy
for each state s
    old = V(s)
    # check all the actions for possible improvements
    for each action a
        value = Q( s, a )
```

```
            # update the estimate if necessary
                if value > V(s) then V(s) = value
        end for
        # remember the magnitude of the adjustment
        max = MAX(max, ABS(old - V(s)))
end for
until max < threshold
```

Intuitively, this corresponds to updating the value of squares in 2D grid one by one, checking the neighbors for better paths.

Monte Carlo Approach

Monte Carlo (MC) methods attempt to learn the optimal policy using experience, unlike the DP approaches that rely on a model of the problem. To do this, MC methods take an episodic approach, where multiple state/action sequences are processed.

Overview

The Monte Carlo technique relies on episodes to find the optimal state values. Because the outcome is known for each episode, the discounted return for each state can be computed *exactly*. However, we want to be able to take into account the probabilistic nature of the problem. For this we need to run through many episodes, and collect statistics for each of the runs.

Monte Carlo methods learn the expected return using these statistics. In fact, the average of the discounted returns from each episode is an accurate estimate of the state value. The more examples we have, the more accurate the final estimate. The optimal policy can then be derived from the estimated returns. Figure 46.6 shows another grid world example.

Algorithm

The pseudo-code in Listing 46.5 assumes we know about the transitions in the world model, so we only need to learn the state values. This is a simple example that is relatively common in games, and also is quicker to learn. A more ubiquitous variation could estimate the Q values for state/action pairs. This would just require replacing each occurrence of s with (s,a)—adapting the data structures accordingly.

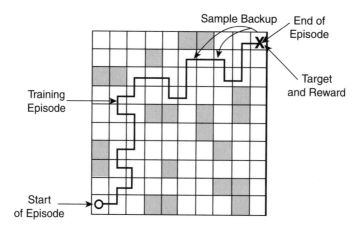

Figure 46.6 A training episode in a simple 2D world. The Monte Carlo technique backs up the expected return from the end of the episode, right to the start.

The first stage of the algorithm is to generate an arbitrary episode given a policy. This returns a sequence of states, and the corresponding rewards encountered. The arrays containing the expected return are initialized to 0 (see Listing 46.5).

Listing 46.5 A Single Pass of the Monte Carlo Approach (The episode has already been generated using a variation of the policy π.)

```
h is the length of the episode
state is the array of states representing the episode
reward is the reward collected at each time step
expected is an array containing the sum of estimated returns
total is an array of integers counting the number of estimates

return = 0
# start at the end of the episode and traverse backwards
for t from h down to 1
        # determine the current state
        s = state[t]
        # accumulate the return and add the reward
        return = reward[t] + return * discount
        # collect statistics for the return of s
        total[s]++
        expected[s] += return
        # and store the current estimate
```

```
     V(s) = expected[s] / total[s]
end for
```

The main loop of the algorithm starts at the end of the episode and runs through each of the states. A running total of the return is kept, and the estimates of each of the states is updated.

Episode Generation

One question arises: How are the episodes generated? The key concept is to make sure that all the state/action pairs are traversed. This is important to ensure optimality. One way to do this is known as *exploring starts*. The idea is that we can generate episodes according to any policy, as long as the first state/action pair is chosen randomly (again, with a good random-number generator).

This is proven to work, but it can be a bit slow. A good policy is to start with random exploration at first, and then decrease the randomness as the results start to improve. This is similar to controlling the temperature with the Boltzman equation in simulated annealing (discussed in Chapter 17).

Summary

In terms of RL algorithms, the Monte Carlo method can be classified as follows:

> ➤ **No bootstrapping**—The estimates of the state value are computed using statistics over many runs, so we don't rely on estimated returns of neighboring states.

> ➤ **Sample backup**—The algorithm does not traverse all the adjacent states. Instead, the randomized episodes imply one arbitrary path is chosen through the states.

> ➤ **Full-depth backup**—MC must wait for the outcome of the episode to determine the return. This return actually includes all the states. When the state values are updated, they take into account the backup all the way from the end state.

Monte Carlo is well suited to problems where no world model is available. The simulation is sufficient to gather statistics. It can take some time to go through enough episodes. Also, some additional memory is needed to store an episode while it is being processed. This makes the approach well suited as an offline process. It is also simple to use on local areas of the state space, so it can be combined elegantly with other approaches.

Temporal-Difference Learning

Temporal differences can be seen as a hybrid approach between DP and MC. It can learn from experience using bootstrapping to estimate the value of states, and benefit from backup to learn quicker.

Concepts

The notion of temporal difference is at the heart of the solution. Instead of waiting until the end of an episode to adjust the estimate, we use the estimates in the next state. From one point in time to another, there may be a difference in the expected return. We can use this temporal difference (Δ_t) to update the estimate:

$$\Delta_t = r_{t+1} + \gamma V(s_{t+1}) - V(s_t)$$
$$V(s_t) \leftarrow V(s_t) + \alpha \Delta_t$$

The second equation expresses that the current reward $V(s_t)$ can be adjusted by the step Δ_t scaled by the constant α (alpha). The step Δ_t itself is the adjustment toward the target estimate; that's the discounted return estimate $\gamma V(s_{t+1})$ of the next state and the reward r_{t+1} collected during the change of state.

The advantage of this approach is that we can learn the policy online, not using an exhaustive dynamic programming approach. This also implies we don't need a world model. The expected rewards are integrated in the learning, and the transition probabilities can be optionally learned (but can be assumed, too).

Algorithm

There are two simple algorithms using temporal-difference learning. *Sarsa* is on-policy because the algorithm relies on the same policy for learning and exploration. On the other hand, *Q-learning* is off-policy because the chosen actions do not affect the learning. (Behavior and control policy can be considered separate.)

There's very little difference between the two algorithms. Both algorithms learn the action values for each state (that is, the Q values). Both use a backup of one deep. However, Sarsa uses a sample backup (only using one Q value to update estimate), whereas Q-learning uses a full backup (all the Q values from the next state are used to update the current estimate). We'll study the Q-learning algorithm because it is the most commonly used, offers better quality learning, and does not rely on a specific exploration policy (see Listing 46.6).

Listing 46.6   The Q-Learning Algorithm That Improves the Estimate of the State/Values Using Full Backup

```
α is a small constant as the learning rate
γ is the discount factor

while learning
      execute action a
      collect reward r
      determine new state s'
      best = -∞
      # scan each of the actions from the new state
      for each a' in s'
            # remember the best only
            if Q(s',a') > best then
                  best = Q(s',a')
            end if
            # update the value of the previous state/action pair
            Q(s,a) += α * (r + γ * best-Q(s,a))
      end for
      # process the next state
      s = s'
end while
```

It's possible to estimate the state values in a very similar fashion, although the algorithm would rely on the transition probabilities from the world model. The learning may be quicker because the Q-values collapse into one state value, but less precise.

Advanced Issues

Given the many different concepts involved in reinforcement learning, it's not surprising that there are many intricacies present in most algorithms.

Approximators

So far, we've assumed that the value estimates—both for states and actions—are stored in an array. This representation has the advantage of allowing most algorithms to converge to the perfect policy. However, a significant amount of memory is necessary, making the approach unsuitable for large problems.

The matrix can be considered as a function estimating the value of states or actions. As such, it's possible to use function approximators to compute a similar result. Perceptrons and decision trees are commonly used for this purpose.

The most effective solution to the problem is to learn the exact estimates using an array, and then to try to approximate it. This would be best suited as an offline computation, because it requires two phases of preprocessing. The advantage is that all the correct data is immediately available, allowing the approximator to achieve the best possible results. The approximator can then be used online as a compact representation of the huge matrix.

Alternatively, the approximator can be the base representation used for learning. Ideally, the technique should be suited to incremental learning—like perceptrons. This approach is slightly trickier and requires more thought. The major problem is that the proof of convergence of most algorithms goes out the window. So obtaining the right results becomes a rather more empirical process.

Hierarchies

Hierarchical solutions have also received a lot of attention recently. One benefit is to divide the problem into levels of problems. The smaller problems are solved first, and then more complex problems are solved using these building blocks. Like hierarchical finite-state machines, the idea is to abstract out common problems and reuse them in a modular fashion [Humphrys 97, Dietterich98].

In most cases, experts handcraft the hierarchy. So it's the engineer who is responsible for simplifying the state/action space of each component, and assembling them together in a convenient fashion. Then, standard reinforcement learning techniques can be used to learn the state/action mapping.

Discussion

Reinforcement learning has benefits and pitfalls in the context of game AI development.

Advantages

Reinforcement learning is based on an extremely simple concept: the reward signal. It usually requires very little effort to express the problem as reward and punishment. Then, it's just a case of modeling the state and actions, and the reinforcement learning can start (easily achieved in computer games). This makes RL an extremely flexible technique.

Given a representation that does not approximate the estimates, most RL algorithms will provably converge to the ideal policy. Naturally, the simulation will require some time, and good exploration of all the state and actions is needed, but the quality of the results still converge asymptotically.

There are different varieties of reinforcement learning algorithms. They can deal without world models if necessary, learning the transition probabilities or expected rewards. However, the algorithms can also make the most of the world model when it is available.

Disadvantages

The naive approach of using a matrix to store the action values scales poorly in terms of memory consumption. Algorithms using a backup depth of one also scale badly in terms of computation. The very nature of "backup" means that numerous forward iterations are required for the reward to eventually reach all the states. This makes it particularly unsuitable for dynamic environments.

The use of approximators is a viable solution in many cases, but the proof of convergence no longer applies. This can lead to unpredictable behaviors and unexpected results, which require much experimentation to resolve.

The reward/punishment paradigm can be surprisingly difficult to work with. For example, expressing humanlike behavior is not something that can be done easily with positive or negative rewards.

Summary

There are fundamental principles that define reinforcement learning problems:

➤ The world is broken into states with different actions available.

➤ Upon the execution of an action, evaluative feedback is received from the environment and the next state is observed.

➤ Some algorithms rely on knowing the probability of reaching another state given an action, and the average expected reward.

➤ The accumulation of reward (discounted over time) is known as the return.

➤ The policy expresses which actions should be taken in which state, either as a probability distribution or as a single action (deterministic).

Using the concept of state and action values, algorithms can be used to determine the benefit of each situation. There are three major RL approaches:

➤ Dynamic programming relies heavily on mathematical knowledge of the environment, updating all the estimates as a set of parallel equations.

➤ Monte Carlo methods use many random learning episodes, using statistics to extract the trends. Full-depth backup is used to propagate the reward from the end of each episode.

➤ Temporal-difference learning techniques update the estimates of state incrementally by using the value of neighboring states (bootstrapping).

Each of these techniques is applicable in different context. The next chapter uses a temporal-difference learning approach to provide adaptive strategies for deathmatch games.

Practical Demo

The animat demonstrating the theory in this chapter is known as *Inforcer*. It uses various forms of reinforcement learning in different parts of the AI architecture. *Inforcer* benefits from having a modular reward signal, which isolates relevant feedback for each component. If learning happens uniformly, the early behaviors are not particularly realistic, but do reach acceptable levels over time.

Chapter 47

Learning Reactive Strategies

This chapter uses adaptation to find the most suitable deathmatch strategies. A variety of reinforcement learning (RL) algorithms are used as tools to craft behaviors automatically. This still requires involvement from the AI engineer, but the role involves designing software instead of implementing it. From a designer's point of view, this new system is easier to adjust implicitly but somewhat harder to control explicitly. From the point of view of gameplay, the RL approach allows adaptation, which provides interesting challenges for the players.

The next few pages cover the creation of an AI architecture to learn high-level behaviors, according to evaluative feedback (that is, the moods).

This chapter covers the following topics:

➤ The practical and theoretical reasons for splitting up the problem into components

➤ The gathering behaviors optimized using immediate reward only, and collection of statistics to estimate the return

➤ How the type of movement is learned using Q-learning, which deals with delayed rewards by improving estimates based on others

➤ An episodic learning algorithm that estimates the benefit of shooting styles at the end of each fight

> ➤ Reasons for *not* using reinforcement learning on other simpler capabilities

> ➤ Testing of the system in a game world and an evaluation of the results from a technical perspective

This chapter creates a fully working reactive animat, using reinforcement signals to adapt its behavior.

Decomposition by Control

Reinforcement learning algorithms are generic tools for finding the mapping between states and actions. They can be applied to learning deathmatch strategies by associating situations with the right behavior. The entire problem could be handled using a single table storing a probabilistic policy, indicating the estimated return for each state/action. Each type of RL algorithm is capable of dealing with this problem successfully.

One major problem with having a large number of states and actions is that the learning happens more slowly. Additional iterations are required to find a suitable policy. As such, splitting up the problem is advantageous from the point of view of computation and memory consumption.

Furthermore, the use of parallel RL means that multiple actions may be dealt with. All the algorithms discussed in Chapter 46, "Reinforcement Learning," are capable of selecting only one action and distributing the reward accordingly. Handling multiple parallel actions and splitting the reward is an active problem in RL research. To get around this issue and deal with tactics made of multiple components, the system requires the use of default behaviors (as discussed in Chapter 45, "Implementing Tactical Intelligence") that are called upon by the RL algorithm—as shown in Figure 47.1.

Splitting up the problem allows the RL algorithms to tackle each component of the behaviors separately, which inserts more flexibility into the design. Any combination of capabilities may form tactical behaviors, and the AI will adapt to find the most suitable approach. This is depicted in Figure 47.2.

In this chapter, we assume the problem is split up into components. Each component controls a different part of the animat, so the decomposition is based on the outputs. It is worthwhile noting that memory consumption may be similar in both cases, because the state space could be designed identically in both cases. The advantages lie in simplifying the reinforcement problem itself.

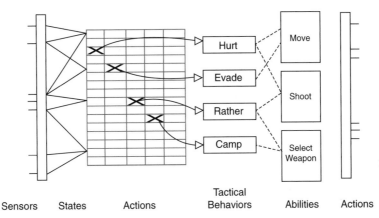

Figure 47.1   A single mapping from state to action used to select the appropriate tactical behavior.

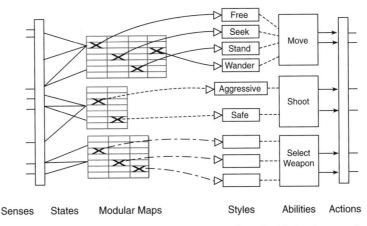

Figure 47.2   Multiple RL algorithms deal with components of tactical behaviors, each corresponding to specific outputs.

As well as decomposing the behaviors into separate capabilities, it's also possible to split the reward signal, distributing it to the components as appropriate. For example, the reward associated with collecting items is sent to the gathering component, and the reward for enemy damage is sent to the shooting component. This is known as *modular reward*, in contrast with *holistic reward* signals (which include all forms of feedback together).

The major advantage of modular reward signals is that the feedback is highly accurate and relevant to the task at hand, reducing the amount of noise present.

The next sections discuss the different learning components individually:

➤ Desire for gathering objects

➤ Types of movement

➤ Shooting styles

➤ Other capabilities, such as selecting weapons

Each is handled using different RL algorithms.

Adaptive Gathering Behaviors

The gathering component of the tactical behaviors is responsible for deciding which type of objects the animat needs to collect. The decision is based on the feedback, which depends on the animat's moods.

Actions

The RL algorithm learns the most suitable actions. In this case, the actions correspond to the possible types of objects that can be gathered: armor, health, weapons, ammo, or none. The empty action is excluded from the learning; instead, it is selected by default if none of the other actions have a positive benefit. The other component learning types of movement are responsible for determining whether gathering is necessary. (For instance, if the health and armor are almost full, gathering may not be worthwhile at all.)

States

All RL algorithms require state variables to learn the policy. For gathering behaviors, the state mostly represents the current inventory: ammo available, number of weapons, health, and armor levels. These factors determine whether it's possible to collect items, but the moods determine whether the animat "feels" it's important. As such, moods are also included in the state used by RL.

Reward Signal

The reward signal is mainly based on the collection of items. If an item affects the player, it's likely there will be some form of reward. Depending on the mood, the reward may have different values. (For instance, health and armor seem insignificant to an angry player.)

Learning Policy

The gathering mode is chosen at regular intervals, triggered by a reward signal (that is, an object is collected) or after a certain amount of time elapses. The learning is achieved with a simple statistical technique. To update the estimate of the return, the reward is added to the total reward accumulator, and the variable counting the number of samples is increased. The estimated return is the total divided by the number of samples (that is, the average).

During learning, a new action is chosen stochastically, with probabilities proportional to their estimated return. When the learning is satisfactory, the gathering behavior may include multiple modes simultaneously (for example, gathering health and armor at the same time).

Modeling Movement

Different types of movement can be used in deathmatch situations. A *Q-learning* component is responsible for mapping the situation to the right type of movement, with the reward signal based on the moods and success in the game.

Actions

The actions correspond to the different types of movement. These include stand, explore, and gather when no enemy is present, but include pursue and evade during combat. Each movement type may be executed at a different speed, so a walking and running variation could be made available. This increases the size of action space, however, so speeds will only be included if there are practical benefits.

States

The definition of states consists mostly of high-level features representing the state of play. For combat, features include the predicted outcome, the current trend, and the physical capabilities for continuing the fight. These are designed by experts to take into account multiple details of the current situation. The state also includes information about the environment when a fight is not active (for instance, nearby sounds).

Reward Signal

The evaluative feedback is based on the outcome of fights (for instance, death, survival, or a kill). Various other events are also considered, depending on the mood (for instance, damage inflicted, fight time, and terrain explored). The reward signal is accumulated over time, but is discounted at regular intervals. Small discounts of few percent (around 10 percent) are used to emphasize recent experiences.

Learning Policy

Unlike the gathering behaviors, the learning for movement must cope with discounted rewards. To achieve this, the reward is propagated from one state to another as time goes by. (This is known as *backup* of depth 1, common in Q-learning.) Because Q-learning uses the estimates of previous return values to compute the value of the current state, it uses *bootstrapping*.

The reward signal is discounted and accumulated over time until the state changes. Then, the value of the previous state is updated based on the current state value.

Learning Shooting Styles

The weapon selection—and shooting behaviors to a lesser extent—can be adjusted to satisfy different requirements (for instance, based on effectiveness or the moods of the animats). This is achieved with an RL approach based on statistics and learning episodes (a.k.a. Monte Carlo; see Chapter 46, "Reinforcement Learning").

Actions

The possible actions selected by the learning algorithm correspond to styles of shooting and weapon selection. For example, common requirements are high damage per second, better hit probabilities, prolonged fights, and highly lethal first shots. The RL algorithm learns the most suitable style for each situation, which is then passed to the respective capabilities.

States

The choice of the states reflects the reward signal, because we want the states to have accurate value estimates. Therefore, the moods are the primary parameters of the state, because the reward—and hence the policy—changes from mood to mood. However, some aspects of the reward may not be subject to moods (for instance, death). So, other strategic features of the situation are included in the model of the state—as for the movement component. This allows the RL to find the correct styles based on moods and other general trends.

Reward Signal

The reward signal is only active during fights, specifically when the animat is firing projectiles. This allows the animat to distinguish between a poor reward from inactivity and a poor reward from unsatisfactory performance (which helps the learning). The reward signal is usually determined by the moods, but some aspects of the reward are independent from emotions (such as the basic desire for survival).

Learning Policy

Shooting styles are selected at regular intervals when a fight is active. The learning is episodic, so the estimates are only adjusted when the fight is over (and the fight usually finishes with extreme reward values, either high or low). All the states and rewards gathered during the fight are processed, and the estimated return for each action is updated accordingly.

Other Capabilities

The moving, shooting, and gathering capabilities are exploited using learning algorithms. These benefit from adaptive AI because the most suitable combination of skills can be found automatically—without the designer's direct involvement. When it comes to other behaviors, such as looking around (for instance, focus or scan), learning does not have any advantages. It's much easier to express such capabilities in terms of the moods, without any form of adaptation.

Reinforcement learning would be suitable for the task, but requires setting up a reward signal and setting up the states and actions. The time overheads outweigh the benefits. Not overusing technology in this way is one way to deal with adaptive behaviors, but this topic is discussed extensively in the next chapter.

Evaluation

Because the learning occurs at a very high level, the resulting behaviors are acceptable regardless of their optimality. So long as animats make consistent decisions, the tactics do not stand out (that is, no hesitating every other second). In the heat of the game, suboptimal moves often go unnoticed from the player's point of view. That said, some exploratory decisions are easily spotted by the trained eye, or an attentive spectator.

On the whole, learning has a tremendous effect on the performance because an animat that has undergone training will easily beat a randomly initialized animat. This is particularly surprising because the animats are mostly optimizing according to their moods—although they do have an implicit notion of performance.

Developing the reinforcement model takes at least as much time as manually crafting behaviors with a subsumption architecture. This is the case even if the learning algorithm has already been implemented. Reinforcement theory is surprisingly simple in code (barely more than equations), and most of the engineer's time is spent adjusting the state/action model with expert features.

Surprisingly, the reward signals do not require much adjustment. The reward signal generally defines the desired behavior implicitly, and the learning algorithm finds a more explicit way to achieve it. For this reason, the reward signal needs to be adjusted by the designer if the behavior is invalid (during the application phase). In this particular case, however, the final behavior is not precisely defined as an "optimal" strategy. Instead, we expect the behavior to emerge from the way the emotions were defined. This more flexible attitude implies that less work is needed, but it's also much harder to reproduce existing strategies with this approach (for example, if the designer wants the animats to exhibit a particular tactic).

Training offline is a good way to hide the learning phase from the human players. However, a minimal amount of validation is necessary to support online learning. Specifically, a good policy needs to be chosen that sacrifices exploration for the sake of exploitation. The policy can be mostly learned offline anyway, removing the need for exploratory moves that give the learning away.

Whether offline or online, the system is unlikely to get stuck in the same state doing the same actions. The emotions are driven independently and change over the course of time. When the animat performs similar behaviors over a small amount of time, the boredom will increase—among others. This means the current state for the reinforcement will change automatically, causing a different action to be chosen.

Despite the various details that must be adjusted and tested, the learning system has a tremendous advantage over the one designed manually: It can adapt to trends in the game. This produces varied gameplay and a more flexible AI that can deal with the enemy better. Because of the way the problem is modeled, however, only general tactics can be learned; no individual patterns can be learned. Reinforcement learning is statistical by nature but could deal with such a problem if the state were modeled comprehensively (that is, with a world model that includes individual patterns). This requires more memory, computation, and learning time, so a planning approach may be more appropriate to countering individual strategies.

From a technological point of view, Q-learning is really simple to implement because it requires no world model (matching the pseudo-code in Chapter 46). The Monte Carlo variation needs a little more code and memory to keep track of the states encountered during the fight. Any dynamic programming approach would take much more effort here, because the transitions and reward probabilities would need to be gathered beforehand.

The system benefits from being decomposed by capability, because learning is faster when dealing with compact representations. There is some redundancy between the movement and shooting capabilities because the states are the same, but keeping them separate allows them to be updated at different frequencies.

Practical Demo

The web site at `http://AiGameDev.com/` offers further insights into the programming behind this system. The animat is known as *Darth Mole* and comes with a guide to launch it within the game. The AI is capable of adaptive deathmatch strategies using a combination of components that are learned from reinforcement.

Summary

The top level of the architecture is decomposed into capabilities that control different parts of the output, which results in the following benefits:

➤ Speeds up the learning by reinforcement and reduces the memory usage

➤ Provides more flexibility in the behaviors instead of relying on default tactics

➤ Avoids the problem of executing multiple actions in RL by separating actions and splitting the reward signal

Each component essentially learns a specific capability based on mood and other information:

➤ Gathering behaviors learn which type of object is desirable based on the inventory status. Statistical analysis is used to estimate the benefits of each object type by collecting immediate feedback (that is, no delayed reward).

➤ The movement component uses expert features specific to the situation to determine whether to pursue, evade, or perform other neutral behaviors. Q-learning allows the algorithm to take into account delayed reward.

➤ The shooting styles (for instance, aggressive, accurate) are learned with an episodic algorithm. Data is gathered during each fight, and the estimates are updated at the end. Expert features about the fight are also used.

➤ Other capabilities are not learned, because they are handled better with standard programming.

Because learning is high level, the decisions have more effect on intelligence of animats than their realism (which remains good throughout the adaptation). Of course, performance is poor before the learning starts, but the results are noticeable after a few iterations. It takes a few precautions before using the system to learn online (for instance, select an appropriate policy). However, most of these are included in the design (for instance, expert features, compact representation). The next chapter looks into the problem of dealing with adaptive behaviors in more depth.

Chapter 48

Dealing with Adaptive Behaviors

In each part of this book dealing with learning technology, prototypes that adapt to solve the problem online are presented. These situations are particularly tricky, and specific solutions are required to deal with them. Building on Chapter 35, "Designing Learning AI," this chapter unravels the problems with adaptation and introduces tricks to deal with them.

This chapter covers the following topics:

➤ The different kinds of problems with adaptive AI, each with its own symptoms and corresponding diagnostic. Possible remedies are presented briefly in the first section.

➤ Particular solutions from software engineering, providing a foundation for analyzing and dealing with adaptation.

➤ The important role of design in terms of adaptation. Modeling the problem is discussed first, along with feedback mechanisms—which are particularly difficult to deal with. Specific architectures are also appropriate to cope with online learning.

➤ Development methodologies that reduce the problems with adaptive AI.

The tricks presented in the next few pages are applicable to most other systems that need to achieve adaptation effectively.

What's the Problem?

Before discussing ways to prevent or cure problems with adaptive AI, we must first identify them. Picking out problems involves a combination of external observation and analysis of the internal workings of the system.

No Learning

Symptom: Learning does not occur, or happens inconsistently.

Example: The decision tree for weapon selection usually selects the weakest weapon, despite better alternatives being available.

Diagnostic: The model or the implementation is (partly) broken.

Remedy:

➤ Debug the code and design.

➤ Verify the source code, comparing it to the theory.

➤ Validate the model by step-through analysis.

Uncontrollable

Symptom: The learning does not match specific results, or degenerates over time.

Example: The reinforcement learning animat does not retreat when it has low health, but instead attempts heroic attacks.

Diagnostic: The system is not equipped to reliably provide the desired control.

Remedy:

➤ Use explicit ways to control the learning with supervision.

➤ Design an architecture to deal with the control problem without learning.

➤ Limit learning to other subsets of behaviors or actions.

➤ Decrease the learning over time as performance reaches satisfactory levels.

Suboptimal

Symptom: Learning does not reach the perfect result.

Example: The average error of a neural network used for target selection is high.

Diagnostic: The design does not assist the adaptation; the system relies on optimality.

Remedy:

➤ Design the system such that suboptimality is not a problem.

➤ Provide hints to the learning by example (supervision) or guidance (feedback).

➤ Model the problem better so it's easier to find the best solution (for instance, expert features).

Unrealistic

Symptom: The behaviors are not realistic enough during the adaptation or at the end of the learning.

Example: Learning to aim causes the animat to spin around in circles for a few seconds.

Diagnostic: There is too much to learn; the policy is not designed for realism; the actions are inappropriate.

Remedy:

➤ Learn as much as possible offline.

➤ Select a better policy that rewards safe exploration and exploitation.

➤ Design the actions at a higher level to reduce the unrealistic combinations.

Solid Software Engineering

To expand on each of these solutions, the first set of tricks that help deal with adaptive behaviors belong to software engineering.

Reliable Programming

When creating a learning system, it's critical for the algorithm's source code to be robust. Programming errors cause much grief during testing because they are difficult to isolate. Therefore, spending additional time to validate the AI code and reduce the number of bugs is a good investment. This can be achieved with unit testing procedures, among others. Then, when a system fails to learn or produces suboptimal results, the code itself is never under question; the accusing finger points to the design without hesitation.

Testing and Debugging

Debugging code can be achieved using standard tools, such as gdb or Visual Studio's integrated debugger. When it comes to testing the AI, however, it's often more convenient to have visual debugging aids. This may include a console or colored primitives within the game (for instance, lines, circles, or boxes).

In addition, a log file proves extremely practical as a dump for AI data in a format that's easier to read and search with text editors (an old favorite among game developers in general). The log may enable an AI developer to deal with bugs that occur on machines of other members of the development team.

An even more robust tool would track and store each of the AI's actions, storing them for later analysis. One of the advantages of this type of subsystem is reproducibility. Each of the AI's actions can be retraced right from the start, so the exact cause of problems can be identified.

In the AI, pseudo-random numbers will often be used to generate the behaviors. Instead of logging each action, the seed of the pseudo-random–number generator can be set to a particular value. With careful implementation of the engine, the simulation will always be exactly the same given identical seeds. This allows any bug to be reproduced with less effort and smaller log files.

A good random-number generator is absolutely essential for AI development, especially for learning systems. Faster and less-predictable alternatives to the default `rand()` are freely available (such as the Mersenne Twister). By setting a random seed every execution of the game, different situations arise during the game's development—stochastically testing the various aspects of the implementation. Such unpredictability often reveals more bugs in the software. The seed can be set deterministically when the game is shipped if necessary.

AI Engineering

The AI software engineer uses more tools than normal programmers. These vary depending on the techniques used, but testing the general performance of learning is useful in most cases. A tool used for such would test the learned model with all the data collected to see how well it performs. This information can be used to perform cross-validation: using part of the data set to see how well the learning algorithm generalizes.

One particularly useful tool will automatically extract the performance of the algorithms over time, and display it as a graph. In fact, it's very practical for the developers to analyze aspects of the learning with visualization packages. Instead of letting the developer format the information in Excel (possibly using macros), command-line tools such as gnuplot are often a better choice because they can be fully automated and easily called from scripts.

Robust Design

Although engineering provides a robust platform for learning and tools to analyze the result, it's the design of the system that solves most of the problems.

Modeling

Successful learning systems are based on strong understanding of both the problem and the solution. Chapter 21, "Knowledge of the Problem," and Chapter 28, "Understanding the Solution," cover this issue in depth. When it comes to adaptation, there are particular ways to deal with problems by modeling the system differently:

➤ The learning can be isolated to small aspects of the behaviors, which are easier to develop and debug.

➤ The search spaces can be left simple and smooth, which increases the speed and effectiveness of learning.

Assisting learning algorithms with expert features helps tremendously from this point of view.

Fitness and Reward

When the learning is not supervised, fitness functions and reward signals define the problem—but can be a surprisingly large source of grief. Learning based on feedback is particularly difficult to achieve realistically and reliably. When done right, however, the design of such feedback mechanisms can assist the learning in many ways:

➤ Smooth functions help learning algorithms by providing continuous and consistent feedback. The noisier these functions, the harder the learning task.

➤ To increase smoothness and provide more hints to the algorithm, reward signals and fitness functions can be set up using levels of magnitude. Essentially, multiple factors are involved in the feedback, and each is scaled according to its importance. Important features will have high weight but will be harder to reach, so simpler features with lower-weight coefficients are used to guide the learning in early stages. This is discussed more in the next chapter, because it benefits AI systems in general—and not only adaptive systems.

These tricks certainly minimize the disadvantages of learning by feedback over supervised techniques.

Architectures

An AI architecture is capable of combining learning components—or fixed components—to provide the desired behaviors. For example, the learning component can be overridden using a subsumption architecture. The essential actions are identified and provided by fixed components while the rest is learned.

Another useful architectural pattern is to provide a fixed component to supervise the adaptation. This can be understood as a learning manager (sometimes referred to as a *critic*); it can adapt the learning rate, verify that key learning examples are not forgotten, or it can determine when the learning algorithm needs to process new patterns.

Methodologies

In addition, different methodologies can increase the likelihood of success in projects based on learning:

➤ Incremental learning allows separate components to learn in separate stages. Simple behaviors are learned first, and then they are frozen while more complex components learn.

➤ To deal with adaptation, learn as many components as possible offline. Only the changes to the default behaviors need to be learned online.

To prevent overfitting and any other forms of degenerate learning, precautions can be taken:

➤ Only learn examples that are unacceptable—adapting the representation so the result becomes acceptable. By loosening the criteria defining valid results, the system will not be as accurate, but will allow better generalization.

➤ Decrease the learning rate over time to maintain consistency. This *cooling schedule* can take into account the system's performance.

Generally, the designer has the most control by trading off exploration and exploitation. Policy adjustment may improve system performance and reliability.

Summary

Adaptive AI can be difficult to deal with because it may not learn, it can be hard to control, it can look unrealistic, and it may be suboptimal. The first set of solutions comes from software-engineering methodologies:

➤ Validate the implementations of the AI techniques to remove any doubt of bugs.

➤ Provide visual debugging aids and standard tools to express AI data in a convenient fashion.

➤ Guarantee reproducibility by using a seeded random-number generator, or by logging all the data.

➤ Use randomized seeds at each execution to test the AI with a variety of different parameters.

➤ For each AI technique, implement tools that can test learning performance (for instance, cross-validation).

When it comes to modeling the system, some designs are better suited to adaptive AI:

➤ Keep the learning localized, splitting it into components when possible.

➤ Reduce the size of search spaces and keep them as simple as possible.

➤ Use fitness and reward functions that are as smooth as possible to provide hints to the adaptation.

Certain methodologies are useful to control the adaptation:

➤ In the game, incremental learning occurs in stages; different aspects of the system are learned separately.

➤ Offline knowledge provides assistance to online adaptation.

➤ Control the adaptation with a learning rate that decreases as performance increases, and not processing when the results are satisfactory.

By combining these tricks, designers can deal not only with adaptation, but they can make it an essential part of the system.

> **Practical Demo**
>
> *Dafty* is an animat that contains many learning components that almost work. *Dafty* attempts to learn capabilities covered in this book with a different approach, but fails. In each case, different tricks from this chapter can be used to identify and repair the problems. The problems are design issues, not implementation bugs.

Part VII

Conclusion

As the last practical application of AI technology to deathmatch games, this part brings together all the existing capabilities within the same architecture. This produces a believable animat capable of rivaling human players in a realistic fashion. Such worthy rivals provide more entertainment to players than bots using classical game AI.

Retrospective Overview

With each of the components in place, it's easier to understand the characteristics of each technique and behavior.

Techniques

The subsumption architecture is a popular approach for implementing robot control. Despite all its limitations, it has many advantages for game developers, including explicit control and design simplicity.

Reinforcement learning is a type of AI problem. Reinforcement learning is applicable to a wide variety of designs, because evaluative feedback is powerful. However, the very concept of reward is also awkward in some situations. Specific algorithms are needed to take into account the reinforcement signal and adapt the representation accordingly. Because reinforcement problems are very broad, there are also many types of algorithms—suited to many designs.

Dynamic programming techniques are very efficient and applicable during the game development. They rely on accurate models of the world. On the other hand, Q-learning techniques are capable of dealing with adaptation during the game—without any knowledge of the environment.

The representation used for reinforcement learning is a mapping from state to action. An array allows the learning to converge to the perfect result, but consumes large amounts of memory. Various forms of abstraction are needed to speed up learning and reduce memory usage—at the cost of accuracy.

Behaviors

The deathmatch behaviors created are effective enough to challenge even the best human players. Because the tactics are a high-level component relying on existing capabilities, the result appears realistic regardless of the quality of the strategy.

Subsumption has the advantage of being designed explicitly, making it easier to adjust. Reinforcement learning finds behaviors suitable for the animat's mood, but could be adjusted to find optimal tactics.

The accumulation of reactive components produces a system that can rival a planning solution—even to the trained eye. Animats with such reflexes are suitable as deathmatch opponents, especially with adaptive skills. However, there are cases that the reactive behaviors cannot handle because of the lack of strong world models and deliberative thinking.

Outlook

Reusing customized capabilities has developed the reactive deathmatch behaviors. This particular system was achieved using common design patterns. These issues are discussed in the next part, which covers reasons to replace components with techniques based on planning and the need for a world model.

Part VIII

Summary

Chapter 49

Game AI Engineering Principles

KEY TOPICS

- Architectures
- Implementations
- Techniques and Their Applicability
- Learning and Feedback Mechanisms

Traditionally, AI techniques focus on very narrow problems; they struggle to solve many problems outside of their intended domain. This weakness is not so much an inconvenience as it is the essence of AI. To get around the limitations, or—from another perspective—to maximize the benefits of AI technology in game development, specific patterns are very helpful. In both design and development, AI patterns provide essential guidance that can save tremendous amounts of time and improve the final system.

Useful principles occur often in game AI development at different levels of the system. This chapter regroups and summarizes the important ideas presented throughout this book.

This chapter covers the following topics:

➤ Architectures common in state-of-the-art game AI systems

➤ Implementation hints to save the developer time

➤ The applicability of each technique, common problems, and possible solutions

➤ Learning systems, and hints on how to design the feedback functions

Such tricks help developers tackle unique problems in their own games.

Architectures

AI architectures allow focused techniques to be assembled together to produce behaviors and capabilities. As levels of intelligence need to scale up, architectures will play an increasingly important role in the development of commercial game AI systems.

The idea behind patterns is to provide guidance for custom architectures using proven designs (reminiscent of software engineering). This book presents a variety of different AI architectures, but most are based on the same pattern. This pattern results from a modular approach that abstracts the common functionality as reusable capabilities, and provides behaviors that are convenient to experiment with.

AI Modules

At the lowest level, AI techniques are encapsulated modules. By abstracting out the implementation behind common interfaces, the techniques themselves become transparent and interchangeable. Therefore, the AI engineer can design the architecture first, and afterward decide which technique is used to provide the functionality.

Many of the AI techniques discussed in this book can in fact provide very similar functionality, such as pattern recognition, regression, or prediction. This includes neural networks, finite-state machines, or rule-based systems, each of which can provide control or problem-solving facilities interchangeably. Because of the tremendous flexibility of such technology, it can be easily reused in many parts of the architecture.

Capabilities

A common set of practical capabilities provides tremendous assistance when creating the illusion of intelligence. For example, movement, shooting, and weapon selection are capabilities. Each of them is a component built upon the AI techniques—generally only one.

There are two different ways to implement the capabilities to make them readily available for nonplayer character (NPC) development:

➤ **Customized components** provide the correct capabilities by passing specific data to the AI technique during the initialization. The capabilities are particular instances of the AI modules.

➤ **Dependencies** allow the capabilities to be implemented as independent components that provides their own interfaces, but that depends on AI modules.

The capabilities have the advantage of being conceptually independent from others, so they are very easy to develop.

Behaviors

The higher-level components provide distinctive behaviors, such as hunting, evading, and camping. Each of these behaviors can be built almost trivially when relying on the capabilities.

Because game AI is based on the appearance of intelligence, visible behaviors are the essence of the problem. Therefore, behavior-based design provides many advantages for game developers, allowing them to use techniques from nouvelle AI such as incremental development and extensive testing.

Arbitration

Finally, the top level of the architecture is a component that arbitrates between the behaviors. Its role is to decide which behavior needs to be activated based on the current situation.

Compared to lower-level tasks, the arbitration is relatively simple because all the details are abstracted out by the behavioral components. This makes them simple to handle from every point of view:

➤ Designers can control the arbitration using static techniques such as finite-state machines or the subsumption architecture.

➤ The AI can learn to control the system using adaptive techniques such as reinforcement learning or classifier systems.

The flexibility in the implementation of the arbitration is an incredible advantage for game AI developers, because they can opt for the simplest solution first—using adaptive techniques to provide interesting behaviors within the game.

Implementations

Naturally, each AI system has its own requirements, and thus each may benefit from a different implementation. However, common techniques tend to improve the development times and the quality of the final product.

The appropriate compromise between the various approaches will not sacrifice performance for development times, however.

Native Code

All the components that are commonly used and have large slices of execution time should be implemented in native C++ code. The only way to identify these performance bottlenecks is through profiling. Standard tools may be used for this purpose, such as Intel's VTune or GNU's gprof, although it's extremely simple to include custom timing routines.

As Donald Knuth points out, "Premature optimization is the root of all evil." The optimizations of the modules should be done only after the system works fully and the bottlenecks have been identified. Ideally, any optimization procedure should not change the results, so ideally, robust unit tests should be available to identify adjustments that break the system.

Scripted

Scripting languages, although they are arguably modern *programming* languages, have much to offer for the development of AI. With the support of either weak or dynamic typing, fewer lines need to be typed and the true purpose of the code shines through. AI algorithms are much faster to prototype and test.

Scripts are ideal for providing small parts of code that are not executed often, or that require strong customization (for instance, an AI dependent on the level of the game). Languages such as Lua or Python support such functionality, although their execution times are much slower than native code. This is the main reason for profiling the entire system and optimizing the crucial components.

Data Driven

Game engines in general—and AI systems in particular—are well suited to a data-driven approach. The entire system is driven by data files that are loaded during initialization, instead of integrating the information within the code. This separation is convenient for all the members of the development team (working independently), and generally leads to more robust systems (clean separation of the code and data).

In particular, the scripts themselves can be stored as files. The data for each of the AI modules is also easily stored on disk (data such as the rules of an expert system or the weights of a neural network, for instance).

Techniques and Their Applicability

During the development of game AI, various problems may occur. Fortunately, we've examined techniques to deal with them. The techniques presented in this book are (mostly) reactive, used ubiquitously throughout the games industry. Often, these reactive techniques can be used transparently as efficient substitutes for deliberative AI— which still have to prove themselves as viable solutions for game AI (with the exception of A* pathfinding).

This section recapitulates solutions that spring to the mind of experienced developers when designing AI. Other "helper" techniques, such as reinforcement learning and evolutionary algorithms, are not discussed here; they can be seen as techniques to help solve each of the following problems.

Problem Solving

Problem solving involves finding an answer to a fixed problem, usually by deducing new facts from the information provided:

➤ **Rule-based systems** are particularly suited to problem solving, because they model the approach of a human expert. In many cases, crisp logic is more than appropriate for representing a majority of problems.

➤ **Fuzzy expert systems** are effective improvements when reasoning requires degrees of truth. However, the fuzzy approach suffers from being less efficient than the crisp alternative.

Sequential Control

Some problems require sequences of actions or behaviors. The position in the sequence needs to be tracked (with a state variable, for example):

➤ **Finite-state machines** have an intrinsic concept of state, so sequences are easily represented. By designing states (potentially nested) and connecting them together, the designers can create behaviors as a chain of actions.

➤ **Probabilistic finite-state machines** add a random element to the sequences, so designers have control over the stochastic actions.

➤ **Fuzzy-state machines** allow degrees of truth in the state activity. Although they provide additional smoothness in the transitions and actions, the computational cost grows with the number of states.

Pattern Recognition

A particular kind of problem in AI is pattern recognition, which involves classifying or recognizing a sample (set of variables). This is also known as estimating a response variable based on predictor values:

➤ **Decision trees** are particularly appropriate for categorical variables (that is, with discrete intervals). The advantage is that the representation is expressive and compact—easily edited by the designer.

➤ **Neural networks**, and particularly perceptrons, are better suited for continuous variables. Multilayer perceptrons are much harder to understand than the single-layer variants, so they should be reserved for the complex problems only.

Sequence Recognition

Recognizing sequences of symbols, or classifying them, is another kind of problem that warrants its own set of techniques:

➤ **Finite-state automata** process the symbols one by one, updating the internal state variable accordingly. Sequences from regular languages can be recognized or classified.

➤ **Probabilistic finite-state automata** can be used to determine the likelihood of sequences occurring.

➤ **Fuzzy-state automata** are used to find the degree of membership of sequences in categories.

Learning and Feedback Mechanisms

Learning technology has a crucial role to play in the future of game AI. Not only does it improve the intelligence of NPCs within the world, it also increases the productivity of AI developers. When using learning AI for offline optimization or online adaptation, there are also common principles to adhere to.

As a rule of thumb, it's best to use supervised learning whenever possible. It provides the best results by tackling the problem directly (for instance, providing patterns for neural networks to recognize). Reinforcement approaches are not as convenient, but should be the second choice. Because there is a constant stream of rewards, reinforcement learning has the advantage of providing hints of which actions are beneficial to the system. Finally, evolutionary techniques should be considered as the last option, because the learning is only evaluated in episodes.

There are many issues with learning based on feedback, one of which is dealing with realism. It's fairly easy to express functionality in terms of reward and fitness, but it's much tougher to express humanlike behaviors. By the time "realism" has been modeled with feedback, many aspects of the behavior have already been interpreted as equations—so the problem is almost solved without much need for learning.

Even learning functionality can be difficult, regardless of realism. An important—if not essential—concept for dealing with such learning involves feedback with levels of magnitude. The designer can provide hints by including simpler concepts in the feedback function, in a way similar to *shaping*. The more important the concept, the more weight it carries. For example, Table 49.1 shows an example for learning deathmatch behaviors from scratch; enemy presence, shooting, damage, and—at the highest level—kills are rewarded.

Table 49.1   Setting Up Feedback with Different Levels of Magnitude Associated with Each Concept

Concept	Weight
Find enemies	0.01
Shoot at enemies	0.1
Damage	1
Kill	10

Summary

Often, the AI engine is split into multiple layers with different responsibilities:

➤ Modules at the base are implementations of AI techniques.

➤ Capabilities of the characters depend on these AI techniques.

➤ Behaviors are expressed in terms of the specific capabilities.

➤ Arbitrators coordinate and select the right behaviors.

The implementation of AI systems benefits from similar trends as game engine development, combining flexibility with efficiency:

➤ Native code is used for expensive common runtimes.

➤ Scripts provide customized layers, simple to implement.

➤ Data files store as much information as possible separate from the codebase.

Table 49.2 summarizes patterns for specific problems.

Table 49.2   Common Problems Encountered in Games and AI Techniques to Handle Them

Challenge	AI Technique
Problem solving	Rule-based system, fuzzy expert system
Sequential control	Finite-state machines variations
Pattern recognition	Decision trees, neural networks
Sequence recognition	Finite-state automata

As far as learning systems are concerned, there are useful guidelines, too:

➤ Prefer supervised approaches, especially when realism is hard to express.

➤ Levels of magnitude in the feedback guide the learning.

Mixing and matching these ideas should enable us to develop any game AI system in a simple but robust fashion.

Chapter 50

The Road Ahead

This book has reached its last chapter, but things are just getting started. Whether approaching game AI development as professionals or hobbyists, we can do many things to follow up on this book, including the following:

> ➤ Experiment—The examples in this book are representative of the techniques and problems, but there are many other combinations to cover.

> ➤ Extend—Although reactive AI is ideal for games in many ways, there are two concepts that could be used to extend the capabilities of the nonplayer character (NPC): world models and planning.

The result of this procedure should be fully autonomous game AI developers!

Practice Makes Perfect

Game AI development is—or soon will be—more a matter of experience than knowledge. There's no doubt that practice is the primary ingredient for becoming a successful AI developer. This book focuses on the practical perspective for this very reason.

The applicability of each AI technique is mentioned during its introduction. Also, the description of every problem includes a comprehensive description of the kind of solution required. To emphasize the versatility of the techniques in a practical fashion, exercises are provided with each part. Hints are available on the web site, along with some solutions.

Open Challenge

About a dozen techniques presented in this book—including variations—and more than 20 problems are mentioned or dealt with. Apart from a few minor exceptions, each technique can be applied to every problem. That leaves approximately 240 combinations to experiment with. Readers are invited to solve the problems they are most interested in as an educational venture and submit them for appraisal by other readers. We intend to collect each of the resulting animats (although the hardest part will probably be to find original names for them all!). You can find more information about contributing and each of the possible combinations on the web site at `http://AiGameDev.com/`.

Game AI Specialists Forum

Readers can access an online forum at `http://AiGameDev.com/`. There are no prerequisites for posting messages except the background knowledge from this book. As such, the discussion is expected to reach intermediate to advanced levels of AI in computer games.

Readers are encouraged to share their experiences throughout this book, regarding both practical and theoretical issues. The forum also provides a means for interaction about the exercises. There are other unrelated public forums for game AI developers, such as GameDev.net, the comp.ai.games newsgroup, and even the AI-Depot.com message boards.

On World Models

Reactive intelligence typically does not have any representation of the world; thanks to the sensors, the world acts as its own model. This proves to be a surprisingly efficient and reliable form of AI. However, AI purely based on reflexes lacks a main characteristic of human intelligence: memory. Therefore, purely reactive animats fail to reach the capabilities of biological players. Although reactive systems may be designed almost as intelligent as ones with world models, they lack realism.

Throughout the development of the animats presented in this book, the animats are given small senses of state (for example, to keep track of the enemy). This not only makes the AI more realistic, it is also much easier to develop. Without relying on advanced concepts behind internal representations of the world, this additional knowledge allows the animats to perform on a human level.

Increasing the capabilities of the AI, however, requires extending the concept of world model—providing each animat with personal knowledge of its environments. The main issue involved is one of representation, because a very flexible and expressive knowledge representation language is needed to store the short- and long-term memories of animats.

As well as providing the potential for nondeterministic behaviors, world models allow the AI engineer to create interesting human phenomena such as forgetfulness and surprise. Advanced world models, beyond those depicted in this book, are extremely rare in professional game AI. That said, there is a wealth of academic information on the subject, originating from classical AI in mid-twentieth century as well as recent research. See the web site at `http://AiGameDev.com/` for some resources.

Planning Techniques

A world model opens up possibilities for the AI. Reactive techniques can operate with memory and significantly benefit from it. That said, there are limitations with reactive techniques (for instance, memory consumption) that make them unsuitable for large problems—hence the need for architectures and decomposition.

Search algorithms shine where reactive techniques fail (rarely in game AI), trading off additional computation for memory. In particular, search techniques are appropriate for establishing plans in the future, considering the consequences of each of the possible actions.

In terms of increasing the capabilities of the NPC, planning techniques based on search algorithms have an important role—although it should not be overestimated. Pathfinding aside, deliberative AI still hasn't found a place in the games industry. (Only a handful of games use deliberative AI.) The web site contains some good starting points for investigating techniques.

Embracing Nouvelle Game AI

At the time of writing, most professional game AI developers are the first to admit that their job involves little AI technology at all. Indeed, techniques such as pathfinding or scripting are generally not considered AI (especially not in the academic sense). Although this classical game AI approach serves its purpose, trends in recent games reveal a need for improved NPCs to increase the entertainment levels. Therefore, advancements in AI technology are necessary to assist the development of realistic and intelligent NPCs.

The solution is partly based on academic AI techniques discussed throughout this book (such as neural networks and decision trees). Although their theory has been researched extensively over the past decades, this in itself is not enough to drive the necessary revolution in AI technology. Future progress in game AI development will be driven by changes in methodologies and practices that are capable of coping with the following:

➤ Cutting-edge AI technology with a complexity superior to classical game AI approaches

➤ Intelligent NPCs behaving autonomously within the game world

This book takes a modern approach to these open problems, inspired by principles from the *nouvelle AI* trend in robotics and concepts reminiscent of *agile development* of software. Both these approaches are popular in their respective domains and are proven to work in professional environments. As demonstrated throughout this book, their applicability to game AI development is unquestionable—notably feature-driven development using evolutionary (incremental) design, with rapid iterations backed by extensive testing.

In fact, this approach is arguably necessary to develop adaptive AI, because of the level of complexity and the unpredictability of the task. Much research still needs to be done on the subject, but this book is written in the hope that the information herein provides a significant step in the right direction.

Bibliography

[Agile01]
Manifesto for Agile Software Development, http://agilemanifesto.org/, 2001.

[AIISC03]
AI Interface Standards Committee, International Game Developers Association,
http://www.igda.org/ai/, 2003.

[Alexander02]
Alexander, B. "The Beauty of Response Curves," *AI Game Programming Wisdom*.
Charles River Media, 2002.

[Alexander02]
Alexander, B. "An Optimized Fuzzy Architecture for Decision Making," *AI Game Programming Wisdom*. Charles River Media, 2002.

[Atherton02]
Atherton, M. et al. "A Functional MRI Study of High-Level Cognition I. The Game of Chess." *Cognitive Brain Research*, 2002.

[Barnes02]
Barnes, J., Hutchens, J. "Testing Undefined Behavior as a Result of Learning," *AI Game Programming Wisdom*. Charles River Media, 2002.

[Bécheiraz98]
Bécheiraz, P., Thalmann, D. *A Behavioral Animation System for Autonomous Actors Personified by Emotions*. Proceedings of First Workshop on Embodied Conversational Characters, 1998.

[Blumberg02]

Blumberg B., Isla D. "New Challenges for Character-Based AI for Games," *AAAI Spring Symposium on AI and Interactive Entertainment*. Palo Alto, CA, March 2002.

[Bourg01]

Bourg, D. M., *Physics for Game Developers*. O'Reilly, 2001.

[Breiman84]

Breiman, L. et al. *Classification and Regression Trees*, Wadsworth International, 1984.

[Brooks86]

Brooks, R. A. "A Robust Layered Control System for a Mobile Robot," *IEEE Journal of Robotics and Automation* 2(1): 14–23, 1986.

[Brooks91a]

Brooks, R. A. "Intelligence Without Reason," *Proceedings of the 12th International Joint Conference on Artificial Intelligence* 569–595. San Mateo, CA, 1991.

[Brooks91b]

Brooks, R. A, "Intelligence Without Representation," *Artificial Intelligence* 47(1-3): 139–160, 1991.

[Canamero97]

Canamero, D. "Modeling Motivations and Emotions as a Basis for Intelligent Behavior," *Proceedings of the First International Symposium on Autonomous Agents*, 148–155, 1997.

[Cawsey94]

Cawsey, A. "Knowledge Representation and Inference," *Databases and Artificial Intelligence 3*, 1994.

[Chalmers90]

Chalmers, D. J. "Thoughts on Emergence," `http://www.u.arizona.edu/~chalmers/notes/emergence.html`, 1990.

[Chen02]
Chen, X et al. "A Functional MRI Study of High-Level Cognition II. The Game of GO," *Cognitive Brain Research.* 2002.

[Conway70]
Conway, J. H, Gardner, M. "The Fantastic Combinations of John Conway's New Solitaire Game 'Life'," *Scientific American*, 223:120–123, 1970.

[Davis93]
Davis, R. et al. "What Is a Knowledge Representation?" *AI Magazine*, 14(1):17–33, 1993.

[Dietterich98]
Dietterich, T. G. "The MAXQ Method for Hierarchical Reinforcement Learning," *Proceedings of the 15th International Conference on Machine Learning*, 1998.

[Ekman79]
Ekman, P., Oster, H. "Facial Expressions of Emotion," *Annual Review of Psychology*, 20:527–554, 1979.

[Elias98]
Elias, H. Perlin Noise Tutorial, `http://freespace.virgin.net/hugo.elias/models/m_perlin.htm`, 1998.

[FEAR03a]
FEAR Language Specification, `http://fear.sf.net/docs/specification/`, 2003.

[FEAR03b]
FEAR C++ User API Reference, `http://fear.sf.net/docs/api/`, 2003.

[FEAR03c]
FEAR Technical Overview, `http://fear.sf.net/docs/overview/`, 2003.

[FEAR03d]
FEAR Library Reference, `http://fear.sf.net/docs/library/`, 2003.

[Forgy82]

Forgy, C.L. "Rete: A Fast Algorithm for the Many Pattern/Many Object Pattern Match Problem," *Artificial Intelligence*, 17–37, 1982.

[Frawley91]

Frawley, W. J. et al. "Knowledge Discovery in Databases: An Overview," *Knowledge Discovery in Databases*, 1–27. AAAI/MIT Press, 1991.

[Gadanho98]

Gadanho, S. C. "Reinforcement Learning in Autonomous Robots: An Empirical Investigation of the Role of Emotions," Ph.D. Thesis, University of Edinburgh, 1998.

[Genesereth95]

Genesereth, M. R. Knowledge Interchange Format Specification, `http://logic.stanford.edu/kif/specification.html`, 1995.

[Gibson77]

Gibson, J. J. "The Theory of Affordances," *Perceiving, Acting, and Knowing*. Lawrence Erlbaum Associates, 1977.

[Gibson79]

Gibson, J. J. *The Ecological Approach to Visual Perception*. Houghton Mifflin, 1979.

[Grünwald98]

Grünwald, P. et al. "Minimum Encoding Approaches for Predictive Modeling," *Proceedings of the 14th International Conference on Uncertainty in AI*, 183–192, 1998.

[Haendel02]

Haendel, L. The Function Pointer Tutorials, `http://www.function-pointer.org/`, 2002.

[Harel87]

Harel, D. "Statecharts: A Visual Formalism for Complex Systems," *Science of Computer Programming*, 1987.

[Harik99]

Harik, G., Lobo, F. "A Parameter-Less Genetic Algorithm," *Proceedings of the Genetic and Evolutionary Computation Conference*, 1999.

[Heuer99]

Heuer, R. J. Psychology of Intelligence Analysis, Center for the Study of Intelligence, `http://www.cia.gov/csi/books/19104/`, 1999.

[Holland75]

Holland, J. H. *Adaptation in Natural and Artificial Systems*. The University of Michigan Press, 1975.

[Humphrys97]

Humphrys, M. "Action Selection Methods Using Reinforcement Learning," Ph.D. Thesis, Trinity Hall, Cambridge, 1997.

[ISAB02]

The International Conference on Simulation of Adaptive Behavior, `http://www.isab.org/confs/`, 2002.

[Isla01]

Isla D. et al. "A Layered Brain Architecture for Synthetic Creatures," *International Joint Conference on Artificial Intelligence*, Seattle, WA, August 2001.

[Jantzen98]

Jantzen, J. "Tutorial on Fuzzy Logic," *Report 98-E 868*, Technical University of Denmark, 1998.

[Kachigan91]

Kachigan, S. K. *Multivariate Statistical Analysis: A Conceptual Introduction*. Radius Press, 1991.

[Kaehler98]

Kaehler, S. D. "Fuzzy Logic: An Introduction," *The Newsletter of the Seattle Robotics Society*, March 1998.

[Kaelbling96]

Kaelbling, L. P. et al. "Reinforcement Learning: A Survey," *Journal of Artificial Intelligence Research*, 1996.

[Koopman95]

Koopman, P. J. A Taxonomy of Decomposition Strategies Based on Structures, Behaviors, and Goals, Proceedings of the Conference on Design Theory and Methodology, http://www.ece.cmu.edu/~koopman/decomp/, 1995.

[Kreinovich92]

Kreinovich, V. et al. "Genetic Algorithms: What Fitness Scaling Is Optimal?" University of Texas at El Paso, Computer Science Department, Technical Reports, 1992.

[Kremer99]

Kremer, S. C. Stacey, D. A. "Artificial Neural Networks: From McCulloch Pitts Neurons to Back-Propagation," Lecture Notes, http://hebb.cis.uoguelph.ca/ ~skremer/Teaching/27642/BP/, 1999.

[Lojban02]

Emotions in Lojban, Online Wiki, http://www.lojban.org/, 2002.

[Manslow02]

Manslow, J. "Learning and Adaptation in Games," *AI Game Programming Wisdom*. Charles River Media, 2002.

[Matumoto02]

Matumoto, Mersenne Twister: A Random Number Generator, http://www.math.keio.ac.jp/~matumoto/emt.html, 2002.

[McCulloch43]

McCulloch, W. S., Pitts, W. "A Logical Calculus of the Ideas Immanent in Nervous Activity," *Bulletin of Mathematical Biophysics 5*, 115–133, 1943.

[Minsky69]
Minsky, M., Seymour P. *Perceptrons; An Introduction to Computational Geometry*. MIT Press, 1969.

[Muggleton90]
Muggleton, S. *Inductive Acquisition of Expert Knowledge*. Addison-Wesley, 1990.

[Norman99]
Norman, D. A. "Affordance, Conventions and Design," `http://www.jnd.org/dn.mss/affordances-interactions.html`, *Interactions*, 38–43, 1999.

[Perkins96]
Perkins, S., Hayes, G. "Robot Shaping - Principles, Methods and Architectures," *Workshop on Learning in Robots and Animals*, AISB '96, University of Sussex, 1996.

[Perlin01]
Perlin, K. Improving Noise, Media Research Lab, 2001.

[Perlin96]
Perlin, K., Goldberg, A. "Improv: A System for Scripting Interactive Actors in Virtual Worlds," *Computer Graphics*, 1996.

[Perlin99]
Perlin, K. Making Noise, GDC Hardcore, `http://www.noisemachine.com/talk1/`, 1999.

[Petta01]
Petta, P., Trappl, R. Emotions and Agents, "Multi-Agent Systems and Applications," *Lecture Note in Artificial Intelligence*, Springer, 2086:301–316, 2001.

[Plutchik80]
Plutchik, R. "A General Psychoevolutionary Theory of Emotion," *Emotion: Theory, Research, and Experience* 1:3–33, New York: Academic, 1980.

[PR02]

Personality Research, Basic Emotions, `http://www.personalityresearch.org/basicemotions.html`, 2002.

[Quake2FAQ]

Quake 2 Weapons and Combat FAQ, `http://www.quake2.com/q2wfaq/q2wfaq.html`.

[Quinlan86]

Quinlan, J. R. "Induction of Decision Trees," *Machine Learning*, 1, 81–106, 1986.

[Quinlan93]

Quinlan, J. R. *C4.5: Programs for Machine Learning.* Morgan Kaufmann, 1993.

[Reynolds87]

Reynolds, C. W. "Flocks, Herds, and Schools: A Distributed Behavioral Model," *Journal of Computer Graphics* 4(21):25–34, 1987.

[Reynolds99]

Reynolds, C. W. "Steering Behaviors for Autonomous Characters," *Game Developers Conference*, 1999.

[Riedmiller93]

Riedmiller, M., Braun, H. "A Direct Adaptive Method for Faster Backpropagation Learning: The RPROP Algorithm," *Proceedings of the IEEE Conference on Neural Networks*, 586–591, 1993.

[Ripley96]

Ripley, B. D. *Pattern Recognition and Neural Networks*, Cambridge University Press, 1996.

[Roberts73]

Roberts, D. D. *The Existential Graphs of Charles S. Peirce.* Mouton, 1973.

[Rosenblatt59]

Rosenblatt, F. *Principles of Neurodynamics*. Spartan Books, 1959.

[Seymour01]

Seymour, J. "A Flexible and Extensible Framework for Modelling and Simulating Physical Agents," Masters Thesis, The University of York, 2001.

[Sharples96]

Sharples, M. et al. *Computers and Thought: A Practical Introduction to Artificial Intelligence*. Bradfords Directory, 1996.

[Sowa92]

John F. Sowa, "Conceptual Graphs Summary," *Conceptual Structures: Current Research and Practice*, 3–52, 1992.

[Sterren00]

Van der Sterren, W. "AI for Tactical Grenade Handling," CGF-AI, http://www.cgf-ai.com/docs/grenadehandling.pdf, 2000.

[Sutton98]

Sutton, R., Barto, A. G. *Reinforcement Learning: An Introduction*. MIT Press, 1998.

[Thomas81]

Thomas, F., Johnston, O. *Disney Animation: The Illusion of Life*. Abbeville Press, 1981.

[Tozour02]

Tozour, P. "The Basics of Ranged Weapon Combat," *AI Game Programming Wisdom*. Charles River Media, 2002.

[Velasquez98]

Velasquez, J. "Modeling Emotion-Based Decision-Making," *Proceedings of the 1998 AAAI Fall Symposium Emotional and Intelligent: The Tangled Knot of Cognition*, 164–169, 1998.

[Ventura98]

Ventura, R. et al. "Emotions—The Missing Link?" Papers from the 1998 Fall Symposium. Emotional and Intelligent: The Tangled Knot of Cognition, 170–175, 1998.

[Waveren01]

Van Waveren, J. P. "The Quake III Arena Bot," Master of Science Thesis, Delft University of Technology, 2001.

[Weisstein03]

Weisstein, E., Eric Weisstein's World of Mathematics, `http://mathworld.wolfram.com/`, 2003.

[Widrow60]

Widrow, B., Hoff, M. E. "Adaptive Switching Circuits," *IRE WESCON Convention Record*, 96–104, 1960.

[Wikipedia03]

Wikipedia, Definition of Information Theory, `http://www.wikipedia.org/wiki/Information_theory`, 2003.

[Wilson94]

Wilson, S. W. "ZCS: A Zeroth Level Classifier System," *Evolutionary Computation*, 1994.

[Wilson95]

Wilson, S. W. "Classifier Fitness Based on Accuracy," *Evolutionary Computation*, 1995.

[Wray94]

Wray, R. et al. Subsumption Architecture Overview, `http://ai.eecs.umich.edu/cogarch0/subsump/index.html`, 1994.

[Yang01]

Yang, S. Y. "Introduction to Intelligent Programming," Lecture Notes, National Taiwan Institute of Technology, Taipei, 2001.

Index

A

F

Q-R

www.informit.com

YOUR GUIDE TO IT REFERENCE

New Riders has partnered with **InformIT.com** to bring technical information to your desktop. Drawing from New Riders authors and reviewers to provide additional information on topics of interest to you, **InformIT.com** provides free, in-depth information you won't find anywhere else.

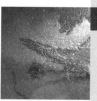

Articles

Keep your edge with thousands of free articles, in-depth features, interviews, and IT reference recommendations—all written by experts you know and trust.

Online Books

Answers in an instant from **InformIT Online Books'** 600+ fully searchable online books.

POWERED BY

Safari

Catalog

Review online sample chapters, author biographies, and customer rankings and choose exactly the right book from a selection of over 5,000 titles.

www.newriders.com

HOW TO CONTACT US

VOICES THAT MATTER

VISIT OUR WEB SITE
WWW.NEWRIDERS.COM

On our web site, you'll find information about our other books, authors, tables of contents, and book errata. You will also find information about book registration and how to purchase our books, both domestically and internationally.

EMAIL US

Contact us at: **nrfeedback@newriders.com**

- If you have comments or questions about this book
- To report errors that you have found in this book
- If you have a book proposal to submit or are interested in writing for New Riders
- If you are an expert in a computer topic or technology and are interested in being a technical editor who reviews manuscripts for technical accuracy

Contact us at: **nreducation@newriders.com**

- If you are an instructor from an educational institution who wants to preview New Riders books for classroom use. Email should include your name, title, school, department, address, phone number, office days/hours, text in use, and enrollment, along with your request for desk/examination copies and/or additional information.

Contact us at: **nrmedia@newriders.com**

- If you are a member of the media who is interested in reviewing copies of New Riders books. Send your name, mailing address, and email address, along with the name of the publication or Web site you work for.

BULK PURCHASES/CORPORATE SALES

The publisher offers discounts on this book when ordered in quantity for bulk purchases and special sales. For sales within the U.S., please contact: Corporate and Government Sales (800) 382-3419 or **corpsales@pearsontechgroup.com**. Outside of the U.S., please contact: International Sales (317) 428-3341 or **international@pearsontechgroup.com**.

WRITE TO US
New Riders Publishing
800 East 96th Street, 3rd Floor
Indianapolis, IN 46240

CALL/FAX US
Toll-free (800) 571-5840
If outside U.S. (317) 428-3000
Ask for New Riders
FAX: (317) 428-3280

New Riders

WWW.NEWRIDERS.COM

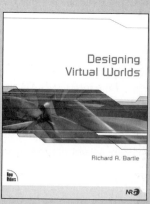